D1585064

City Edition

The Daily Record.

NEW COMPETITION. SEE WEEKLY RECORD, FRIDAY. £5 PRIZE.

To Win £5. Original Competition. Friday's Weekly Record. One Halfpenny.

LARGEST SALE OF ANY MORNING OR EVENING NEWSPAPER IN SCOTLAND.

No. MCCCXII—SIX EDITIONS.   GLASGOW, THURSDAY, JANUARY 4, 1900.   PRICE ONE HALFPENNY.

"The Daily Record" is sent direct by post from the office to any country within the Postal Union at the rate of 1d. a day (which includes postage), payable in advance. A subscription is taken for any number of days. The subscription for one month is 2s. 6d.; for 6d. for three months, 13s. for six months, or 26s. for a year. Cheques or postal orders should be "crossed" and made payable to the Manager, "The Daily Record," 126 and 128 Union Street, Glasgow.

BUSINESS NOTICES.

The CHIEF OFFICE of THE DAILY RECORD is 126 and 128 Union Street, is open for the transaction of business from 9 a.m. till 11 p.m. each day (Saturday and Sunday excepted). On SATURDAY the business hours are 9 a.m. till 4 p.m. On SUNDAY the office is open from 4 p.m. till 9 p.m. After these hours ADVERTISEMENTS may be received at the Printing Works, 4 Frederick Lane, North s-ederick street.

TELEPHONE NUMBERS—Editorial, 4695; Commercial, 4740.

TELEGRAPH ADDRESS—"Daily Record, Glasgow."

All Notices require the Signature and Address of Sender. All Advertisements received are subject to the approval of the Manager. If an Advertisement be paid for and not approved, the money will be returned.

Advertisers and Subscribers are particularly requested to use POSTAL ORDERS instead of stamps.

DIRECTORIES of CHIEF TOWNS of SCOTLAND, ENGLAND, IRELAND, and WALES may be CONSULTED at the DAILY RECORD Offices, 126 and 128 UNION STREET, GLASGOW.

THE DAILY RECORD is on Sale at every BOOKSTALL in SCOTLAND, and COMMERCIAL TRAVELLERS and others experiencing any difficulty in obtaining THE DAILY RECORD at any Bookstall would much oblige by communicating with the MANAGER, DAILY RECORD.

BIRTH, MARRIAGE, DEATH, and IN MEMORIAM NOTICES.

18 Words or Under, is 6d PREPAID. And for every additional word, 1d.

BIRTHS.

CUTHBERT.—On the 2nd inst., at Hawarden, Port-Glasgow, the wife of Captain CUTHBERT, R.N.R., a "Suffolk;" a daughter.

FISHER.—On the 2nd inst., at Thornton Cottage, Rosewell, Mid-Lothian, Mrs. FISHER; a daughter.

JOHNSON.—On the 2nd inst., at Forrest Buildings, Llanerchmon, the wife of JOHN JOHNSON; a daughter.

REID.—On the 2nd inst., at 158 Renfrew Street, the wife of MATTHEW REID; twin daughters.

RISK.—On the 2nd inst., at 1 Saltoun Gardens, Kelvinside, the wife of ROBERT K. RISK; a son.

WATSON.—On the 2nd inst., at 142 Cumbridge Drive, Kelvinside, N., the wife of J. DOUGLAS WATSON; a daughter.

WILSON.—On the 3rd inst., at 25 Corporation Buildings, M'Leod Street, Gorgie Road, Edinburgh, Mrs. JAMES WILSON; a son—both doing well.

MARRIAGES.

BROWN—BEDFORD.—On the 3rd inst., at Edinburgh, by special licence, WALTER SHEWBREAD BROWN, hairdresser, Burntisland, to ANNIE JEMIMA MACINTOSH, daughter of George Bedford, Milltown, Bedford, Banffshire.

CAMPBELL—M'CULLOCH.—On the 3rd inst., at Glasgow, by the Rev. David Brown, St. Enoch's Parish Church, CHESSER CAMPBELL, Fenwick, to JUNE, only daughter of the late John M'Culloch and Mrs. Wylie, Knockewart, Dairy, Ayrshire, and granddaughter of the late Matthew White, Glasgow.

GOLDEN WEDDING.

STEVENSON—FORREST.—On the 31st December, 1849, at Muir Street, Motherwell, by the Rev. J. T. M'Farlane, of Brandon Street U.P. Church, Hamilton, WILLIAM STEVENSON, to MARGARET, only daughter of William P. West; now of Stevenson & Co., photographers, 109 Bothwell street, Glasgow.

DEATHS.

ADAM.—On the 2nd inst., at 80 Barrington Drive, JANET URIE BLIND (JURA), aged 15, beloved daughter of William Adam.

BORLAND.—On the 2nd inst., at Auldcot, Polkskshaws, after a short illness, JOHN DAVIDSON, Jun.

COWIE.—On the 3rd inst., at 4 Bruce Road, Polkshields, in her 81st year, MARY AITKEN, relict of John Howie, Townhead, Irvine. Funeral To-Morrow (Friday), from 4 Bruce Road, at 12 Noon, and from Caledonian Railway Station at Kilwinning at 2.15 p.m. Friends please accept this intimation and invitation.

JOHNSTONE.—On the 2nd inst., at 3 Marchmont Terrace, of pneumonia, Mrs. JOHNSTONE, faithful servant and friend of Mr. and Mrs. Lewis O. Smith and family.

MANSFIELD.—On the 2nd inst., at 3 Abercromby Place, Edinburgh, MARY ANNE LUTYENS, widow of Thomas Mansfield, chartered accountant, Edinburgh, aged 86 years.

MILLAR.—On the 2nd inst., at 25 Albert Drive, Crosshill, ELIZABETH RODGER BURNETT, wife of John Hutcheson Millar.

MONK.—On the 2nd inst., at 1 Renfrew Street, Glasgow, ANNIE PIERCE, aged 46 years, beloved wife of George Bone, burgh surveyor, Clydebank.

SCOTT.—On the 2nd inst., at 41 Castle Street, Edinburgh, suddenly, JANET BROWN, aged 70, widow of Richard Scott, Haddington.

SCOTT.—On the 2nd inst., at 16 Gibson Street, Hillhead, JANET BROWN, aged 70, widow of Thomas Scott, late of Laggah, Barrhill.

SCOTT.—On the 3rd inst., at Glenbrook, Dullatur, ANNE BILSLAND, aged 55 years, dearly beloved wife of Duff Simpson.

WALLACE.—On the 3rd inst., at Royal Bank House, Leven, FORBES THOMSON WALLACE, banker.

WYLIE & LOCHHEAD, LIMITED,
FUNERAL UNDERTAKERS
AND
CAB AND POST MASTERS.
CAB AND CARRIAGE HIRERS
45 UNION STREET
AND
20 BERKELEY STREET.
All ARRANGEMENTS MADE for CREMATION at the GLASGOW CREMATORIUM.
Telegraphic Address—WYLIE, GLASGOW.
TELEPHONES FOR WAREHOUSE........No. 786
    STABLES............. 820
    HEARSE............... 4693

PUBLIC NOTICES.

GLASGOW UNITED EVANGELISTIC ASSOCIATION.

GLASGOW EVANGELISTIC CAMPAIGN, 1900.

SPECIAL UNITED SERVICES For Week, Jan. 4-5. To-night at 8 o'clock. Brunswickhill U.P. Church, Lancefield Street—Mr. JAMES MARSHALL. Cowcaddens Free Church—Mr. J. W. PASCOE.

EVANGELISTIC CAMPAIGN.

CHRISTIAN CONVENTION WILL BE HELD IN CHRISTIAN INSTITUTE, 70 BOTHWELL STREET, TO-MORROW (FRIDAY), 5th JANUARY, 1900.

Noon.—"The Secrets of Spiritual Power." 3 p.m.—"The Enduement of Power." 8 p.m.—"An Appeal for Absolute Surrender and

REV. F. B. MEYER.

CANVAS, SAIL CLOTH, CLOTHING, TWINES, &c., &c.

TENDERS will be received until Noon on the dates named below for the under-mentioned articles, or which Forms of Tender, containing conditions of Contract, and all particulars, may be obtained on personal application at this Office, or by Letter addressed "Director of Navy Contracts, Admiralty, London, S.W." Full-size patterns of the articles may be seen, and small samples of most of them obtained, at the Admiralty Pattern Rooms, 72 Great Queen Street, Lincoln's Inn, London, W.C.; and at the Chambers of Commerce at the places specified against the items, on application to the Secretary, from whom Forms of Tender may also be obtained, viz.:—

		Date for receipt of Tender.
Worsted, Blue....	27,000 lbs.	(Bradford), (Cleakheaton), (Dewsbury),
White, &c.	1,410 „	Glasgow, Halifax, Leeds, Leicester, and Wakefield. 16th Jan.
Caps, Blue Cloth...	60,000 No.	Glasgow, Leeds, and Manchester.
Duck Covers for Caps....	60,000 „	
Hessen....	182,000 yds.	
Linen, Bleached, &c.	58,700 „	Barnsley, Belfast, Dundee, and Leeds.
„ Black	17,200 „	
Osnaburgh	17,500 „	
Towelling	62,008 „	Barnsley, Belfast, Dundee, Leeds, and Manchester.
Duck cloth, ordinary	1,050,000 „	
„ fine white	85,400 „	
Canvas Sail Cloth—		
(Royal Navy)...	1,403,800 „	Belfast, Dundee, Glasgow, and Leeds.
(Merchant).....	424,600 „	
For Seamen's Bags	201,000 „	
Coal Sack Cloth...	300,0 0 „	
Hammock Cloth...	500,000 „	Belfast, Bristol, Dundee, Glasgow, and Leeds.
Twines	780 cwt.	
Threads	16,500 lbs.	
Jute Thread	23,000 „	Belfast, Glasgow, and Leeds.
Hair, Curled.....	105,00 „	Dundee, Glasgow and Leeds.
Waterproof Sheet—		Glasgow, Halifax, and Manchester.
Packing Paper...	155,800 yds.	
Calico	179,400 „	
Cotton Waste,]	11,240 cwt	Glasgow and Manchester.
Packing, &c..		
Sponge Cloths.....	200,000 No.	

Manufacturers only will be accepted.

T. GWYN, Director of Navy Contracts. Contract Department, Admiralty, London, S.W., 1st January, 1900.

YOU CANNOT DO BETTER THAN ALWAYS USE
COOPER & CO.'S CELEBRATED TEAS,
BECAUSE THEY HOLD THE LEADING POSITION, REPRESENT THE BEST VALUE, GIVE GREATEST SATISFACTION.

LEADING PRICES:— 1/2, 1/4, 1/6 1/8, and 1/10 PER Lb.

8 TO 25 HOWARD STREET (AND BRANCHES), GLASGOW.

THOROUGH CLEARANCE SALE DURING JANUARY. OF ALL SURPLUS WINTER STOCK AT GREATLY REDUCED PRICES AND EVERY DEPARTMENT INCLUDED.

SMITH, SONS & LAUGHLAND, 78—UNION STREET—82

THE NATIONAL TELEPHONE COMPANY, LIMITED.

GOVAN TELEPHONE RATES.

The DIRECTORS of the above Company have decided from JANUARY 1st, in order to bring EXCHANGE TELEPHONES WITHIN THE REACH OF ALL CLASSES, to offer to all subscribers and intending subscribers to the Govan Telephone Exchange the following:—

EASY TERMS as an alternative to the present inclusive annual rental for unlimited local service:—

THREE GUINEAS A YEAR, Plus Government Royalty, 7s. = £3 10s. for the installation and maintenance of an Exchange line to an address within the prescribed distance from the Exchange. The above annual payment INCLUDES the RIGHT OF BEING CALLED UP WITHOUT FURTHER CHARGE by any Subscriber to the Company's system throughout the Kingdom.

ORIGINATED LOCAL MESSAGES, ONE PENNY PER CALL.

Full particulars may be obtained on application to the DISTRICT MANAGER, ROYAL EXCHANGE, GLASGOW. Head Offices—Oxford Court, Cannon Street, London, E.C. W. E. L. GAINE, General Manager.

THE SALE OF GREENLEES & SONS' "EASIEFIT" HORSE-SKIN BOOTS

Still increases by leaps and bounds, and the reason is simply because they are the Best All-round BLACKING LEATHER BOOTS in the World. They are made from Specially Dressed HORSE HIDE, which will Outwear all other kinds of Leather, and at the same time take on a very much finer Polish. The first time you require Boots try the "EASIEFIT," and you will never go back.

THE PRICES ARE—

LADIES'   GENTLEMEN'S
10s 6d and 14s 6d   10s 6d, 15s 6d, 19s 1d.

BRANCHES:
454 Argyle Street.   196 Dumbarton Rd., Partick.
335 Cowcaddens Street.   104 Duke Street, Dennistoun.
576 New City Road.   21 High Street, Paisley.
73 Paisley Road West.   24 King Street, Kilmarnock.
445 Bauchiehall Street.   194 High Street, Ayr.
68 SOUTH BRIDGE STREET, AIRDRIE.

THE MOST POPULAR AND FASHIONABLE. PEEBLES HYDRO. AND HOTEL. 550 Feet above Sea Level. Every Home Comfort. Pure, dry, and bracing Air. A most Successful Resident Specialist for the Treatment of Rheumatism, Gout, Sciatica, Liver and Kidney Complaints. Air, Sun, Electric Light, Turkish, Russian, Needle, and Electric Baths, and Roentgen Rays. A. THIEM, Proprietor; also of the Windsor Hotel, Glasgow.

PATENT OFFICE.

Patents for Inventions, and Registration for Designs and Trade Marks obtained by Messrs. JOHNSONS, 115 St. Vincent Street, Glasgow; and 4 Osborne Terrace, Haymarket, Edinburgh. Handbook "Hints to Inventors" gratis and post free.

PUBLICATIONS.

A PRICELESS GEM. Address for the

NEW-YEAR GIFTS AT
THE TRON HOUSE.
USEFUL FURNITURE, AND ORNATE SEASONABLE PRESENTS.

MESSRS. DALY & CO. cordially thank the many thousands of Customers who have participated in the Charming, Useful GIFTS provided for their world-wide connection, and reiterate that never before has such a really Grand Collection of Choice and Elegant Presents been collated by any Firm in the Kingdom, the following being merely an illustration of what our Patrons may expect:—

WORKBOXES AND WRITING DESKS.

Hundreds of Beautiful Variegated Designs, Inlaid Mahogany, Satinwood, &c., from 11½d to 51 12d, the latter being an exceptionally high-class article production, worth double the price, and most suitable for a handsome New-Year Gift.

PHOTO FRAMES.

Lovely CUT-GLASS PHOTO CABINET FRAMES, 5½d and 11½d each. Plush Photo Frames in all the newest shades from 6½d up to 5l 6d each. These make very nice inexpensive presents to relations or friends or acquaintances.

MANTEL BORDERS.

ELEGANT FELT MANTEL BORDERS in new artistic designs, 1s 11½d, 1s 11½d, 2s 6d, to 4s 11d; also RICH PLUSH BORDERS, very superior quality, beautifully sewn in Silk, with nice Silk Fringe, 6s 11d to 10s 6d each.

NEW YEAR CARDS.

Thousands of Neat Fancy Boxes of lovely artistically designed NEW-YEAR CARDS, with all the most appropriate greetings. Arranged in boxes of 10, 15, 25, and 50, with envelopes to match, 6½d and 11½d per box.

DOLLS! DOLLS!

THOUSANDS of PRETTY DOLLS, WOOD and WAXEN, DRESSED and UNDRESSED, from 4½d up to 21s 6d.

EVENING GAMES AND PUZZLES.

An Unique and Magnificent Collection of New and Most Amusing GAMES and PUZZLES for Young and Old, suitable for festive and social evening amusement; your choice at 6½d and 11½d each.

OCCASIONAL CHAIRS.

These Chairs are specially prepared in Artistic Frames, Polished Chippendale Mahogany, and beautifully upholstered Silk, Tapestries, or Velvet, 7s 11d, 10s 6d, 15s 6d, 21s, 25s 6d, and 20s 6d each.

FOR BABY.

Our Famous BABY CHAIRS are made in the most approved style, combining a High and Low Chair, Rocker, and Coach complete, each 10s 6d; or with nice Stuffed Backs, 12s 6d and 14s 6d.

BAMBOO TABLES.

HUNDREDS to SELECT FROM!

Nice Strong BAMBOO TABLES, artistically made, and finished with Matting Tops, 1s 11d; with Two Leaves, 2s 11d; and with Four Leaves, 5s 11d. Also, Bamboo Tables with best Lacquered Tops—real works of art—(square or octagonal), without Trays, 6s 6d; with Two Trays, 10s 6d; and with Four Trays, 12s 6d. An Immense Variety of BAMBOO CABINETS and WHATNOTS, in all sizes and designs, 12s 6d, 14s 6d, 15s 6d, to 61 6d. BAMBOO MUSIC CABINETS, 12s 6d, 15s 6d, and 21s.

BEAUTIFUL AND HANDSOME PRESENTS.

CAKE BASKETS.

A Splendid Selection in all the Very Latest Shapes, with Rich and Choice Engravings, at 10s 6d, 15s 6d, 20s 6d, up to 50s.

TEAPOTS.

Lovely ELECTRO-PLATED TEAPOTS in all the Newest Designs and Shapes, at 7s 6d, 8s 6d, 10s 6d, 15s 6d, 21s 6d, up to 25s each.

DINNER CRUETS.

Charming Assortment of best Silver-plated and beautiful Cut Crystal BOTTLES at 5s 6d, 7s 6d, 15s 6d, 19s 6d, 25s 6d, up to 50s each.

DINNER SETS.

Lovely 61-Piece DINNER SETS, real Gem of Art, artistically designed in all the most fashionable colours, 17s 11d, 19s 11d, 12s 11d, and 25s 6d; also a very superior selection of beautifully gilt 61-Piece Dinner Sets, every piece gilt, at 27s 6d, 32s 6d, and 32s 6d per set. NOTE—LETTER ORDERS Carefully Executed. Send for Illustrated House Furnishing Catalogue. Post Free.

MESSRS. DALY & CO., TRON HOUSE, 60 to 70 TRONGATE.

PRICE ONE SHILLING.
WATSON'S FAMILY EXPENDITURE BOOK For 1900.
G. WATSON & SON, 162 Ingram Street.

WINTER OVERCOATS.

THE WINTER IS APPROACHING, And every Man wishes to be inside a good warm Overcoat, so we are determined to supply an article that will be found

WARM AND COMFORTABLE.

There is no doubt that nowhere in the Three Kingdoms can there be found so well turned out an article, made of the Best Material and Fit, as we make for the same money.

Our Stock is so large that there will be no difficulty in our Customers "suiting" themselves to a T.

THE PRICES WE CHARGE FOR OUR OVERCOATS are from 35/ to 75/, Wool, Mixed, and Silk Fringe.

And we are in our Order Department turning out SUITS TO MEASURE for 42/, the materials of the Best Wool (Patterns to be chosen by our Customers), splendidly made. It is perfect, and we confidently state that NO SUCH VALUE CAN BE HAD ELSEWHERE, the great and extensive Business done by us in our several Houses in Edinburgh, Belfast, and Dublin affording us great facilities.

B. HYAM, 124 and 126 HIGH STREET, EDINBURGH.

WATCH YOUR EYES.

TRY ALLISON'S FAMED SIGHT-RESTORING SPECTACLES and EYE-GLASSES. Best Value in the World. Thousands of Testimonials. Address—ALLISON, MANUFACTURING OPTICIAN, 57 EGLINTON STREET. Branches—2 Bridgeton Cross, 171 New City Road. 411 Sauchiehall Street. Established over Half-a-Century.

FURNITURE PAYABLE BY INSTALMENTS. NO DEPOSIT REQUIRED. LARGE STOCK TO SELECT FROM. ALL GOODS MARKED IN PLAIN FIGURES.

GLASGOW FURNITURE CO., 142 WEST NILE STREET, GLASGOW. OPPOSITE EMPIRE PALACE THEATRE.

NEW-YEAR HOLIDAY ATTRACTIONS AT JOHN ANDERSON'S
ROYAL POLYTECHNIC, LIMITED,
OVER 62 YEARS ESTABLISHED, AND NOW MORE POPULAR THAN EVER.

GREAT HOLIDAY ATTRACTIONS. UNPRECEDENTED BARGAINS, IN ALL DEPARTMENTS.

THE MAGIC CAVE. THE CHILDREN'S FAIRYLAND. ENTIRE REMAINING STOCK OF TOYS OF EVERY DESCRIPTION TO BE SOLD WITHOUT RESERVE.

THE COSMORAMIC VIEWS OF THE WAR. REALISTIC AND EXCITING.

THE MARIONETTES PERFORM EACH HOUR FROM 11 O'CLOCK A.M. THOUSANDS HAVE PRONOUNCED THEM EXCEEDINGLY CLEVER. SEE THEM.

EDISON'S GRAND CONCERT PHONOGRAPH, THE MARVEL OF THE AGE. HEAR IT. ADMISSION FREE. ALL WELCOME.

BOOKS. BOOKS. WE INTEND TO MAKE A BIG HOLE IN THE BOOK STOCK. ALL REMAINDERS TO BE CLEARED REGARDLESS OF COST. A RARE CHANCE TO BUY GOOD BOOKS CHEAP.

JOHN ANDERSON'S ROYAL POLYTECHNIC, LTD., 91 to 99 ARGYLE STREET, GLASGOW.

PIANOFORTES, ORGANS, MUSIC. Music Accessories.

BAMBOO TABLES.

The Largest and Finest Selection of Musical Instruments in the United Kingdom by all the well-known Makers. Liberal Discounts for Cash, and favourable terms on the Hire System.

SPECIAL INSTRUMENTS AT A MODERATE PRICE.

Extensive dealings with the best Manufacturers of the cheaper class of Pianofortes and Organs enable PATERSON, SONS & CO. to offer the best value in the market. Special Catalogue of these Instruments on application.

TUNING, REGULATING, AND REPAIRING.

This Department employs none but careful attention. Only competent men employed who have the special training necessary for the effectual carrying out of the work. Estimates for Repairs free of charge.

MUSIC AND MUSIC ACCESSORIES.

A large and varied stock of Standard, Popular, and Classical Music.

A selection of Violins, Guitars, Banjos, Mandolines, &c. Cases, Bows, Strings, and other Fittings.

CATALOGUES ON APPLICATION.

PATERSON, SONS & CO., 152 BUCHANAN ST., GLASGOW. AYR, DUMFRIES, PAISLEY, KILMARNOCK AND GREENOCK.

SALE OF FURNITURE
BY ORDER OF THE TRUSTEE, Mr. WM. H. JACK, Accountant, 99 West Regent Street, Glasgow. ALL GOODS NOW SELLING AT ABOUT HALF ORIGINAL COST.

ALL FURNITURE belonging to the TRUST ESTATE of Messrs. JOHN AINSLIE & SON, Manufacturing Cabinetmakers, 65 Stirling Street, Glasgow, can now been finished and removed to 68 and 74 Union Street for convenience of Sale; also, a good portion of the SEQUESTRATED ESTATE of Messrs. JAMES SWAN & SON, Cabinetmakers, and Upholsterers, Byres Road, Hillhead; and are now selling at 68 and 74 Union Street.

The above goods comprise Drawing-room, Dining-room, Parlour, Bedroom, Hall, Library, and a great variety of other Furniture.

Also a quantity of Silk Brocatelles, Tapestries, Velvets and other Art Furniture Coverings.

NOTICE.—The above goods having been made for a high-class trade, are well worth the attention of intending purchasers of Furniture.

Goods purchased now will be stored Free till Whitsuntide if required.

UNION FURNITURE CO., 68 AND 74 UNION STREET.

THOUSANDS OF POUNDS Sterling HAVE BEEN SAVED to OUR CUSTOMERS IN THE COST OF

MEDICINES.

PHYSICIANS' PRESCRIPTIONS DISPENSED BY QUALIFIED CHEMISTS. ONLY DRUGS OF BEST QUALITY USED.

FRANCIS SPITE & CO., LTD., ST. ENOCH SQUARE, and GLASGOW.

NETTOYAGE A SEC. (Dry Cleaning) GIBSON & REID, PEUVENT NETTOYER PARFAITEMENT, ROBES DE BAL ET ROBES DE SOIREES. A la mode Française sans être détachées.

THE PAISLEY DYE WORKS. RECEIVING OFFICES— 508 Argyle Street. 55 Govan Road, Govan. 81 St. George's Road. 227 Dumbarton Road. 142 Eglinton Street. 33 Kilbowie Rd. 90 Cambridge Street. Also at Edinburgh, Leith, Coatbridge, Hamilton, Wishaw, Port-Glasgow, and Paisley.

SULPHOLINE SKIN LOTION. The only effective remedy for SKIN TROUBLES. Sulpholine quickly drives away Eruptions, Pimples, Eczema, Acne, Blackheads, and all Disfigurements, developing a fair, spotless skin and beautiful complexion.

EDWARD SCOTT'S GREAT ANNUAL CLEARING SALE! NOW FOR THE BARGAINS!!!

I AM CLEARING OUT ALL THE LADIES' OVERSHOES, 8 and 8½, at...	1/
I AM THROWING AWAY ALL THE LADIES' ALPINE SNOW BOOTS at...	4/6
I AM THROWING AWAY ALL THE GENTLEMEN'S SNOW BOOTS, Extra Large Sizes, at...	3/3
GENTLEMEN'S OVERSHOES PITCHING AWAY at...	2/11

THE SNOW HAS COME!!!

GENTLEMEN'S WATERPROOF BOOTS, "ZUG" LEATHER, ABSOLUTELY IMPERVIOUS TO DAMP—Now IS YOUR CHANCE—from	17/6
GENTLEMEN'S ALL-WATERPROOF BOOTS, THE "WOLHAM" HIDE, THOROUGHLY DAMP PROOF—from	14/6
GENTLEMEN'S "KELTIC" LACING BOOTS, WORTH 19s 6d, Going at	12/6
GENTLEMEN'S SPLENDID BOOTS FOR this SEVERE WEATHER from	7/6 10/6

GAITERS, GAITERS, GAITERS, FROM 1s PER PAIR!!!

LADIES' DRESS SLIPPERS—at Absurd Prices to Clear COLOSSAL STOCKS—from 1/

NOW FOR THE DANCE! GENTLEMEN'S PATENT DANCING SHOES, all going (Marvellous!) from 3/6

GENTLEMEN'S SLIPPERS for New Year Presents! COME ALONG! THE PRICES ARE EXTRAORDINARY! Clark's Goods, Reece & Picard's Goods. All the Finest and Best in the World—THROWN AWAY.

LEGGINGS. LEGGINGS. LEGGINGS. THERE NEVER WAS A BETTER TIME TO PURCHASE. FROM IS 11d.

FOR WORKING MEN! THE WHOLE STOCKS OF TRANSVAAL ARMY BOOTS, DOUBLE SOLED, Clearing out at 4/11

LADIES' "KELTIC" BOOTS and SHOES, CHEAPER THAN EVER, from 5/11

BOYS' and GIRLS' BOOTS Thrown Away, to suit ages 5 to 14 years, from 3/9

TRAVELLERS' SAMPLES! TRAVELLERS' SAMPLES!! 25 per Cent. less than former Cost. INFANTS' BOOTS and SHOES, LOVELY GOODS, from 10½d

THE "GRAND CENTRAL" IS BOOMING!!! 193 ARGYLL STREET. THE BARGAINS HERE ARE PHENOMENAL!!! THE WHOLE STOCK THROWN ON THE MARKET TO BE REALISED!!!

SEE THE HANDSOME WINDOWS!!!

EDWARD SCOTT, 8 and 32 JAMAICA STREET, 109 and 795 NEW CITY ROAD, 6 and 7 CHARING CROSS MANSIONS, 353 VICTORIA ROAD, CROSSHILL, AND BRANCHES.

TELEPHONES.

A NECESSITY OF THE AGE.

To everyone who wishes to be abreast of the times a Telephone is a necessity. It is a mistake to think that a Telephone is only value for its cost to a large firm. The want of a telephone prevents many small businesses from getting into touch with the larger houses.

MONEY IS SAVED.

About 6d per day represents the INCLUSIVE COST of an Exchange Telephone anywhere in Glasgow. It is worth this to many, although only used to make or cancel appointments.

TIME IS SAVED.

There are over 7000 of the best firms in Glasgow connected. You have no doubt customers amongst these whom you desire to convenience, and you can talk to the lot for less than ½d per annum per subscriber.

READ THIS.

While you are thinking about having a Telephone others are taking it, and you do not always know whose business is thus going past you.

NOTE SPECIALLY, That the Company can also Supply PRIVATE WIRES to DISTRICT MANAGER.

For Rates and Details of Service, apply to DISTRICT MANAGER.

THE NATIONAL TELEPHONE CO., LTD., ROYAL EXCHANGE, GLASGOW.

NETTOYAGE A SEC. LADIES' DRESSES and GENTLEMEN'S SUITS. Also, all Kinds of Household Furnishings DRY CLEANED, by BRAND & MOLLISON, CITY OF GLASGOW DYEWORKS. RECEIVING SHOPS— 54 UNION STREET 21 Elmbank Street. 61 Victoria R.', Govan. 367 Byars road, Hillhead. 433 Gallowgate. 231 Dumbarton Road. 119 Cowcaddens Street. 45 Princes St., Polkshields. 39 Napiershall Street. 181 Eglinton Street. 138 Great Hamilton Street. 505 Duke St., Dennistoun. 79 Broomielaw, W. Cross. 208 Paisley Rd., W.

SNOW BOOTS and OVERSHOES PROTECTION AGAINST DAMP AND COLD FEET. LADIES, GENTLEMEN, and CHILDREN CAN CHOOSE FROM OUR LARGE STOCK AT MODERATE PRICES. Our Patent Safety-Filled HOT WATER BOTTLES in the Best Rubber, make useful CHRISTMAS PRESENTS. Prices—3s 6d, 4s 6d, 5s 6d, 6s 6d, and 7s 6d. INSPECTION INVITED. CURRIE, THOMSON & CO., 45 JAMAICA STREET.

HEALTH, STRENGTH, ENERGY. PEPPER'S QUININE and IRON TONIC is bracing, vivifying, sustaining, dispels depression, cures indigestion, neuralgia, and all aches or pains. Pepper's Quinine and Iron the only real tonic. Shilling Bottles.

FURNITURE PAYABLE WEEKLY, FORTNIGHTLY, or MONTHLY, AS ARRANGED. ALEXANDER GRANT, 91 GARSCUBE ROAD, GLASGOW. ESTABLISHED 1824.

BOW'S EMPORIUM.

We are prepared for our usual Rush of Business at the TOY DEPARTMENT, and would again ask our Patrons to Come Early and get well served. SEASONABLE PRESENTS to Suit Everybody. There is NO BETTER PLACE than BOW'S EMPORIUM.

TOYS. TOYS. TOYS. SKIN ROCKING HORSE (Real Models), 8s 11d, 12s 9d, 15s 6d, 17s 6d, 22s 6d, 27s 6d, 32s 6d, 3s 6d. Tricycle Horses, 22s 6d, 25s 6d. Toy Perambulators, 5½d, 10½d, 1s 6d, 2s 11d, 5s 6d, 6s 11d, 9s 6d, 12s 6d. Horses and Carts, 6½d, 10½d, 1s 3d, 1s 9d, 2s 9d, 3s 6d, 4s 6d. Dolls an Immense Variety, Dressed and Undressed, from 2d to 6s 6d each. Drums, Guns, Trumpets, Engines, Tops, Mechanical Toys, most interesting to the Children, 3d, 6d each.

PRESENTS! PRESENTS! A Magnificent Range of ALBUMS, Work-Boxes, Writing Desks, smokers' Cabinets, Meidesms, Concertinas, Photo Frames, Dressing Cases, Bags, Purses, Pocket Books, Cigar Cases, Ladies' Plush Companions (fitted). Silk Lined Work Baskets—all at our wellknown Cash Prices.

CHINA TEA SETS. We have constantly displayed about 50 TEA SETS, all plainly priced from 4s 11d to 21s 6d, so that intending Purchasers can walk along our Department and see them all at a glance. Dinner Sets also displayed for the convenience of Customers, 12s 11d, 17s 11d, 19s 11d, 22s, 25s 6d, 32s. Moustache Tea Sets, 3s 6d, 4s 6d, 5s 11d to 10s 6d.

TABLE GLASS AND VASES. EPERGNES, Vases, Decanters, Water Sets, Jellies, Sugars and Creams, Butters, Tumblers, Wine Glasses, Fairy Lamps, Water Jugs, Carafe and Tumblers, Gas Moons, Shades and Stands, Shades of Fruit—all at the Lowest Possible Cash Prices.

SIDEBOARDS. 4-FEET SIDEBOARDS, 3 Bevelled Mirrors on Back, Canopy Top and Pillars, Carved Doors, £4 10s; Do in Solid Oak, £4 19s 6d; 4ft. 6in., details as above, £4 17s 6d; 5 ft 6in of solid Oak Sideboard, Canopy Top, Reeded Pillars, Carved Doors, Pediment, and Panels, £10 10s. We guarantee all our sideboards thoroughly seasoned material.

WARDROBES. 3-FEET 6-IN. WARDROBE, Bevelled Plate-Glass Door, Carved Panels and Long Drawer, £4 7s 6d. 4 Feet Wardrobe, with Mirror Door, Long Drawer, Carved Panels, £4 15s. This is our special Robe. Solid Walnut Wardrobes, 4ft., £7 19s 6d; 4ft. 6in., £9 15s 6d; 5ft., £11 5s. All fully guaranteed.

PARLOUR SUITES. 7-PIECE PARLOUR SUITES, Saddle Made, Birch Frames, Upholstered in Leather Cloth, £5 17s 6d. Do. in Rich Saddlebags, £8 10s; Hairoloth, Tufted Back, £10 10s each. £5 19s 6d. Rich Saddlebag Suites, Heavy Oak Frames, £16 16s. Do. Figured Velvet, £19 10s; Do. in Morocco, £22 10s. These are undoubtedly the best Possible Value for Cash.

CARPETS. TAPESTRY CARPETS, Finest Patterns, 3 by 2½ yards, 15s 6d; 3 by 3 yards, 18s 6d; 3 by 3½ yards, 19s 6d; 3 by 4 yards, 25s 6d. Do. Brussels, 3 by 2½ yards, £2 1s 6d; 3 by 4 yards, £3 1s 6d; by by 4 yards, £2 5s 6d. Velvet Squares, 3 by 2 24s 6d; 3 by 4 yards, £2 8s 6d. Axminster Squares, 3 by 4, £4 19s. Stair Carpets, 18 Inches wide (Hemp), 6½d per yard; Tapestry, 10½d, 1s per yard. Stair Runner, Brussels, 2 yard wide, 2s 6d.

FLOORCLOTH. FLOORCLOTH, 1 yard wide, 5¾d; ¾d; 8¼d per yard; 1 yard wide, 11½d; 14 yard, 1s 2d; 1½ yard, 1s 5d; 2 yards wide, 2s per running yard. Floorcloth Squares, 2 by 2 yards, 3s; 3 by 4 yards, 6s 6d; 4 by 4 yards, 8s. Linoleum Squares, 3 by 2 yards, 4s 10d; 3 by 4 yards, 9s.

KITCHEN FURNITURE. KITCHEN CHAIRS, 2s 6d, 2s 11d, 4s 3d, 4s 6d; Arms to match, 6s 6d, 7s 6d, 8s 6d. Kitchen Tables, 1s 6d, 12s 6d, 14s 11d. Kitchen Dressers for Country Houses, 22 10s, £3 3s, £3 10s.

PARAFFIN LAMPS. TABLE LAMPS, with Metal Stands, Fancy Oil Container, and Globe Complete, 2s 3d, 1s 6d. Do. with Duplex Burner, Chimney, and Fancy Outside Globe, 2s 6d, 2s 10½d, 3s 6d, 4s 9d, 5s 6d. Hanging Lamps, 1s 8d, 2s 6d, 3s 6d, 4s 6d, 5s 11d, 6s 6d, 7s 6d. The Wall Bracket Lamps, 6½d, 9½d, 1s 3d, 1s 6d, 2s 3d, 3s 6d, complete with Globe and Wick.

CHRISTMAS CARDS. See our Stock of CHRISTMAS CARDS. The Designs are Lovely, the Value the best possible. Buy at Bow Cases.

WRINGERS. ACME WRINGERS, with all the Latest Improvements, and warranted best quality. Rubber Rollers—14in., 17s 6d; 15in., 19s 6d; 16in., 21s.

NOTICE.—Please note, we Close Each Evening at 7, on Saturdays at 9.

GOODS DELIVERED FREE BY OUR VANS TO SHETTLESTON BAILLIESTON TOLLCROSS BROOMHOUSE UDDINGSTON COATBRIDGE, GOVAN, RENFREW, PAISLEY, WHITEINCH, CLYDEBANK, CATHCART RUTHERGLEN, AND CAMBUSLANG.

WILLIAM BOW, 61 to 71 HIGH STREET, GLASGOW (CORNER OF BELL STREET) MIDWAY BETWEEN COLLEGE STATION and CROSS STATION.

TREES AND SHRUBS. We invite attention to our Extensive and Well-Grown Stock of FOREST TREES, also ORNAMENTAL and FLOWERING SHRUBS, suitable for Parks, Lawns, Villa Grounds, &c. FRUIT TREES AND BUSHES IN A BEARING CONDITION. ROSES. A Large Collection of Strong, Well-Grown Plants, including all the Newest and Best Varieties. Catalogues free on application. Special Quotations for Large quantities, and Estimates for Planting. Our Nurseries are within 3 minutes' walk from Cathcart Station. Trains from Central every 10 minutes.

AUSTIN & M'ASLAN, 89 MITCHELL STREET, GLASGOW. ESTABLISHED 1717.

FURNITURE BY EASY PAYMENTS. £5 to £1000 WORTH SUPPLIED.

PAYABLE WEEKLY, FORTNIGHTLY, or MONTHLY. 1 ROOM & KITCHEN Furnished....£10 13 9 2 ROOMS & KITCHEN Furnished....£14 6 0 FOUR APARTMENTS for £27 10s, £32, £40. Larger Houses in proportion.

SOLID OAK SIDEBOARDS, from £5 10s to £45, payable deposit and fortnightly instalments. OAK SUITES in real leather, 6 pieces. Reliable goods, £12 12s. Payable deposit and weekly. TELESCOPE TABLES, heavy make, 6 legs, Solid Oak, 4 feet, £2 12s. Easy payments. OVERMANTELS from 18s 6d. Bedsteads from 21s. Carpets from 12s 6d. Oval Tables, 25s. CALL OR WRITE FOR ILLUSTRATED PRICE-LIST AND TERMS. Kindly mention "THE DAILY RECORD."

BROWN, BARKER & BELL, 79 UNION STREET (1 up), GLASGOW.

PATENTS FOR INVENTIONS. How to Obtain and Maintain them. A Handbook on Patent Law and Practice, by WALLACE FAIRWEATHER, C.E. Chartered Patent Agent. May be had, Post Free, on application to CRUIKSHANK & FAIRWEATHER, 62 ST. VINCENT STREET, Glasgow.

A WONDERFUL MEDICINE.

BEECHAM'S PILLS.
BEECHAM'S PILLS. Worth a Guinea a Box.
BEECHAM'S PILLS. For Bilious Attacks.
BEECHAM'S PILLS. For Nervous Disorders.

FULL AND WONDERFUL PARTICULARS TO-MORROW (FRIDAY).

THE RE-BUILDING OF
PETTIGREW AND STEPHENS' WAREHOUSE.

THE VAST EXTENSION NOW APPARENT TO ALL.

THE OUTLINES OF WHAT IS TO BE THE "STORE OF THE CENTURY" NOW BEGINNING TO APPEAR.

THE CLEVER ARRANGEMENTS FOR CONDUCTING BUSINESS DURING RECONSTRUCTION ARE IN EVERYONE'S MOUTH.

SO FAR, ALL IS WELL! BUT UNFORESEEN DIFFICULTIES HAVING ARISEN

ANOTHER DRASTIC MOVE AND ANOTHER FORCED SALE IS FOUND NECESSARY.

IMPORTANT NOTICE. TO ENABLE THE CONTRACTORS WHO ARE CARRYING THROUGH THE VAST EXTENSION SCHEME OF PETTIGREW AND STEPHENS TO FULFIL THEIR UNDERTAKING, AND HAND OVER A PORTION OF THE NEW BUILDING IN TIME FOR THE SPRING TRADE, THEY HAVE DEMANDED A FURTHER SURRENDER OF A PORTION OF THE PRESENT PREMISES FOR A SHORT PERIOD. THIS MEANS THAT AT ALL COSTS, A STOCK VALUED AT £40,000 MUST BE REDUCED IN THAT TIME TO ONE OF £20,000, AND THAT A GREAT FORCED SALE OF A MOST IMPERATIVE AND DRASTIC CHARACTER MUST BE HELD. NO TIME CAN BE LOST IN THIS MATTER.

THE FIRM HAVE THE REPUTATION OF DOING NOTHING BY HALVES, AND WHEN THEY SAY THAT THIS IS TO BE ONE OF THE GREATEST EFFORTS IN THEIR

The Last Word
in RACING
is found in the
NOON RECORD

Daily Record
and Mail.
The All-Scotland Newspaper. Sale Twice That of Any Other Morning Paper.
ESTAB. 1847—No. 22,562 GLASGOW, THURSDAY, MAY 8, 1919 ONE PENNY

Are you Reading our great New Serial:
The Great God Chance?
OPENING CHAPTERS
On PAGE 13.
A Story that will Charm and Delight you.

PEACE TREATY FOR GERMANY STERN BUT JUST.

THE ALLIES' TERMS.

FRENCH FRONTIER OF 1870 RESTORED.

£5,000,000,000 INDEMNITY.

ALLIED TROOPS ON RHINE FOR FIFTEEN YEARS.

Terms Presented.—The Germans were presen ed with the Allied Peace Treaty at Versailles yesterday afternoon. The sitting did not last an hour, and the time was occupied with the speech of M. Clemenceau, in handing over the Treaty to the enemy delegation, and with Count Brockdorff-Rantzau's reply.

"The time has come when we must settle our accounts," said M. Clemenceau, adding that the Germans had asked for peace, and the Allies were ready to give it. But, he added, the Second Treaty of Versailles had been bought at too great a price to allow the Allies to do other than guard themselves against a recrudescence of another war.

Count Rantzau, in reply, repudiated the suggestion that the entire responsibility for the war rested on Germany's shoulders, and asserted that Germany alone had not been guilty of atrocities.

£5,000,000,000.—By the terms of the Treaty, for the consideration of which fifteen days are allowed, Germany is made responsible for indemnities amounting to £5,000,000,000. £1,000,000,000 is due within two years, and bonds to the amount of £4,000,000,000 are to be held by the Allies.

Back to France.—The French frontier of 1870 is restored, with a reservation regarding the Saar Valley. The restoration of Alsace-Lorraine to France is described as dating from the signing of the Armistice. In return for her ruined mines, France receives the full ownership of the mines in the Saar Valley.

Belgium and Poland.—A section of Prussian territory is to be ceded to Belgium. To Poland must be given Upper Silesia, Posen, and part of the province of West Prussia. Danzig is to be a free city under the League of Nations.

New German Army.—Germany's new Army must not exceed 100,000 men, including not more than 4000 officers. No reserve of officers with war experience will be permitted. Armament production must be limited in accordance with the size of the Army.

Rhine Occupation.—To guarantee the execution of the Treaty, German territory to the west of the Rhine, together with the bridgeheads, will be occupied by Allied forces for 15 years. If, before the expiration of 15 years, Germany complies with all the Treaty undertakings, the occupying troops will be withdrawn immediately.

TREATY HANDED OVER.

HISTORIC SCENE AT TRIANON PALACE.

Versailles, Wednesday.

The meeting between the Allied and German delegates for presentation of the peace terms to the latter opened at a minute past three and the actual presentation took place a few minutes later.

The proceedings lasted less than an hour. The meeting terminated at 3.51 p.m.

President Wilson, with the other American delegates, arrived about ten minutes to the hour, and was closely followed by Mr Lloyd George and the other British representatives. The reception of both was very cordial, both outside the Trianon Palace and by those allowed inside the grounds.

Almost on the stroke of three o'clock the German elegates arrived in three cars, the first containing Count Brockdorff-Rantzau.

Their reception was, to say the least, cold.

On the steps of the main entrance to the Trianon Palace were grouped the officers of the Allied armies. It was noticed that, while some turned their backs, evidently to avoid saluting, those who did salute did so in a most formal and perfunctory manner.

The sitting having been declared open, M. Clemenceau read a document, a copy of which had been handed to every delegate in advance informing the Germans that they would be given a fortnight in which to present their observations on the Treaty.

While M. Clemenceau's speech was being translated into English, M. Dutasta, Secretary-General of the Peace Conference, slipped quietly across the space between the tables and handed to Count Brockdorff-Rantzau, who rose to receive it, the bulky volume containing the text of the Treaty.

M. CLEMENCEAU'S SPEECH.

"The Time Has Come to Settle Our Accounts."

M. Clemenceau, speaking in French (his speech was translated as he proceeded into English and German at convenient intervals), said:—

Gentlemen Plenipotentiaries of the German Empire—It is neither the time nor place for superfluous words. You have before you the accredited plenipotentiaries of all the small and great Powers united to fight together in the war that was so cruelly imposed on them.

The time has come when we must settle our accounts. You have asked for peace. We are ready to give you peace.

We shall present to you now a book which contains our conditions. You will be given every facility to examine those conditions and time necessary for it.

Everything will be done with the courtesy that is the privilege of civilised nations. To give you my thought completely, you will find us ready to give you any explanation you want, but we must say at the same time that this Second Treaty of Versailles has cost us too much not to take on our side all necessary precautions and guarantees that this peace shall be a lasting one.

FIFTEEN DAYS ALLOWED.

I will give you notice of the procedure that has been adopted by the Conference for discussion, and if anyone has any observation to offer he will have the right to do so. No oral discussion is to take place, and the observations of the German delegation will have to be submitted in writing.

The German plenipotentiaries will know that they have the maximum period of fifteen days within which to present in English and French their written observations on the whole of the Treaty.

Before the expiration of the aforesaid period of fifteen days the German delegates will be entitled to send their reply on the particular headings of the Treaty or to ask questions in regard to them. After having examined the observations presented within the aforementioned period the Supreme Council will send their answer in writing to the German delegation and determine the period within which the final answer must be given by that delegation.

I wish to add that when we receive, after two or three or four or five days any observation from the German delegation on any part of the Treaty, we shall not wait until the end of the fifteen days to give our answer; we shall at once proceed in the way indicated by this document.

THE GERMAN REPLY.

Spirited Repudiation of Blood-Guiltiness.

Count Brockdorff-Rantzau, speaking in German (the speech was translated into French and English), said:—

Gentlemen,—We are deeply impressed with tho sublime task which has brought us hither to give a durable peace to the world. We are under no illusion as to the extent of our defeat and the degree of our want of power. We know that the power of the German arms is broken. We know the power of the hatred which we encounter here, and we have heard the passionate demand that the victors shall make us pay as the vanquished and shall punish those who are worthy of being punished.

It is demanded of us that we shall confess ourselves to be the only ones guilty of the war. Such a confession in my mouth will be a lie.

We are far from declining any responsibility for this great world war having come to pass and for its having been made in the way in which it was made by the attitude of the former German Government at the Hague Peace Conference.

Its action and omissions in the tragic twelve days of July certainly contributed to the disaster, but we energetically deny that Germany and its people, who were convinced that they were making a war of defence, were alone guilty. Nobody will want to contend that the disaster took its course only in the disastrous moment when the heir to the throne of Austria-Hungary fell the victim of murderous hands.

In the last fifty years the Imperialism of all the European States has poisoned the international situation. The policy of retaliation and the policy of expansion and disregard of the rights of peoples to determine their own destiny have contributed to the illness of Europe which reached its course in the world war.

NOT THE ONLY CRIMINAL.

The Russian mobilisation took from Statesmen the possibility of healing, and gave the decision into the hands of military powers. Public opinion in all the countries of our adversaries is resounding with the crimes which Germany is said to have committed in the war. Here also we are ready to confess the wrong that may have been done. We have not come here to belittle the responsibility of the men who have waged the war politically and economically and to deny any crimes which may have been committed against the rights of peoples.

We repeat the declaration made in the German Reichstag at the beginning of the war. That is to say, "A wrong has been done to Belgium, and we are willing to repair it." But in the manner of making war also Germany is not the only guilty one. Every nation knows of deeds of people which the best nations only remember with regret.

I do not want to answer by reproaches to reproaches, but I ask them to remember when full reparation is demanded not to forget the Armistice. It took you six weeks till we got it at last, and six months till we come to know your conditions of peace.

THE ALLIED BLOCKADE

Crimes in war may not be excusable, but they are committed in the struggle for victory and in defence of national existence, and passions are aroused which make the conscience of peoples blunt. The hundreds of thousands of non-combatants who have perished since November 11 by reason of the blockade were killed with cold deliberation after our adversaries had conquered and victory had been assured to them. Think of that when you speak of guilt and of punishment.

The measure of the guilt of all those who have taken part can only be stated by an impartial inquest before a neutral commission, before which all the principal persons of the tragedy are allowed to speak and to which all the archives are open.

We have demanded such an inquest, and we repeat this demand again at this Conference, where we stand facing our adversaries alone and without any allies.

We are not quite without protection. You yourselves have brought us an ally, namely, the right which is guaranteed by the Treaty, by the principles of the Peace. The Allies and Associated Governments foreswore in the time between the 5th of October and 5th of November, 1918, a peace of violence, and wrote a "peace of justice" on their banner.

On October 5th, 1918, the German Government proposed the principles of the President of the United States of North America as a basis of peace, and on the 5th of November their Secretary of State, Mr. Lansing, declared that the Allied and Associated Powers agreed to this basis with two definite deviations.

The principles of President Wilson have thus become binding for both parties to the war—you as well as for us, and also for our former Allies. The various principles demand from us heavy national and economic sacrifices, but the holy fundamental rights of all peoples are protected by this Treaty. The conscience of the world is behind it. There is no nation which might violate it without punishment.

You will find us ready to examine upon this basis the preliminary peace which you have proposed to us with a firm intention of rebuilding, in common with you, that which has been destroyed, and repairing any wrong that may have been committed—principally the wrong to Belgium—and to show to mankind new aims of political and social progress.

Considering the tremendous number of problems which arise, we ought, as soon as possible, to make an examination of the principal tasks by special commissions of experts on the basis of the Treaty which you have proposed to us. In this it will be our chief task to re-establish the devasted vigour of mankind, and of all the people who have taken part by an international protection of the life, health and liberty of the working classes.

As our next aim, I consider the reconstruction of the territories of Belgium and of Northern France, which have been occupied by us, and which have been destroyed by war. To do so we have taken upon ourselves a solemn obligation and we are resolved to execute it to the extent which will have been agreed upon between us.

MUTUAL HELP.

In this task we cannot do without the co-operation of our former adversaries. We cannot accomplish the work without the technical and financial participation of the victorious peoples, and you cannot execute it without us. Impoverished Europe must desire that the reconstruction shall be fulfilled with the greatest success and with as little expense as is in any way possible. This desire can only be fulfilled by a clear understanding about the best methods to be employed.

It would be the worst method to go on and have the work done by German prisoners of war. Certainly this work is cheap, but it would cost the world dear if hatred and despair should seize the German people when they consider that their brothers and sons and fathers who are prisoners are kept prisoners, beyond the preliminary peace, in the former penal work.

Without any immediate solution of this question, which has been drawn out too long, we cannot come to a durable peace. Our experts of both sides will have to examine how the German people may come up to their financial obligations to repair without succumbing under the heavy burden. A crash would bereave those who have a right to reparation of the advantages to which they lay claim, and would draw after it an irretrievable disorder of the whole of the European economical system.

Vanquishers as well as the vanquished people must guard against this menacing danger, with its incalculable consequences. There is only one means of banishing it—unlimited confession of economical and social solidarity of all peoples in a free and rising League of Nations.

ONE SUBLIME THOUGHT.

Gentlemen, the sublime thought to be derived from the most terrible disaster in history of mankind is the League of Nations. The greatest progress in the development of mankind has been pronounced, and will make its way. Only if the gates of the League of Nations are thrown open to all who are of goodwill can this aim be attained, and only then the dead of this war will not have died in vain.

The German people in their hearts are ready to take upon themselves their heavy lot if the bases of Peace which have been established are not any more shaken. The Peace which cannot be defended in the name of right before the world always calls forth new resistances against it.

Nobody will be capable of subscribing to it with a good conscience, for it will not be possible of fulfilment. Nobody could be able to take upon themselves the guarantee of its execution which ought to be in its signature. We shall examine the document handed to us with goodwill and in the hope that the final result of our interview may be subscribed to by all of us.

M. Clemenceau said:—"Has anybody any more observations to offer? Does no one wish to speak? If not, the meeting is closed."

PROTECTION FOR FRANCE.

ASSURANCE BY BRITAIN AND AMERICA.

Paris, Wednesday.

The following official statement was issued this evening:—

In addition to the securities offered in the Treaty of Peace, the President of the United States of America has pledged himself to propose to the Senate of the United States, and the Prime Minister of Great Britain has pledged himself to propose to the Parliament of Great Britain, an engagement, subject to the approval of the Council of the League of Nations, to go immediately to the assistance of France in the case of an unprovoked attack by Germany.—C.N.

FATE OF GERMAN COLONIES.

MANDATES GIVEN TO ALLIES.

BRITAIN'S SHARE.

Paris, Wednesday.

The following official announcement is made this evening:—

The Council of Three—M. Clemenceau, President Wilson, and Mr. Lloyd George—yesterday decided as to the disposition of the former German Colonies as follows:—

Togoland and the Cameroons.—France and Great Britain shall make a joint recommendation to the League of Nations as to their future.

German East Africa.—The mandate shall be held by Great Britain.

German South-West Africa.—The mandate shall be held by the Union of South Africa.

The German Samoan Islands.—The mandate shall be held by New Zealand.

The other German Pacific Possessions South of the Equator, excluding the German Samoan Islands and Nauru.—The mandate shall be held by Australia.

Nauru.—The mandate shall be given to the British Empire.

The German Pacific Islands North of the Equator.—The mandate shall be held by Japan.

OUTLINE OF TERMS.

END OF CONSCRIPTION IN GERMANY.

The Treaty of Peace now handed to the Germans is not by itself the final document on which the reconstruction of the world after the War will be based.

It is designed, in the first instance, to set forth the conditions upon which alone the Allied and Associated Powers will make peace with Germany, and along with these to establish those institutions which the co-operative efforts of the Allies have devised for the prevention of wars in the future and the betterment of mankind.

For this latter reason it includes the Covenant of the League of Nations and the International Labour Convention, but it does not deal, except incidentally, with the complicated problems arising out of the liquidation of the Austrian Empire, nor with the arrangements to be made in the territories of two enemy Powers, Turkey and Bulgaria, except in so far as it binds Germany to accept whatever subsequent settlement may be decided upon by the Allies in the case of these belligerents.

The Treaty is divided into 13 sections. The first contains the Covenant of the League of Nations, to which functions are assigned in various places by the Treaty.

The second describes the geographical frontiers of Germany, beginning at the north-eastern point of the present Belgian frontier. The third, which consists of twelve clauses, binds the Germans to accept the political changes in Europe brought about by the Treaty. It establishes two new States, Czecho-Slovakia and Poland, and provides for their recognition.

It revises the basis of Belgian sovereignty and alters the boundaries of Belgium. It establishes new systems of government in Luxembourg and the Saar Basin, and restores Alsace-Lorraine to France.

The Fourth Section deals with the political reconstruction of the territories outside Europe affected by the war. It contains a general renunciation on the part of Germany of her possessions and rights abroad.

The Fifth Section sets forth the military, naval, and air conditions of peace, limits the size of the German Army and Navy, and abolishes compulsory recruiting in Germany as a first step towards general disarmament.

The Sixth Section inposes on all the signatory Powers the obligation to maintain all the graves of the fallen, and regulates the return of prisoners of war.

The Seventh Section deals with Responsibilities and Punishment, and provides for the trial of the ex-Emperor William.

The Thirteenth is made up of a series of operative clauses; the termination of

Continued on Page 2.

ALL the News
ALL the Pictures
ALL the Time

Daily Record and Mail.
The All-Scotland Newspaper. Sale Twice That of Any Other Morning Paper.
ESTAB. 1847—No. 22,601 GLASGOW, MONDAY, JUNE 23, 1919 ONE PENNY

Advertise YOUR WANTS IN OUR CLASSIFIED COLUMNS 1d per word.

GERMANS SINK SCAPA FLOW FLEET BEFORE SIGNING!

ENEMY TREACHERY.

GERMANS SCUTTLE FLEET AT SCAPA.

ADMIRAL UNDER ARREST.

On the eve of the signing of Peace, the Germans have sunk or beached all their seventy-one warships interned at Scapa Flow.

Scuttlers Ignore Orders.—After the Germans had scuttled their ships, they set out in boats for the shore. Some of the boats, refusing to stop when ordered, were fired on, and a few of the enemy were killed and wounded.

No British on Board.—By the terms of the Armistice, there were no British guards on board the German ships, which were interned with skeleton enemy crews as caretakers. The Germans may have opened the sea cocks.

ENEMY FIRED ON.

GERMAN FLAG RAISED BEFORE SHIPS SANK.

The events at Scapa Flow were disclosed in the following statement issued by the Admiralty on Saturday night:—

This afternoon certain of the interned German ships at Scapa were sunk and abandoned by their crews.

The crews will be detained in safe custody.

A later announcement by the Admiralty states:—

According to the latest reports received from Scapa Flow, all the interned German battleships and battle cruisers have sunk, except the battleship Baden, which was still afloat.

Five light cruisers have been sunk, but the other three have been beached.

Eighteen destroyers have also been beached by the local tugs, and four destroyers were still afloat.

The rest of the destroyers have sunk.

The German Rear-Admiral and most of the Germans from the ships are in custody on board H.M. ships.

Some boats from the ships refused to stop when ordered were fired on, and a small number of Germans were killed and wounded.

In accordance with the terms of the Armistice, the German ships were interned with skeleton German crews as caretakers, and without British guards on board.

Highly-placed British Naval officers say the Germans may have opened the sea cocks and thus filled the ships, or may have bored holes through the vessels' bottoms.

It will take hundreds of thousands of pounds to float the ships, and to clear them out of the way at Scapa by blowing up would be an expensive process.

TOO MUCH TRUST.

The German ships at Scapa Flow have been treated as interned and not surrendered. The vessels had skeleton German crews on board under their own admiral, and while the Admiralty had the right to send inspecting parties aboard to see that the conditions of the internment were carried out, no other visits were ever permitted.

The German crews were only inspected periodically by British naval officers.

It is stated that arrangements had been made to board the German fleet on Monday should peace be signed, the ships then passing automatically to the Allies.

A British proposal at the Peace Conference was that the surrendered enemy fleet should be sunk in mid-ocean. The French objected to this, pointing out that the French Fleet had been neglected during the war owing to the necessary national concentration on their military effort. They, therefore, proposed the distribution of the surrendered fleet among the Allies.

RED FLAG AS SIGNAL.

A Thurso correspondent gives the following particulars:—

The hoisting of a red flag appears to have been the pre-arranged signal amongst the German crews for the scuttling of their respective ships, an act fully in keeping with the traditions of the German race.

The signal was responded to by the crews taking to their boats and making for the shore, whereupon the guard ships immediately opened fire for the purpose of getting the men to return, but they jumped out of their boats and swam ashore, where they were rounded up.

"SERVES US RIGHT."

Admiral Sir Percy Scott, discussing the Scapa Flow outrage with a Press representative in London, said:—

"It serves us right for trusting the Huns throughout the war.

"They have shown they are not a civilised race, and they never ought to have been treated as such. They are barbarians."

STORY OF THE COUP.

BATTLESHIPS CAN BE SEEN BOTTOM UP.

(From Our Own Correspondent.)

Kirkwall, Sunday.

The German coup at Scapa Flow was brought off about noon on Saturday, when many of the British ships had put out to sea for exercises, and, therefore, when the Germans, no doubt, thought the watch over them was somewhat relaxed.

The present position seems to be that one German battleship remains afloat, three light cruisers are beached—two in Swanbister Bay and one off Cavako, and a few destroyers are beached off Fara.

Of the sunk battleships three may be discerned from the shore lying bottom upwards. The battle cruiser Hindenburg sank whilst an attempt was being made to beach her. She is not lying in deep water, and her funnels and masts can be easily seen from the shore, so that probably it will not prove a very difficult task to raise her.

The Emden is among the cruisers which were beached. One of these cruisers was saved very simply by casting her adrift and allowing the wind to drive her ashore.

Of the light cruisers which sank, one went down in deep water whilst an attempt was being made by a tug to run her aground.

Information in regard to occurrences at the destroyer anchorage is somewhat difficult to obtain.

FIRE OPENED.

It is stated that the German ensign was run up and the crews of the destroyers were seen to be leaving in the small boats which were moored astern. Certain British vessels were ordered to open fire, whereupon the Germans remaining aboard immediately jumped into the sea.

A number of them were picked up by our craft which were ordered to the scene.

The number of casualties which occurred is not yet available.

As soon as news of the situation had been received by the authorities on shore, steps were taken to intercept the Germans who were making for the shore, and a body of royal marines, fully armed, took up positions along the beach. None of the German sailors who succeeded in reaching the shore were allowed to land, but were taken prisoners and sent to the British ships, some to H.M.S. Imperieuse and others to H.M.S. Victorious.

Eye-witnesses of the proceedings give various accounts of what occurred. People living in the vicinity of Houton Pier declare that the German Admiral succeeded in reaching Houton quite early, and that he asked the men at the aviation station to go out and rescue some of the German sailors who were in difficulties.

Several men were seen to jump into the water while the Emden was being towed shorewards.

One of these Germans made for a buoy, and reaching it sat astride it for some hours before he was taken off by one of our small craft.

VIOLENT EXPLOSION.

Early this morning a violent explosion occurred off Houton at the spot where one of the German warships was sunk.

An eye-witness states that the explosion threw up a pillar of water and a large quantity of debris several hundred feet.

The single battleship which remained at anchor last night has been put on the ground in Swanbister Bay beside the two light cruisers beached there on the previous afternoon.

The enemy ships which are not completely under water are all flying the British ensign. The prisoners are now on board the Royal Sovereign. The remainder of the British Fleet have sailed.

Further stories from our own correspondent of the sinking of the German Fleet will be found in Page 9, column 3.

COAL INQUIRY REPORTS.

JUSTICE SANKEY FOR STATE CONTROL.

OWNERS AGAINST.

The findings of the Coal Commission were issued yesterday, and are now in the hands of the King.

The principal recommendations in each of the four reports are thus briefly summarised:—

Mr. Justice Sankey—"I recommend, on the evidence before me, that the principle of State ownership of the coal mines be accepted. I recommend that Parliament be invited immediately to pass legislation acquiring the coal Royalties for the State, and paying fair and just compensation to the owners."

Mr. Robert Smillie. Justice Sankey.

Mr. Smillie's Group—Substantial agreement with Mr. Justice Sankey's report. Messrs. Smillie, Hodges, and Smith, however, do not agree that any compensation whatever should be paid to the present mineral owners, but would grant compassionate allowances in cases in which small Royalty owners were expropriated in such a way as to deprive them of their means of livelihood.

Sir Adam Nimmo's Group—"Evidence submitted to the Commission affords no ground for belief that nationalisation would have the effect of reducing the price of coal. We have carefully weighed the whole of the evidence, and have come to the conclusion that the nationalisation of the coal industry in any form would be detrimental to the development of the industry and to the economic life of the country."

Sir Arthur Duckham—"A Ministry of Mines should be set up which should, at a later date, form one of a group of Ministries attached to a Ministry of Industry to supervise and control all mineral rights throughout Great Britain, and to ensure the proper working of all minerals."

Details of the reports will be found on Page 2.

71 ENEMY WARSHIPS.

The interned German Fleet at Scapa Flow consisted of:—

Five battle cruisers.
Nine battleships.
Seven light cruisers.
50 destroyers.

The battle cruisers were the Seydlitz, Hindenburg, Derfflinger, Moltke, and Von der Tann.

The battleships were the Friedrich der Grosse, Konig Albrecht, Kaiser, Kronprinz Wilhelm, Kaiserin, Bayern, Markgraf, Prince Regent Luitpold, and Grosser Kurfurst.

The light cruisers were the Karlsruhe, Frankfurt, Emden, Nurnberg, Brummer, Kohn, and Bremse.

The destroyers were all of the newest types, but all the ships were in a more or less dilapidated state internally.

It will be recalled that it was on November 21, 1918, that the pride of the Kaiser's navy surrendered to Admiral Beatty's Grand Fleet.

The German fleet came from Kiel to a point 50 miles east of the May Island, where prize crews were put on board, and they were escorted to Scapa Flow and interned with skeleton crew of German sailors.

NEW GERMAN MOVE.

OFFER TO SIGN IF KAISER GOES SCOT FREE.

ALLIES REMAIN ADAMANT.

The new German Cabinet has offered to sign the Peace Treaty on certain conditions, but the Allies insist on the acceptance of all their Terms by seven o'clock to-night.

Guilt of the War.—One of the conditions, it is stated, on which Germany professed willingness to sign was that she should be absolved from the sole guilt of the world war.

Trial of War Lords.—Another reservation the Germans proposed was that the Peace Treaty should not provide for the punishment of the guilty, amongst them the ex-Kaiser.

TIME UP TO-DAY.

TREATY MAY BE SIGNED ON THURSDAY.

Paris, Sunday.

The "Echo De Paris" understands from a member of the Peace Conference that a further extension of forty-eight hours may be allowed to the Germans, provided the new German Government gives a formal undertaking before to-morrow evening that it will sign the Peace Treaty unconditionally.

The same paper also anticipates that the signing of the Treaty will take place next Thursday afternoon.

Everything is now ready in the Hall of Mirrors for the signing of the Peace Treaty.

In the middle of the immense hall, on a platform, will be placed a large table around which the plenipotentiaries will take their seats.

In front of M. Clemenceau, who will preside, will be placed a small table on which will be laid the diplomatic documents which each representative of the Powers, who will be called forward in the alphabetical order of their countries, will sign.

The chief of each delegation will place the seal of his Government on the documents, and, as there are more than a hundred delegates, the ceremony, which will begin early in the afternoon, will last about an hour and a half.

FINAL GERMAN PROTEST.

It is not certain that M. Clemenceau will deliver a speech, but the chief of the German delegation will doubtless wish to make a final protest.

About four hundred people will be present at this historic scene.

M. Pichon, the Minister of Foreign Affairs, has requested that everything shall be ready by Tuesday, although it is not considered that the ceremony can take place before the end of the week, at the earliest on Thursday.

The resumption of diplomatic relations will not follow immediately on the signature of the Treaty, but only after its ratification.

Authority for German citizens to come to France will also not be granted until after ratification.—P.A.

CONFESSION OF WAR GUILT.

Berlin, Saturday.

The new Ministry is believed to be in favour of signing the Peace Treaty on the basis agreed upon between the Majority Socialists and the Centre, namely, that the signature will not cover points which are incompatible with Germany's honour; that is to say, the confession of sole guilt for the war, and the surrender of German nationals to an Entente tribunal.

The "Cologne Gazette's" Weimar correspondent is responsible for the report that Herr Erzberger has asked in Versailles what the Entente's attitude would be towards these points, and the Entente, it is alleged, gave him informally to understand that it would not be disinclined to yield on the points affecting Germany's honour. An official demarche has now been made in this direction, the "Gazette" says, and it is hoped the Entente's reply will be received by Monday.

An official telegram from Weimar denies that any such Note as reported by the "Cologne Gazette" has been sent to the Allies.—P.A.

SLOVAK-BOLSHEVIK MOVE.

Copenhagen, Sunday.

A Kaschau telegram, received via Budapest, says that a Slovak Revolutionary Governing Council has been constituted with Anton Janousek as President.

The Council, which has decided on the title of the Slovak Soviet Republic, has telegraphed its greetings to Lenin and the Hungarian Soviet Government.—Reuter.

WEIMAR DECISION.

PEACE TO BE SIGNED WITH RESERVATIONS.

Berlin, Sunday.

In the National Assembly at Weimar to-day, Herr Bauer, the Premier, stated that the Government would give full powers for the signing of the Peace Treaty in the following form:—

"The Government of the German Republic is ready to sign the Peace Treaty, without, however, thereby admitting that the German people is the author of the war and without undertaking the obligation of Articles 227 to 230."

A vote of confidence was passed in the Government by 236 votes to 89, with 68 abstentions.

The Articles referred to relate to the trial of the ex-Kaiser and the surrender of other Germans.—P.A.

ANSWER FROM THE ALLIES.

Paris, Sunday.

M. Clemenceau, Mr. Lloyd George and President Wilson met to-night at Mr. Lloyd George's house to consider the German Note of conditions, as announced by Herr Bauer, on which Germany would sign the Peace Treaty.

The answer was made after the meeting to the effect that the Allied and Associated Powers could accept no qualification or reservation, and must require from the German representatives an unequivocal decision as to their purpose to sign and accept the Treaty as a whole or not to sign and accept it as finally formulated.

After signature, Germany would be held responsible for the execution of every stipulation of the Treaty.—Reuter.

POINTS IN GERMAN NOTE.

According to the "Germania," the new Foreign Minister, Herr Hermann Mueller, will make known to the National Assembly to-day the text of the Note which is to be sent to the Entente, and which will be despatched immediately on its being approved by a majority of the National Assembly.

The "Germania" professes to be able to declare that in this Note Germany does not accept Article 231 of the Peace Treaty, by which Germany accepts all responsibility for the world war, and, further, does not accept Articles 227 to 230, the sections entitled "Penalties."

Germany cannot assent to the Peace Treaty from its inner conviction, because it contains conditions that cannot be fulfilled and cannot be borne.

Germany, therefore, does not sign voluntarily, but only yields to force.

The Note also declares that the economic and financial terms exceed the limits of Germany's capacity.

Germany, therefore, will sign only under reserve, and with the best will in the world will not undertake full responsibility for the execution of the Terms.

The Cabinet has not yet decided on the manner of signing.—P.A.

PEACE VOTE AT WEIMAR.

Amsterdam, Sunday.

According to a telegram from Weimar received here, Herr Bauer, the new Premier, announced at to-day's session of the National Assembly that the Imperial Government had decided to sign the Peace Treaty, "provided it were ratified by the National Assembly."—P.A.

Copenhagen, Sunday.

A telegram from Weimar says:—

The National Assembly to-day, by 237 votes to 138, resolved "that the National Assembly agrees to sign the Treaty."

Five deputies abstained from voting.—P.A.

MR. CHURCHILL IN PARIS.

Paris, Sunday.

Mr. Churchill and Mr. Montagu, the Secretary of State for India, arrived here yesterday evening, and dined with Mr. Lloyd George.—Reuter.

Daily Record and Mail

The All-Scotland Newspaper. Sale Twice That of Any Other Morning Paper.

SPECIAL PEACE EDITION

ESTAB. 1847—No. 22,607 GLASGOW, MONDAY, JUNE 30, 1919 20 PAGES. ONE PENNY.

BLOCKADE TO BE LIFTED IF GERMANY PLAYS FAIR.

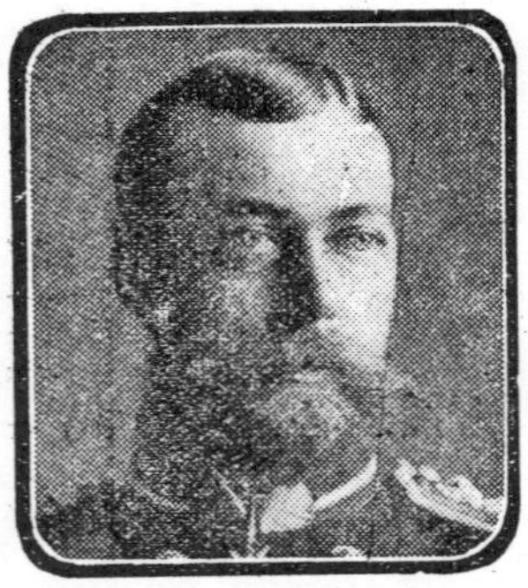

King George, who has sent messages of congratulation to his Allies.

PEACE PACT SIGNED AT LAST.

IMPOSING SPECTACLE IN HISTORIC PALACE OF FRENCH KINGS.

BETHMANN HOLLWEG'S DRAMATIC OFFER.

The German delegates signed the Peace Treaty at Versailles on Saturday afternoon at 3.15.

Simple Ceremony.—Thus was brought to a close the great war with Germany, which commenced on August 1, 1914, and lasted four years and 328 days. The historic ceremony, which took place in the ancient Palace of the French Kings, where the German Empire was proclaimed 48 years ago, was completed in half an hour.

Hollweg's Request.—Declaring that during his period of office as German Chancellor he was solely responsible for the ex-Kaiser's political acts, Herr von Bethmann-Hollweg has made a request to the Allies that he be put on trial instead of William II. (See page 2.)

The Allies have intimated to Germany their readiness immediately to raise the blockade as soon as they have been officially advised of the complete ratification of the Treaty by the German Republic.

Germany asks a meeting of the Plenipotentiaries of both parties to "supplement and correct the provisions of the Peace Treaty."

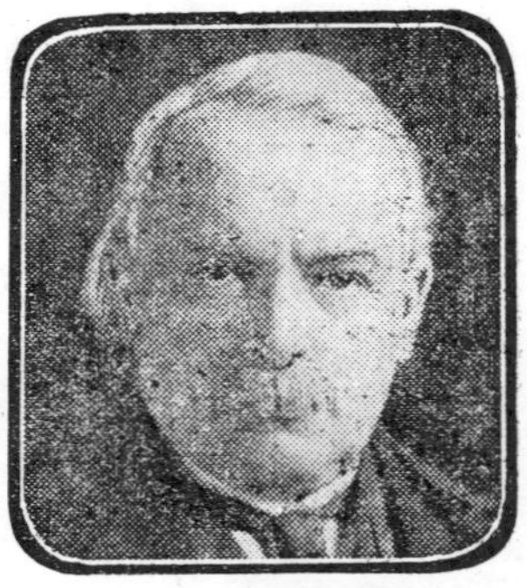

Mr. Lloyd George, who signed the Peace for Great Britain.

THE KING TO HIS PEOPLE.

ROYAL WORDS OF HOPE TO ALLIES.

The King has delivered to his people and his Allies messages as follows:—

TO HIS PEOPLE

"The signing of the Treaty of Peace will be received with deep thankfulness throughout the British Empire.

"This formal act brings to its conclusive stages the terrible war which has devastated and distracted the world.

"It is manifest of the victory of the ideals of freedom and liberty for which we have made untold sacrifices.

"I share my people's joy and thanksgiving, and earnestly pray that the coming years of peace may bring to them every increasing happiness and prosperity."

TO PRESIDENT OF FRANCE.

"On this happy occasion, when our enemies have finally acknowledged defeat, I beg you, Monsieur le President, to accept the expression of my heartiest congratulations and good wishes.

"Under your able guidance, and the magnificent leadership of her great soldiers and statesmen, France has at length achieved her final aim, and after all the cruel sufferings of the last five years has earned her glorious reward. France and her valiant children may now surely feel that the night has passed and hail the consummation of the greatest triumph in history.

"The British people, M. le President, share the joy and triumph of France, as they have shared her sorrows and anguish.

"Our arduous task has been gloriously accomplished, but still there remains much work before us, and upon the ruins of this mighty conflict a new and a better Europe must arise.

"I am confident that France, and my Empire, will also work hand in hand in this great regeneration, and I doubt not that, mindful of their common sacrifices and their common triumph, the mutual love and respect of our two countries, resting on the sure foundation of the strenuous comradeship of war, will grow ever stronger in the benign fellowship of peace.

"In all sincerity Britain thanks France and wishes her God speed."

TO PRESIDENT WILSON.

"In this glorious hour, when the long struggle of nations for right, justice, and freedom is at last crowned with a triumphant peace, I greet you, Mr. President, and the great American people in the name of the British nation.

"At a time when fortune seemed to frown, and the issues of the war trembled in the balance, the American people stretched out the hand of fellowship to those who, on this side of the ocean, were battling for the righteous cause.

"Light and hope at once shone brighter in our hearts and a new day dawned. Together we have fought to the happy end, together we lay down our arms in the proud consciousness of valiant deeds nobly done.

"Mr. President, it is on this day one of our happiest thoughts that the American and British peoples, brothers in arms, will continue for ever to be brothers in peace. United before by language, traditions, kinship and ideals, there has now been set upon our fellowship and sacred seal of common sacrifice."

OUR OTHER ALLIES.

Messages couched in a similar strain have been sent to:—

The King of Italy, the King of the Belgians, the Emperor of Japan, the President of the Portuguese Republic, the King of Rumania, the King of Greece, the President of the United States of Brazil, the President of Poland, the King of the Serbs, Croats, and Slovenes, the President of the Czecho-Slovak Republic, the President of the Republic of China, the Sultan of Egypt, the King of Siam.

WHAT THE GERMANS LOSE BY SIGNING THE PEACE PACT.

By signing the Peace Treaty Germany loses—

1—30,000 square miles of territory, including Alsace-Lorraine, Malmedy Posen, parts of East and West Prussia, and of Silesia (should the plebiscite in the last-mentioned area go against her).

2—6,670,000 of her population of 68,000,000. Alsace-Lorraine alone accounts for a loss of 1,874,000 and Posen for 2,000,000.

3—Among the large towns lost to Germany are Strasbourg, Metz, Thorn, Branberg, Oppeln, Lissa, Konitz.

4—The German overseas Empire goes, the Allies having appointed mandatories for the various colonies, who are responsible to the League of Nations.

5—Germany hands over to the Allies all her merchant ships over 16,000 tons, and half of those between 16,000 tons and 1000 tons. She has also to build merchant ships for the Allies up to 200,000 tons annually for five years, a total of 1,000,000 tons.

6—The Army of Germany is to be reduced to 200,000 men within three months. Her stipulated police army is in future to be 100,000 men.

7—The final amount of reparation due from Germany is not yet fixed, but for the first year a payment of £1,000,000,000 is to be made.

THE TREATY SIGNED IN SILENCE IN THE HALL OF MIRRORS.

GERMANS AGREE LOYALLY TO ABIDE BY TERMS.

(From Our Special Correspondent.)

Versailles, Saturday.

"The signature of the conditions of Peace between the Allied and Associated Powers and the German Empire is now an accomplished fact, and the proceeding are thus closed."

In this brief sentence, M. Clemenceau this afternoon at 3.35 intimated the consummation of the protracted labours of the Peace Conference of imposing peace upon Germany.

The President of the Conference opened the proceedings very briefly. He said:—

"The Allied and Associated Governments have come to an agreement on the conditions of Peace. The text has been written, and the President of the Conference has stated in writing that this text which is now to be signed is identical with the text of the 200 copies that have been distributed to the German Delegation.

"The signatures will be affixed now undertaking to abide loyally and faithfully by the condition of Peace."

DRAMATIC MOMENT.

Here there was an interruption when M. Clemenceau made reference to the Delegation of the "German Republic." A cry that was almost a shout of "Reich! Reich!" (Empire) was hurled at him across the room from the German table

M. Clemenceau immediately corrected himself, and repeated the words, "Reich Allemand."

He then called upon the German Plenipotentiaries to sign.

Herr Hermann Mueller and Dr. Bell at once rose and walked to the table on which the Treaty was laid, and signed. Mueller, German Foreign Minister, attaching his signature first. They made no speech.

It was a quarter past three when they signed, and as they returned to their places a smile and a sigh of relief ran round the room.

The Germans had signed and peace was at last a tangible reality. The waters of the fountains in the Park lept into the air and guns announced the news to the crowd outside.

The first Allied Delegation to sign was the American headed by President Wilson, who was followed by Mr. Lansing, Colonel House, Mr. Henry White, and General Bliss.

How our Peace-Signing Pictures reached Glasgow. —See Page 2.

The next delegation to sign was the British—Mr. Lloyd George, Mr. Bonar Law, Mr. Balfour, Lord Milner, and Mr. Barnes.

A huge Ormulu inkstand, from which protruded two preposterously light and feathery quill pens, marked the central table on which lay the main Treaty.

The British delegates were followed by those of the British Dominions who signed in a body. Messrs. Doherty, Selton and Foster for Canada first: then Mr. Hughes and Sir Joseph Cook for Australia; then Mr. Massey for New Zealand; Generals Smuts and Botha for South Africa; Mr. Montagu and the Maharajah of Bekanir for India.

THE GREAT FIVE YEARS.

June 28, 1914: Archduke Franz Ferdinand murdered by Prinzep, who fired the shot which set the world aflame.

Aug. 1, 1914: Germany declared war.

Nov. 11, 1918: Armistice signed.

May 7, 1919: Draft Treaty presented.

June 16: Allies' reply to German counter-proposals, fixing time-limit.

June 23: Time-limit expired, 7 p.m. Peace accepted, 5 p.m.

June 28: Peace Treaty signed.

The next delegation to sign was the French headed by M. Clemenceau, who was followed by MM. Pichon, Klotz, Tardieu, and Jules Cambon.

It must be admitted that the ceremony was curiously unimpressive from a spectacular point of view. The groups of invited guests and Pressmen at the opposite endsof the Hall could see little, and what they saw was a constant passage to and fro of elderly gentletmen in sombre attire, who seemed to be doing nothing particularly interesting to themselves, and whose appearance harmonised singularly with the old and dim gold of the tables and the walls and the flaming colours of the ceiling.

After the delegation of the Great Powers had signed the interest largely died out, for it then became much a procession of the representatives of the smaller Powers advancing and adding their names. It was quite impossible for those looking on to come to any idea how the process of signing was going on, because, between them and the table were the document mass lying awaiting signature.

VICTORY BOOM.

The first intimation that the last delegate of Czecho-Slovakia, which was the last Power to sign, had added his name, and that Peace was at last a fact, came when the cannon from Fort Satory was heard firing a salvo and raucous sirens shrieked reminding one of the nights of past German air raids.

When the cannon stopped there came a sudden hush over the room. Everybody became seated as if some magician had waved a wand.

One could see that M. Clemenceau was again on his feet. His final words were as brief as those which he opened the sitting.

The scene which followed outside the Chateau was much more dramatic, and appealed much more to the crowd than the rather dull and unimpressive proceedings within the Hall of Mirrors. Cheers were raised from the front of the terrace as everyone came out from the Hall of Mirrors, and the remarkable historic scene was witnessed of M. Clemenceau, President Wilson, and Mr. Lloyd George walking side by side down the broad pathway between the fountains spurting spray, hemmed in by a cheering crowd, while from the distance the cannon of Fort Satory fired a second salvo, and a flock of aeroplanes hummed overhead.

It would be impossible to say who of the Big Three was the most popular, but the British noted particularly that the cheering crowd hung on to Mr. Lloyd George's car and followed it several hundred yards

It transpired later that the Treaty had not been signed by the Chinese Delegation as a protest against the settlement of the Shantung question.

PREMIER SENDS THE NEWS.

MESSAGE TO THE KING BY AEROPLANE.

A special messenger arrived in London by aeroplane from Paris on Saturday evening with a letter for the King from the Prime Minister, as follows:—

Galiere des Glaces, du Château de Versailles.

"**Mr. Lloyd George**, with his humble duty to your Majesty, has the honour to announce that the long and terrible war, in which the British Empire has been engaged with the German Empire for more than four years, and which has caused such suffering to mankind, has been brought to an end this afternoon by the Treaty of Peace just signed in this hall.

"He desires, on behalf of all the plenipotentiaries of your Majesty's Empire, to tender their heartfelt thanks to your Majesty on the signature of a treaty that marks the victorious end of a terrible struggle which has lasted so long, and in which your Majesty's subjects from all parts of the Empire, have played so glorious a part."

The information was conveyed to Buckingham Palace that the foregoing message was written by Mr. Lloyd George at the actual Peace Conference table, and was immediately dispatched to London by aeroplane.

PREMIER'S RETURN TO LONDON.

Mr. Lloyd George, accompanied by others of the British and Dominion Peace delegates, returned to London last night, and after being received at the station by the King, the Prince of Wales, and others, was heartily acclaimed by great crowds throughout his drive with the King from Victoria Station to Buckingham Palace and from there to Downing Street.

On alighting from the train, the Premier shook hands with the King and greeted many of his old friends, and the party immediately thereafter left the station.

The Royal carriage had proceeded only a few yards when its progress was arrested by a party of some 500 Colonial soldiers, who had formed themselves into an unofficial guard of honour.

They made desperate efforts to get at close quarters and shake hands with the King and the Premier. Their object was frustrated, but a New Zealand soldier succeeded in throwing an autograph album into the carriage, which both His Majesty and Mr. Lloyd George signed before throwing it back. The carriage then proceeded on its way amid thunderous cheers.

From the window overlooking the porch at No. 10 Downing Street the Premier made a short speech in reference to the signing of Peace, in which he said:—

"Let us rejoice in this great victory, not in the spirit of boastfulness, which was the downfall of Germany, but in a spirit of reverence, which is worthy of the noble sacrifices which have been made." (Cheers.)

SECURITY OF FRANCE.

NEW PACT WITH BRITAIN AND AMERICA.

Paris, Sunday.

Before leaving Versailles yesterday, President Wilson and Mrs. Wilson paid a visit to President and Madame Poincare, with whom they had a long and cordial interview.

President Wilson expressed once more to President Poincare his gratitude for the reception he had received in France, and on his side President Poincare thanked Dr. Wilson for having that very morning signed a Treaty guaranteeing France the assistance of the United States in case of a non-provoked attack, the same text being signed by Mr. Lloyd George in the name of Great Britain.—P.A.

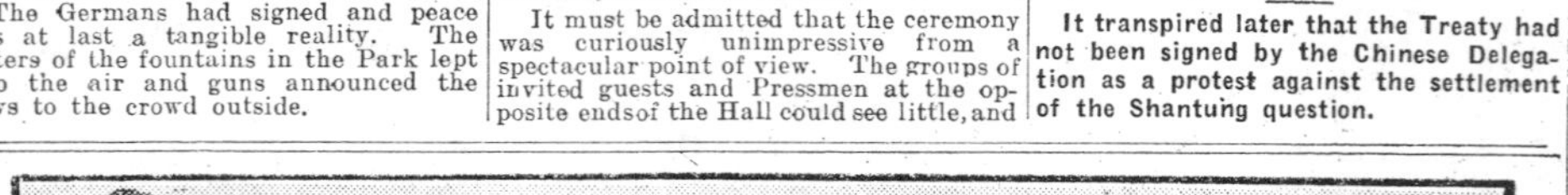

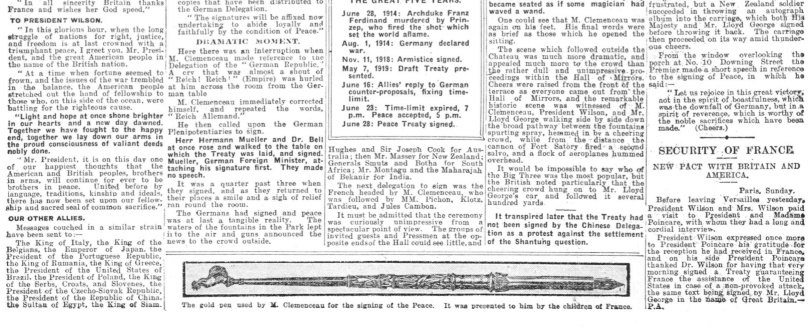

The gold pen used by M. Clemenceau for the signing of the Peace. It was presented to him by the children of France.

THEIR OWN "SEASIDE."

No seaside, alas, for these poor kiddies. But they were not downhearted, and enjoyed their paddle even in London—in Trafalgar Square fountain.

TAKING THE SALUTE.

Aberdeen Girl Guides held a successful rally, when they were reviewed by Mrs. Davidson, County Commissioner. Our photograph shows her taking the salute.

THE POPULAR CHECK.

Checks are more popular than ever this season. This is how one smart Parisienne conformed to the vogue of the moment. Effective, isn't it?

DO YOU ENVY HER?

In this hot weather she prefers to remain cool and be quite independent of fashion's capricious fancies. To most of us, however, her coolness is tantalising.

SEEN IN PARIS.

This smart frock, "snapped" on a Paris boulevard, is in a navy shade with an elaborately embroidered design in gold on the skirt.

TWO OF THE QUEER TASMANIAN ANIMALS WHICH WILL BE PRESENTED TO THE PRINCE OF WALES.

Among other mementos of his tour which the Prince of Wales will bring home are several Tasmanian animals. A collection of rare marsupials has been made, and will be presented before he leaves Tasmania. Two of them are the Tasmanian devil (left) and the Tasmanian wolf.

WOMAN WHO FIGHTS MEXICANS.
Page 11.

Daily Record and Mail.

The All-Scotland Newspaper. Sale Three Times That of Any Other Morning Paper.

ESTAB. 1847—No. 24,180. GLASGOW, SATURDAY, JULY 12, 1924. ONE PENNY.

WASH FROCKS FOR THE HOLIDAYS
in a large variety of designs and styles in Ratine, Sponge Cloth and Striped Zephyrs. In all leading colour effects and offered in two lots at HOLIDAY PRICE...... 10/- & 15/-
The BONANZA Ltd. 173 to 185 ARGYLE ST.

HANDING OVER TSARIST £10,000,000 TO SOVIET.

TSARIST MILLIONS.

GIVING SOVIET BANK OF ENGLAND DEPOSITS.

CONFERENCE PROPOSAL.

GOVERNMENT "WATCHING" BRITISH CREDITORS' INTERESTS.

IF an agreement under consideration by the Anglo-Soviet Conference in London is finally approved, the Soviet will get the £10,000,000 or £12,000,000 deposited in the Bank of England and other banks by the Tsarist Government.

It is understood that if an agreement, which is at present being considered by the Anglo-Soviet conference in London, is finally approved, it will have the effect of benefiting the Soviet Government to the extent of probably £10,000,000 or £12,000,000.

If the Treaty of Commerce is concluded, it will supersede the old trade agreement drawn up in 1921, and will enable the Soviet Government to claim money, now in the Bank of England and other banks, which belonged to the Russian Imperial Government.

The drawing up of the Treaty, so far as the British Government is concerned, has been left by the Prime Minister in the hands of Mr. Ponsonby, Under-Secretary for Foreign Affairs.

Well-informed circles in London state that there is nothing unexpected in the Treaty, since one of the principal objects of the conference was to put the Soviet Government in the position formerly occupied by the Tsarist Government.

The Treaty of Commerce has not yet been finally approved, and no further plenary session of the conference has been fixed.

It was pointed out last night that the agreement was not a separate matter, but was part of the general Treaty, which it would be the endeavour of the conference to draw up.

In the event of complete agreement being reached by the conference on all points, including Soviet indebtedness to this country, sums in the possession of the former Russian Government would be released in favour of the Soviet Government, but not as part of any partial agreement.

In this connection it was mentioned that it has been stated in the House of Commons that the Government were fully aware of the situation and were watching the interests of the people who had lost money in Russia.

HERRIOT REPLIES TO POINCARE.

BIG SENATE VOTE OF CONFIDENCE.

Paris, Friday.

M. Herriot replied this afternoon, in the Senate, to the speech made by M. Poincare yesterday.

If the Allies were not to agree on the Dawes plan, were they, he asked, to return to the policy of enclosing the Ruhr and mass expulsions.

The French Government must hurry up and substitute an inter-Allied Agreement for the Agreement which now exists between France and Belgium.

He pointed out that Germany, in January next, would retake her economic liberty so far as France was concerned, and it was therefore in the interests of France that some agreement should be arrived at.

GERMAN LOAN.

It was not sufficient to issue bonds in connection with the Dawes plan.

It was necessary to place these bonds—and the British and American Governments were constantly occupied with this task—so that there would be no loss of confidence between the interests of the future bearers of bonds and the Govrnment.

The Experts' Report depended clearly on the co-operation of the Allies and Government.

M. Poincare interrupted, and said M. Herriot implied that each Government was left with its political freedom.

M. Herriot maintained that if one accepted the Dawes plan, one must also accept its directing principles, and one of those principles was that the problem of Reparations must henceforth pass into the economic domain.

There was another interruption regarding Mr. MacDonald's speech yesterday.

M. Herriot said he had not read the text of the speech.

He explained that it was the Reparations Commission which would present to the London Conference suggestions for the putting into operation of the Dawes Plan, and that the Commission would say when the plan was really put into operation.

The Premier added that Italy and Belgium had already accepted the bases of the Franco-British Note.

M. Herriot received a vote of confidence by 246 votes to 18.—C.N.

BRITISH MEETING.

A meeting was held in the Premier's room at the House of Commons yesterday to consider questions connected with the forthcoming Inter-Allied Conference. There were present:—

Mr. Ramsay MacDonald.
Mr. Philip Snowden.
Mr. J. H. Thomas.
Mr. Sidney Webb.
Hon. Peter Larkin (High Commissioner for Canada).
Sir Joseph Cook (High Commissioner for Australia).
Sir James Allen (High Commissioner for New Zealand).
Mr. James M'Neill (High Commissioner for Irish Free State).
Lord Olivier (Secretary of State for India).

SCOTCH EXPRESS.

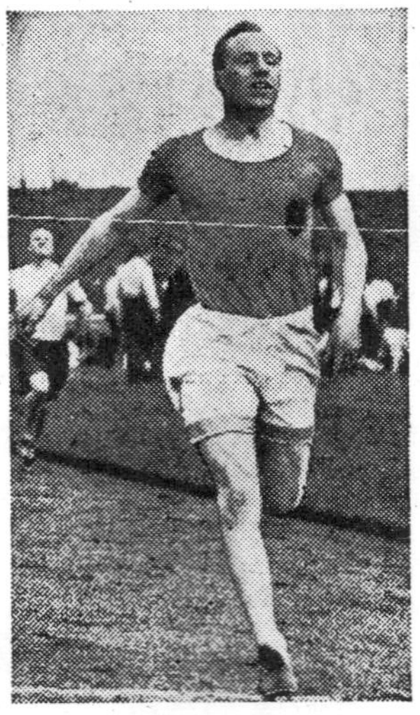

Eric Liddell, the Scottish champion, yesterday won the 400 metres Olympic race in the world's record time of 47 3-5 secs.

METAGAMA AGAIN ASHORE.

CRIPPLED LINER'S FATE.

St. John's (N.F.), Friday.

The crippled Canadian-Pacific liner, Metagama, which has been undergoing repairs here since June 20, after her collision with the Italian steamer, Clara Camus, off Cape Race, went ashore this afternoon off the entrance to the harbour.

The Metagama was leaving for Quebec for permanent repairs. The vessel is now surrounded by tugs trying to get her off.

The ship took on a bad list. It became difficult to control her, and the wheel chains broke when she was swinging around for exit.

It will be remembered that after the collision on June 19, the Metagama contrived to reach port, but the captain, owing to her sinking condition, had to beach her on a mudbank.—Reuter.

LLOYD GEORGE'S ALTERNATIVE TO STATE MINES.
Page 5.

REBELS' COUP.

BRAZIL CITY HELD, DESPITE HEAVY GUN FIRE.

Buenos Aires, Friday.

A message to "La Nacion" states that the Government of Sao Paulo has been deposed, and that a revolutionary junta headed by General Rondon has formed a temporary Government.

The rebels are reported to be continuing their operations successfully, and it is feared the movement may extend.

Efforts by the Federal Authorities to take Sao Paulo have failed in spite of violent bombardments which have inflicted many casualties on the inhabitants.

Disquieting reports from other quarters indicate that the Federal troops are joining the rebels, and even the navy is believed to be tainted with the revolutionary spirit.—C.N.

VERA CRUZ MURDER.

New York, Friday.

A message from Mexico City states that a British subject named Herbert Vereker has been killed at Potrera Bellano (in the northern district of the State of Vera Cruz) by bandits because of his refusal to give over his money to them.—C.N.

SCOTS RUNNER'S FEAT.

E. H. LIDDELL'S TRIUMPH AT OLYMPIC GAMES.

WINS 400 METRES RACE.

CREATES NEW WORLD'S RECORD AFTER THRILLING FINISH.

ERIC H. LIDDELL, an Edinburgh University student, and Scottish champion sprinter, won a notable victory for Britain at the Olympic Games in Paris, yesterday. Not only did he win the 400 metres race, but he created a new world's record by covering the distance in 47 3-5 secs.

A GREAT RACE.

LIDDELL BREAKS TAPE THREE YARDS AHEAD.

Paris, Friday.

The Union Jack flew in proud majesty over the Colombes Stadium to-day, for the only final down for decision, the 400 metres flat, resulted in a great victory for Britain.

The brilliant running of E. H. Liddell, the Edinburgh University sprinter, was responsible, and in covering the distance in 47 3-5 seconds he created the third world's record in two days for this event.

Guy Butler, the old Light Blue was third, being separated from the winner by Fitch, the American, who, in the semi-final returned 47 4-5 seconds, beating Imbach's 48 seconds dead of yesterday.

SKIRL OF THE PIPES.

The race was the one bright spot in the afternoon's sport, for with the Decathlon events occupying most of the programme, the crowd had sunk into more or less apathy.

There had been nothing to applaud. The 100 metres times were all mediocre compared with the recent performances of the cream of the world's sprinters in the event proper.

It looked like being a dull afternoon. Suddenly the pipers of the Cameron Highlanders, who had assembled in the middle of the stadium began playing, and the crowd broke into cheers at the lively strains of a Scotch air.

SEMI-FINAL THRILL.

It was the prelude to better things. It was time for the 400 metres semi-finals, and the Decathlon was relegated to the centre of the stadium.

The first was a thrilling race. Butler, one of the British representatives, reproduced his brilliant form of yesterday, and confident of qualifying, slowed up nearing the tape, to finish a comfortable second.

Even then he was only beaten by inches by Fitch, who returned a world's record time.

The crowd were stirred, and when the time was announced there was a remarkable demonstration of enthusiasm.

STIRRING RACE.

However, there was better to come, for the final was even more thrilling.

There was a gasp of astonishment when Eric Liddell, one of the most popular athletes at Colombes, was seen to be a clear three yards ahead of the field at the half distance.

Nearing the tape Fitch and Butler strained every nerve and muscle to overtake him, but could make absolutely no impression on the inspired Scot.

With 20 yards to go Fitch seemed to gain a fraction, but Liddell appeared to sense the American, and with head thrown back and chin thrust out in his usual style, he flashed past the tape to gain what was probably the greatest victory of the meeting.

So far, certainly, there has not been a more popular win.

FRENZY OF ENTHUSIASM.

The crowd went into a frenzy of enthusiasm, which was renewed when the loud speaker announced that once again the world's record had gone by the board.

The day really closed on this glorious note.

Far away in a remote corner of the Stadium a few decathlon competitors were hurling themselves at the high jump, but they were almost unobserved for the crowd had gone with the thrill of Liddell's victory fresh in their minds.

'VARSITY STUDENT.

HOLDER OF THREE SCOTTISH CHAMPIONSHIPS.

Eric H. Liddell, who was born in Tientsin, China, on January 16, 1902, comes of a sterling sporting ancestry.

His father was a missionary in the Far East, but before that he was a gymnast and fencer of marked ability. His father had strong family associations with Greenock and Loch Lomondside, while his mother was born in the Scots Border country.

Young Liddell received his early education at Eltham College and succeeded his brother, R. V. Liddell, as captain of the school.

In his youthful schooldays he gave promise as an athlete, but it was when he went to Edinburgh University that he showed his real mettle.

TRIPLE SCOTS CHAMPION.

He has held the 100 yards and 220 yards Scottish amateur championships since 1921, and last month at Hampden at the S.A.A.A. championship meeting he completed the triple event by adding to his list of triumphs the 440 yards race.

Two years ago Liddell gave the English athletes a taste of his ability by romping home in the 100 yards and 220 at the British championship gathering, and this year he won the 440 yards.

If there have been ups and downs in his running career, it is due to the fact that he is a student first and an athlete afterwards.

NOT TO WRECK IT.

MR. ASQUITH AND THE HOUSING BILL.

Speaking at Norwich last night in connection with the Liberal campaign, Mr. Asquith said neither of the opposite parties was for the moment in good trim for aggressive work.

The Labour Government had produced a good, wholesome Free Trade Budget, but what else was there to their credit?

Their path week by week was strewn with unfulfilled pledges and broken promises. While they had enjoyed the almost unexampled tolerance and no lack of good will or helpful co-operation, they had shown a singular incapacity for constructive statesmanship.

Referring to housing. Mr. Asquith declared that no attempt had been, or would be, made by the Liberal Party to wreck the Government Bill.

They wished it well so far as it was an effort to deal on a comprehensive and continuous scale with a grave and urgent national problem. Mr. Asquith, however, strongly criticised the finance of the scheme.

RAILMEN'S BILL.

LEADERS TO FRAME MEASURE FOR NATIONALISATION.

The National Union of Railwaymen, sitting in conference at York, yesterday, adopted a re-drafted resolution:—

(1) Welcoming the grouping of the railways, and

(2) Calling upon the Executive to frame a Bill to be submitted to Parliament having for its object the nationalisation and democratic control of the railways.

Mr. Figgins, of Glasgow, opposed the resolution as not going far enough.

The working class, he contended, had very little to learn in regard to the control of industry.

It was not the few men who sat on Boards of Directors and drew big salaries who really administered the Railway industry.

It was the workers, and particularly the supervisory grades who were organised in that Union who were responsible for the actual administration.

TO-DAY'S WIRELESS PROGRAMMES Page 5

Daily Record and Mail.

PREMIER WITH A "DOUBLE" Page 7

ESTAB. 1847—No. 24,744. GLASGOW, TUESDAY, MAY 4, 1926. ONE PENNY.

LAST MINUTE PEACE BIDS FAIL.

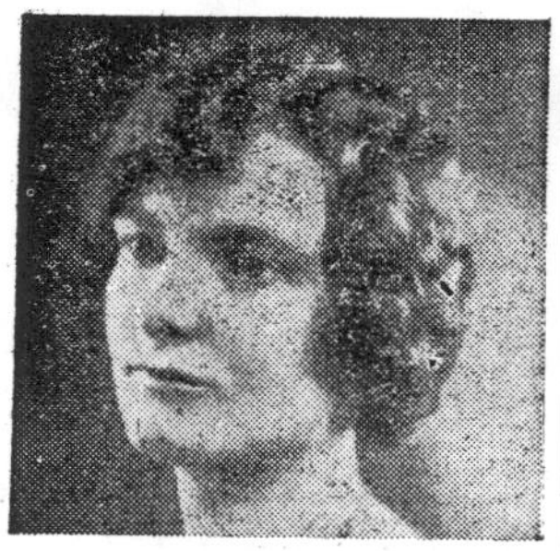

The Hon. Mrs. Hoare, daughter of Viscount and Viscountess Deerhurst, who will be presented at Their Majesties' Court this season.

BIG STRIKE BEGUN.

LAST MINUTE PEACE MOVES END IN FAILURE.

PREMIER'S REVIEW OF CRISIS.

"THE General Strike is on." This dramatic message was flashed over the wires from London shortly after 11 o'clock last night. Earlier in the evening an optimistic feeling prevailed that a settlement might be reached when it was reported that the Prime Minister was again in contact with the miners' leaders and the T.U.C. Negotiating Committee.

A faint flicker of hope was also raised by a short exchange between Mr. Churchill and Mr. Thomas in the concluding stages of the Chancellor's speech in the House of Commons. The significant passages were these:—

Mr. Churchill said that the Government were bound to face the position unflinchingly, rigorously, rigidly, and resolutely to the end.

"Then this is the end?" inquired Mr. Thomas. "The door is always open," replied the Chancellor. "The T.U.C. have only to cancel the general strike challenge."

"Does that specific statement apply equally to the lock-out notices?" asked Mr. Thomas.

These exchanges afforded a slight hope that negotiations would be resumed. As a matter of fact no further negotiations took place, and the House of Commons dissolved in the knowledge that all efforts at a settlement had completely failed.

Members of the Miners' Executive who had been waiting in the Committee corridor during the evening left the House of Commons soon after the House rose at 11.7. Mr. Thomas and several other members of the T.U.C. remained, as did one or two members of the Cabinet.

There was a great crowd outside the Houses of Parliament, a section of which sang the "Red Flag," and raised cheers for the miners. Another section sang "God Save the King." The police kept the crowd in check. There was no disorder.

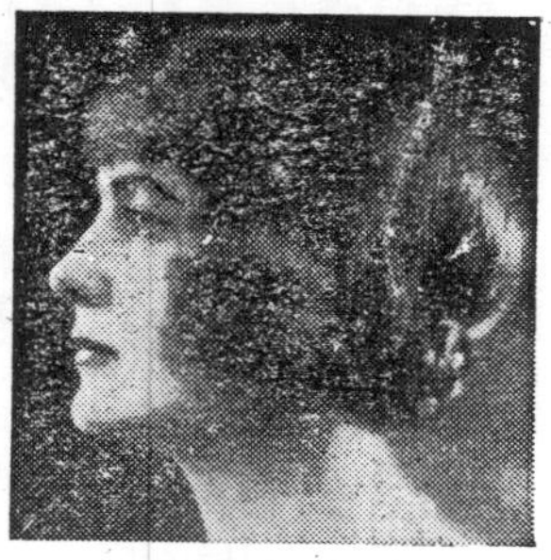

Lady Cunliffe, wife of Lord Cunliffe of Headley, who will be presented at Their Majesties' Court.

TRAINS & TRAMS.

STATE APPEAL TO MOTORISTS.

POSITION TO-DAY.

Reports received from areas in Glasgow and the West of Scotland early this morning indicated that the strike of all classes of transport workers has been more or less complete. The exact situation, however, will not be known until about noon.

The trains from Glasgow to the South left as usual under the control of drivers whose home stations are in England, and, despite the fact that they were warned that the companies could not guarantee that the trains would reach their destinations, large numbers of passengers travelled. The Belfast and Dublin boats left as usual.

'BUS SERVICES.

With regard to the 'bus services the position last night was very obscure. A large proportion of the drivers are non-union men and they may be at work as usual to-day. It is said that the local authorities operating the emergency measures may take over the 'buses

The Scottish Motor Transport Company will run 'buses on all routes from Kilmarnock to-day.

All work was stopped at the docks at an early hour this morning, only certain "safety" men being permitted to remain on duty.

GLASGOW TRAMS.

Following instructions from their society, the Transport and General Workers' Union, Glasgow tramwaymen are expected to join in a sympathetic strike to-day.

By the programme, drivers and conductors on late cars were expected to finish duty at midnight, and the all-night men were due to finish at 4 a.m.

The Subway, which is also under the management of the Tramways Department, is similarly involved in the dispute.

To-day people who rely on these conveniences are likely to experience great difficulty in getting to their destination, as, at the best, only a skeleton service could be provided.

OFFICIAL'S EXPLANATION.

Tramway employees, to the number of nearly 400, including a dozen conductresses, met in the Berkeley Hall, Glasgow, last night, to hear an explanation of the situation from Mr. Arthur Gee, group secretary of the Transport and General Workers' Union.

Mr. Gee stated that the meeting was ot called for the purpose of taking a ecision on the question of a strike or o strike, but to pass on instructions.

Instructions had been given to strike, and they were carrying out these.

Subsequently, meetings for a like purpose were held at the tramway depots throughout the city.

A meeting of the Road Transport Secon of the Transport and General Workers' Union was held in Glasgow last ight, when all the stables and garages sented in this organisation endorsed ion of the British Trade Union t to commence work this

DRASTIC ORDERS.

AUTHORITIES' WIDE POWERS.

Wide discretion given to authorities under the Emergency Powers Act is revealed by the regulations published last night. In addition to powers taken to maintain services essential to the life of the community, such as the supply and distribution, of food, coal etc., and organisation and direction of transport, there are stringent penal provisions.

Persons will be held guilty of offence against the regulations by any attempt to cause mutiny, sedition, or disaffection among His Majesty's Forces, or forces under civic authorities, or to interfere with organisation and distribution of supplies, the usual exception being made for participation in a strike or peaceful persuasion.

HEAVY PENALTIES.

Measures are included to provide against the possession, for the purposes of circulation, of documents aiming at a contravention of the regulations, and the Secretary of State, or persons authorised by him, may prohibit or disperse any public meeting or procession likely to occasion grave disorder.

There is a regulation against unlawful drilling, and the billeting sections of the Army and Air Force Act may be enforced.

Failure to comply with, or an offence against, the regulations, entails liability on summary conviction to imprisonment for three months, or a fine not exceeding £100, or to both imprisonment and fine.

The police may arrest without warrant any person acting in such a manner as to endanger the public safety, and are given extensive powers of search in this connection.

IN CLYDE YARDS.

CONFUSING POSITION OF THE UNIONS.

What is going to nappen in the shipbuilding and engineering establishments on Clydeside is not yet known.

Some of the unions have issued instructions to their men to stop; others have not.

In any case, the works may very soon be affected by the shortage of power supplies

PROFITEERING WARNING

Sir Arthur Rose, the emergency commissioner for Glasgow, issues a warning regarding food profiteering.

Prices, he said yesterday, appeared to be inclined to rise generally, and it was difficult to see any real justification for that at the moment. He had powers to fix maximum prices, and if material increases took place it might be necessary to put these powers into operation, although they did not want to do so.

"If prices run away, however," he concluded, "drastic action will have to be taken."

PETROL SUPPLIES.

RATIONING OR PERMITS NOT NECESSARY.

It is considered unlikely that a system of rationing or permits for motor spirit will be necessary, says an official announcement.

The principal motor spirit distributing companies state that the r tail price of motor spirit will remain unaltered.

No action will be taken by the police during the present emergency in respect of the use of a mechanically propelled vehicle for which an Excise licence is not in force, or one which is used for purposes not covered by any such licence, provided that the vehicle is registered and carries its proper number plates.

The police will not, however, permit a vehicle to be used in any manner inconsistent with the safety of the public.

APPEAL TO MOTORISTS.

The Ministry of Transport appeals to the owners of motor vehicles of all kinds for assistance in maintaining national and local services essential to the wellbeing of the community.

Owners of commercial and mechanical transports not fully used should notify the haulage committees of their areas.

It should be clearly understood that the Government is prepared to assist in the transport of foodstuffs and other essential services.

STRANDED.

RAIL PASSENGERS' ADVENTURE.

A large number of Scottish travellers to the South found themselves in an awkward predicament in the early hours of the morning as a result of the cessation of railway traffic.

Late trains left Glasgow and Edinburgh with fairly large complements who had decided to take the risk attached to travel under such conditions.

When Carstairs was reached, however, the trains proceeded no further. They were coupled to another train which arrived from Aberdeen and run back to the Central Station, Glasgow.

It appears that they were unable to go as far as Carlisle on account of the large number of trains already held up there.

NIGHT IN CARRIAGES.

When a *Daily Record* representative visited the Central Station about 2 a.m., he found that most of the passengers had remained in the carriages.

Some of them had resigned themselves to the situation and had settled down as comfortably as possible for the night.

Others were too worried as to how and when they were to get to their destinations to follow this philosophical example.

One family with whom the *Daily Record* representative chatted were gravely concerned about the prospects of their reaching London in time to catch a boat which was to convey them to Natal.

"It we have to take a taxi all the way, we must get to London," was how the matron of the little party expressed herself.

COAL FOR BRITAIN.

DUTCH DOCKERS URGED NOT TO HANDLE IT.

Rotterdam, Monday.

The Transport Workers' Federation to-day distributed a manifesto to the Rotterdam dockers exhorting the men not to assist in coal loading to Great Britain from Tuesday next, nor to work vessels entering the New Waterway for bunkering which, under normal conditions, would have bunkered in Great Britain. The manifesto also urges the men not to enrol for British ships.—Reuter.

PREMIER'S POSITION.

HOW HE FOUGHT FOR PEACE.

WAGES CRUX.

There was a tense atmosphere in the House of Commons when the business began yesterday.

The Prime Minister was greeted with loud cheers when he entered the House. A Conservative member shouted "Here he is," and the whole of the Ministerialists rose and cheered and waved their order papers.

Mr. J. H. Thomas entered the House shortly after the Prime Minister, and on his entrance the whole of the Labour Party rose and cheered him.

On the motion for the adjournment the Prime Minister said—

"I would like to express my view at the outset that these difficulties have been considerably increased for many years past by the organisation of the industry itself and the extraordinary machinery they have for wages adjustment."

TWO ESSENTIALS.

There were no doubt historical reasons for this—the nature of the industry and the isolation of many of the mining villages had something to do with it. But the industry would have caused far less anxiety to itself and to the nation had it succeeded in conducting its affairs through such organisations as were employed in the cotton and iron and steel industries and the railways.

Moreover, the conditions of the industry had been interfered with many times by successive Governments. ("Hear, hear.") He was quite convinced there would be and could be no settlement in that industry until two things were attained—

First, a very different spirit, and

Secondly, a very different organisation for the discussion and arrangement of wages. ("Hear, hear.")

The whole machinery required, in his view, a radical overhauling.

"One Government prescription after another has been tried and administered, and yet the health of the patient has been but little improved.

INTO DECIMALS.

"Something is done at the last moment because up to that last moment both sides have been too prone to manœuvre for a favourable position with the public, and the public themselves are incapable of forming a sound judgment because the mysteries of minimum percentages and datum lines, bonus terms, and percentages and allowances and subtractions going into two decimals.

"One of the great difficulties is that you can never get the agreed amount the miner is earning, for neither the miner nor owner will ever agree on a figure, and then a Cabinet Minister, not necessarily a mathematician or a chartered accountant by profession is called in, and expected to understand these matters and expected with a divine impartiality to make these two sides agree —and this is the peculiar feature time after time—at the last minute of the eleventh hour that is left.

Continued on Page 2, Column 1.

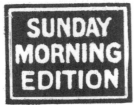

SUNDAY MORNING EDITION

SUNDAY MAIL

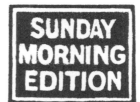

SUNDAY MORNING EDITION

No. 975. Registered at the General Post Office as a Newspaper. Entered at the New York Post Office as Second-Class Matter. SUNDAY, MAY 22, 1927. Telephone Number: CENTRAL 9880 (12 Lines). PRICE TWOPENCE.

AMERICAN AIRMAN ARRIVES SAFELY IN PARIS.

ATLANTIC FLIER'S OVATION IN FRENCH CAPITAL.

SUCCESSFUL END TO LONELY JOURNEY FROM AMERICA TO EUROPE.

By a late hour last night it was made evident from messages received from various quarters in England and Ireland that Captain Lindbergh, the daring young American airman, was succeeding in his New York to Paris flight.

Extraordinary scenes of enthusiasm marked the arrival at Le Bourget aerodrome last night of Captain Lindbergh, the young American airman, after his great flight. About 100,000 people mobbed him when he descended from his aeroplane.

CROWDS ASSEMBLE TO MEET AIR HERO.

Paris, Saturday Night.

Amidst scenes of indescribable enthusiasm, Captain Lindbergh, the young American airman, landed at Le Bourget aerodrome at 10.22 to-night after his amazing Transatlantic flight. He brought his machine to earth about four hundred yards from the concrete platform reserved for landing purposes.

He alighted from his machine looking remarkably fresh after his arduous experience, and was immediately surrounded by a dense crowd who surged round the machine shouting, singing, and cheering deliriously.

The scenes baffled all description. Never before has the like been seen here. Motor cars were everywhere, and the roads around the air port were blocked with vehicles and with people. A system of invitations and special passes had been organised, but for a long time the places reserved for the public were filled to overflowing. People swarmed up the adjacent buildings and sheds and even balanced themselves on the slender branches of trees. The whole scene was illuminated by searchlights and flares dotted all over the aerodrome

TROOPS CHARGE CROWD.

OVER-ZEALOUS ATTENTIONS OF ADMIRERS.

When the machine ran along the aerodrome track there was such a rush of people towards the aviator that the 34th Regiment of Aviation which was keeping order had to charge the crowd and drive them back in order to save the airman from their over-zealous attentions. Mr. Myron Herrick, the American Ambassador, was present, and a way was made for him through the crowd to the aeroplane. Mr. Herrick was the first to greet Lindbergh as he stepped from his machine, and he heartily shook the hand of the aviator and kissed him on the cheek.

It was with the greatest of difficulty that the crowd could be kept back so great was the enthusiasm. People swarmed round the machine, each one trying to shake the aviator by the hand.

MACHINE CARRIED OFF.

DEMONSTRATION WHILE DOCTORS REVIVE AIRMAN.

In their enthusiasm the crowd seized hold of the machine and carried it for a distance of 200 yards. Captain Lindbergh was carried to the quarters of the officers of the Flying Corps where doctors at once set to work on giving him restoratives and injections. The "Spirit of St. Louis" was practically undamaged.

Lindbergh was delighted with the warmth of his reception, and smiled his acknowledgments to the almost hysterical cheering of the multitude. He was in danger of being badly mobbed, but he took it all in good part, and was heard to remark that he was not called a "lucky fool" for nothing.

He had had, he said, a wonderful flight, and had been aided by excellent flying conditions. He had never had the slightest doubt but that he would win through, and he never felt the least apprehension even when he was making his solitary way over the Atlantic wastes. He admitted, however, that he was relieved when he came in sight of Ireland, for he knew then that it was all over bar the shouting.

WIDESPREAD INTEREST.

WORLD'S EAGERNESS TO KNOW LINDBERGH'S FATE.

The news of Lindbergh's arrival at Le Bourget was announced to thousands of listeners-in by the B.B.C., who broke into a dance selection to give out the news. The interest taken in the flight in London was manifest by the incessant enquiries to-night regarding the airman's progress, and scores of inquiries were made at the London and Glasgow Offices of the *Sunday Mail.*

Mr. Raymond Orteig has cabled to Captain Lindbergh his congratulations, and informing him officially that he has won the 5000 dollar prize at stake.

Colonel Harry Day has wired Captain Lindbergh the following request:—"Will you explain in person to the people of Great Britain your experiences and sensations during the flight? Will give you £1200 for six lectures, one to take place in each of the following towns:—London, Glasgow, Liverpool, Manchester, Birmingham, and Cardiff."

The reports from Transatlantic vessels and various parts of Ireland to-night made it clear that Captain Lindbergh, the young American flier, had succeeded in negotiating the greatest dangers of his desperate bid to fly from New York to Paris.

The Empress of France reported sighting Lindbergh about 5 a.m. this morning at a point one-third of the way between Newfoundland and Ireland.

The next message came from a postman in the village of Dungarvan, in Ireland, who informed the civic authorities that whilst on his rounds about noon to-day he sighted an aeroplane one mile north of Dungarvan heading from a north-easterly direction

At 5.20 p.m. the American 'plane was reported as seen passing over Smerwick Harbour, in County Kerry, at an altitude of 1000 feet. He was flying towards the Cork coast. The machine appeared to be flying well, and the conditions were favourable.

At 5.30 p.m. he was reported to have passed over Goleen in the south-west corner of County Cork heading south east.

The Central News Plymouth correspondent telephoned at 7.40 this evening that an aeroplane, believed to be that of Capt. Lindbergh, flew over St. Germans, Cornwall, nine miles west of Plymouth and about two miles inland.

The aeroplane came from a due northerly direction and flew straight out to sea, disappearing almost due southwards over the Channel. It was flying at too great a height for any distinguishing marks to be visible from the ground but spectators say it was a large light-coloured machine.

Preparations in France to receive Captain Lindbergh included all-night flying facilities on the air line route between Paris and London, while emergency landing fields were prepared at Beauvais, Poix, Abbeville, Berckplage, and Calais.

The thousand million candle-power lighthouse on Mont Valerian, which can be seen for nearly 200 miles, was lit up from the moment Captain Lindbergh was due to arrive, and the aerodrome at Le Bourget was marked by great lights.

The Committee of Reception had decided that in order to avoid any demonstration in the streets of Paris Captain Lindbergh was to be rushed in a closed motor car through side streets from Le Bourget to his hotel, arrangements having been made that he could, if he wished, be in bed within twenty minutes of descending from his machine.

(Continued on Page 2.)

Inside Items

	Page
Otley Sweep Dilemma ...	2
Sir Harry Lauder's Woes ...	6
Screen Stars' Assets	9
Financial Page	16
Racing Page	19
£750 Racing Contest	23

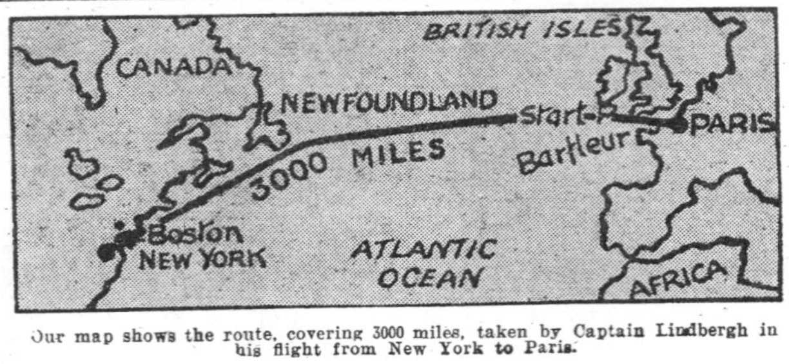

Our map shows the route, covering 3000 miles, taken by Captain Lindbergh in his flight from New York to Paris.

ATLANTIC FLIGHT.

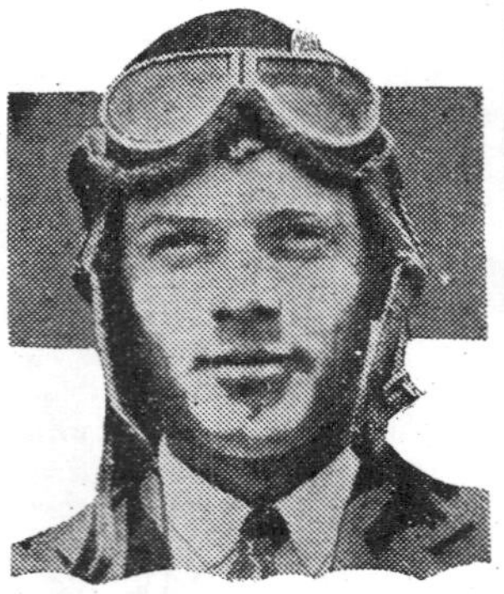

Capt. Lindbergh, the young American, who arrived safely in Paris last night after his daring flight across the Atlantic.

ROAD SMASHES.

Two Serious Collisions in Glasgow Streets.

TAXI-CAB WRECKED.

GLASGOW, Sunday Morning.

Shortly before midnight two serious collisions occurred in Glasgow streets. The first, between a taxi-cab and a tramcar, occurred in Pollokshaws Road, resulting in two persons being injured, one of them very seriously.

It appears that an empty taxi on its way to the city swerved, and collided with a tramcar proceeding in the opposite direction. So severe was the impact that the front part of the tram was smashed, and the steering-gear pushed back several inches.

The taxi-cab was completely wrecked, and both front wheels severed, one of them resting on the footboard of the tramcar.

The driver of the taxi-cab, Murdoch Nicholson (30), 660 Dalmarnock Road, Glasgow, and severely injured, and was conveyed with all speed to the Victoria Infirmary in a private car, while the tram-driver, who suffered from shock, was treated at the local police office.

The wrecked taxi lay in a heap across both sets of tram rails, with the result that traffic was held up for about half an hour.

A second smash of an alarming nature occurred about the same time near the junction of Broomielaw and Oswald Street.

In this instance a two-seater car carrying two ladies and gentlemen, was proceeding eastward along Clydeside when it crashed through a barrier erected around road-mending operations which are being carried out in Broomielaw.

Although the vehicle fell sideways into a large hole five or six feet deep, none of the four passengers was injured, their escape from serious injury being a remarkable one.

DUNDEE MAN MISSING.

POLICE HELP IN SEARCH FOR CORPORATION EMPLOYEE.

DUNDEE, Saturday.

Dundee Police are investigating the disappearance of Charles Henry Hunter (54), foreman painter, who was employed at the Dudhope Corporation Housing Scheme and who resided at Craigiebank, Dundee.

He left his home to go to work at 7.30 a.m. on the 14th inst., and since then he has not returned. His relatives have had no word regarding him.

GOLF INTERNATIONAL.

HOYLAKE, Saturday.

Although Scotland held the lead in today's golf international at the Royal Liverpool links, England made a great recovery in the closing matches and drew level in the final game.

Andrew Jamieson, the young Pollok player, distinguished himself in both his matches.

(Full Report on Page 21.)

NEW SEARCH IN TRUNK CRIME.

CLUE OF LODGER WHO VANISHED.

SURPRISE STATEMENT TO SCOTLAND YARD.

POLICE APPEAL FOR HELP.

LONDON, Saturday Night.

As a result of the police appeal to the public to come forward with any information they may possess in regard to the Charing Cross trunk crime mystery, a man has made a statement regarding a lodger who formerly lived at his house

This man, he said, came to him some three weeks before the discovery of the body and answers the description of the man who bought the trunk at Brixton.

He did not know the man's occupation, but his hours were very irregular, and on the day after Mrs. Bonati's death he appeared to be very agitated and unable to answer questions coherently. He left without giving any indication of where he was going, why he was leaving, or whether he intended to return. The police have decided to follow up this information with a view to discovering whether this is the man for whom they are looking in connection with the case.

CELLARS SEARCHED.

Meanwhile, the police are still completely in the dark as to where the crime was perpetrated. For twelve days they have searched garages and probed into the recesses of coal cellars in the hope of gleaning some information, but all their efforts have been in vain.

One fact emerges strongly from the inquiries, namely, that while hundreds of persons have come forward with information, the one person whom it appeared certain would be the first to be discovered is still unknown. This is the porter who wheeled the trunk from the taxi to the left luggage office at Charing Cross on the afternoon of May 6.

The Hon. Trevor Bingham, assistant commissioner in charge of the Criminal Investigation Department, has now taken control of the inquiries.

About forty acquaintances of the dead woman have been seen by the police. But none of them has been able to throw any light on the mystery. One man still sought is "Jim the chauffeur," who wrote a letter to Mrs. Bonati from "Earl's Court Mews," a non-existent address.

Continued on Page Two.

PRINCE FOR GLASGOW?

MAY OPEN MOTOR SHOW IN KELVIN HALL.

GLASGOW, Saturday.

It is probable that the Prince of Wales will visit Glasgow to open the forthcoming motor show in the Kelvin Hall. The Duke of York, in 1923, performed the opening ceremony, and since then no similar shows in Glasgow have been so favoured by Royalty.

Should he come to the Second City for the big automobile exhibition there is every likelihood that the Prince will attend the dinner of the Scottish Motor Trade Association.

The previous visit of the Prince of Wales to Glasgow was in 1921, when he received the freedom of the city. On that occasion he made a tour of the British Industries Fair in the Kelvin Hall.

JEWELLERY
More than merely to be worn for the decoration of the person should provide that dainty, delicate and delicious effect, such as the fragrance of an Eastern perfume—in a word—
DAVID DOW & SON
Jewellers & Silversmiths
68 ARGYLE STREET and
325 SAUCHIEHALL ST.

Daily Record and Mail

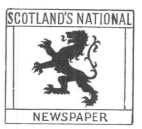

SCOTLAND'S NATIONAL NEWSPAPER

ESTAB. 1847—No. 26,063. GLASGOW, TUESDAY, AUGUST 5, 1930. ONE PENNY.

BRITAIN'S WELCOME HOME TO INTREPID AIR GIRL

WONDERFUL AMY HOME.

GIRL FLIER MET BY CROWD OF 250,000 AT CROYDON.

HER KISS FOR MOTHER.

SELDOM has a greater or more enthusiastic welcome been given a national hero than that accorded to Miss Amy Johnson, the lone flier to Australia, on her arrival at Croydon, near London, last night.

"CALL ME 'JOHNNIE,' SAYS AMY."

PUBLICITY SHE DETESTS.

GREAT crowds had gathered at Croydon aerodrome hours before Miss Johnson was due to arrive.

Mr. and Mrs. Johnson, Amy's father and mother, and their daughters Mollie, aged 18, and Betty, aged 11, reached the aerodrome about 4.30, with nearly a dozen relatives.

They went straight to the Aerodrome Hotel, where they were soon joined by the Lord Mayor of Hull (Councillor Richardson), and the Sheriff of Hull (Councillor Frederick Till).

Other arrivals at the aerodrome were Mr. C. W. Crocker and Mr. Wood, partners in the firm by whom Amy was employed before taking up flying.

They brought eight members of the staff, mostly young women friends of the intrepid airwoman, who were anxious to be on the aerodrome to welcome their old companion.

HISTORIC 'PLANE.

Lord Wakefield congratulated Mr. Johnson on his daughter's wonderful feat.

A few minutes later, the Jason, the tiny aeroplane in which Miss Johnson made her historic flight, was wheeled out to the aerodrome, and was the object of great interest, gleaming green and silver in the bright sunshine.

Packed six deep in the roadway, past the aerodrome, and in dense masses in the enclosure, the crowds (estimated at a quarter of a million people) waited patiently, joining in the chorus of the song, "Amy, Wonderful Amy," broadcast from loud speakers in the Air Ministry control tower.

AMY ARRIVES.

Special arrangements had been made by the Air Ministry to give Miss Johnson a great reception, and there was a big public enclosure and every precaution taken to prevent a recurrence of the scenes which marked Colonel Lindbergh's arrival at Croydon, when the crowd broke through the police cordon.

At five minutes past nine, the Imperial Airways liner, City of Glasgow, in which Miss Johnson had completed the last stage of her journey home from Australia, landed at Croydon.

Hatless, her brown hair shining in the brilliant rays of a searchlight, Amy made a strikingly pretty picture as she stepped from the great air liner to receive the homage which awaited her.

KISS FOR MOTHER.

Cheers—and such cheers—rent the air; but when the girl flier stepped from the 'plane her first act was to fling her arms around her mother and embrace her affectionately. Then her father and sister were also embraced.

It was a scene which few present will forget.

Lord Thomson (Secretary of State for Air), Miss Bondfield (Minister of Labour), Sir Sefton Brancker, Mr. Montague, Lord Wakefield, and a host of others pressed forward to give her their congratulations.

"HULLO!"

In the light of the giant floodlights, Amy walked laughingly, happily, with Sir Sefton Brancker, Director of Civil Aviation, to a platform covered with Union Jacks.

Entirely unaffected, and with no trace of nervousness, she walked to the edge of the dais, and stood in front of the three or four microphones.

Again and again she waved to friends whom she recognised in the crowd, laughingly calling out "Hullo!" until Lord Thomson started his speech.

Lord Thomson said that she had added lustre to the British Empire and to the cause of aviation by her epoch-making performance.

He expressed his delight that she had returned among her people, and expressed the hope that for many many years her star would be in the ascendant.

DETESTS PUBLICITY.

Miss Johnson then walked about again, shaking hands with everybody.

A few minutes later Lord Thomson spoke over the wireless, and paid a splendid tribute to Miss Johnson.

When it came to her turn to reply, she produced a long manuscript, to read before the microphone.

Time and again she emphasised how astonished she was that people had come out to greet her wherever she had gone on her return home.

Then she said, with vigour: "I hate all this publicity. I detest it. I am sure you are fed up with the name of Amy Johnson, and I don't blame you.

"I don't want this advertisement. I like to be free in my 'plane, up among the clouds. That is where I find the greatest joy."

HAPPIEST IN A 'PLANE.

Expressing her pleasure in being back in Britain, she said that during the next few months she would be flying round the country with a view to encouraging flying, especially among the youth of the nation.

"I am never so happy," she went on, "as when I am alone in the silent, wide, open spaces of the sky. These are my tastes, and it requires all my courage to face public applause and to make speeches.

"I am told, over and over again, wherever I go, that I am never what people think I am.

"WELL DONE, JOHNNIE."

"Cannot we drop the 'Miss Johnson' and start from to-day with the name of 'Johnnie,' the name by which I was known to the London Aeroplane Club, where I learnt all my flying?"

Then she expressed her thanks to various people who had assisted and encouraged her during her flight, including Lord Wakefield and her father.

She also thanked the King for his cable to her and the decoration he conferred; Lord Inchcape and the Imperial Airways for arranging her homeward journey.

Sir Sefton Brancker added his tribute, and Miss Bondfield, speaking for the women of Britain, said: "Well done, Johnnie; I want to say how glad we are."

After the speeches, Miss Johnson drove in an open car along the enclosure, waving her hand in response to the acclamation of the vast assembly.

AMAZING ENDURANCE.

Owing to the dense and excited throng along the route Miss Johnson did not arrive at Park Lane until almost midnight.

The amazing powers of endurance of this wonder girl were fully proved. After all the fatigue of her journey, she travelled the whole twelve miles from Croydon to Grosvenor House Hotel standing up in the open motor-car, waving to the cheering throngs—a journey which took at least two hours to accomplish.

After appearing on the balcony of her hotel she retired to change.

At midnight she appeared in the lounge dressed in a simple frock of yellow satin, and was once more greeted with cheers.

Still smiling she acceded to the cries for a speech, but it was short and to the point.

"Thanks ever so much," she said. "It is all so kind. I cannot say more."

(Wireless Programmes—Page 3.)

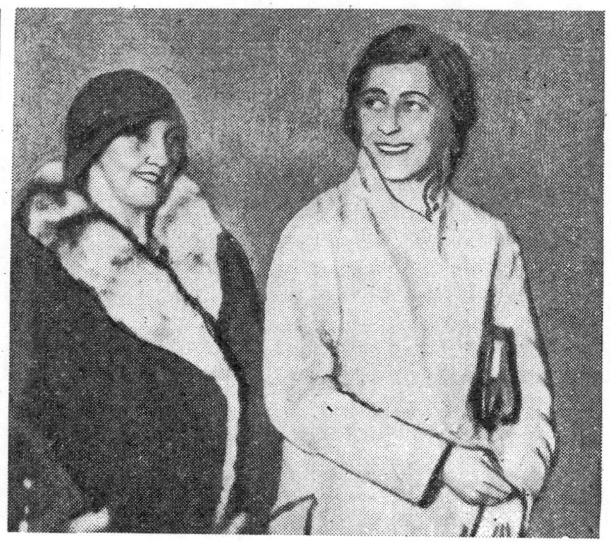

Miss Amy Johnson and her mother on the arrival of the famous girl flier at Croydon last night.
By "Daily Record" Special Photo-telegraphic Service.

PRINCESS'S GIFT.

DUCHESS OF YORK 30 YESTERDAY.

GLAMIS QUIET

(From Our Own Correspondent.)
Glamis, Monday.

THE peace and seclusion in which the Duchess of York spent her 30th birthday anniversary at Glamis Castle to-day were in sharp contrast to the way in which Her Royal Highness's birthday was passed exactly 16 years before, on the occasion that brings sombre memories.

On the night of her 14th birthday the Lady Elizabeth Bowes-Lyon celebrated the event by going to one of London's biggest theatres.

THE CONTRAST.

There, from a box, she and her brother looked upon one of the manifestations of war excitement which were characteristic of theatre audiences in these fateful days.

To-day her hours were spent tranquilly at the Castle of Glamis in the company of her husband, her little Princess daughter, her parents, the Earl and Countess of Strathmore, and her favourite brother, the Honourable David Bowes-Lyon, constant companion and playmate of her childhood years at Glamis.

Possibly the thoughts of the Duchess went back to that evening in 1914, and perhaps to the long days that followed when Glamis Castle was used as a military hospital and her home life became closely linked with the war and war's ravages among mankind.

Because of the circumstances which have brought Her Royal Highness to her ancestral home in the heart of Strathmore, to-day's celebration of the Royal birthday was of the quietest and most personal kind.

From each member of her family the Duchess received a birthday gift. The one she will cherish most came from her daughter. What it was had been kept a deep secret from her Mamma by the curly-headed Princess.

Although quietly celebrated at Glamis, the occasion was widely recognised outside by many friends who telegraphed greetings to Her Royal Highness.

Messages from the King and Queen were included in the bunch of telegrams sent up to the Castle from the village Post Office.

GLASGOW'S MESSAGE.

The Lord Provost of Glasgow sent the following telegram:—

"On behalf of your fellow-citizens of Glasgow, permit me to offer your Royal Highness most hearty congratulations on the anniversary of your birthday.
Lord Provost Kelly, Glasgow."

Lord Provost Kelly received the following reply:—

"Please convey to my fellow-citizens my warmest thanks for their birthday greeting. Elizabeth."

As already stated in the *Daily Record*, Sir Henry Simpson, of London, has taken up residence at the Castle accompanied by a surgeon, also from London.

To-morrow (Tuesday) morning, the Home Secretary, Mr. J. R. Clynes, is due to arrive at Glamis, having left London to-night.

He will be met by the Earl of Airlie and others at Glamis station.

DUKE ON LOCH.

The Duke of York, accompanied by the Hon. David Bowes-Lyon and Admiral Brooke (the Duke's Equerry) enjoyed a forenoon's shooting on Forfar Loch to-day.

The Duke was dressed in sports outfit and was wearing shorts. He had with him his pet Labrador.

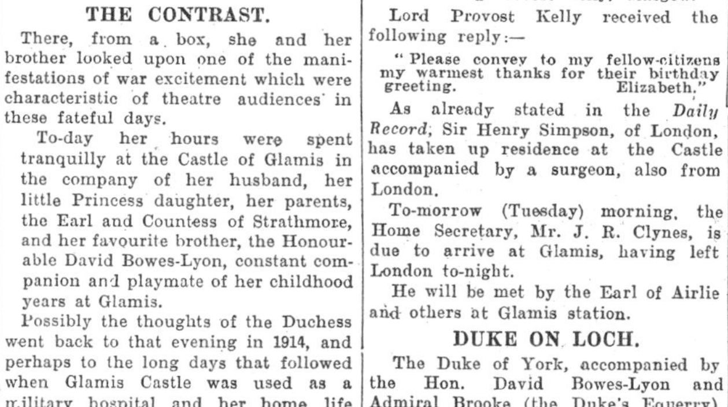

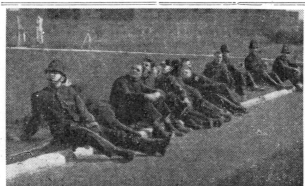

Policemen held in readiness to control the crowd gathered at Croydon last night to welcome Miss Amy Johnson on her return.—By "Daily Record" wire.

PAGEANT OF HIGHLAND HISTORY.

EPITOMISED IN EXHIBITION.

ENCHANTED LAND.

WHEN the history of the Celtic revival in Scotland comes to be written it is certain that the great Highland Exhibition, which was opened in Inverness yesterday, will have an honoured place in the story.

Many chiefs and representatives of noted families of the North were there, but in the weeks to come Inverness will be the Mecca not of Highlanders alone, but of many from overseas also who are expected to visit this Exhibition.

The relics shown recall more vividly than words could tell not only the glamour and romance of the enchanted land, as Sir David Y. Cameron, who opened the Exhibition, called it. They show us pictures of the Highlanders and their country through the ages, in peace as well as in war.

We see how the clansfolk tilled the soil, how they sang at their work, what they read and wrote, how they made music, how they loved and worked and fought and died. We are enabled to follow the social and economic development of the people up to the present day.

BATTERED RELICS.

As Sir David said, it would take days to see this Exhibition as it should be seen, and it is a pity that this wonderful collection, to which castle and cottage alike contributed, must be dispersed so soon.

It is to the battered relics of the battlefield that the eye is first attracted. Each weapon and trophy has its story. There is the sword of Donald Fraser, the blacksmith who, with five companions, ambushed the men who would have taken Prince Charlie at Moy Hall. Donald and his men attacked in the darkness shouting the battle-cries of various clans so that the enemy thought they were being attacked by an army. Strange to say the only man killed in that fight was Donald Ban Maccrimmon, The Macleod's piper, who, before leaving Skye, composed his death lament.

We pass on to where an iron pot hangs from a tripod. As we watch we see that it is in a cave, and round it are the seven men of Glenmoriston with Prince Charlie in their midst. The Prince is awaiting news of the vessel that is to carry him to France.

CULLODEN SHIELD.

There are many other relics that mark the progress of the Prince. There is the lock of his hair cut by Mrs. Macdonald of Kingsburgh when he sought refuge there with the companion of his wanderings. There is, after his escape from Uist, the punch bowl which he broke while struggling in jest with Kingsburgh himself. Near them is the silver ornamented shield, worth thousands of pounds now, which he is said to have carried at Culloden.

Claymores once wielded in battle by Lochiel and Sir Rori Mor MacLeod, and many another Highland warrior of old days are there.

As we pause before a dented corslet a picture arises before the inward eye of Bonnie Dundee at Killiecrankie, a gallant figure on horseback as he raises his arm to urge his men forward and exposes the chink in his armour to the fatal bullet.

We look at a walking stick and think of Simon, Lord Lovat as he stands nonchalantly on the scaffold and hands the cane to his kinsman with a bland farewell. Further on is a drum with the warcry "Stand Fast" on it. This drum was beaten when last the fiery cross was carried in the Highlands.

There are weapons on view which were used by the great Marquis of Montrose; there are Andrea Ferara swords and other fine weapons which show how

(Continued on Page 2, Column 5).

H.T. BATTERIES
"O-KAY" 60 volts...2/11
"O-KAY" 100 volts...5/11
Postage 1/3.
Everything for Wireless.
Cash or Easy Payments.
YOUNG'S
(GLASGOW) LTD.
40 STOCKWELL STREET
Tel.: Bell 2419 'Grams: 'Aerial,' Glasgow

Daily Record
and Mail

ESTAB. 1847—No. 26,116. GLASGOW, MONDAY, OCTOBER 6, 1930. ONE PENNY.

SCOTLAND'S NATIONAL

NEWSPAPER

AIR WRECK: 46 DEAD

Lord Thomson,
the Air Minister, killed in the great
airship disaster.

HORRORS OF R101 DISASTER.

ONLY EIGHT SURVIVORS.

BLAZING LINER'S 1000 FEET FALL IN FRANCE.

Air Vice-Marshal Sir Sefton Brancker,
who was killed in the R101 disaster.

KING AND THE BEREAVED.

"THIS NATIONAL DISASTER."

DAY OF PRAYER.

AS news of the terrible disaster to the R101 became known, yesterday was turned into a day of sorrow for the nation.

In a great number of churches and chapels in the country the news of the calamity was broken by priests and ministers, and prayers were said by crowded congregations.

The King and Queen, who are at Sandringham, received the news by telephone. His Majesty immediately sent the following telegram to the Prime Minister:—

I am horrified to hear of this national disaster which has befallen airship R101 and the consequent serious loss of life, including that of Lord Thomson, my Air Minister. The Queen and I sympathise deeply with the relatives and friends of those who have perished in the service of their country, and also with the injured survivors.—George R.I.

The King and Queen joined with humble village folk in the Parish Church at Sandringham yesterday in special prayers for those bereaved by the R101 disaster.

OIL IN HEDGES.

STARTLING THEORY OF THE DISASTER.

Beauvais, Monday Morning.

There has been a startling development in the investigations into the disaster.

Late last night it was reported that the fields and hedges over which the airship passed, shortly before the calamity, bore traces of oil.

This discovery has changed the whole line of the inquiries which were begun last evening and are to be continued to-day.

It is taken to indicate that those in control of the airship were aware that she was losing altitude to a dangerous extent and were prepared to go the extreme of throwing a quantity of fuel overboard in order to lighten the ship.—C.N.

CAMBUSLANG TRIBUTE.

An impressive tribute to those who perished in the R101 was paid by close on 2000 people at Cambuslang last night. They had assembled in the Savoy cinema theatre to hear a performance of Handel's "Messiah" by the local choral and operatic society.

Rev. Dr. R. S. Calderwood, who presided, asked the company to bow their heads and join with him in prayer, beseeching for the bereaved relatives of the R101 victims the sympathy and guidance and care of Almighty God. The tribute was reverently paid.

THE greatest airship in the world, R101, the pride of British aeronautical engineers, is lying in a French orchard, a mass of twisted, blackened wreckage.

Of the 54 men who sailed away in her so cheerfully from Cardington on Saturday evening, confident that they were about to achieve an epoch-making flight to India, all but eight are dead.

Lord Thomson, Secretary of State for Air; Air Vice-Marshal Sir Sefton Brancker, Director of Civil Aviation; Wing-Commander Colmore, Director of Airship Development; and Major G. H. Scott, inventor of the Airship Mooring Mast, are among the dead.

Of the eight survivors, A. Disley, a wireless operator, and W. G. Radcliffe, a rigger, are the more seriously injured; but the life of none of the eight is considered in danger.

SHATTERING EXPLOSION IN STORM.

The disaster occurred shortly after two o'clock yesterday morning near Allone, a village about four miles south of Beauvais. Inhabitants were awakened from sleep by the roar of the airship's engines overhead and saw her flying low, apparently in difficulties and battling with the heavy wind and rain. Shortly afterwards there was a shattering explosion, followed by a blinding flash. R101 fell 1000 feet.

One of the theories of the cause of the disaster is that the gas containers may have been holed by friction against the metal part of the hull.

DESPERATE BATTLE FOR LIFE.

SURVIVOR'S STORY OF DISASTER.

By Our Special Correspondent, J. A. CANNELL

"Beauvais, Sunday.

WITHIN a few hours of wishing good luck to Major Scott and waving good-bye to the R 101 at Cardington, last night, I saw her again, to-day, a burnt out skeleton, lying at the edge of a wood six miles from here.

Last night the airship, as she floated from the mooring mast and hovered over Bedford, made a brilliant picture.

To-day, she is a tragic pile of metal, though still retaining her gigantic shape. The shape and outline of the huge vessel is all that is left of her.

VIEWED FROM 'PLANE.

I came by specially chartered 'plane from London, to-day, following almost the same route which the airship took last night.

After we had reached Beauvais Aerodrome, my pilot turned north and,

(Other R 101 disaster news on Pages 2, 5, and 6.)

within a few minutes, I was looking down on the tragic skeleton which, last night, was the R 101, the world's largest airship.

I am certain that I have never seen such a stupendous and vivid contrast, and I am sure that I shall never see its like again.

From the air I could see the great skeleton of the airship lying obliquely across a huge field, with its nose into hilly woods. Only the elevators at the extreme rear of the machine were left unburned.

A concentrated collection of wreckage could be seen near the centre of the airship, where the navigating gondola would be.

From my aerial view point I could see thousands of people, in a huge semi-circle, watching near the airship, and, not far from the ship itself, a line of covered objects, which were the corpses taken from the airship earlier in the day.

The roads from Paris, Beauvais itself, and other neighbouring towns were

packed with motor cars, conveying people to the scene where the R101 met her terrible fate.

The view of the wreckage of the R101 which I had from the air was more telling and poignant because with the crowds surrounding it and miles of motor cars, it made a complete yet awful picture.

Beauvais is like a city of mourning, and all the flags are at half-mast.

S URVIVOR INTERVIEWED.

Seven of the eight survivors of the wreck are in a small hospital, not far from the aerodrome. I went to see them shortly after my arrival, though I had the utmost difficulty in obtaining permission to do so.

The Mayor of the town, who had taken charge at the hospital, told me that the British Consul had expressly asked him to refuse permission to anyone desiring to interview or photograph the survivors, as it was necessary for them not to become too excited.

I was, however, granted the necessary permission, and first had a talk with Mr. A. Disley, one of the four wireless

(Continued on Page 2.)

NOTED MEN WHO PERISHED.

R34'S ATLANTIC COMMANDER.

LABOUR PEER.

AMONGST the many notable men who lost their lives in the R101 disaster were the following:—

LORD THOMSON, Secretary of State for Air.

Was 55 years of age and a bachelor. He had a distinguished career as an engineer officer. He served in the Mashonaland campaign and in the South African War. In the Great War he was at the G.H.Q. in France. He received his peerage on taking office in the first Labour Government as Secretary of State for Air, taking the title of Lord Thomson of Cardington. He returned to the Air Ministry on the formation of the present Labour Government in June, 1929. He regarded the cost of State airships as money well spent. He was the author of a book entitled "Air Facts and Problems." In it he quoted instances showing the dangers of airship work, and gave a striking table of Zeppelin casualties. He was a member of a party which flew to India and back.

AIR VICE-MARSHAL SIR WILLIAM SEFTON BRANCKER, K.C.B., Director of Civil Aviation.

Director of Civil Aviation at the Air Ministry since 1922. He was 53 years of age, and was made K.C.B. in 1919. He was a frequent visitor to Glasgow, as the Scottish Flying Club, the only light aeroplane club in Scotland, was his pet enterprise. His last visit to Renfrew was in July during the Fair Holidays, when he took the opportunity of a visit to Falkirk with a view to spreading aviation propaganda in that district.

MAJOR G. H. SCOTT, C.B.E., A.F.C., Director of Airship Development (Flying).

Born in 1888 in Catford, Kent. At the outbreak of the War he joined the Royal Naval Air Service. In 1917 he became Captain of R9, the first British rigid airship to fly. On the formation of the Royal Air Force he was given the rank of Major. Towards the end of 1918 he was chosen to command R34, and was awarded the A.F.C. In 1919 he commanded R34 on its flight from East Fortune, Scotland, to the United States and back to Pulham. For this he was awarded the C.B.E. This was the first flight of any aircraft to America. He took part in the Canadian flight of R100 during July and August this year, and was officer in charge. Major Scott had close associations with the West of Scotland, and it is only a fortnight since he left Glasgow for the south at the conclusion of a visit to his father-in-law, Mr. A. J. Campbell, who resides at Mambeg. Major Scott was married to Miss Jessie R. Campbell, whose father for a number of years was manager of the shipbuilding yard of Messrs. Wm. Beardmore & Co., at Dalmuir.

Firemen searching for bodies in the debris of the giant airship R101, which at the time was still burning in places.—Picture from Paris by "Daily Record" wire.

Wireless Programmes—Page 23.

 Daily Record
and Mail.

SCOTLAND'S NATIONAL NEWSPAPER

ESTAB. 1847—No. 27,063.   WEDNESDAY, OCTOBER 18, 1933.   ONE PENNY.

MUSSOLINI'S ADVICE TO EUROPE

H.R.H. the Duchess of York leaving the Lord Roberts Memorial Workshops, Dundee, after her visit of inspection yesterday.

TASK FOR BRITAIN AND ITALY.

Peacemakers Between France And Germany.

IL DUCE'S TALK WITH THE "DAILY RECORD."

SIGNOR MUSSOLINI gave our Special Representative in Rome a personal interview, speaking with impressive candour of the consequences of a breakdown at Geneva such as actually occurred a few hours later.

Il Duce may at any moment summon the signatories of the Four-Power Pact, of which he is chief author, to review the crisis and its possibilities.

All his references to the Hitler Government and the suspicion between nations assumed that big things were at that moment ready to burst on the world.

"WE ARE ON THE BRINK."

Germany Cannot Afford War.

By W. J. Blyton.

WITH his burning dark eyes upon me, Signor Mussolini said—"The most important problem for the world to realise is this—how to make the position safer and better between Germany and France.

"The task of Britain and Italy is to make the position there easier.

"We are on the brink of serious developments. My opinion is that Germany is not now in a situation to afford any policy which can make for war, unrest, or insecurity.

"Germany has been through a good deal in the last few years. After such events what is wanted is a building-up and a settlement.

DANGEROUS SPEECHES.

"Perhaps there have been speeches made in Germany when it had been better if speeches had not been made—that is to say, by the under chiefs and the minor leaders."

In the interests of the Third Reich itself, he said prophetically, it was time to restore unity in speech and action, together with a sense of Europeanism, otherwise deplorable consequences would rapidly ensue.

Fascism deplored the recent disturbing warlike speeches in certain German quarters—both as disquieting to the world and as tending to discredit the original Fascism in world eyes.

LIMIT IN DISARMAMENT.

"If the Disarmament Conference really and finally fails, new groups will be formed, acute differences may arise, and new uncertainties—even of a social nature—will begin in the history of Europe and the world. That is why, regardless of everything, an agreement must be reached.

"Perhaps too much has been said at Geneva of total disarmament. It is rather a question of reduction all round and adjustment, seeing that there is a limit beyond which no state can pass without exposing itself to serious dangers.

"It is clear and logical, for instance, that Britain should look on naval armaments differently from land armaments.

GERMANY'S NEED.

"But difficulties could even now be overcome if there were more reciprocal understanding and confidence between peoples."

When he warned Germany that her

supreme need is a long period of peace—and peaceful behaviour—it was as if he meant—" Let them take a leaf out of the book of the Italian revolution."

The less responsible speakers must be kept in line. Italy, I gather, is annoyed at certain developments which tend by implication to discredit Fascism generally.

Fascism is all for steadiness and peace, and obtaining by diplomacy what need not be got by war. It is against the new German doctrine of an "elect" race.

NOT A FAILURE.

The Disarmament Conference must be regarded as postponed, not a failure—as consequences too grave would ensue from failure.

Signor Mussolini puts the emphasis on direct agreements and friendships between strong governments. But, like a profound realist, he lets these beliefs be understood rather than brandish them.

SIR JOHN SIMON AND VON NEURATH.

Direct Challenge to Allegations.

(By Our Political Correspondent.)

Following the return of Sir John Simon from Geneva yesterday, there was a discussion of the situation preliminary to to-day's Cabinet meeting between the Foreign Secretary, the Prime Minister, and Mr. Baldwin.

The allegations made by Baron von Neurath, the German Foreign Minister, about Sir John Simon's speech at Geneva, which immediately preceded the German withdrawal from the Conference, are directly challenged in official circles in London.

The German Foreign Minister's statements are regarded in London as an attempt, by the German Foreign Office, in blaming Sir John Simon for Germany's action at Geneva, to create political dissension in this country and make a breach in the unity of the National Government.

Such an effort is merely another example of Germany's blundering diplomacy.

DRAMATIC STROKE PLANNED.

The fact is, of course, that the German Government had planned their dramatic stroke before Sir John Simon's speech at Geneva. They took this decision because they were not prepared to accept the proposals upon which the British, French and American Governments had agreed.

BRITISH LINER AGROUND.

Salvage Ships Rush To Rescue.

MISHAP IN FOG.

Marseilles, Tuesday.

THE steamer City of Paris, belonging to the Ellerman City Line, with 200 passengers on board, is aground at Faraman, near Marseilles. The mishap occurred at 6.15 p.m., and was due to a dense mist which prevented the captain from seeing the Faraman lighthouse.

The following wireless message has been received from Captain Jackson of the City of Paris:—

"Situation of steamer not dangerous although aground. Passengers not in danger."

PASSENGERS ENTERTAINED.

Several salvage steamers from Marseilles have rushed to the rescue. The City of Paris (10,902 tons), which is bound for Bombay, left Liverpool about ten days ago but had to put into Swansea with engine trouble on October 8.

The 200 odd passengers were entertained and taken for sight-seeing trips in South Wales until the damage was repaired and the vessel set sail on Thursday of last week.—Reuter.

HOSPITAL SERVICES.

Centralisation Scheme For Inverness.

The Public Health Committee of Inverness County Council yesterday decided to approve a scheme of joint hospital services with the Burgh of Inverness.

Lochiel, Convener of the County Council, said the County Council about three years ago decided to go in for joint hospital services, because it thought this would be cheaper and better. It was the advice of their Medical Officer and also the wish of the Scottish Department of Health that the treatment of all infectious diseases should be centralised.

WIRELESS—Page 21.

ODDS TO BE CUT.

English "Bookies'" Losses.

FOOTBALL BETS.

SUCH heavy losses have been sustained by Lancashire and Cheshire bookmakers on football bets, during the five weeks which have elapsed since the football season began, that a special meeting of layers in Manchester, last night, decided to reduce the odds.

The losses are due to the phenomenal success of backers of the "three home teams."

Bookmakers in the area mentioned are estimated to have lost well over £100,000 since the season began, and scores of small bookmakers have been compelled to suspend entirely the football side of their business.

HOPELESS PROPOSITION.

The hundred leading bookmakers who attended last night's meeting decided unanimously to reduce the odds on "the three home teams" from 10 to 1 to 8 to 1.

In some districts the "three home teams" bet has been abandoned altogether as a hopeless proposition.

One reason for the success of short-list backers on football matches is said to be the new off-side rule, which has resulted in fewer drawn games.

"BLAZING 'PLANE" SCARE.

Leuchars Pilot Lands with Flare.

Great excitement prevailed in St. Andrews last night when a message was received that an aeroplane had come down in flames in a field near The Grange.

St. Andrews Fire Brigade and the local motor ambulance hurried to the spot, but before they reached the scene of the supposed disaster they were turned back.

It was learned that a 'plane from Leuchars had been engaged in night flying, and the pilot, having missed his way in the darkness, had decided to make a landing with the aid of a flare. In this he had been successful, but the light gave the impression that the 'plane had burst into flames.

RADIUM AS CURE FOR CANCER

Framers Of Report Very Guarded.

TOO EARLY YET.

THERE is not much to satisfy those who believe in the ultimate efficacy of radium as a cure for cancer in the fourth annual report of the National Radium Trust and Radium Commission. The compilers of the report are very guarded in their phrases, and indicate that no statistical evidence as to the true value of radium treatment in cancer can be available for five years. Probably at the end of three years the Commission may be able to publish an interim report which may suggest the best methods of irradiating cancer, and give some provisional expression of opinion as to the value of radium in this treatment.

OTHER TREATMENTS.

"The proportion of cancer cases which can be adequately treated by radium alone," states the report, "is comparatively small, and other treatments are frequently necessary, such as operative surgery, and the use of X-rays. Pathological examinations are also constantly required.

"All these methods of diagnosis and treatment require an adequately trained personnel, whose services, with the necessary apparatus and suitable laboratory accommodation, can only be made available in large and fully equipped hospitals. . . .

"Treatment must be accompanied by research, involving the physical character and biological effects of radium, the assessment of the results attained by treatment, and access to technical literature of the subject."

INQUIRY INSTITUTED.

In order that comparisons may be made, arrangements have been completed for comparing the results of excisional surgery in cancer and radium treatment.

Radium has been used in the treat-

(Continued on Page 32.)

Which means a George Younger

George Younger & Son, Ltd.,
BREWERS, ALLOA.

Daily Record
and Mail.

SCOTLAND'S NATIONAL

NEWSPAPER

ESTAB. 1847—No. 27,105.   WEDNESDAY. DECEMBER 6, 1933.   ONE PENNY.

LOCH NESS MONSTER PHOTOGRAPHED

WHAT IS IT?

Sworn Statement By Foyers Photographer.

A PUZZLING PICTURE.

Let Our Readers Judge.

WHAT will be the most discussed photograph of our time appears on the back page of the "Daily Record" to-day. The photographer is Hugh Gray, employed at the British Aluminium Works, and living at The Bungalow, Foyers.

Yesterday, before a magistrate of Inverness, and other witnesses, he swore to the fact that his remarkable snapshot was taken of the monster which he saw in all its great length moving on the surface of Loch Ness.

The "Daily Record" leaves the picture itself and the evidence which has been collected to the judgment of its readers.

WHAT THE EXPERTS SAY.

Negative Not Tampered With.

YESTERDAY the *Glasgow Herald* published the following report about the Loch Ness monster:—

The Loch Ness monster has been photographed by Mr. Hugh Gray, fitter, Aluminium Works, Foyers.

The negative reveals a creature about 30 feet long with a head like a seal and an elongated body like an eel, with two lateral fins.

Mr. Gray was walking on the afternoon of Sunday, November 26, when he saw the monster in the loch a distance of about 100 yards away. He had his camera with him and took five snapshots, only one of which has been successful.

The monster was seen no fewer than four times last week, once by Alexander Shaw, roadman, Whitefield, who saw it on a previous occasion during the summer. It was also seen from the opposite side of the loch on Wednesday and Thursday.

The distance mentioned in the above report does not coincide with Mr. Gray's considered statement. He can only say that he was standing some distance off and at a certain height. It looks as if the photographer had taken the picture at a distance of some 50 feet and that the elevation from which he took it meant he had to point his camera downwards.

Investigation.

A similar report appeared in the Aberdeen *Press and Journal*, which added that Hugh Gray was being made offers from many sources for the negative. Actually, offers involving large sums of money were received by Mr. Gray, but as the *Daily Record* had already secured the picture on Monday afternoon these offers were ineffective, Mr. Gray preferring that the reproduction should be made in our columns.

Nothing was published about the case yesterday, as it was felt that the fullest possible investigation was necessary. Immediately the negative arrived in the *Daily Record* Office from Foyers, a group of photographic experts were invited to inspect the film. These gentlemen were:—

Mr. M. C. Howard, of Kodaks.

Mr. C. L. Clarke, of "The Kodak Magazine."

Mr. S. Ballantyne, of Lizars.

Mr. Cameron, of Blackadder's.

Experts' Views.

They one and all agreed that the negative bore no trace of having been tampered with in any way, although, naturally, they expressed no opinion on the nature of the object photographed, having no means of verification. The attempted verification had to be conducted, yesterday, in Foyers, where the *Daily Record* representative, along with Bailie Hugh MacKenzie, J.P., of Inverness, and Mr. Peter Munro, an official of the British Aluminium Coy., interviewed Mr. Gray.

For the purpose of taking a sworn statement Mr. MacKenzie, J.P., was specially asked by the *Daily Record* to accompany our representative, and they travelled from Inverness to Foyers by motor car to see Mr. Gray.

It was felt that the statement made by Mr. Gray should amount to a sworn statement.

Our readers will be as puzzled as ourselves as to the nature of the object which is contained in this photograph. A print was submitted to Professor Graham Kerr, M.A., F.R.S., Professor of Zoology at Glasgow University, and he and his staff were naturally non-committal.

Does Not Recognise It.

Professor Graham Kerr said:—

"I see nothing in the photograph with a head like a seal, nor do I see a body like an eel, nor do I see two lateral fins, such as have been described by the photographer.

"What I do see is a curved

(CONTINUED ON PAGE 2.)

The winter sport season now being on, both in Scotland and on the Continent, makes sports fashions important. Here is a really smart all-wool winter sports outfit in brown and orange.

MAN WHO TOOK THE PICTURE.

Mr. Gray Tells His Story.

"GLAD TO HELP."

(From Our Own Reporter.)

Inverness, Tuesday.

A DAILY RECORD representative who visited Foyers was told how the photograph of the Loch Ness monster was taken.

Mr. Hugh Gray, one of the employees of the British Aluminium Company at Foyers, had had a glimpse of the monster on a previous occasions, but often after that he was very dubious that the object was a real monster, so many stories had been published.

However, it was his custom on Sundays to go along the Loch Ness side, especially where the River Foyers enters the loch, and scan the loch, if the water was very calm.

"Four Sundays ago," Mr. Gray said, "after the church service, about one o'clock, I went to a part of the lochside where I could get a good view of the loch, taking with me my camera, as was my usual custom.

"The loch was as still as a mill pond, and the sun was shining brightly. I had no idea that I would see the monster, or the great black object that has so often been reported as making its appearance in the loch.

Up It Comes.

"I had hardly sat down on the bank overlooking the loch, when, lo and behold! an object of considerable dimensions rose out of the water not so very far from where I was sitting. I immediately got my camera into position and snapped the object, which was two or three feet above the surface of the water. I did not see any head, but there was considerable motion from what I thought was the tail.

"The object only appeared for a few minutes. I cannot give any definite opinion as to its size or appearance except that it was of great size, and had apparently come up to the surface then sank out of sight.

"I afterwards went home thinking that, from the brief view I had of the object, so far as the photograph was concerned, nothing would show on the surface of the water. The spool lay in my mother's house at Foyers until Friday of last week, when my brother took it to a chemist's business in Inverness, where the negative was developed, and I understand that a very good picture of the monster, or whatever the object is, was seen.

"No one was with me," said Mr. Gray, "when the photograph was taken.

A Delight To Him.

"I might have had it developed long before I did, but I was afraid of the chaff which the workmen and others would shower upon me if I said I had a photograph of the monster, as there are many who do not give credence to the story that there is anything unusual in the loch."

Asked by Bailie Mackenzie, J.P., if he swore to all he had said, Mr. Gray said that he did.

"In fact," he said, "if the photograph shows something that will be helpful in elucidating the identity of the strange thing in the loch, it will be a delight to me. I am glad that the *Daily Record* has shown such a great interest in the strange creature that has got into the loch, and I am glad to give them the negative to be published."

ABERDEEN CYCLIST KILLED.

In Collision With Motor Car.

ANOTHER street fatality occurred in Aberdeen last night.

The victim was David Main Youngson (37), who resided at 141 Ruthrieston Circle, Aberdeen, the same area as that in which a little girl who was killed by a motor lorry the previous night resided.

Youngson, who was an attendant at Woodend Hospital, was cycling down Anderson Drive, and when nearing its junction with Great Western Road he was struck by a motor car.

He was conveyed to Aberdeen Royal Infirmary where it was found that life was extinct. He is survived by his widow and a family of three.

MR THOMAS REPLIES TO MR DE VALERA

If A Republic Is Declared.

IRISHMEN'S STATUS.

"THE contingency has not arisen, and, I hope, will never arise."

Mr. J. H. Thomas, the Dominions Secretary, made this statement in the House of Commons yesterday in replying to a question on the status of Irish Free State subjects after the declaration of a republic.

Subsequently Mr. Thomas read despatches on the subject between the British Government and the Free State Government, and stated that the British Government could not believe that the Free State Government contemplated final repudiation of their Treaty obligations.

"HAS NOT ARISEN."

The Dominions Secretary was asked by Major-General Sir Alfred Knox if he would take immediate steps to bring to the notice of the natives of the Irish Free State, both in this country and the Free State, the disadvantages which they will suffer, both in status and in the way of

PROHIBITION KILLED.

New York, Tuesday.

After some delay, Utah, the last of the States to act, has ratified the repeal of Prohibition, which is now dead.—Reuter.

entering this country, from the declaration of the Irish Free State as a republic.

Mr. Thomas: "No, sir. I do not feel that any steps such as those indicated are necessary. The contingency has not arisen, and, I hope, will never arise. Further, the advantages enjoyed by British subjects, as compared with aliens, in this country are sufficiently well known and appreciated to need no emphasis from me." (Cheers.)

DISADVANTAGE OF ALIENS.

Sir Alfred Knox—Is it not a fact that, in the event of the declaration of a republic by the Irish Free State, no longer immigrants from Ireland would be allowed to come here and compete in the British labour market. or take advantage of our schemes of social insurance? Is it also not a fact that all natives of the Irish Free State domiciled in this country would be liable to be returned to Southern Ireland if they do not accept British nationality?

Mr. Thomas—There can be no doubt whatever as to the disadvantages of aliens in this country compared with British citizenship.

"DOOR NEVER CLOSED."

Sir William Davison—Will he assure the House that the status of British citizens, which was guaranteed by the Treaty to the loyalists in Southern Ireland, will be guaranteed by this House whatever happens?

Mr. Thomas—I have already said that I still refuse to believe that such a contingency will ultimately arise. When it does the Government will deal with it.

Mr. Hannon—May I ask whether the House is to understand that the door is still open for negotiations if the Irish Free State desire it?

Mr. Thomas—The door has never been closed.

Full Text of Despatches—Page 11.

WIRELESS—Page 20

LOUNGE FURNITURE
We are offering several models at very keenly cut prices. These Suites are all of superior workmanship. Example:—
"The Gloucester" 3-Piece Set, in Heavy Quality Fadeless Damask. Settee with 2 Interior Spring Cushions and Easy Chairs with Spring Cushions. **£32.10**

A. GARDNER & SON, LTD.
36 JAMAICA ST., GLASGOW, C.1

Daily Record
and Mail.

ESTAB. 1847—No. 27,767. TUESDAY, JANUARY 21, 1936. ONE PENNY.

SCOTLAND'S NATIONAL

NEWSPAPER

 # THE KING IS DEAD

Weakened Heart Stilled

Peaceful Passing In Midst Of Family

BULLETIN AT MIDNIGHT

The "Daily Record" deeply regrets to announce that His Majesty King George died five minutes before midnight at Sandringham.

The official bulletin stated:—

Death came peacefully to the King at 11.55 p.m. to-night in the presence of Her Majesty the Queen, the Prince of Wales, the Duke of York, the Princess Royal and the Duke and Duchess of Kent.

(Signed) Frederic Willans
Stanley Hewett
Dawson of Penn

Death-bed Scene—the Queen In Tears

The King remained without pain right to the end. He passed away in complete peace.

When the doctors realised that the end was only a matter of minutes, they summoned the Queen and her family to the sick-room.

The Queen and the Royal Princes, with the Princess Royal and the Duchess of Kent, came up to the room.

They were all present in the room itself when the King breathed his last.

The Archbishop of Canterbury also was present during the final sad scenes.

QUEEN BREAKS DOWN

The Queen, whose iron self-control had kept her calm throughout the long, anxious days, broke down then.

Tears welled into her eyes as she thought of the long years of her happy married life and the 25 years of reign she had shared with the King.

Then the Queen turned to her son—the new King—and mother and son exchanged an affectionate embrace.

Edward Windsor up to last night, and now King Edward VIII., turned to his brothers and his sister with sad face.

The Royal party moved out of the King's death chamber to an adjacent room, to talk over what was to be done.

THE NEW KING

The Queen, the Duke of York and the Duke of Kent, who for less than 12 hours had held Sovereign

DRAMATIC FOREWARNING FOR NATION

REALISATION that the King had not long to live came with the dramatic intimation flashed by the official bulletin at 9.25 last night:—

"The King's life is moving peacefully towards its close."

An earlier bulletin, at 5.30, had given the first indication of the critical turn in the King's illness, stating:—"The condition of His Majesty the King shows diminishing strength."

After these two messages a stunned nation waited—for the end.

---

power as Counsellors of State, spoke together in low tones.

Their sovereign authority, delegated to them by King George in the last official act of his busy life, had now passed to the new King, who, to-day, will be proclaimed to the nation.

The slender, fair-headed, and still almost boyish-looking Prince, now a King, seemed to have at once bravely shouldered the new and tremendous responsibility which had devolved on him as Head of the British Empire.

HER MAJESTY 'PHONES

Immediately the death was announced, the Queen herself spoke over the telephone to members of the Royal Family who were not at Sandringham.

The Duke and Duchess of Gloucester at Buckingham Palace, the Duchess of York at Windsor, the Duke of Connaught at Bath, and Queen Maud of Norway at Oslo—the only surviving child of King Edward and Queen Alexandra—were all informed.

A few minutes later, the silence over Sandringham was broken by the roar of a powerful car, speeding through the night towards London, carrying Lord Wigram, King George's secretary, on his way to see the Prime Minister.

Once all that was necessary had been done, the Queen went to her sorrowful bed.

The Princess Royal and the Duchess of Kent tried in vain to console her. The Queen's grief was too great for comfort.

The happy union that had lasted for so many years was over. Queen Mary, now the Queen Mother, wept and sorrowed for her dead husband like any other loving wife.

THE LYING-IN-STATE

The new King remained up until the early hours of the morning. He was in consultation with his brother, the Duke of York, about the arrangements for the funeral of King George, the lying-in-state and other matters.

The new King will journey to London to-day for the Accession Council, at which the Archbishop of Canterbury and the Home Secretary will be present.

This morning the body of King George will be taken from Sandringham to the little church of St. Mary Magdalene, where he so often worshipped.

"EDWARD," THE NEW KING

Dramatic Signature On Telegram

THIRTY-THREE minutes after the death of the King, the son who has succeeded him—no longer the Prince of Wales—used his signature—"Edward"—as King for the first time.

His telegram telling the Lord Mayor of London that the King had passed away was signed in that way.

Hitherto his signature has been "Edward P."

The telegram to the Lord Mayor was timed 12.28.

The new King is the first bachelor to ascend the throne since George III.

See Page 2

Here it will remain until future arrangements have been completed.

It is expected that plans for the lying-in-state in London, presumably in Westminster Abbey, will be made known to-day.

The Duke of Connaught, the King's uncle, in the hotel at Bath, where he is spending the winter months, listened to the successive wireless messages relating to the King's gradual sinking, and did not retire to his bed until after the last sad bulletin was broadcast announcing the King's death.

TWO HUGE
MONEY
CONTESTS
PAGES 30 and 31

Sunday Mail

Scotland's National Sunday Newspaper

"Abune them a'"
LANG'S
LIQUEUR
Scotch Whisky

No. 1433   WIRELESS—P. 33   SUNDAY, MARCH 8, 1936   48 PAGES   TWOPENCE

GERMANY MARCHES AGAIN—AFTER 18 YEARS

Goose-Stepping To—?

RHINELAND FRENZY OF PATRIOTISM

GERMAN troops marched into the Rhineland again yesterday.

Thus, after 18 long years, Germany finally regained full sovereignty over all her territory.

In Frankfort, Mainz, Coblenz and Cologne there were scenes of wild enthusiasm when the first soldiers of the Fatherland seen there since the war proudly goose-stepped along the crowded streets.

Thousands marched with the men, singing, cheering and shouting madly in their excitement. Red banners with the swastika appeared over most of the buildings, while high above warplanes droned a joyous salute.

Thousands more troops and guns will pour ceaselessly into the Rhineland to-day, and by night the reoccupation will be complete.

COLOGNE has been empty of troops since the last units of the British Army of Occupation retired several years ago. Yesterday the tramp of armed men was once again heard in the city, deafened at times by the surging tide of cheering that swept along the route of the German units' advance.

In front of the Excelsior Hotel, once British General Headquarters, General von Kluge, commanding the Munster

25,000 TROOPS "TOOK POSSESSION"

TWENTY - FIVE thousand troops, it is unofficially estimated, have been moved to the Rhineland — infantry, cavalry, armed cars and guns.

Military District, reviewed the German troops from a spot over which British sentries paced day and night for years.

As the German troops swung into the cathedral square sharp words of command were given and the men started the goose-step. They shook

the asphalt as they stamped past, eyes right, saluting the German General.

They revealed how the German Army has been reorganised on modern lines.

With the infantrymen came anti-aircraft guns, anti-tank guns, field kitchens and some mechanised equipment.

Coblenz, the city built where the Mosel River enters the Rhine, went wild with joy when the first German troops entered. The children saw their first German soldiers. Many of the old people who had lived through the days of national tribulation watched the Fatherland's soldiers march in. Tears coursed down their cheeks.

The scenes are likened to those which were witnessed in the early days of the war, when the Germans passed through the Rhineland on the way to the front.

Thousands of people lined the routes taken by the troops and threw flowers at the men, who caught them and stuck them in their uniforms and the bores of their rifles.

NEAR FRONTIERS

News that the troops were coming to Trier (Treves), up the Mosel River, towards the French frontier, an old garrison town, was conveyed to the inhabitants through loud speakers, which blared the information across the squares. Thousands of people massed in the streets and there were scenes of wild jubilation.

At Aix la Chapelle, Trier (Treves) and Saarbrucken, which are close to the French and Belgian frontiers, only a few troops will be stationed.

PICTURES FROM THE RHINE

The Mayor of Cologne, Dr. Riesen, greeting the German troops who entered the demilitarised Rhineland zone yesterday.—Picture by air to London and transmitted to Glasgow by telephoto wire.

Hitler leaving the Kroll Opera House yesterday after making the speech that rang round the whole world.—By telephoto wire from Berlin to London and thence to Glasgow.

EUROPE'S REACTION

France—"Sanctions" Britain — "Wait And See"

EUROPE to-day is seething with excitement over Germany's tearing up of the Locarno Treaty, even coupled as it is with the offer of a new 25-year pact of non-aggression between France, Germany and Belgium, with Britain and Italy as guarantors.

Already informal discussions have taken place in Paris between M. Flandin, the French Foreign Minister, and the Ambassadors of the Locarno Powers—Britain, Italy and Belgium, the talks developing into separate conferences with France's military allies.

Here are the reactions to the news of the entry of the demilitarised zone, as reported from the countries most concerned :—

FRANCE'S DECISION

M. Flandin has announced that it has been decided to bring Germany's rejection of Locarno before the League of Nations.

The French Foreign Office spokesman told the British United Press after the meeting of Ministers and Military Chiefs:—" France will ask the League and the signatories to the Treaty of Locarno to apply financial and economic

sanctions against Germany, as well as measures of a military character if necessary."

The League Council has been summoned tentatively for Thursday.

The French Government intends to insist on the evacuation of German troops from the demilitarised zone, and will demand the support of Great Britain, Italy, and Belgium.

M. Flandin intends to call a meeting of the Powers signatory to the Locarno Treaty in Paris on Monday evening to fix a common attitude for Geneva. It is hoped that Mr. Eden will attend after Monday's Cabinet.

Fortifications are being strengthened in Eastern France, it is learned from Paris, and detachments of mobile guards have been sent to reinforce the frontier police.

All Army leave in Eastern France has been stopped, and telegrams have been sent to officers and men on leave ordering them to return. Some reports state that Army leave in general is cancelled over the week-end.

The Kehl Bridgehead over the Rhine near Strasburg, which was evacuated by the French under the Locarno agreement, has now been re-occupied by French troops. German troops had already reached the Rhine at this point and to-day French and German soldiers will be facing each other in this area.

M. Deat, the French Air Minister, accompanied by General Pujo, Chief of the Air Staff, and other high officers yesterday inspected the Eastern air defence system at Metz and discussed the new situation with officers in charge.

BRITAIN'S ATTITUDE

Mr. Anthony Eden went yesterday to Chequers, and with the Prime Minister studied the situation.

It has not been considered necessary to call an emergency meeting of the Cabinet, as a Cabinet meeting had already been arranged for to-morrow

(Continued On Back Page)

ANXIETY FOR BEATTY

THE following bulletin was issued at nine o'clock last night:—" Lord Beatty's condition gives rise to increased anxiety."

The bulletin is signed by Lord Horder, Sir Maurice Cassidy and Dr. C. N. Groves.

A bulletin during yesterday morning had stated that Earl Beatty, who is lying at his home in Grosvenor Square, London, had had a fairly good night, but that his condition remained grave.

His brother, Major Beatty, visited the house yesterday.

Soon after Dr. Groves came by taxi. Later he was joined again by Dr. Groves. Lord Horder arrived about eight o'clock last night to join the two doctors.

TOMMY ROSE LANDS

Marseilles, Saturday.

Flight-Lieutenant Tommy Rose, who is attempting to break the record for a flight from the Cape to England, landed at Benghasi, Tripoli, at 10.40 a.m. to-day.

He is not flying on until to-morrow.—Reuter.

The first German soldier, of the troops who entered the Rhineland yesterday, looks at Cologne. In the background can be seen Cologne Cathedral. Picture by air to London and transmitted to Glasgow by telephoto wire.

PRAMS
Lists Free
Inspection Invited
CASH OR EASY PAYMENTS
YOUNG'S
STOCKWELL ST. GLASGOW

Daily Record
and Mail.

ESTAB. 1847—No. 27,898.   MONDAY, JUNE 22, 1936.   ONE PENNY

SCOTLAND'S NATIONAL

NEWSPAPER

ANOTHER COLOUR REVOLUTION

THE EMPEROR AT WEMYSS CASTLE WITH PRINCESS TSHAI CHI AND MRS. OLIVE MUIR, OF GLASGOW

First News Photograph
In Nature's Hues
Ever Published

TO-DAY, for the first time in the history of world journalism, the *Daily Record*, Scotland's National Newspaper, has pleasure in reproducing in this issue, along with its ordinary news, a colour photograph of an actual news event.

No colour photograph has hitherto been reproduced by any newspaper in the course of its ordinary run, and at high speed.

For two years, the *Daily Record* has been pioneering in the use of full colour, both for editorial and for advertising purposes.

This unique development is a vastly different thing from the use of a flat colour tint along with black—a process exploited by

Associated Scottish Newspapers so far back as 1909.

The success of the *Daily Record* colour reproductions has been acclaimed in every country of the world. To-day, colour photography of a news event marks another revolution in newspaper achievement.

It is gratifying to the *Daily Record* that, through its initiative, Scotland should thus take the foremost place in journalistic progress.

The photograph was taken by an

ordinary full-plate camera using the wonderfully successful Dufaycolor film, which on being developed gives a transparency of Nature's full colour.

This transparency was then subjected to the elaborate *Daily Record* system of colour engraving, stereotyping and printing, resulting in the remarkable print above

EMPEROR LEAVES TO-DAY

THE Emperor of Abyssinia, who is the subject of the first photograph in colour ever reproduced by a newspaper, leaves Wemyss Castle to?day along with his suite for London.

He spent a delightful week-end on the Firth of Clyde, and expressed himself as charmed with everything.

Full story of the Emperor's weekend is given on Page 9.

I.R.A. CALL OFF BANNED MEETING

Countryside Like France In War-Time

The Irish Republican Army, faced with the Government proclamation declaring the organisation an illegal one, yesterday called off the banned demonstration, which they had planned to take place at Bodenstown Churchyard, County Kildare.

Free State troops in full war kit turned the little countryside cemetery into an armed camp. Civic Guards kept watch with them.

Aeroplanes, which were in wireless communication with the ground headquarters, swept the sky.

Sallins, the nearest village of any size, looked like a French village behind the lines during the War.

Full Story—Page Three.

RADIO—Page 8

BIG GOLF
CLASH REALLY
IS "OPEN"

Hoylake's Stern Test

By HENRY COTTON,
Open Golf Champion 1934

Hoylake, Sunday.

EVERYONE agrees that the Championship is really "Open"; but there is no doubt in my mind that the man who wins the title will have every claim to consider himself the best golfer in the field.

That has not always been the case in big championships; but Hoylake, in its present condition, 7078 yards from the back tees, is a formidable test that admits of no "flukes."

Long driving, accurate second shots (particularly with wooden clubs and the longer irons) will be telling factors this week.

Particularly, if there is a wind, I cannot see any player beating 287 for the 72 holes.

Henry Cotton.

287 The Limit

And, if Hoylake provides one or two of its "breezes," it may be difficult to get anywhere near an average of 4's.

Gene Sarazen arrived to-day, after travelling from London, and went round the championship course in 71, afterwards playing at Wallasey.

Gene has not left himself much time to get into trim, but a last-minute trip across the Atlantic is no novelty for him, and I know of no overseas challenger who is more dangerous.

Padgham's Chance

My own form has been satisfactory, to me, and I pride myself on being a stern critic where my golf is concerned.

Padgham I regard as having the best chance among British professionals, with Burton as a possible.

In his present form, Perry cannot be regarded as likely to retain the title.

Greatest Test

I repeat, however, that whoever wins will have the satisfaction of knowing he has triumphed in one of the greatest tests of golf ever devised.

The recent rains have brought Hoylake to perfection, and every man who is long, strong and accurate will be among the leaders at the finish.

And now for the battle.

Nanking Leader's Move

Canton, Sunday.

GENERAL CHIANG KAI-SHEK, leader of the Nanking Government, is reported to have sent an ultimatum to the Kwangsi (Canton) leaders, ordering them to withdraw all their troops from Hunan within a week, failing which they will be forcibly expelled.—Reuter.

Mr. Baldwin's Smoke

Presbyterian Mixture
A. GALE & CO.
1 Dundas Street,
GLASGOW C.1

Daily Record
and Mail.

ESTAB. 1847—No. 28,045.   THURSDAY, DECEMBER 10, 1936.   ONE PENNY

SCOTLAND'S NATIONAL
NEWSPAPER

MRS. SIMPSON

A full colour study of Mrs. Simpson, the most talked-of woman in the world. This colour plate is the finest portrait yet issued of the woman who has figured in the greatest constitutional crisis of our time.

COMFORT IN SPECTACLES
Shell frames give nose comfort.
Toric lenses give eye comfort.
This combination gives the ideal
reading spectacle
JOHN TROTTER
LIMITED
40 Gordon Street, Glasgow
and 100 George St., Edinburgh

Daily Record
and Mail.

ESTAB. 1847—No. 28,046.   FRIDAY, DECEMBER 11, 1936.   ONE PENNY

SCOTLAND'S NATIONAL
NEWSPAPER

A SCOTS QUEEN

King George VI And Queen Elizabeth To Be Proclaimed

CORONATION NEXT MAY

FUTURE PLANS OF EDWARD VIII.

AS the unparalleled drama of the abdication of King Edward VIII. unfolded itself yesterday, a wave of relief swept over the country, spreading right throughout the Empire, the succession of the Duke and Duchess of York to the Throne being hailed as not only the best but the only solution to the crisis.

To Scotland the crowning of the Duchess of York as Queen Elizabeth will be particularly gratifying and the Empire will welcome, with warmest loyalty a Scottish Queen.

KING GEORGE VI.

The new King will be Proclaimed to-morrow afternoon.

It is understood he will assume the title of King George VI.

The Coronation will probably take place on the date arranged for King Edward—May 12.

The House of Commons will meet at 2.45 to-morrow afternoon for members to take the Oath of Allegiance to the new King. The swearing-in will be continued at Monday's sitting.

King Edward will renounce with the Throne all his titles. After abdicating, he will be plain Mr. Windsor.

ACCESSION PLANS

The *Daily Record* learns that, while the Duke of York, who will be 41 on Monday, has not yet made a final decision as to what title he will take, it is likely that he will choose to be known as George VI., rather than Albert I.

Princess Elizabeth

When her father comes to the Throne, Princess Elizabeth will be Heiress Presumptive, as the Duke of York has been Heir Presumptive during his brother's reign.

Princess Elizabeth will not be Heiress Apparent, as this title would follow to any future son who might be born to the new King and his Queen

For this reason, it is considered unlikely that Princess Elizabeth will be given the Duchy of Cornwall. Most probably she will continue to be known as Princess Elizabeth.

It was authoritatively stated last night that the Accession Council at St. James's Palace will be held by the new King as the first act of his reign to-morrow morning.

The Proclamation of the new King will take place to-morrow afternoon.

Queen Mother

It is probable that, with the accession of the new King and the presence of a Queen Consort again, Queen Mary will be known as Mary the Queen Mother.

"MR. WINDSOR"

King Edward, the *Daily Record* understands, will leave the country as soon as he has completed his abdication by signing the Act of Abdication,

Continued On Back Page

King Edward To Broadcast To-night

KING EDWARD will broadcast to-night at 10 o'clock.

An announcement made by the B.B.C. last night stated:—

"King Edward desires, immediately he has ceased to be King, to broadcast. His broadcast to-morrow evening will be in the character of a private person owing allegiance to the new King.

"Arrangements have been made to enable what he says to be transmitted all over the world."

The King will make his broadcast from outside London, it is understood. He may broadcast from Sunningdale, or, alternatively, it is possible that, should he leave the country earlier in the evening, he may speak to his peoples from abroad.

After the King has spoken all B.B.C. transmitters will close down.

The New King

MOVING SPECTACLE STIRS HEARTS

Premier's Ordeal In Memorable Commons Scene

BY OUR PARLIAMENTARY REPRESENTATIVE
WESTMINSTER, THURSDAY.

NEVER IN THE LONG HISTORY OF PARLIAMENT, EXTENDING OVER 700 YEARS, HAS THERE BEEN THE SCENE AND THE DRAMA COMPARABLE WITH TO-DAY, WHEN KING EDWARD VIII. RENOUNCED THE THRONE OF THE GREATEST EMPIRE IN THE WORLD.

So moving was the spectacle that not only women were moved to tears, but members of Parliament, seasoned in public affairs, wiped their eyes as the irrevocable decision was made known.

Cheers For Premier

At 3.35, Mr. Baldwin came in by the doors behind the Speaker's chair. He carried two sheets of typescript bearing the red Royal Seal at the head.

He hesitated for a moment before emerging into the full view of the House, as if somewhat nervous. Two or three colleagues patted him on the back and, as if encouraged, he stepped forward. When the House saw him they cheered long and mightily.

The demonstration of loyalty and affection was unanimous exceeding anything seen like it previously.

Mr. Baldwin looked a trifle haggard. His hands moved rather nervously. Sitting down between Mr. Ramsay MacDonald, Lord President of the Council, and Mr. Neville Chamberlain, Chancellor of the Exchequer, he talked with them at some length.

Wife's Encouragement

While waiting for questions to finish, Mr. Baldwin looked up and saw his wife in the Gallery above. Both exchanged a slight smile—it seemed as though it was a smile of encouragement.

Question time ended at 3.42. When the Speaker, looking very grave, stood up and said, "Mr. Baldwin," a great hush fell upon the proceedings. The very silence itself stirred the emotions.

Mr. Baldwin nervously rose to his feet, and with the typescript in his hand walked to the far end of the Chamber and stood at the Bar. The three clerks

(Continued on Page 2, Column 4)

Great Ovation For Duke

THE DUKE OF YORK was given a loyal ovation when he returned by car to his London residence, 145 Piccadilly, last night.

Many hundreds of people had assembled in the locality, and when the Duke arrived he was cheered lustily. So enthusiastic was his reception that the police, in spite of their numbers, were unable to clear a passage for the Royal car for nearly five minutes.

The Duke, who was sitting in the back of the car, raised his hat repeatedly and smiled his acknowledgements to the tremendous crowd.

After the Duke had entered the house a man in the crowd started to sing the National Anthem, which was immediately taken up by the hundreds of people thronging the vicinity.

Men and women climbed the railings around the house, and every vantage point was used to catch a glimpse of the Duke. Traffic was unable to proceed for several minutes.

The New Queen

RADIO—Page 27

You'll enjoy McEWANS Better!

Daily  and Mail. Record

SCOTLAND'S NATIONAL NEWSPAPER

ESTAB. 1847—No. 28,047.   SATURDAY, DECEMBER 12, 1936.   ONE PENNY

LAST FAREWELL

"Prince Edward's" Tribute To Brother

"THE WOMAN I LOVE"

Ex-King At The Microphone

Ex-King Leaves The Country

THE MOST DRAMATIC OF ALL BROADCASTS IN THE 20 YEARS' HISTORY OF RADIO WAS HEARD BY THE WHOLE WORLD, LAST NIGHT.

It was a message of farewell to the people of Britain and the Empire, and of allegiance to the new King by "Prince Edward" by which title the ex-King was introduced to his listeners by Sir John Reith.

FOUR HOURS LATER CAME THE NEWS THAT THE EX-KING LEFT BRITAIN'S SHORES ABOARD THE H.M.S. FURY.

Yesterday afternoon the Duke of York became Sovereign, and this afternoon, in London, he will be proclaimed as King George VI.

GREATEST LOVE STORY

Our Correspondent at Cannes, Edward F. Balloch, telegraphed last night :—

They are saying in Cannes to-night that the ex-King's radio talk is the greatest love story that has ever been told.

A MOTHER'S MESSAGE—
From Queen Mary To The People

"I HAVE BEEN SO DEEPLY TOUCHED BY THE SYMPATHY WHICH HAS SURROUNDED ME AT THIS TIME OF ANXIETY THAT I MUST SEND A MESSAGE OF GRATITUDE FROM THE DEPTH OF MY HEART. THE SYMPATHY AND AFFECTION WHICH SUSTAINED ME IN MY GREAT SORROW LESS THAN A YEAR AGO HAVE NOT FAILED ME NOW . . .

"I NEED NOT SPEAK TO YOU OF THE DISTRESS WHICH FILLS A MOTHER'S HEART WHEN I THINK THAT MY DEAR SON HAS DEEMED IT TO BE HIS DUTY TO LAY DOWN HIS CHARGE . . . .

"I KNOW THAT YOU WILL REALISE WHAT IT HAS COST HIM TO COME TO THIS DECISION . . . ."

Message In Full—Back Page.

Ex-King's Midnight Dash To Portsmouth

From Our Special Correspondent
Portsmouth,
Saturday Morning.

A CAR, believed to contain Prince Edward, dashed through the Unicorn Gates at Portsmouth Dockyard at 12.10 this morning.

The car was the one which left the Royal Lodge at Windsor, escorted by five others, and a shooting brake stacked with luggage, and rushed through the night to the coast immediately after the ex-King had made his last dramatic farewell to the nation.

When the car approached the gates at last speed, two Admirals who had been pacing up and down inside for half-an-hour sprang to attention and saluted, and the procession entered.

Destroyer Alongside

Moored alongside in the dockyard was H.M.S. Fury, waiting to take Prince Edward abroad for a secret destination.

Immediately the cars entered the dockyard, the ex-King stepped out and spoke to Admiral Fisher, who invited him into his house. He emerged a little later.

His departure was brief and informal. He shook hands with those of his staff who were not accompanying him on his journey.

The ex-King walked aboard without any ceremony, and almost immediately the destroyer cast off.

Doubt existed as to whether the ex-King had left in a destroyer or aboard the Admiralty yacht Enchantress. It was later definitely learned that he had left aboard a destroyer.

RADIO—Page 19

Edward's Broadcast In Full

THE ex-King's broadcast was from Windsor Castle, and the announcer's introduction was:—"This is Windsor Castle — His Royal Highness Prince Edward."

The full text of the broadcast is as follows: —

At long last I am able to say a few words of my own. I have never wanted to withhold anything, but, until now, it has not been constitutionally possible for me to speak.

A few hours ago I discharged my last duty as King and Emperor; and now that I have been succeeded by my brother, the Duke of York, my first words must be to declare my allegiance to him. This I do with all my heart.

You all know the reasons which have impelled me to renounce the Throne, but I want you to understand that, in making up my mind, I did not forget the country or the Empire which, as Prince of Wales and lately as King, I have for 25 years tried to serve.

"THE WOMAN I LOVE"

But you must believe me when I tell you that I have found it impossible to carry the heavy burden of responsibility and to discharge my duties as King as I would wish to do, without the help and support of the woman I love.

But I want you to know that the decision I have made has been mine and mine alone. This was a thing I had to judge entirely for myself.

The other person most nearly concerned has tried, up to the last, to persuade me to take a different course.

I have made this, the most serious decision of my life, only upon a single thought of what would, in the end, be best for all.

TRIBUTE TO MOTHER

This decision has been made less difficult to me by the sure knowledge that my brother, with his long training in the public affairs of this country and with his fine qualities, will be able to take my place forthwith, without interruption or injury to the life and progress of the Empire.

And he has one matchless blessing enjoyed by so many of you and not bestowed on me—a happy home, with his wife and children.

During these hard days I have been comforted by Her Majesty, my mother, and by my family.

Ministers of the Crown, and in particular Mr. Baldwin, the Prime Minister, have always treated me with full consideration.

GRATEFUL TO PEOPLE

There has never been any Constitutional difference between me and them, and between me and Parliament.

CONTINUED ON BACK PAGE

1937
END EVERY
DAY WITH
A Y
GEORGE YOUNGER'S
ALLOA ALES

Daily Record
and Mail.

SCOTLAND'S NATIONAL

NEWSPAPER

ESTAB. 1847—No. 28,079.　　WEDNESDAY, JANUARY 20, 1937.　　ONE PENNY

GLASGOW BOXER'S WORLD TITLE
Benny Lynch's £2600 Share Of Record Purse

Lynch (right) ducks to avoid a lead to the jaw during his fight with Small Montana in London last night.
—Picture by wire.

NOW UNDISPUTED CHAMPION

Montana's Craft Saves Him From Knock-Out

By ELKY CLARK, Ex-European Flyweight Champion

London, Tuesday Night

BENNY LYNCH OF GLASGOW IS NOW THE UNDISPUTED FLYWEIGHT CHAMPION OF THE WORLD.

At the Wembley Pool, here, to-night he defeated Small Montana of America on points over fifteen rounds.

Lynch won, I thought, with a bit in hand. Benny has always been noted as a fighter depending mostly on a big punch to bring him victory, but on his display to-night he surprised his most ardent admirers by the way he boxed and brought into play a clever craftsmanship.

Lynch throughout was the aggressor, and although he failed to land a knock-out punch, he obviously worried Montana with wicked lefts and rights to the body.

Against a less crafty fighter, Lynch would surely have gained his objective, as he did against Jackie Brown and Pat Palmer.

The purse for the contest amounted to £6000, of which Lynch claimed £2600. Several hundreds of pounds were guaranteed Montana for travelling and training expenses in addition to what the Filipino actually received.

There were 13,600 people at the fight, and they paid £14,000.

MONTANA did not prove the lightning spark he was cracked up to be, but nevertheless he proved to be seven stone nine pounds ten ounces of tough material.

The Filipino, although not so fast on his feet, possessed a nice swerve from the hip that was delightful to watch. It was with this movement that he prevented the Scot from landing a knock-out. Montana was coolness personified throughout the Scot's rugged onslaught. It was by keeping a cool head that he managed to stay the distance.

Montana proved a splendid boxer, but

(Continued on Back Page)

U.S. Offer To Lynch

NORMAN HURST, Boxing Correspondent of Allied Newspapers, writes that yesterday afternoon he received a message from the manager of Madison Square Garden, New York.

"Tell Lynch that if he defeats Montana in a clear-cut manner he will be matched for a fight at Madison Square against Sixto Escobar for the bantamweight championship of the world."

This would give Lynch an opportunity of gaining the unique distinction for a British boxer of holding two world titles at the same time.

"I'M MIGHTY PROUD"

Benny Lynch's Message To The "Daily Record"

By "WAVERLEY"

In the early hours of this morning I had a telephone conversation with Benny Lynch, who was then in the Euston Hotel, London, where he is staying. He returns home to-morrow, arriving in the Central Station, Glasgow, at 9.35 p.m.

"How are you, Benny?" I queried.

"I'm feeling very fit. Let me give this message to the 'Daily Record.' I'm not the least bit damaged, and I'm mighty proud that once again I have won for Scotland. Just now I feel proud I am a Scot, and that I have kept the title for my country."

"It was a hard fight, I believe."

"I found him very elusive, but I think I have proved that I can both box and fight, and that I am not just a strong puncher as some people seem to think. It was a battle of tactics.

"There was a time, nearing the half-way stage, when Montana foxed that he was tiring. I pretended I was weary, too. In the seventh round he let go, but I was ready for him, and proved myself as strong as he was. I think he realised that.

"Was he a hard puncher?"

"He was guilty of hitting with the inside of the glove and I suspected that those in his corner warned him about it. But he was a great little sport, and one who fought fairly and squarely, asking for no mercy and proffering none.

"And now I'm off to bed, but tell your readers once again that I'm so happy at keeping the championship in Scotland."

Tommy Morgan, the famous Scots comedian, who is a close friend of Benny, was with me during the conversation. He also had a word with the champion.

"We're all waiting to give you a great welcome," said Tommy.

TRAGEDY OF DEATH OF COL. BAILLIE-WRIGHT

Was Preparing For Ex-Officer Son's Release From Jail

LIEUTENANT-COLONEL C. H. BAILLIE-WRIGHT, father of Norman Baillie Stewart, known as the "Officer in the Tower," died at his home in Woodstock Road, Redland, Bristol, yesterday.

The tragedy of his death is that he and his wife had just begun making preparations for the homecoming of their son.

Baillie Stewart is serving a sentence of five years' penal servitude for imparting information to a foreign Power, and is expected to be released early next month from Maidstone Prison, it being assumed he will be granted the usual good conduct remission.

It is understood that an application has been made to the Home Office for the release of Baillie Stewart earlier than would otherwise have been the case owing to his father's death.

Recent Serious Illness

Inquiries early this month at the home of Col. and Mrs. Baillie-Wright met with the response that they had both left Bristol for the time being, and apparently Col. Baillie-Wright returned to Bristol only a few days before his death.

Col. and Mrs. Baillie-Wright were living at Southsea when their son was tried by court-martial in April, 1933, found guilty, sentenced and cashiered.

On two occasions since Col. Baillie-Wright had had serious attacks of illness, and only the hope of seeing his son free again and established on another career had enabled him to recover. He had received offers from several people to take his son into business.

Throughout ex-Lieutenant Baillie Stewart's imprisonment his father and mother, who have lived very quietly and in seclusion in Bristol, have maintained their belief in his innocence.

"My son still maintains his innocence, and so do I," his mother once wrote.

Mrs. Baillie-Wright has been seeing

Lt.-Col. Baillie-Wright.

Baillie Stewart in prison fairly regularly—the last time early this month.

His father stated recently, "I know my son has a talent for writing, and I understand that while at Maidstone he has been writing lyrics and some music which showed considerable promise."

It was as a result of the publicity of the trial of the "Officer in the Tower" that Lieut.-Colonel Baillie-Wright adopted the name of Lieut.-Colonel C. H. B. Wright.

Royalty And Youth Festival

It is officially announced from Buckingham Palace that the King and Queen will visit the Festival of Youth at Wembley Stadium, on Saturday, July 3.

Well, Gorbals Have It...

By MISS BILLIE HOUSTON

WELL, Gorbals have it. When I saw little Benny, our own Benny, pursue the Filipino, Montana, round the ring, sticking out that gorilla left of his as though measuring the distance between Montana's nose and the floor, I thought what a pity this Filipino is portable.

Benny seemed to be hitting the top of Goat Fell. Every punch was a paralyser had it landed. But the Filipino had all the pimpernels skinned from the row of gooseberries. He was a ghost who would not be handcuffed to anything that was coming from Gorbals.

Lynch A Fighter

I was desperate. My own feeling was that Montana is the greatest boxer I have ever seen in the ring, but Lynch was a fighter. The beauty and mathematical precision of Montana amazed me. But Lynch had guts. I think he won on the last two rounds, because Benny suddenly went all out.

But, partisanship aside, Montana is the most marvellous thing I've ever seen.

Come On, Glasgow

Now I can breathe freely, as I did at the ringside when Benny Lynch's arm was held up as the winner. I felt like the fellow at the back of the hall who kept yelling, "Come on, Glasgow."

Every bone in my body, everything I had got in me, echoed that shout. Right or wrong, I wanted Gorbals to win . . . and it did win.

Lynch, with his dour, wee face, that awful punch coming up that seemed to threaten—did it connect—to knock Montana toward Hollywood, was my one hope. How I wanted Lynch to win. And he won. So here's to us.

STIRLING TO PLANT "ROYAL" TREES

The Commissioners of Crown Lands have informed Stirling Town Council that they are prepared to pay for the planting of a tree in the King's Park, Stirling, in commemoration of King George V.

RADIO—Page 8

COMFORT IN SPECTACLES

Shell frames give nose comfort. Toric lenses give eye comfort. This combination gives the ideal reading spectacle

JOHN TROTTER
LIMITED
40 Gordon Street, Glasgow and 105 George St., Edinburgh

Daily Record
and Mail.

SCOTLAND'S NATIONAL

NEWSPAPER

ESTAB. 1847—No. 28·171.   FRIDAY, MAY 7, 1937.   ONE PENNY

ZEPPELIN HINDENBURG EXPLODES; 100 DEAD

75 Feet From Safety; Four Leap To Ground

BIGGEST IN THE WORLD

GERMAN ZEPPELIN HINDENBURG BURST INTO FLAMES AS SHE MOORED AT LAKEHURST, NEW JERSEY, LAST NIGHT, AND EXPLODED WITH A ROAR WHICH SHOOK THE ENTIRE NEIGHBOURHOOD.

IT IS REPORTED THAT NEARLY EVERY ONE OF THE 100 PEOPLE ON BOARD HAS BEEN KILLED.

So far as is known, there were only four survivors, who owed their lives to their jumping from windows as the blazing wreckage fell towads the ground.

One survivor, Herbert Loughlin, said—" There was a blinding flash, but the people on the ground would know more about that than we would inside. I jumped when the ship was close to the ground."

It is understood that the airship was preparing to disembark passengers when it exploded.

Sobbing Spectators Watch Army Trucks Race To Airship

The airship had tossed her nose-lines (ropes by which she is moored) towards the ground when suddenly there was a terrific burst of flame from the stern. The airship immediately crashed and fell. Within a few moments her twisted steel frame had collapsed to the ground.

Spectators stood sobbing, many of them hysterical, as Army trucks with screaming sirens sped to the still-blazing wreckage.

The airship had cruised above the airport for more than an hour within sight of spectators waiting for the weather to clear to permit the mooring.

The ship had earlier flown over New York through a heavy electrical storm, and it is thought that this caused her to explode.

It is understood that it will be impossible to reach the wreckage until this morning, as it is still burning fiercely.

A wide area around has been roped off. Ambulances are unable to get through. Newspaper-men have been barred.

Scenes of indescribable confusion prevail at Lakehurst, it is understood in New York.

All telephone wires are jammed, leading to difficulty at the moment in ascertaining exact news of the disaster and the exact number of casualties.

The Hindenburg's envelope was filled with hydrogen.

The envelope of the Zeppelin had been treated with an aluminium powder to minimise the effect of heat rays from the sun.

A photographer, Mr. Murray Becker, said: " I had my camera trained on the ship when the explosion occurred. Everything went up in flames. In a second there was nothing much left of the airship except the skeleton.

" I saw one man who had no clothes on assisted by two others, and one woman lying on a stretcher."

Captain Max Pruss was in command of the Hindenburg and Captain Lehmann assisted in an advisory capacity. According to a late message both officers are reported to have escaped.

Captain Lehmann is reported to be in hospital with serious burns. It appears that he leapt from the control cabin.

The passengers included Charles Seymour Higgins, of London, and J. Grant, assistant-manager Hamburg-American Line in London.

The President Hindenburg, Germany's super zeppelin, the advent of which had given promise to revolutionize Transatlantic travel.

GERMANY STUNNED

Berlin, Friday.

THE report on the Hindenburg was received in official circles in Berlin soon after midnight, at first with disbelief, and steps were being taken to check its accuracy beyond dispute before any news was issued to the German papers.

An official of the Propaganda Ministry said to Reuter:

" We can make no comment until we have full details. It seems hardly credible."

The zeppelin's flight has been regarded in Germany as having been proved perfectly safe, and no one has expected any such accident to be even possible.—Reuter.

DELAYED BY STORM

Two Hours Would Have Meant Safety

FROM OUR OWN CORRESPONDENT

New York, Thursday.

THE Hindenburg was delayed at the landing field by a heavy storm, and for two hours she cruised around until the gusts of wind had died down.

These two hours would have saved the lives of those who perished in the explosion.

The airship passed over Lakehurst Field in a heavy storm, with gusts of rain and wind, at 5.25 p.m. and could not land. She set off towards the coast and hovered around there for some time and just after seven oclock approached the air field again.

She was over her mast at 7.20 and had dropped two of her landing lines from the nose which was immediately seized by the ground staff.

The mooring line which was to go on to the big mooring mast was also thrown out and was just about to be attached to the mast when it was seen that there were flames shooting out of the dirigible two-thirds of the way down.

The passengers were looking out of the ship and waving to their friends when there were screams of horror, as within five seconds practically the whole of the giant ship was demolished.

Crowd Scorched

The flames roared hundreds of feet into the air and the ship crashed to the ground nose first within a few yards of the horrified spectators, who began to run for their lives.

The heat was so intense that many of the people on the ground were scorched before they could get away, but it is not known yet that any have been seriously harmed.

Meanwhile the airship lay on the ground a blazing mass, unapproachable for a hundred yards.

It was impossible for those inside to escape because the disaster occurred within a few minutes of the ship being moored.

They had to be left to their fate.

Built From The Frame Of The Tragic R 101

THE R 101's twisted framework had actually been embodied in the construction of the Hindenburg. The scrap metal was purchased by the German Government and shipped from France.

THE Hindenburgh had been specially designed to avoid a fate similar to that which overtook the British R 101 at Beauvais in 1930.

There was hardly an inch of wood in the ship. Everything was built of featherweight metal duralmin. The walls were all of balloon fabric.

She was the first Zeppelin in which passengers were able to smoke.

She had been in commission for just a year operating the North Atlantic service between Frankfurt and Lakehurst, New Jersey. She could accomplish the round trip in less than a week.—Reuter.

Safety Measures

She had a capacity of 7,070,000 cubic feet of helium gas divided into 16 separate compartments so that the destruc-

But Designed To Avoid Similar Fate

tion of one or two would not force her down. As a furthe rprecaution against fire she used Diesel oil engines.

She was 813 feet long, and had a diameter of 135 feet. Her cruising speed was about 80 miles an hour.

The accommodation for passengers was on two decks, the upper deck containing the dining-room, saloon, writing and reading rooms and state rooms. On the lower deck was accommodation for the crew.

The Hindenburg was partly constructed at the time of the R.10 disaster, but work was suspended so that plans could be drafted to eliminate the possibility of a similar disaster.

The Hindenburg could travel 8000

miles without refuelling, while her cruising speed of 80 miles an hour was about ten miles an hour faster than that of the Graf Zeppelin.

Her hull was 815 feet long and her total height inclusive of gondolas was 145 feet, nearl yas high, that is, as Nelson's Column.

The ship's empty weight was 100 tons, while she carried on an average voyage nearly 50,000 pounds of mail and other cargo, together with a total passenger weight of between 7000 and 8000 pounds.

MORE MEMBERS IN DRAPERS' SOCIETY

A growing membership roll was reported at the annual general meeting of the Drapers' and Warehousemen's Friendly Society in Glasgow last night.

The chairman, Mr. Weir, reported that a total of benefits valued at £6700 had been distributed during the year.

Accumulated funds, he said, were £56,689. Mr. James Weir was re-elected president.

RADIO—Page 27

EMPIRE
EXHIBITION
SPECIAL

Daily and Mail. Record

SCOTLAND'S NATIONAL
NEWSPAPER

ESTAB. 1847—No. 28,475   THURSDAY, APRIL 28, 1938   ONE PENNY

THE CLACHAN

Empire Exhibition.
Glasgow 1938

Night and Day

TOWERS DOMINATE THE EMPIRE S

Tower of Empire and one of the fountain cascades floodlit.

Guardian lion at the United Kingdom Pavilion.

THIS IS THE VIEW SEEN BY THE GOLDEN RAM WHICH S

NIGHT TIME MAY BE THE CHIEF GLORY OF THE EXHIBITION. CROWDS ON THE AVENUES WILL SEE THE MARVEL OF THE FOUNTAINS AND CASCADES FLOWING IN CEASELESS COLOUR CHANGES. THE FLOODLIT BUILDINGS WILL HOLD THEIR SOARING SHAPES UNTIL THE CROWDS GO HOME.

"I'll do my bit every night," says Mac, "by burning the candle at both ends."

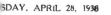

Two Years Ago—A Glasgow Park; To-day—The Heart Of The Empire

Bellahouston Park—a survey view seen in 1936.

To-day's view of Bellahouston from the air—a wonder town housing the achievements of Empire.

TOP OF THE WOOL PAVILION. BELOW—THE FOUNTAINS ON

" Confidence of the Home Government was demonstrated by the magnificence of the building which they have erected."—Earl of Elgin. This is the building—the United Kingdom Pavilion.

BERLIN'S NIGHT OF TERROR—Page 2

Good Whisky—
JOHNNIE WALKER
BORN 1820—STILL GOING STRONG

Daily Record and Mail.

ESTAB. 1847—No. 29,373   FRIDAY, MARCH 14, 1941   ONE PENNY.

AMERICA TO SEND US 99 WARSHIPS

PROLONGED SCOTS RAID: ONE NAZI 'PLANE SHOT DOWN BY FIGHTER

Hospital Hit: Fires Quickly Controlled

High explosive and incendiary bombs were dropped in several places when enemy aircraft carried out a prolonged raid in central Scotland last night. A hospital in one town in the area was hit.

Early this morning it was known that three German bombers had been shot down during the night's raids throughout the country.

During a lull in the heavy barrage put up in an East Scotland town when enemy aircraft were over, roof spotters watched an air battle in the bright moonlight.

Closely pursuing a German machine, a British fighter got in several bursts of machine-gun fire and the German began to lose height rapidly and observers believe it crashed.

The Woman's Speciality Shop with Popular Prices: The New Whitneys

Be sure to visit the 1st floor devoted to Costumes and Coats with the new drop-shoulder line as sponsored by Schiaperelli.

•

Model Suits, Frocks 2-pc. Cloth Coats 9 months to pay

•

Model Furs & Fur Coats 18 months to pay

Greenock
Last 2 Days
Britannia Halls
10 a.m.—6 p.m.

The New Whitneys

54 & 64 Buchanan St Glasgow
53 So. Bridge Edinburgh

Send post free Catalogue of Costumes
Suits, Frocks, Cloth Coats, Fur Coats
(Strike out items not desired)

Name ....

Address ....
D.R. 14/3/41
howats

Heavy Fire By Defence Guns

IN THE RAID ON CENTRAL SCOTLAND THE CRASH OF ANTI-AIRCRAFT FIRE RESOUNDED THROUGHOUT THE NIGHT AND THE SKY OVER ONE TOWN WAS LIT UP WITH THE FLASH OF GUN BURSTS, AND TRACER BULLETS WERE COLOURFUL PATTERNS ACROSS THE MOONLIT SKY.

Incidents reported included damage to a hospital, schools, dwelling houses and churches. Some casualties were removed to hospital.

In a Central Scotland town a hospital was reported hit and damaged. Doctors and nurses looked after patients while enemy aircraft roared overhead. A school in the same area was also damaged.

In the same town a block of dwelling houses was hit, the casualties including a member of the family of a doctor who was attending to injured.

Roof watchers in the town saw the sky starred with shell bursts as A.-A.

SIX R.A.F. MEN DEAD IN MID-AIR COLLISION

Bond Head, Ontario, Thursday.

SIX R.A.F. men were killed in a mid-air collision between two Avro-Anson bombers here to-day. Two others were seriously injured and taken to hospital.—Reuter.

guns brought heavy fire to bear on the raiders.

Many flares were dropped including a number of the chandelier type. A.-A. guns and machine guns shot some of them out as they hung in the sky.

After one particularly heavy burst

Continued on Back Page
Column 5

PATRIOT FORCES' SUCCESS CONFIRMED

IT is now confirmed that Abyssinian patriot forces have occupied Yavello, 70 miles north of Mega, said an official communique from Nairobi last night. The patriots, said the communique, are following up the enemy's retreat in co-operation with our forces from Dolo (Italian Somaliland Border).

"In Italian Somaliland," the communique adds, "our forces surprised the enemy at Daghabur, a post 100 miles south of Jijiga and captured some prisoners and lorries in which they were preparing to leave."

An Arab dhow which approached Mogadishu on Wednesday with a cargo for the Italians attempted to escape when it was realised that the port is in British hands.

With the co-operation of the air force it was quickly intercepted and captured.

The Cairo communique issued from British G.H.Q., yesterday, stated that in Libya, Eritrea, and Abyssinia, there was "nothing of importance to report."

"Italian Somaliland.—Our advance continues in all sections."

1300 Freed From Italian "Devil's Island"

A GRIM STORY OF THE HARDSHIPS BORNE BY 1300 MEN AND WOMEN, INCLUDING A FEW BRITISH INDIAN TRADERS, IN AN ITALIAN CAMP AT GENANE, ON THE SEASHORE 25 MILES SOUTH OF MOGADISHU, HAS JUST BEEN REVEALED BY ONE OF THE RELEASED PRISONERS.

The prisoners were mainly Abyssinians, some of whom had been imprisoned there for five years. Two hundred Somalis, suspected of anti-Fascist activities, and 79 Indian seamen from the crews of ships sunk by raiders, were also locked up there. The camp was found by British troops after the fall of the Italian Somaliland Capital.

The prisoners suffered from inadequate rations, except the Indians, who were more comfortable, as they paid the guards for extra food.

Place An Order For Your "Daily Record"

THE directors of the Newsprint Supply Company, Ltd., representing the national, provincial and Scottish newspapers, have made a further announcement regarding the reduction in the consumption of newsprint by all newspapers.

The effect of the first cut, which comes into operation on Sunday, March 16, will be to reduce the present size of the Daily Record from six 12-page issues per week to three of 12 pages and three of 8 pages per week.

Other daily and weekly and Sunday newspapers will be correspondingly reduced in size.

It is anticipated—the Director states—that a further substantial cut in newsprint consumption will be necessary probably by the middle of April.

To make sure of your copy of the Daily Record it is absolutely necessary to place a firm order.

SOME 99 warships will be transferred by the United States Government to Britain during 1941, it was stated authoritatively in Washington yesterday.

These will include 17 over-age destroyers, 55 submarine chasers, and nine over-age submarines, it is understood.

The building of 500 cargo ships for Britain is provided for in the new emergency programme of the U.S. Maritime Commission, states a New York message quoting the New York "Journal of Commerce."

The United States Office of Production management announced yesterday that of 972 'planes delivered during February 879 went to Britian.

PETROL AND OIL

These cheering items of news followed quickly on the information that, according to a Washington despatch to the New York Daily News, the U.S. Government has authorised the unlimited export of high-test aviation petrol and oil to all parts of the British Empire, in addition to lubricating oils for 'planes.

A high administrative official in Washington disclosed yesterday that financial responsibility for between

GREEK DESTROYER SINKS SUBMARINE

A COMMUNIQUE issued yesterday by the Greek Ministry of Marine stated that the destroyer Psara (Commander Costan) escorting a convoy in the Aegean Sea, has sunk a submarine which attempted to attack the convoy.

The Psara is a vessel of 1389 tons, built at Genoa for the Greek Government in 1932.

300,000,000 and 350,000,000 dollars worth of unfilled British orders for war materials and British-owned facilities for munition production in the United States may be transferred to the United States Government.

TWO-OCEAN NAVY

Mr. Sam Rayburn, Speaker to the House of Representatives, told reporters in Washington, yesterday, that he planned to have the 7000 million dollar (£1,750,000,000) Bill ready for action by the House on Tuesday next.

Efforts would be made to pass the Bill the same day, he added.

The Appropriations Committee of Representatives began hearings on it yesterday.

Speedy completion of a two-ocean Navy was urged by Colonel Knox. Secretary of the Navy, and Naval and Air Chiefs who testified before the Committee.

They warned Congress that the international situation might continue to grow worse.

Speedy completion of a two-ocean Navy was necessary because the combined German, Italian and Japanese Fleets at the beginning of this year totalled 1,835,000 tons, against the 1,250,000 tons of the U.S.

This did not take into account French ships.

Colonel Knox told the Committee that the United States had to face the possibilities of the defeat of Britain and the participation of Japan as a belligerent.

Good Morning! Another Day Nearer Victory!

BLITZ PICTURES—Pages 2, 3, 9

CLEARLY SUPERIOR

MU GIN

ALONE OR ALLIED

Melrose-Drover Ltd., Leith

Daily Record and Mail.

ESTAB. 1847—No. 29,374   SATURDAY, MARCH 15, 1941   ONE PENNY.

SECOND CLYDE BLITZ HEAVIER

SECOND night Clydeside blitz was even more intense than the first.

★

Residential areas which had shaken off the debris of Thursday night's attack a few hours earlier were once more on the enemy's "military target."

★

RAIDERS APPEARED TO BE MORE NUMEROUS, AND DEFENCE BARRAGE WAS HEAVIER.

WOMAN KILLED

THE ATTACK WAS MORE WIDESPREAD, AND IN A RURAL AREA A COTTAGE WAS BOMBED AND A WOMAN KILLED.

★

Incendiaries dropped were quickly extinguished. English districts, too, shared the raiding, but on a less serious scale than the Scottish attacks.

★

Two bombers were brought down in the East and West of England.

Clydeside has been blitzed. But the spirit of the people is "Clyde-built"— Scotland's Civil Defence Commissioner said of the raid victims last night: " I have never seen men and women behave with such courage."

The spirit is typified in our picture. The dinner must be cooked—Luftwaffe or no—even if the kitchen has disappeared and the job has to be done in the open air.

HOUSES THE TARGET

Dwelling houses and civilians were again the principal sufferers last night when Clydeside underwent its second prolonged raid in two nights.

Early incidents reported were:—

A hit on a tenement building in a town in the area. Extensive damage was done, and rescue squads were rushed to the spot.

A hit on a cottage in a rural district—one dead, two hurt.

A hit on a first aid post. Casualties unknown so far.

Enemy raiders were also reported over towns in east and central Scotland, but the main weight of the attack seemed again to be directed against Clydeside. Several long lulls in the opening stages of the raid were succeeded by a period of intense activity, during which A.-A. fire reached much greater intensity than during Thursday night's raid.

FLARES DROPPED

Waves of raiders passing over the district seemed to be stronger. Searchlights swept the sky and at moments gun flashes blending into a

Continued on Back Page, Col. 4.

BRITONS ASKED TO LEAVE HUNGARY

Vichy, Friday.

BRITISH nationals who are not in possession of diplomatic passports have been asked by the British Consulate to leave Hungary shortly, states a Budapest despatch to the official French News Agency.

McLAREN DAKS

During the month of March all DAKS Trousers in stock of which we hold a very large number in all sizes— fittings—and in a great variety of shades and textures—these famous trousers will be sold FREE OF PURCHASE TAX

at

37/6

And there is a McLaren DAKS Sports Jacket to tone or contrast at prices from

42/-

There are still large stocks in all departments at prices FREE OF TAX

McLAREN
AND SON (GLASGOW) LIMITED

Civil and Military Outfitters

42 - 50 GORDON STREET
GLASGOW

OPEN SATURDAY TILL 7 P.M.

GREEKS' NEW DEADLY WEAPON

Cairo, Friday.

GREEK fishing smacks manned by the ablest seamen in the Aegean, and armed with machine-guns and light cannon, have begun to operate in the odecanese, according to private messages I received to-day. Rhodes is now virtually cut off from the neighbouring bases of Leros and Stampalia.

While they hold off Italy's military attacks, the Greeks are rushing ahead with entrenchments in a few remaining weak points on the Bulgarian border. German troops in Bulgaria have been ordered to stay some miles from the frontier, and the Greeks have left no room for doubt that they will fight if the Nazis come on. No immediate clash is expected.

Man To Guard Cargoes

A NEW Naval appointment to meet the much-boosted Nazi Spring offensive by U-boats was disclosed by the Admiralty last night, in the announcement that " Admiral Sir Percy L. H. Noble has recently taken up the appointment of Commander-in-Chief Western Approaches."

The appointment means that Sir Percy will lead Britain's Naval forces in the titanic struggle to be waged against enemy raiders harrying British, Allied and American shipping in the Atlantic.

The Western Approaches Command has long existed, but has been extended to meet the German threat, and a new title has, therefore been given to the post.

Admiral Sir Percy Noble, who was 61 in January, may properly be described as " just the man for the job." He is a strategist, a " strong

Continued on Back Page, Column 2

Two More Nazi Night Bombers Down

TWO more Nazi bombers were brought down early in the moonlight raids which were renewed on several parts of Britain last night.

The crew of four were killed when one crashed in a Western area. The other burst into flames, and fell in the sea off the East coast.

Raiders circled in pairs over a South-West coast town, which was heavily attacked. Here as in other parts where enemy aircraft passed over in force, A.-A. guns put up a heavy barrage.

Admiral Sir Percy Noble.

Somaliland War Nearing The End

Nairobi, Friday.

OPERATIONS in Italian Somaliland are rapidly ending. To-day's official communique from Nairobi says:—

" Operations in Abyssinia continue

according to plan.

" Mopping-up operations in Italian Somaliland are rapidly ending with the capture or surrender of the last remnants of the enemy.

" Since the advent of the topees

and slouch hats of our Imperial troops, which are now as familiar a feature in Italian Somaliland as they recently were in Kenya, fresh confidence has been instilled into many of the native inhabitants

---

Good Morning! Another Day Nearer Victory!

BEAUTIFUL
ballito
STOCKINGS

Sunday Mail

Scotland's National Sunday Newspaper

No. 1705　　　　　SUNDAY, MAY 25, 1941.　　　F　　TWOPENCE

IT'S TWICE AS NICE WITH H·P SAUCE

H.M.S. HOOD SUNK

BIGGEST NAZI SHIP CHASED

H.M.S. HOOD, THE WORLD'S MIGHTIEST BATTLESHIP, HAS BEEN SUNK. IT IS FEARED THERE WILL BE FEW SURVIVORS.

This dramatic news was flashed to the world last night by the British Admiralty a few hours after Hood had gone down in a big sea battle with German naval forces off the coast of Greenland.

Bismarck Damaged

The Bismarck, Germany's biggest battleship of 35,000 tons, was also engaged in the battle It has been damaged, and last night other British warships were racing across northern seas to put the finishing touch to the pride of the Nazi Fleet

The official Admiralty communique states:—

" British naval forces intercepted early this morning off the coast of Greenland German naval forces, including the battleship Bismarck. The enemy were attacked and during the ensuing action H.M.S. Hood (Capt. R. Kerr), wearing the flag of Vice-Admiral L. E. Holland, C.B., received an unlucky hit in a magazine and blew up.

" The Bismarck has received damage and the pursuit of the enemy continues. It is feared there will be few survivors from H.M.S. Hood."

All-Day Battle

The German forces were first sighted by the British Navy early yesterday morning.

Our warships went into action immediately. The guns of two of the greatest battleships afloat roared into the morning. Their biggest shells were hurled across miles of sea.

The battle raged all day.

It was as the action developed that Hood was hit.

The normal complement of Hood was 1341 officers and men.

The German forces soon retired and dashed for their home bases, our ships in hot pursuit.

CONTINUED ON BACK PAGE.

H.M.S. HOOD.

SHOTS AT ITALIAN KING

THE King of Italy had a narrow escape from death while visiting Tirana, capital of Albania, a week ago, it was revealed in an official communique issued in Rome yesterday. A Greek, who fired several shots at the Royal car, was arrested.

The shooting took place on May 17, while King Victor Emmanuel was motoring to an airport, accompanied by M. Verlaci, the "Quisling" Premier of Albania

The communique said the shots went wide, and nobody was injured.

The Greek, who is said to have given his name as Mihanloff Vasillaci, was saved from being lynched by the crowds, as he was arrested immediately.

He will be tried by a military court

Vasillaci is said to have stated

that he had a personal grievance against members of the Albanian Government because he had not been given employment.

Although the shots missed the King and M. Verlaci, it is reliably learned in Rome (says the B.U.P.) that one bullet hit a rear tyre of the King's car.

The tyre went flat, but the car did not stop.

This is the third attempt made on the life of King Victor Emmanuel The first was in 1911, and the second at Milan in April, 1928.

AJAX IN CRETE SEA BATTLE

H.M.S. cruiser Ajax, of Graf Spee fame, it became known yesterday, took part in the smashing naval action against a German troop convoy on its way to reinforce their air borne troops in Crete.

This is the fifth naval engagement in which the Ajax has fought.

First was the ignominious defeat of the Graf Spee. Next she attacked three Italian destroyers in the Mediterranean, sinking two of them.

Thirdly, she engaged an Italian heavy cruiser, with which were four destroyers, one of which she severely damaged.

Ajax also took part in the sweeping victory of the Battle of Matapan.

Gib. Navy Sets Sail

Berlin, Saturday.

ALL the warships at Gibraltar, including an aircraft-carrier and three submarines, have left the fortress and are steaming in the direction of the Mediterranean, according to an official German News Agency dispatch from Algeciras.

MECHANISED H.G.

The first Home Guard unit in Scotland to have mechanised equipment will be inspected at Garscube House Estate this afternoon

R.A.F. Fighters Over Crete

NAZI PLANES SMASHED

R.A.F. long range fighters and bombers are dealing shattering blows at the German invasion 'planes in Crete where the great battle which has raged for five days and six nights is reaching a decisive stage.

On Maleme airfield, which has been the object of the Nazis' main drive, the R.A.F. created havoc among Junkers troop-carrying 'planes and on the beach others were destroyed as they disgorged troops and artillery.

TWO LONE RAIDERS

TWO lone raiders bombed and machine gunned districts in the South and South-East of England last night.

Diving from low clouds, one raider loosed bursts of machine-gun fire over a South-East Coast district and shortly afterwards dropped a number of bombs. No damage or casualties have been reported.

The other raider, a Junkers 88, also dropped a stick of bombs and machine-gunned roads in a South of England town.

The only casualty was a Home Guardsman, who was slightly injured.

An Air Ministry communique stated that there had been little enemy activity over Britain during the day.

A few bombs were dropped and there was a small number of casualties in a South-East coast town.

Many of the Junkers went up in flames and at least 14 were destroyed.

German attempts to land reinforcements at Heraklion and Retimo failed. The enemy has been cleared out of the former town and our men have shot down 16 troop-carrying aircraft since May 21 in this area.

In and around Maleme intense fighting is continuing. The Germans have launched their main effort in this area to extend their original foothold.

Bold intervention by our Air Force at a crucial moment in the battle, when the Nazis were beginning to receive heavier armament by air, occurred on Friday.

NO RESPITE

The Germans at Maleme have not been given a moment's respite.

Now, standing up with resolute courage to the horrific ordeal of intensive dive-bombing and facing an enemy now equipped with light artillery and mortars, General Freyberg's men nevertheless continue to inflict heavy casualties on the enemy from our positions east of the aerodrome.

In an interview in Egypt one of the R.A.F. pilots who took part in the fighting over Crete said, " The Germans were landing troops from the air with cynical disregard for their lives.

" Some have fallen into the sea and others were tangled in trees

Continued on Back Page

French Air Deserters

A WHOLE squadron of good modern French bombers have deserted from Syria and landed on an R.A.F. aerodrome in Palestine, according to a broadcast from the Free French radio station at Brazzaville, French Equatorial Africa, picked up by the Columbia Broadcasting System yesterday.

The French commentator declared that this news had been received from Cairo.

PREMIER TELLS

To Beat Invaders

STAND FIRM! CARRY ON!

In these four dramatic words the Premier crystallises a personal message to every man and woman in Britain as to their duty if the German hordes attempt invasion of our island home.

His exhortation, by way of preface to a leaflet, "Beating the Invader," which will be in the hands of us all this week, is both an assurance and a guidance.

And the guidance comes in this final note:—

Give all the help you can to our troops.

Do not tell the enemy anything

Do not give him anything.

Do not help him in any way

SEE PAGE 4.

ZAMZAM—U.S. ACTS

Madrid. Saturday.

Two representatives of the U.S Embassy have arrived at San Sebastian on their way to occupied France to negotiate with the Nazis for the repatriation of the 140 American passengers on the sunk Egyptian liner Zamzam. According to the Swiss radio, the passengers are now in Piarritz.

FREE!

Important Guide To Successful Engineering Careers

Containing pages of practical guidance " ENGINEERING OPPORTUNITIES" is beyond argument the finest and most complete handbook on Successful Engineering careers ever compiled It is a book that should be on the bookshelf of every person interested in engineering, whatever his age, position or experience

The Handbook contains among other intensely interesting matter details of B.Sc., A.M.I.C.E., A.M.I Mech E., A.M.I.E.E. A.M.I.A.E., A.M.I.W.T. A.M.I.P.E., A.M.I.R.E., CIVIL SERVICE and other important Engineering Examinations, outlines courses in all branches of AUTOMOBILE RADIO AERONAUTICAL, CIVIL, MECHANICAL, ELECTRICAL, and PRODUCTION ENGINEERING, DRAUGHTSMANSHIP, TRACING, INSPECTION, GOVERNMENT WORK, BUILDING (the war and after war career), R.A.F., MATHS., etc. and explains the unique advantages of our Employment department.

WE DEFINITELY GUARANTEE **'NO PASS—NO FEE"**

If you are earning less than £10 a week you cannot afford to miss reading " ENGINEERING OPPORTUNITIES" You should write for a copy of this 208-page guide to the best-paid posts immediately - FREE and post free

BRITISH INSTITUTE OF ENGINEERING TECHNOLOGY

171 Shakespeare House
17 Stratford Pl., LONDON. W.1

The German attack by parachute-troops on Crete lends interest to this picture of American parachute-troops taken during a training flight just before they left the 'plane. Grim and silent, fully ready for their jump into space, they sit in their Douglas C 39 army transport 'plane.

ACTION STORY OF GREAT SEA CHASE PAGE TWO

Look for the—
the sign of
GOOD BEER
YOUNGERS OF ALLOA

Daily Record and Mail.

ESTAB. 1847—No. 29,437   WEDNESDAY, MAY 28, 1941   E   ONE PENNY

Roosevelt's Dramatic Broadcast

UNLIMITED NATIONAL EMERGENCY EXISTS

President Roosevelt

"GET BISMARCK" —AND HOW NAVY DID!

THE Admiralty last night told the full story of the greatest sea chase in history when they revealed that the Bismarck was pursued for 1750 miles before being sunk.

In avenging the Hood the Navy gave one of the most devastating exhibitions of Britain's sea power ever seen.

Relentless Pursuit

For nearly 2000 miles 'planes of Coastal Command, battleships, cruisers, destroyers and aircraft-carriers carried on a relentless pursuit of the Bismarck.

The main body of the Home Fleet, under the leadership of Admiral J. C. Tovey, aboard H.M.S. King George, one of our new and mighty battleships, a force from Gibraltar led by Vice-Admiral Sir James Somerville on the Renown, and two more powerful men-of-war, the Rodney and Ramillies, escorting convoys in the North Atlantic, all answered the call, " Get the Bismarck."

Sealed Her Fate

H.M.S. Dorsetshire, which had the honour of ending Bismarck's career, is one of the post-Washington 10,000-ton 8-inch gun cruisers first commissioned in 1930. Captain B. C. S Martin spent ten years on the lower deck and won his commission at Jutland.

The only one other bluejacket who has become captain in modern times was a messmate of the King, then Prince Albert, in the Malaya during the last war.

Other big ships in the chase were:—

Renown. — The 32,000 tons battleship which hit the Scharnhorst in April last year.

Rodney.—33,900 tons flagship, completed in 1927. Carries nine 16-inch guns, twelve 6-inch guns, six 4.7 A.A. guns, 26 smaller guns, two torpedo tubes and two 'planes. Thirteen months ago a heavy bomb struck her in " battleship v. bomber " fight off Bergen.

King George V. and Prince of Wales.—35,000 tons battleships and world's most formidable fighting units.

Victorious.—23,000 tons aircraft carrier launched in first month of war.

Ark Royal.—Aircraft carrier, " sunk " several times by German and Italian propaganda.

Ramillies.—29,150-ton battleship, twice " sunk " by Rome radio.

From Britain, from Newfoundland, from the aircraft-carriers Ark Royal and Victorious, 'planes swept the skies, reporting every twist and turn of the Bismarck as she tried desperately to break through the net.

Damaged in the earlier engagement and repeatedly struck by aerial torpedoes, the Bismarck limped painfully through the mists.

Tribal class destroyers closed in and delivered a further volley of torpedoes and she appeared to be stopped. But she made a plucky effort to escape her final doom.

WOUNDED GIANT

After some time her engineers managed to get the wounded giant moving again, and reconnaissance aircraft reported that her fire power was still formidable.

In the last desperate encounter she engaged our destroyers, but soon our heavy ships came up, and to H.M.S. Dorsetshire, a cruiser, fell the task of administering the coup de grace.

At 11.01 yesterday morning Bismarck sank beneath the waves.

Roosevelt's Monetary Powers

Washington, Tuesday.

OVER stiff Republican opposition, the administrative forces to-day won the approval of the House of Representatives for legislation continuing President Roosevelt's emergency monetary powers for two additional years.

The Bill now goes to the Senate.

The cruiser H.M.S. Dorsetshire had the honour of giving the final blow to the Bismarck.

NAZI ADMIRAL LOST WITH BISMARCK

Admiral Luetjens (above) and Captain Lindermann of the Bismarck were killed during the action which avenged the Hood. There were only a few survivors from the Nazi battleship.

Crete Situation Serious

BRITISH IN NEW LINE IN REAR

AIRCRAFT CARRIER AT GIBRALTAR

ONE aircraft carrier, one old cruiser, and five destroyers have arrived at Gibraltar, says an Algeciras message, quoted by Algiers radio.

CAIRO, TUESDAY.

VERY SEVERE FIGHTING IS GOING ON AROUND THE MALEME-CANEA AREA IN THE PLAIN BETWEEN THE TWO PLACES, SAID AUTHORITATIVE MILITARY CIRCLES HERE LATE TO-NIGHT.

The Germans continue landing troops at Maleme, and the situation is serious.

They are suffering very heavy losses, but the Germans never care about losses if they can achieve their object.

The question is, how long they are going to continue pouring men and aircraft into Crete?

The troops arriving are not parachutists, but land in troop-carriers on Maleme aerodrome, which is littered with the wreckage of burnt-out 'planes.

(Continued on Back Page, Col. 1)

'Complete Revenge'—U.S.

New York, Tuesday.

IN huge black streamer headlines, the newspapers here tell of the end of the Bismarck.

The New York Sun in a leading article headed, " speedy revenge." says that although at the time of writing a full account of how the Bismarck was sunk is lacking, " no details are needed to give the British and German public alike the impression of speedy and complete revenge."

" America has real cause to rejoice with Britain over her latest naval feat," says the Washington Star. ' The Royal Navy's vengeance," it adds, " has tremendous psychological potentialities."

Commenting on the sinking of the Bismarck, Mr. Cordell Hull, U.S. Secretary of State, said he supposed that the law of retribution arose to some extent at least.

PRESIDENT ROOSEVELT IN A MOMENTOUS BROADCAST TENSELY AWAITED BY THE WORLD AS ONE OF THE GREAT TURNING POINTS IN AMERICAN HISTORY, THIS MORNING ENUNCIATED IN BLUNT PHRASES THAT LEFT NO ROOM FOR DOUBT THE POLICY OF HIS GOVERNMENT IN RELATION TO THE WAR.

Speaking from a reception room in the White House, the President announced that he proclaimed an " unlimited national emergency exists."

The President said: " We assert the ancient American

WINANT GOING BACK TO U.S. TO REPORT

Washington, Tuesday.

MR. J. G. WINANT, the U.S. Ambassador to Great Britain, is leaving for the United States this week-end to report, it was disclosed by the State Department to-day. —P.A.

doctrine of the Freedom of the Seas.

" We reassert the solidarity of the 21 American Republics and the Dominion of Canada in the preservation of the independence of the Western Hemisphere.

" We pledged material support to the other Democracies and we will fulfil that pledge.

" We in the Americas will decide whether, when and where our American interests are attacked or our security threatened.

" USE ARMED FORCES "

" We are placing our armed forces in strategic military positions and we will not hesitate to use our armed forces to repel attack.

" The pressing problems that confront us are military problems. We cannot afford to approach them from the point of view of wishful thinkers or sentimentalists.

" What we face is cold, hard facts. The first fundamental

(Continued on Back Page, Col. 3)

This was Hitler's pride—the Bismarck photographed in a heavy sea.

Scots Town Day-Bombed

FOUR hours after a low-flying German raider dropped bombs on an East of Scotland town yesterday afternoon, the body of Mrs. John Clark was recovered from the wreckage of the cottage in which she and her husband lived.

The husband, Mr. John Clark, a 65-year-old fire-watcher, sustained injuries to the chest and bruises

Machine-gun fire was heard and fighters chased the raider out to sea.

In the vicinity of the house which was struck the wreckage was quickly cleared away.

Splendid work was done by the police and other services, particularly the rescue party.

RADIO— PAGE 4

Good Morning! Another Day Nearer Victory!

HP SAUCE
APPETISES THE FOOD
then helps to digest it

World War—6 a.m. Edition
Daily Record
and Mail.

ESTAB. 1847.—No. 29,603   MONDAY, DECEMBER 8, 1941   ONE PENNY

"WITHIN THE HOUR"

MR CHURCHILL in his Mansion House speech on November 10 made the following declaration:—

"We do not know whether the efforts of the United States to preserve peace in the Pacific will be successful.

"But if they fail I take this occasion to say—and it is my duty to say—that should the United States become involved in war with Japan the British declaration will follow within the hour."

JAPS LAND IN MALAYA: SINGAPORE RAIDED

Air And Naval Attacks On U.S. Pacific Bases; Heavy Casualties By Bombing

One U.S. Battleship Ablaze: Jap Air Carrier Down: British Gunboat Sunk

Roosevelt sent a message to the Emperor—

JAPAN HAS DECLARED WAR ON THE UNITED STATES AND GREAT BRITAIN IN THE WESTERN PACIFIC AS FROM DAWN TO-DAY.

But before the declaration could come into effect Japan had struck with startling suddenness at both countries, bombing the Hawaiian naval base at Pearl Harbour, Honolulu, and sinking a British gunboat in the Whangpoo River at Shanghai.

The Columbia Broadcasting System picked up a message early this morning saying that Singapore had been attacked by Japanese 'planes and that two cruisers were hit, but so far this lacks confirmation.

SINGAPORE 5 A.M. COMMUNIQUE (SEE COLUMN 5 BELOW) ANNOUNCED A MALAYA LANDING BY JAPS.

—But the Emperor replied with bombs.

LORDS AND M.P.s TO MEET TO-DAY

AN announcement from 10 Downing Street last night stated that the Lord Chancellor, after consultation with the Government, has summoned the House of Lords to meet at 3 p.m. to-day, and the Speaker, after consultation with the Government, has summoned the House of Commons to meet at the same time. A statement will be made in both Houses.

According to the Tokio correspondent of the Japanese "Osaka Mainichi," Imperial Headquarters in Tokio have announced that a naval battle between Japanese and British and American naval units is going on in the Western Pacific.

The U.S. Fleet has steamed out of Pearl Harbour, according to a radio report received at Washington. Another radio report states that U.S. forces have already accounted for six Japanese 'planes and four submarines. It is also stated that a Jap aircraft carrier has been sunk off Honolulu.

It is officially announced in Washington that 104 were killed and 300 wounded as a result of the Japanese bombing of Island of Oahu, the main island of the Hawaiian group, on which Honolulu stands

EYE-WITNESS'S STORY OF RAID

Fort Shafter, Hawaii, Sunday.

HERE is an eye-witness account of the Japanese attack on Hickman field and Pearl Harbour.

"We saw a group of four-motored bombers (Note—if four-motored bombers operated from aircraft carriers this is something new in this type of operation) approaching us, with the rising sun sign painted on their wings.

"They came over Honolulu itself, and were at once met with anti-aircraft fire from Pearl Island, Ford Island, Wheeler Field, Honolulu municipal airport, Hickman Field, and the new navy repair base.

"A terrific barrage was put up, but all the points I mentioned appeared to have been attacked.

"We saw one 'plane crash in flames. Later we got reports that three fires were raging at Pearl Harbour after the first attacks, and that at least three ships were hit, but there has been no confirmation of this.

"The Fleet steamed out. Then we heard they were after Japanese aircraft carriers from which the attacks were being launched

"These were said to be off Barber's Point, west of Pearl Harbour. Despite the bombing there was no panic.

"The attacks on the island began at 7.55 a.m., rousing people from their Sunday morning sleep. Many were still in pyjamas by midday.

"The way the bombers attacked Pearl Harbour was this:—They came in from the north-east over the range of mountains that overshadows the base. Thus they were almost over the base before they were detected"

ADVERTISER'S ANNOUNCEMENT

I SEND THE BEST OF LUCK

I Have Recommended
YEAST-VITE
To All My Friends When Feeling Below Par.

Holbrook,
Nov. 11th, 1941.

Dear Sirs.—I have been taking Yeast-Vite tablets and cannot speak too highly of them.

Before taking them I was suffering from indigestion, headaches, also various other aches and pains due to middle age. I now feel quite different, and would not be without these valuable tablets.

Wishing you every success in the sale of your wonderful tonic, for which I send the best of luck—I have recommended these tablets to all my friends when feeling below par.

(Sgd.) Miss H. S

Bristol.
Nov. 6th. 1941.

Dear Sirs.—Since I have been taking Yeast-Vite tablets for rheumatism I feel much better, and am still taking them I would not be without them, as they are a good pick-me-up.

(Sgd.) Mrs F M

Yeast-Vite tonic tablets bring quick relief from Headaches, Nerves. Lassitude, Depression, Insomnia, Rheumatism, Indigestion, etc. Sold everywhere at 7d 1/4, 3/3 and 5/4, including Purchase Tax

U-BOATS OUT
U.S. Transport Torpedoed

A U.S. Army transport carrying timber has been torpedoed 1300 miles west of San Francisco, it is announced in Washington.

The White House also announced that an American cargo vessel had been sending out distress signals approximately 700 miles west of San Francisco.

"This indicates that Jap submarines are strung out in this area," commented Mr. Stephen Early, the President's Secretary.

RIGHT ABOUT WHEEL-ER

Montana, Sunday.

ISOLATIONIST Senator Burton Wheeler, after learning of the Japanese attack, said to-night:—

"The only thing now is to do our best to lick hell out of them."

Mr. Cordell Hull, after reading Tokio's official reply to the American Note of November 26, declared last night:—

"In all my public life I have never seen a document more crowded with infamous false hoods and distortions, on a scale so huge that I never imagined until to-day that any Government on this planet was capable of uttering them."

Wheeler.

New Raid On Honolulu:
Jap Attack On Guam

The White House announced that a new raid on Honolulu began at 5.30 p.m. American time, and that the island of Guam, in the Pacific, had been attacked.

Three U.S. vessels, including the battleship, Oklahoma, were attacked in the first raid on Pearl Harbour, according to a report from Honolulu to the N.B.C. The Oklahoma is reported to have been set on fire but no statement has been issued by the Navy Department in Washington.

When the Japanese 'planes swept over a private American aircraft was sprayed with machine-gun bullets, but the owner managed to land safely.

The United States War Department has ordered the mobilisation of all military personnel throughout the country.

Axis radio broadcasts from Shanghai stating that Manila army and naval bases had been heavily dive - bombed on Sunday night and Monday morning were picked up by the Columbia broadcasting system in New York

An unconfirmed report states that three American battleships have been hit in the first day's fighting, including the West Virginia and Oklahoma. states our Washington correspondent. who adds that the U.S. Government has received unconfirmed reports

Continued on Back Page, Col. 5

Japs Land In Malaya

AN OFFICIAL COMMUNIQUE, ISSUED IN SINGAPORE AT 5 O'CLOCK THIS MORNING, STATES THAT THE FIRST ATTEMPTED LANDING WAS MADE SHORTLY AFTER 01.00 LOCAL TIME AND REPULSED BY SMALL ARMS FIRE AND AIR ACTION.

Enemy troops succeeded in landing on a beach near Padang. Sabek, and were reported to be infiltrating towards the Kota Bahru aerodrome, on the east coast of Malaya.

They are being engaged by land forces and aircraft. Our aircraft are also attacking enemy ships and enemy troops which have landed. Ten ships are reported off Bangkok

Singapore was also raided by air shortly before dawn this morning.

There was slight damage and a few civilian casualties.

Two bombs fell in the centre of the city and a number of others were heard to explode in various parts of the island.

Japan has also attacked Hong Kong, according to a Tokio radio report

CHEERS FOR FLEET

"Thousands of people stood in the streets and on the hilltops as the Fleet steamed out —and how they cheered. It did you good to hear them.

Good Morning! Another Day Nearer Victory!

"My thoughts grow in the aroma of that particular tobacco" (Earl Baldwin, Dundee. 1925)

DR. WHITE'S GLASGOW Presbyterian Mixture

THIS TOBACCO WAS FAMOUS AS EARL BALDWIN'S

A.CALL & CL. Ltd Bond St GLASGOW

Daily Record

and Mail.

EST. 1847—No. 29,887   BLACK-OUT—Back Page   THURSDAY, NOVEMBER 5, 1942   RADIO—Page 6   ONE PENNY F

They call it 'Bottled Sunshine'!
DAYTONA
PURE WINE OF SOUTH AFRICA
ASK YOUR WINE MERCHANT FOR SUPPLIES AND SUPPORT
PRODUCE OF THE EMPIRE
DAYTONA WINES LTD

AXIS FORCES ROUTED: IN FULL RETREAT—Official

9000 Prisoners: 260 Tanks: 270 Guns: 600 Planes: 100,000 Tons Of Shipping Sunk Or Damaged

ROMMEL'S DESERT ARMY IS IN FULL RETREAT, WITH THE 8TH ARMY IN CLOSE PURSUIT OF HIS "DISORDERED" COLUMNS IN THEIR FLIGHT TO THE WEST.

Cairo G.H.Q. reported this dramatic development of the battle last night after 12 days of ceaseless attacks by the Allied land and air forces. Formidable Axis losses detailed in the communiqué are:—

Over 9000 prisoners, including General Ritter von Thoma, Commander of the Afrika Korps; more than 260 German and Italian tanks destroyed; at least 270 guns captured or destroyed; over 600 enemy planes destroyed or damaged; and over 100,000 tons of Axis supply shipping sunk or damaged by naval and air forces.

A Cairo message says that the Italians on one sector have asked for an armistice to bury their dead. The enemy pocket on the coast is now ironed out

Gen. Alexander, C.-in-C. Middle East, planned the strategy of the Eighth Army's brilliant attack

Official Communique

THE Axis forces in the Western Desert, after 12 days and nights of ceaseless attacks by our land and air force, are now in full retreat, states the Middle East joint war communique issued last night.

Their disordered columns are being relentlessly attacked by our land forces and by the Allied air forces by day and night.

General Von Stumme, a senior General who is said to have been in command during Rommel's absence in Germany, is known to have been killed.

So far we have captured over 9000 prisoners, including General Ritter Von Thoma, Commander of the German Afrika Korps, and a number of senior German and Italian officers.

HEAVY LOSSES

It is known that the enemy's losses in killed and wounded have been exceptionally high.

Up to date we have destroyed more than 260 German and Italian tanks and captured or destroyed at least 270 guns.

The full toll of the booty cannot be assessed at this stage of the operation. In the course of these operations our air forces, whose losses have been light, have destroyed and damaged in air combat over 300 aircraft and have destroyed or put out of action a like number on the ground.

At sea our naval and air forces have sunk 50,000 tons and damaged as much again of shipping carrying Axis supplies to North Africa. The Eighth Army continues to advance.

TO-DAY

The Signal To Strike

From ERIC LLOYD WILLIAMS,
Reuter's Special Correspondent, at a forward aerodrome.
Tuesday Night (Delayed).

FIRST signs of the Axis rout were reported back to this aerodrome early this afternoon when a message flashed from the 8th Army's land forces announced that the enemy was beginning to fall back towards the west. It was the moment for the Allied forces to strike.

The call went out to the squadrons to "send in every available bomber and every available fighter." This was a dramatic moment — the moment everyone here had been waiting for a long time.

Though the weight of our air attacks had been very heavy for the past few days the tempo of our operations seemed to be doubled in a few minutes. From every desert landing ground waves of planes took off.

Great dust plumes rose as one plane after another took off, heading west with throttles wide open. Down on the aerodromes tired ground crews, the sweat running down their faces grimed with oil and dust, paused for a few seconds in their work to give the "thumbs up" sign to the pilots.

Everyone was in on this great show. British airmen, Americans at their aerodromes, where the Stars and Stripes fluttered in the dust clouds, Australians, South Africans—every squadron mustered every possible plane, loaded them with bombs and sent them in to pound the enemy.

Even at night the bombing squadrons joined in.

Within a matter of 15 minutes or so, when the first waves returned, the ground crews went feverishly to work to put the planes back into the air in the fastest possible time.

Continued on Back Page, Col. 4

Lt.-Gen. Montgomery took over command of the Eighth Army in the field on Aug. 18. He is 54.

King Sends Thanks

THE King has sent the following message to General Alexander:

The Eighth Army, magnificently supported by the Royal Air Force and units of the Royal Navy has dealt the Axis a blow of which the importance cannot be exaggerated.

"For the last fortnight we have all been following with anxious interest the progress of the hard-fought battle and I can assure all three Services—embracing as they do the many representatives of the British Commonwealth and our Allies—of the admiration and pride of the whole Empire in their brilliant victory, in the name of your fellow countrymen all the world over.

"I express to you, to Air Chief Marshall Tedder, to General Montgomery, to Air Vice-Marshal Coningham, and to the commanders and all ranks of the three Services, my thanks for the far-reaching success which, by your untiring co-operation, you have so decisively achieved."

ROAD OPEN TO TRIPOLI

THERE is no doubt that Rommel's army has been largely destroyed and the road to Tripoli may soon be open, writes a military correspondent.

The destruction of the Axis striking power may be considerably greater in extent than is suggested in the official figures, big as they are.

The Afrika Korps has small chance of reforming.

MASSED AT GIB.

German News Agency stated last night that among the ships massed at Gibraltar are the aircraft-carriers Furious and Argus and another of unknown type, six cruisers, 26 destroyers, four submarines, one monitor, two large transports, 26 freighters and 12 tankers.

Scots In Thickest Of Battle

THE toughest fighting on the Alamein line fell to a re-formed Highland Division having its first taste of desert fighting.

Scotsmen and men from all parts of the United Kingdom who now make up this fighting arm of Montgomery's army came against the most heavily defended of all the enemy's positions along the Alamein line.

Time and again they attacked several strong points which stubbornly barred their way forward, and time and again they had to come back after being within an ace of success

At last the heroic attacks and repeated barrages put in by our massed guns began to tell. The enemy's nerves inevitably became frayed and one by one strong-points were overcome and the Highland Division was able to report that it was up to its objectives.

At one time during these attacks it was feared that the division was suffering very heavy casualties indeed. Big numbers of its men were missing, but then came good news. Many of them turned up.

In the end it was seen that the Highlanders' casualties were quite light considering the heaviness of the task they had been doing.

RUSSIA

All Attacks Smashed

HEAVY German attacks with tanks and infantry were smashed yesterday by Stalingrad's defenders.

More than 1000 German officers and men were killed, declared Moscow's midnight communique.

"North-west of Stalingrad there were clashes with small enemy groups.

"On one sector our troops captured five blockhouses and one dug-in enemy tank. Seven enemy planes were brought down."

South-east of Nalchik (Caucasus) Red Army troops fought fierce defensive engagements. On one sector one unit repelled the enemy attack and killed 350 Germans. Seven tanks were destroyed."

North-east of Tuapse, the Black Sea port, Soviet troops carried out active operations and captured several German points of resistance.

SOLOMONS

Advance By U.S. Forces

WITH Army and Navy planes bombing and strafing the retreating Japs, U.S. forces on Guadalcanal are pushing westward step by step, occupying fresh ground and capturing discarded equipment.

Last night's U.S. Navy communique stated that on Monday and Tuesday United States troops on the island attacked the Japs to the west making small territorial gains.

"About 20 enemy machine-guns and two small pieces of artillery were captured.

"There is no report of troop activity on the eastern flank of our positions."

U.S. ELECTIONS

Senate. — Republicans, 17 elected; Democrats, 15 elected. Results to come, two.

House of Representatives.—Democrats, 205; Republicans, 194. Results to come, 33.

The Democratic Party finally secured control in the new House of Representatives last night as slowly accumulating returns assured it of the 218 members necessary for a majority.

What Election Means—Page 2.

ADVERTISER'S ANNOUNCEMENT

You've earned your Guinness —it'll do you good

A GLASS OF GUINNESS IS A CHEERFUL SIGHT

G.E.1124.E

FAMOUS FOR NEARLY 200 YEARS.
GEORGE Younger's
Alloa BEER

Daily Record and Mail.

EST. 1847—No. 30,382 RADIO—Page 7 WEDNESDAY, JUNE 7, 1944 BLACK-OUT—Back Page ONE PENNY F

GOURLAY'S for TYPEWRITERS
AT REASONABLE PRICES
44 ST. VINCENT PLACE
GLASGOW, C.1
PHONE: CENTRAL 7944-5
BUY SELL or EXCHANGE

LATEST COMMUNIQUE

S.H.A.E.F. Communique No. 2.
23.30 Hours, June 6.

Shortly before midnight on 5th June, 1944, Allied night bombers opened the assault. Their attacks in very great strength continued until dawn.

MINEFIELDS SWEPT

The naval forces, which had previously assembled under the over-all command of Admiral Sir Bertram Ramsay, made their departure in fresh weather and were joined during the night by bombarding forces which had previously left northern waters. Channels had to be swept through the large enemy minefields.

This operation was completed shortly before dawn, and, while mine-sweeping flotillas continued to sweep towards the enemy coast, the entire naval force followed down swept channels behind them towards their objectives.

Shortly before the assault three enemy torpedo boats with armed trawlers in company attempted to interfere with the operation and were promptly driven off. One enemy trawler was sunk and another severely damaged.

The assault forces moved towards the beaches under cover of heavy bombardment from destroyers and other support craft while heavier ships engaged enemy batteries which had already been subjected to bombardment from the air.

Some of these were silenced. Allied forces continued to engage other batteries. Landings were effected under cover of the air and naval bombardments and airborne landings involving troop-carrying aircraft and gliders carrying large forces of troops were also made successfully at a number of points.

Reports of operations so far show that our forces succeeded in their initial landings. Fighting continues.

Allied heavy, medium and light and fighter bombers continued the air bombardment in very great strength throughout the day with attacks on gun emplacements, defensive works and communications.

CONTINUOUS COVER

Continuous fighter cover was maintained over the beaches and for some distance inland and over naval operations.

Allied reconnaissance aircraft maintained continuous watch by day and night over shipping and ground forces.

Our aircraft met with little enemy fighter opposition or anti-aircraft gunfire.

Naval casualties were regarded as being very light.

LANDINGS ON 100-MILE FRONT ARE REPORTED

Germans Say Paratroops Of Both Sides Are Battling West Of Le Havre

First day of the Allied assault on the Western "Wall" has gone well. A communique from Allied Supreme Headquarters at midnight announced: "Reports of operations so far show that our forces succeeded in their initial landings." These landings, according to German accounts, are taking place at a series of points extending over a 100 miles line from Cherbourg to Le Havre.

According to a German news agency report shortly after the midnight communique the Allies now hold bridgeheads on both sides of the Orne estuary, roughly midway between Cherbourg and Le Havre and further west in the area north-west of Bayeux.

A small Allied group consisting of light tanks and armoured scout cars now stands a few kilometres in the dunes north-east of Bayeux and is trying to establish contact with the main bridgehead, according to the Germans.

FIGHTING 10 MILES INLAND

Allied paratroops have been dropped on the road between Carentan and Valognes-Cherbourg-Paris road, said Paris Radio last night. "Very heavy fighting is going on here," the radio said.

Mr. Churchill reported to the House of Commons last night that landings along the whole front have been effective and that fighting is taking place in the town of Caen, ten miles inland.

At Allied H.Q. the invasion army was stated to be "over the first four or five hurdles" in its tremendous opening task in the liberation of Europe.

The Allied troops went in at dawn yesterday under the greatest air umbrella in history and got on to the beaches without the coastal defences proving nearly as effective as was expected.

The Luftwaffe made only 50 sorties in reply to the Allies' devastating air blow, in which over 10,000 bombs were hurled by the R.A.F. at the German defences between midnight and 8 a.m., and 7000 sorties flown by air armadas supporting our ground troops during the day.

Airborne troops engaged in the biggest parachute descent in military history suffered little loss and are now established.

Losses among the huge naval armada which accompanied the invaders have been "very very light."

Air and ground battles between Allied and German paratroops took place yesterday afternoon west of Le Havre, according to Berlin.

"PARIS SIEGE"

Several British and Canadian battalions of paratroops and airborne troops in gliders were being landed when German gliders landed German paratroops. Heavy fighting took place partly while the men were still in the air, said the radio.

The German Overseas News Agency said last night: "Un-

Continued on Back Page, Col. 1.

INVASION PICTURES
Pages 3, 4, 5, and 8

Greatest Air Armada
Out Again Last Night

THE greatest air armada of the war was crossing the East Coast for two hours yesterday evening.

The thunder of the first wave of heavy bombers flying south-east brought people running into the streets from their tea tables and stampeded cattle.

The armada continued without a moment's respite as fighters and heavy bombers flew out in a dozen streams simultaneously in every part of the sky.

"It dwarfs anything we have ever known here," said an observer on the coast. "It is like all the heavy night attacks of the last few weeks put into one."

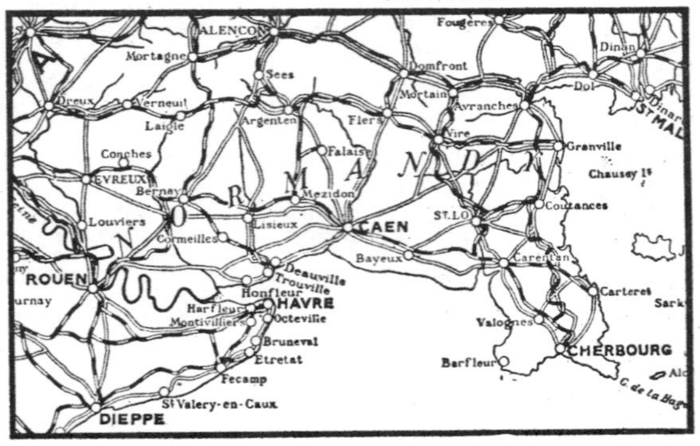

In looking at this map of the invasion areas, the southern English coast is behind you

First German Prisoners

FIRST German prisoners and first casualties to reach a British port were landed late yesterday afternoon, states a correspondent representing the combined American press.

They belonged to the 352nd infantry division, holding the sector between Isigny and Bayeux and to the 21st panzer division from the Caen sector, it was stated.

"5th" Beyond Ostia

Allied H.Q., Italy.

Allied troops advancing south of Rome advanced beyond the Tiber at all points and cleared Ostia harbour.

See Story—Page 6

Weather Worry

WEATHER is still biggest worry of invasion, reports Reuter's correspondent. A strong north-west wind shows no sign of moderating.

It will not halt flow of reinforcements, but an improvement would make the operation very much easier.

Threat To French

THE Commander of the German forces in France last night broadcast this order to the people of France:

German troops have been given the order to shoot at any person who is seen to be co-operating with the Allied invasion forces or who gives shelter to Allied soldiers, sailors or airmen.

Frenchmen who co-operate with Allied troops will be treated as bandits.

—And Appeal

Radio France (Algiers) addressed this appeal to the French police and gendarmerie last night.

Policemen, gendarmes, and members of the Garde Mobile join the Patriot forces with all your equipment.

Police officers and prison wardens, political prisoners are in your charge. When opportunity presents itself, open the doors and let them go!

U.S. BOMB GALATZ

Scores of U.S. heavy bombers heavily escorted by fighters, took off from the American Heavy Bomber Base in the Soviet Union yesterday, and roared over the Soviet-German front to shower many tons of high explosive and incendiary bombs on aerodrome installations at Galatz.

Saw 100 Gliders 15 Miles In
TANKS MOVING ON CAEN

From LAWRENCE FAIRHALL, "Daily Record" Air correspondent with the Allied Expeditionary Air Forces in England.

Tuesday Night.

THE Air Vice-Marshal this afternoon visited airfields under his command and spoke to Typhoon pilots who have been flying over the invasion beaches since dawn this morning.

He heard first-hand stories of how the Luftwaffe has failed to put up any resistance to the great fleets of Allied aircraft which have kept up a day-long offensive against targets in the invasion zone.

Two high-flying ME's were the only enemy aircraft which have so far been reported over the landing areas. One of these, after finding itself flying in the middle of some Spitfires, shot up into the clouds and was lost.

We Hold Beaches

Flying Officer F. M. Botting, a Canadian, reported seeing a number of gliders lying in a big field.

"The field was about 10 to 15 miles inland, and I saw somewhere between 50 and 100 gliders lying all over the ground," he added.

R.A.F. pilots who had been flying at low level over the fronts all day told me this evening that they saw our tanks moving on Caen, ten miles up the River Orne.

"In the area inland we saw several fires which may have been petrol dumps going up," they said.

When we left after our last sorties we could see no enemy infantry at this point near the coast."

There was no longer any opposition on the beaches, which were in our hands.

Lack of Opposition

The lack of air opposition was fantastic, they added.

"We saw our ships closing in on the beaches as we went over the French coast. When we turned at the end of our patrols and were over them again a few minutes later we could see them already unloading supplies which were moving off from the beaches inland almost as we watched.

"The whole business from the

Continued On Back Page—Col. 4

"WE ARE HERE NOW," SHOUTED PARATROOPS AT LE HAVRE

From CYRIL MARSHALL, "Daily Record" Special Correspondent.

Stockholm, Tuesday.

"WE are here now!" shouted Allied paratroops as their feet touched ground at Le Havre, and the same shout came from more of them as they reached the earth at Caen, according to a Berlin report.

The paratroopers immediately started shooting, putting up a barrage behind which they tried to get possession of a number of concrete forts.

In this, the Berlin report says, they were not successful, but they managed to entrench themselves and the greater part of them resisted death or capture until other Allied troops, coming by sea, landed and joined them.

Berlin opinion is that Eisenhower's aim is to drive straight for Paris if he succeeds in establishing strong beach-heads. The places chosen for landing, in the neighbourhood of Caen, in the region between the mouths of the rivers Orne and Vire, give rise to this opinion.

Big paratroop formations which landed west of Le Havre and near Boulogne are supposed to have had for their task, the luring of large numbers of German troops from the landing beaches but the Germans claim that the ruse was not successful.

"Dummies"

It is reported that German divisions have been locked in fierce combat since the morning with both paratroops and disembarked troops.

One Berlin report says that parachute troops were made to appear more numerous by the sending down of life-sized dummies.

Large German air forces have been dispatched to the scenes of the landings and are hotly engaged with Allied naval and air forces.

Later Berlin reports declare, that there were 12 landing places and that the Allies penetrated three miles inland at three or four points.

Bailey's
Quality Wine Merchants
GLASGOW. EDINBURGH.
PAISLEY, GREENOCK,
AYR, IRVINE, TROON.

Daily *and Mail* Record

EST. 1847—No. 30,554   RADIO—Page 5   MONDAY, DECEMBER 25, 1944   BLACK-OUT—Back Page   ONE PENNY F

FOR COUGHS, COLDS & INFLUENZA.
LANG'S
GOLD MEDAL
BANANA RUM
GUARANTEED
PURE JAMAICA

MIGHTIEST AIR ASSAULT OF WAR

10,000 Tons Hit Front Supply Lines

ALLIED 4500 AIRMADA:
116 NAZIS DOWN

APPROXIMATELY FOUR THOUSAND FIVE HUNDRED ALLIED PLANES YESTERDAY STRUCK SMASHING NEW BLOWS AGAINST RUNDSTEDT'S SUPPLY LINES IN THE GREAT BATTLE OF THE BULGE, PROBABLY THE GREATEST-EVER AIR ASSAULT OF THE WAR.

The Allied Air Forces flew between 6500 and 7000 sorties mainly against the German counter-offensive.

They dropped about 10,000 tons of bombs and destroyed at least 116 German planes in the air, as the Germans sent up opposing fighters for the second succesive day.

"CRACK MAY TURN TIDE"

Incomplete reports show 39 bombers and six fighters missing from yesterday's operations, states U.S. air communique.

A spokesman at Shaef last night: "The Air Force has dealt the enemy a terrific crack to-day, and may turn the tide of the German counter-offensive.

HITLER:
By Goebbels

DR. GOEBBELS, broadcasting to the German people, last night, said:

"The German people vow that they will continue to stand firm as a wall by the Fuhrer.

"When I took him the Christmas greetings of the German people he asked me to convey his greetings to you, to every one of you who endures with pride and dignity.

Sleepless Nights

"His thoughts are always with his people, to whom all his feelings go by day and during the many sleepless nights.

"When our enemies depict him as sick, the wish is the father to the thought.

"The Fuhrer is enjoying the best of health and is, as always, filled with the utmost mental and spiritual driving force.

"I never saw the Fuhrer so full of plans and visions for the future

"He will not fail to give them a fitting answer at the appropriate time."

Christmas Wishes

of the usual kind may well seem something of a mockery in these grim, abnormal times. But, as the Very Rev. Dr. James Black says on Page 2 to-day:—

"Be sure of this— that your husbands and sons in France, Italy, or Burma will be only too happy to know of your happiness."

And it is the privilege of

The Daily Record

to associate itself sincerely with that message to all its readers.

CANADIAN 1st ARMY — ARNHEM — Maas — NIJMEGEN — CLEVE — BRITISH 2nd ARMY — VENLO — DUISBURG — ESSEN — U.S. 9th ARMY — AACHEN — JULICH — COLOGNE — LIEGE — DUREN — BONN — BELGIUM — COBLENZ — U.S. 1st ARMY — **RUNDSTEDT'S LINES OF ATTACK** — LUXEMBOURG — TRIER — SAARBURG — VERDUN — SAARLAUTERN — U.S. 3rd ARMY — METZ — SAARBRUCKEN — SARREBOURG — NANCY — STRASBOURG — ST DIE — U.S. 7th ARMY — Moselle — FRANCE — SELESTAT — COLMAR — FRENCH 1st ARMY — MULHOUSE — BELFORT — Miles 0 10 20 30 40 50 — BASLE — SWITZERLAND

Over 2000 Flying Fortresses and Liberators of the U.S. 8th Air Force, the greatest force of heavy bombers ever flown on a single mission, attacked communication supply centres, aerodromes and other military installations.

4690 TONS ALONE

The U.S. "heavies" alone dropped approximately 4690 tons of bombs on road and rail supply lines from Euskirchen south to Trier and on 11 Luftwaffe aerodromes in the Frankfurt area, states USSAFE Headquarters.

More than 900 Mustangs and Thunderbolts accompanied the U.S. bombers, and the giant force made a column 400 miles long.

R.A.F. KEEP IT UP

As the head of the column entered Germany the tail was just leaving England. It took over two hours for the procession to cross the coast.

In the afternoon the offensive was maintained by strong forces of R.A.F. Halifaxes and

Why There's No "Basic" Ration

THE great forces of U.S. planes on yesterday's mission consumed an estimated 4,250,000 gallons of petrol—enough to fill 425 U.S. railway tank cars.

Lancasters, protected by Spitfires and Mustangs.

After dark last evening, Lancasters of R.A.F. Bomber Command attacked railway targets at Cologne and an airfield at Bonn.

The concentrated attacks on two airfields in the Ruhr were made in clear weather.

Continued on Back Page, Col. 5

"Decided Turn For Better"—Supreme H.Q.

Supreme H.Q., Sunday Evening.

The situation at the front has to-day taken a decided turn for the better, it was reported here to-night.

The German drive into Belgium has been halted, at least temporarily, and Stavelot is in American hands.

This good news may be the direct result of the increased air operations which have been made possible by a great improvement in the weather conditions in the last two days.

Hundreds of fighter-bombers, in their greatest strength since the weather clamped down on them eight days ago, took off for the second successive day against enemy armour and transport.

Dive-bombers were there as well, carrying out missions designed to keep the enemy from moving into the battle area.

Bastogne is still in our hands as well as Stavelot, although fighting is going on for this town.

Allied troops are exerting strong pressure on both flanks of the German drive.

Heavy fighting was reported to have taken place yesterday near Grosbous, 14 miles north-west of the city of Luxembourg, according to the latest available information.

Several strong German counter-attacks were repulsed in that area.

Allied Gains

Allied forces pressing on the southern flank of the German advance through the Ardennes have made gains.

The American position at Stavelot which is separating the two German westward thrusts is holding firm in face of numerous German attacks which have been repulsed.

Allied troops pressing northwards from Luxembourg against the southern flank of the German advance gained a mile or two along a 25-mile front.

Most important development to-day was the continued stepping-up of Allied air attacks.

Generally the Germans have made no further progress westward and the situation is shaping well.

Germans 40 Miles In

American troops continued their stubborn resistance in face of Rundstedt's mighty pressure and made local gains in the area of Maubach, nine miles south of Duren.

The Germans cut the road from Hotton to the north-east, although Hotton itself is still in Allied hands.

Hotton is 25 miles south of Liege and the German advance to this area represents a drive of 40 miles from their starting point.

Enemy Thrust Held

Enemy tanks are near Rosieres, seven miles south-west of Bastogne, says an official communique.

Other enemy troops have

Continued on Back Page, Col. 3

Last Nazi Gamble

THE text of the call which the American Army has made to the Wehrmacht in the west, as broadcast by Luxembourg Radio, said:—

"The German High Command has made its last gamble. All available reserves have been flung into this throw to break open the steel ring around Germany.

"This latest German counter-attack will be completely effectivless and so will all other attempts."

ANTI-GERMAN GOVT. FORMED IN HUNGARY

A NEW Hungarian Government has been formed with Bela Miklos as Prime Minister and Dr. Vasari as Finance Minister, said a statement quoted by Moscow radio last night.

The members of the new Government gave the traditional pledge to the Assembly to work for the nation. A Government proclamation was then adopted by the Assembly. It said:—

"Our country is going through difficult times having been dragged by Germany into war against the United Nations. Owing to Szalasy, Hungary is the last satellite of the hated Nazis. Szalasy is a usurper and the country has been left without leaders.

"This great national crisis has forced the Patriots to take steps and a national assembly has been chosen by free election

"The Provisional National Assembly has formed a Provisional Government of Hungary.

Asks For Truce

"It will ask for an armistice with the United Nations and undertakes to restore all damage done by Hungary in the war. It will restore neighbourly good relations with all the United Nations.

"Our interests demand that the armed forces of the Hungarian people take part in the destruction of the Nazis and thus expiate their guilt before the United Nations.

"The Provisional Government regards as important the mobilisation of all forces of the country for the war.

"A democratic Hungary is essential to our independence.

"Thus all decrees against the people and the Jews are annulled, freedom of speech and Press restored, and the Arrow Cross organisation disbanded.

"Democratic transformation opens the way to the rebirth of our nation and shall lay the

Continued on Back Page, Col. 4

North V-Bombs May Be Feint

IT seems fairly certain that the Germans gambled on surprising our defences in the first V-bomb attack on Northern England recently, writes an air correspondent.

The new tactics may be taken as an admission by the enemy of the great difficulties they experience in piercing our intercepting "shield" in the South and as a tribute to the strength of our defences in that part of the country.

It may well be that this blow at the North was merely an attempt to compel us to redispose our intercepting forces so as to make an attack on London easier.

It is unlikely that the range of the V bombs has been increased. If these bombs were launched from "parent" planes it is probable that the bomb-carrying aircraft ventured farther out to sea, hoping that on this new route they would escape detection and destruction.

Stories Of Attack—Page 5.

Noted Band Leader Is Missing

MAJOR GLENN MILLER, the American band leader, is reported missing. The announcement was made on Sunday night during a "Forces Favourites" broadcast of records.

It is learned that the other members of Glenn Miller's band are all safe.

Glenn Miller and his band went to France in the autumn. The 50 musicians in the band are all members of the U.S. Forces.

Among the requests received for the programme was one for a record by Glenn Miller and his band, and the compere expressed the sorrow that would be felt by Major Miller's admirers over the news.

MAY BE CAPTURED

"The Moonlight Serenader," as he is known in the States, is one of America's foremost band leaders.

It is thought that while he was arranging for a troops' concert he may have been captured.

To-day the band will be broadcasting in the "A.E.F. Christmas Show" at 7 p.m in the Home Service. It will be conducted by the deputy leader, Sergeant Jerry Gray.

ADVERTISER'S ANNOUNCEMENT

Spa
REGD
NYLON   OR BRISTLE
TOOTHBRUSHES

made to give your teeth a good brush

JOHN FREEMAN & CO., LTD.,
Spa Brush Works, Chesham, Bucks.

V2 Sites Hit

SPITFIRES of R.A.F. Fighter Command attacked V2 storage, erection and launching sites in enemy-occupied Holland yesterday.

Polish Spitfires attacked one site with their cannon, and saw shell bursts over all the area.

RELY ON THE QUALITY
ballito STOCKINGS

Sunday Mail

Scotland's National Sunday Newspaper

WHAT NOW? NEW PEACE PROBLEMS SEE PAGE 8

Bottled Proverbs
HP sauce
waste not, want not; it's scarce.

No. 1898   SUNDAY, FEBRUARY 4, 1945   RADIO—PAGE 7   TWOPENCE   A

THE WAR'S GREATEST DAY OF TERROR IN BERLIN

THIS WAS BERLIN BEFORE IT WAS DOOMED—

And The Russians Are Still Driving On

LATE last night flames were still licking the battered ruins of Berlin—a city of chaos and despair, a city still dazed by terror after the most dreadful day in the history of war.

The day had started badly for the jittery Berliners. The Russians, moaned the Capital's loudspeakers, were still advancing. They went to work dejectedly. Then, just before noon, the sirens wailed—and the greatest-ever raid on the centre of Berlin was on.

U.S. Burst Through Siegfried Pillboxes

SHAEF, Saturday.

TWO American divisions to-day burst completely through the first pillboxes of the Siegfried Line.

As the First Army pushed deep into the Siegfried defences to-day the Germans threw in a few infantry counter-attacks with one or two tanks in support and heavy hand-to-hand fighting is going on in the area of the Gerolstein Forest.

In spite of this First Army troops have blasted their way through the outer defences of the line at one point at least, and are keeping up relentless pressure along the whole of their 35-mile advancing front.

Stiff fighting is now raging through the German town of Drieborn, seven miles east of Monschau.

In this area the First Army is across the Roer river in strength and is fighting its way through hilly, wooded terrain.

A 2000-yard advance through stubborn German resistance last night took Allied troops into the town of Harterscheild, on the Monschau-Schleiden road, and the village of Schoneseifseen, a mile from Harterscheild, was also taken.

Further south, in the sector east of Bullange, other First Army troops have beaten off German counter-attacks.

9-Mile Front

Fighting from one pillbox to the next, the Americans fought their way through to Udenbreth, just across the German border in this sector and cleared the Germans out of this town. Advances of between two and three thousand yards are reported from this sector.

General Patton's Third Army has established a front of nine miles across Germany across the Our River, south-east of St. Vith, and is closing in on the main Siegfried defences.

Pincers Closing

Four more German villages have fallen to the 3rd Army troops in this area as they press back stiff German resistance, to enlarge their bridgehead, which is now some four miles deep in places.

3rd Army troops are now fighting two miles further north-east in the vicinity of Bleihalf, an important control point on the main highway running north-west from Prum to Schonberg.

American and French troops have launched the final attacks to wipe out a pocket of Germans

Continued on Back Page, Col. 6

Democracy Comes To Germany

Western Front, Saturday.

DEMOCRACY came back to a little corner of Germany this week. It was on a small and experimental scale, but it was democracy—a miniature free election in the Aachen area of Germans, by Germans, for Germans.

There were only 14 voters and only two men to be elected, and for limited powers, but it was an election with a secret ballot, the first the Germans have had for a long time.

An interpreter told the voters what the meeting was about and what they had to do. Then they elected Joseph Driessen, their representative—not leader.

Into the battle for Berlin roared the might of the Allied Air Forces. More than 1000 Flying Forts streamed over the capital and rained about 2500 tons of bombs on targets in the heart of the city. And all in 45 minutes.

No wonder Berlin panicked. It was a cascade of death. The airmada flew into the Reich in a column 300 miles long.

Rumbling overhead, the bombers had driven from the minds of Berliners thoughts of the ever-increasing threat to their city.

But as soon as they emerged, trembling, from their air-raid shelters their radios brought new fear.

German announcers revealed that the "Battle of Germany" had reached a climax.

Final Blow

And late news from correspondents in Moscow support that opinion.

Marshal Zhukov's spearheads are already attacking to secure a bridgehead across the Oder at Kuestrin.

Behind them armour and infantry, massing little more than 40 miles from the Reich capital's Volksturm - manned trenches, are being welded together for the blow which will carry them across the Oder—and the decisive attack on the city.

Two years and a day from the final triumph of Stalingrad, which Marshal Zhukov helped to plan, and after

Continued on Back Page, Col. 4

Jap Savagery Could Not Break Down British Grit

MORE than half of the 30,000 British, Australian and Dutch prisoners forced by the Japanese to build the Bangkok—Moulmein railway through the jungles of the East, died in the two years ending June, 1944.

This terrible story of suffering and Jap savagery in the prison camp hells to which our soldiers were condemned since the capture of Singapore was revealed yesterday.

Its brightest feature is its evidence that the flame of British resistance could never be put out, despite disease, torture and death.

Pte. George Heeley, 1st Battalion Cambridgeshire Regiment, one of the men rescued on Luzon last week, told a B.U.P. war correspondent that the Japanese treatment was savagely inhuman.

Heeley said that British officers were formed into special squads and given the heaviest and the filthiest work of all to do.

U.S. Army Trials

Sentences ranging from 35 years' imprisonment to five years' were imposed in Paris yesterday on six American soldiers for black marketeering in U.S. Army goods.

All were dishonourably discharged from the Army by the court-martial.

One man was found with £800 in his possession

—AND THIS IS THE MAN WHO STARTED IT

ALL-OUT AIR BLOWS ON REICH

ALL Germany is being hammered from the air. Allied bombers were over the Reich for $7\frac{1}{2}$ hours continuously in daylight yesterday, according to the Nazi radio. The raid on Berlin itself was the greatest ever on the centre of the city.

Two great waves of the armada of more than 1000 Flying Fortresses swept over the German capital just before noon and rained about 2500 tons on military, Governmental and communication targets, says the U.S. Eighth Air Force headquarters.

Great Fighter Protection

At the same time more than 400 Liberators of the Eighth struck at the Brabag synthetic oil plant at Rothernsee, a suburb of Magdeburg, and at the Magdeburg railway yards. The Forts and Liberators were protected along their route by more than 900 Mustang and Thunderbolt fighters.

And Stuttgart, Munich, Berlin and Leipzig were off the air at 2 p.m. and did not relay the usual Deutschlandsender news broadcast, says the "Sunday Mail" Listening Station.

Out Again At Nightfall

Another powerful striking force of heavy R.A.F. bombers passed over Eastern England before nightfall yesterday, heading out over the North Sea in long procession for the Continent, said a late flash.

The attack on Berlin was aimed at disrupting communications through the capital city and at disorganising the control of military forces within the Reich at this crucial time. Berlin is the hub through which flow vital communications lines between the Eastern and Western Fronts.

The concentrated attack on Berlin lasted about 45 minutes. Objectives included the Anhalter and Potsdamer railway stations and the Templehof marshalling yards, all in the centre of the city.

Continued on Back Page, Col. 6

"The Capital Will Be Defended"

SWEDISH correspondents inform their editors that they are ready to leave Berlin, as tension is increasing daily and things are happening which "will shortly make reporting more difficult."

Volksturmers, women, and old folk are digging tank-traps in the Frankfurter Allee, one of the big working class thoroughfares.

In other districts — Communist despite 12 years of Nazi rule—workers are chalking up hammer and sickle signs.

Sappers are mining buildings and machine-gun nests and barricades are being built from raid debris.

Berliners and refugees read yesterday in the two-page newspapers that they must stretch their thin rations further—eight weeks' supplies must last nine.

Mad dogs are running round the city as a result of an outbreak of rabies.

Reports from Berne say the

Gestapo have arrested a number of personalities to prevent their collaborating with the Russians and forming a new Government.

"The capital will be defended stone by stone," said a Berlin military spokesman, "and arrangements for mass evacuation will not be put into practice until things get really hot."

The Government would stay in Berlin, he added.

SIGN END IS NEAR IN WEST

America is planning to move her troops from Europe to fronts in the Pacific—

See "It Was News in New York Last Night."—Page 4.

International Report By Rex—Back Page

Y·O·U·N·G·E·R
Spells warmth in the cold spell
WILLIAM YOUNGERS BEER

Daily Record
and Mail.

"BLACK & WHITE"
It's the Scotch!
MAXIMUM PRICES:
Fixed by the Scotch Whisky Association
25/9 per bottle   13/6 half-bottle
Gt. Britain and N. Ireland only

EST. 1847—No. 30,596   RADIO—Page 4   TUESDAY, FEBRUARY 13, 1945   BLACK-OUT—Back Page   ONE PENNY F

BIG THREE DECIDE FATE OF GERMANY

Momentous Declaration; Polish Settlement

VITAL DECISIONS FOR THE FINAL DRIVE TO VICTORY IN EUROPE AND THE POST-WAR SETTLEMENT WERE ANNOUNCED BY THE "BIG THREE" LAST NIGHT.

MR. CHURCHILL, PRESIDENT ROOSEVELT AND MARSHAL STALIN HAVE MET NEAR YALTA, IN THE CRIMEA, FOR EIGHT DAYS.

The main decisions of the Conference which ended during the week-end are:

Unconditional surrender terms for Germany have been agreed, but will not be made known until final defeat.

Germany will be ruled by the three Supreme Commanders from Berlin and each Power will occupy a separate zone, France to be invited to take a zone of occupation and to join the Control Commission.

Disarming All Germany

All German forces will be disarmed and disbanded, military equipment removed or destroyed, war industry eliminated or controlled and all war criminals punished.

Germany must pay reparations in goods. Future world security will be organised at a conference of United Nations at San Francisco in two months' time; Agreement on the formation of a new Polish Government of National Unity and on the Curzon line as approximately the eastern frontier of Poland, and a declaration of concerted policy and joint action in meeting the political and economic problems of liberated Europe.

The conference also reached an agreement on reciprocal repatriation of liberated prisoners of war.

Mr. Churchill went to Yalta by air.

The conclusions of the "Big Three" conference exceed expectations. It has been able

FULL TEXT ON PAGES 3 and 6

to reach agreements which go beyond vague phrases and indicate specific courses of action, writes Frederick Truelove, "Daily Record" diplomatic correspondent.

One of the striking features of the official statement is the agreement on Poland.

SETTLED THEIR DIFFERENCES

The three Leaders have announced that they went to the conference resolved to "settle their differences" on this subject.

The world is now informed how they have done so. There is to be a new Polish Provisional Government on a broader democratic basis and free elections.

The eastern frontier of Poland is to follow the Curzon Line, there are to be territorial compensations in the north and west, but the final western limits are to
Continued on Back Page, Col. 3

CRIMEA DELEGATES' DECISION

Freed P.O.W. Agreement

THE Big Three Conference in the Crimea has reached agreement on the repatriation of prisoners of war and civilians of the British Empire, the Soviet Union, and the United States, liberated by the Allied forces.

The agreement concluded was drawn up in two separate but identical texts, one drawn between the Governments of the British Commonwealth and the Government of the U.S.S.R. and the other between the Government of the United States and the Government of the U.S.S.R.

Allies Provide

Under these arrangements each Ally will provide food, clothing, medical attention and other needs for the nationals of the others until transport is available for their repatriation.

In caring for British subjects and American citizens, the Soviet Government will be assisted by British and American officers. Soviet officers will assist British and American authorities in their task of caring for Soviet citizens liberated by the British and American forces, during such time as they are on the continent of Europe or in the U.K. awaiting transport to take them home.

Finally, by the agreement reached, the three Governments are pledged to give every assistance consistent with operational requirements to help to ensure that all these prisoners of war and civilians are speedily repatriated.

Children Were Burned Alive

SIX truck loads of children were burned alive by the Germans at the Auschwitz-Oswiecim concentration camp, and mothers who witnessed the spectacle went mad, according to the Yugoslav War Crimes Commission.

The Commission's report, quoted by the Yugoslav Telegraph Agency, said that 2,500,000 people perished in the camp up to October, 1943.

It placed responsibility for the atrocities on Hitler, Himmler, the Nazi Party, and camp officers.

The camp had installations for speedy mass annihilation of prisoners.

Mr. Churchill, President Roosevelt and Marshal Stalin photographed in the grounds of the Livadia Palace, Yalta, where the Three-Power Conference was held.

Nazis Learn Their Fate

From "Daily Record" Listening Station

SHORTLY before midnight last night the Allies opened up a radio barrage against the Germans, broadcasting the text of the Crimean communique from all quarters of the globe.

New York, Algiers and Luxemburg joined in with Paris, Cairo and Bari. Germans at the Italian front heard the news in a special broadcast by the British Eighth Army station.

Double West Front Punch Rocks Nazi Defences

From WILLIAM STEEN, Reuter's Special Correspondent

Supreme H.Q., A.E.F., Paris, Monday.

MONTGOMERY in the north and Bradley in the centre are to-night rocking the German defences with a one-two punch at the chin and the solar plexus.

British troops have already overrun Cleve. Gains continue to be won along the entire Canadian Army offensive front, and more than 4000 prisoners are now in the cages.

North of Cleve the Canadians are well up to the line of the Spoy Canal. Scottish troops took Gennep, south of the Reichwald Forest.

Third Army men have slashed their way through Prum after heavy concentrations from artillery had paved the way.

Scots Bore Brunt

Scottish troops who have borne the brunt of General Crerar's battle are through the first defended belt of the Siegfried zone. Facing south below the Reichswald they are to-day up against strong concrete villages above the Goch-Gennep railway line, cables Doon Campbell.

These men have added another page of glory to their battle honours.

They overran the first acres of Western Germany. They

hurdled the concrete bunkers, the mines, and the anti-tank ditches of the Siegfried Line between Kranenburg and Cleve in five hours.

Since six o'clock last night, in two small battles round Hekkens and Kessel the latter, a small village on the Niers, Scottish troops have taken some 200 prisoners—not just "rag tag and bobtail" but the best infantry the German Army can put into the field, and men who at this time of day cannot be replaced.

Stalking 'Chutists

These Scottish troops are to-day stalking through firs, silver birches, and mine-filled mud to penetrate positions that Rundstedt has ordered his crack parachutists to hold to
Continued on Back Page, Col. 1

KONIEV'S FLANK THREAT TO BERLIN

MARSHAL KONIEV'S northern armies, far beyond the Oder, are fanning out into two major thrusts menacing the whole German front from the Baltic to Czechoslovakia.

If the German High Command cannot stem the tide—and there is no indication so far that Guderian has slowed the Soviet advance — the situation will become catastrophic.

Koniev's tank spearheads, in a threat to Berlin from the flank, are driving north-west, roughly parallel with the Oder and are already fighting behind the main Oder line fortifications.

Simultaneously the tank armies of one of the Soviet's greatest exponents of armoured warfare are driving west and may soon engulf huge areas of South-Eastern and Central Germany. Dresden and Leipzig may soon be in the danger zone.

Road To Berlin

This drive coupled with the battle now raging over the Pomeranian Lakeland, may open the road to Berlin quicker than any frontal assault, cables Duncan Hooper, Reuter's special correspondent in Moscow.

The Oder line now exists as an effective barrier only in the northern and central sectors, and even there it is believed to have been heavily dented.

Above and below Breslau it has ceased to have any further value for the Germans and it might be said that the steel-hooded forts and giant pill-boxes have passed into history.

Ring Round Breslau

Koniev has succeeded in getting huge tank forces across the river in one of the biggest bridging operations of all time. His armies are now shooting out like so many tentacles, snapping German communications and wrapping themselves round strongpoints vital for the defence of this sector.

It is expected that the ring round Breslau will finally be
Continued on Back Page, Col. 5

ADVERTISER'S ANNOUNCEMENT

Snowfire Girls: NAN

Nan — fair, petite and cuddlesome — has a slightly helpless manner which appeals to men. In fact, she has boy friends everywhere. Her skin is lovely — and she knows it! Nan also knows that not for worlds would she be without her Snowfire Beauty Makers — cream, powder and lipstick.

Snowfire

BEAUTY MAKERS
For ever and a Date!

CREAM · POWDER · LIPSTICK

Spring for— **WILLIAM YOUNGERS BEER**

Daily Record
and Mail.

EST. 1847—No. 30,668   1d   TUESDAY, MAY 8. 1945   A KEMSLEY NEWSPAPER

"BLACK & WHITE"
It's the Scotch!
MAXIMUM PRICES
Fixed by the Scotch Whisky Association
25/9 per bottle. 13/6 half-bottle
Gt. Britain and N. Ireland only

SURRENDER TERMS SIGNED

WAR NOW OVER—THIS IS VE-DAY

The children did not wait for the official announcement of the end of the war. They just went to it—and set their bonfires alight. Celebrations like this were going on in many parts of Glasgow and Edinburgh last night.

THE war is over. Unconditional surrender has been received from Germany by Britain, America and Russia.

But the official announcement from the lips of Mr. Churchill will not come until this afternoon, when the Prime Minister will broadcast at three o'clock.

H.M. the King will broadcast to the peoples of the British Empire and Commonwealth to-night at 9 o'clock. Parliament will meet at the usual time to-day.

In view of this fact, to-day will be treated as Victory in Europe Day and will be regarded as a holiday. To-morrow, Wednesday, May 9, will also be a holiday.

Ed Murrow, of the Columbia Broadcasting System, in a broadcast from London last night, said that Mr. Churchill and President Truman were ready to make an official surrender proclamation at any moment, but Marshal Stalin declared that he was not ready and it was agreed to postpone the announcement.

WAR CHIEFS ON RADIO

Fifteen people will take part in "Tribute to the King," the broadcast which will precede the King's broadcast to-night.

They include representatives of the Dominions and Colonies, the three fighting Services, the Merchant Navy, the Police and Civil Defence forces, a nurse and a London housewife.

It is hoped that the voices of the following will be heard in "Victory Report," the broadcast which will follow the news after the King's speech—Eisenhower, Montgomery, Alexander, Tedder, Bradley, Admiral Tovey and Mountbatten.

SURPRISE DELAY

Explanations of the surprising delay in announcing VE-Day, in spite of the complete capitulation by the Germans, lies in the importance which is attached to synchronising the news in London, Washington and Moscow.

Telephone calls went on all through the day between Mr. Churchill, President Truman and Marshal Stalin. Differing views were apparently held on when the public should be told.

Continued on Back Page, Col. 3

Why VE-Holiday Was Changed

*T*HE decision that to-day (Tuesday) should be regarded as a whole holiday is a departure from the original plan, under which VE-Day was to have been a holiday only from the time an announcement was made.

This change was occasioned by the feeling in official circles that news of the German announcement of complete surrender had spread throughout the country and would be pointless to continue as though the Premier's announcement of final victory in Europe would be a surprise.

Mrs. Henderson, of Carshalton, who will introduce the King on the radio when he makes his speech to-night.

Clyde Ships V-Daft; Sirens, Rockets, Flares

AT midnight last night hundreds of ships—warships, merchant ships, tugs, steamers, motorboats and anyone possessing a horn, a hooter or an old A.R.P. rattle opened up in the Firth of Clyde to create the most tremendous victory din likely to be heard in any part of the country.

For miles around and far inland the noise was heard and people on the coast, excited by the din and the spirit behind it, suddenly defied the coast blackout ban and allowed their lights to blaze out into the streets.

The Tail of the Bank was ablaze with light from multi-coloured flares, while rockets discharged from ships gave a display reminiscent of peace-time illuminations.

Church bells from the Cowal shore were heard ringing.

GLASGOW GAIETY

Glasgow became a city of revelry last night. Crowds packed the main streets, dancing and singing to the accompaniment of organs, mouth organs, and other instruments.

A British and an American soldier led community singing in George Square, where many people added to the gaiety by wearing paper hats.

The night sky all over the city was aglow with the light from hundreds of bonfires.

Late city transport could not cope with the homeward-bound crowds.

" Blazing Bonfires Anticipate VE-Day "—Page 3

No 'Daily Record' on Thursday

The " Daily Record " will be published to-morrow (Wednesday) but not on Thursday. Publication will be resumed on Friday.

The " Evening News " comes out as usual to-day, but publication is suspended on Wednesday, with resumed publication on Thursday.

---

48 BRITISH SHIPS OFF OSLO
NAZI CHIEF ORDERS 'NORWAY SURRENDER'

" **G**ERMAN soldiers in Norway, the German Foreign Minister, Count von Schwerin-Krosigk, has ordered the unconditional surrender of all German forces," said General Boehme, commander of German forces in Norway, over Oslo radio last night.

Allied naval units are reported to have arrived in Oslo Fjord. It is believed they will form the first nucleus of the British Mission there, says a message from inside Norway.

Although the Norway surrender has not yet been confirmed from Allied official

Continued on Back Page, Col. 1

BRESLAU FALLS.
U.S. 7 Miles From Prague

THE Patriot Prague radio at 11.36 last night reported that advanced U.S. tank units, presumably General Patton's, had just passed the town of Reporyje, about seven miles south of Prague.

It was officially announced last night that hostilities have ceased on the French 1st Army front, sa'd Paris radio.

Russians Take Breslau

Stalin in an Order of the Day last night announced: " Forces of the First Ukrainian Command after a prolonged siege, to-day, May 7, completely captured the town and fortress of Breslau.

" Up to 7 o'clock our troops had taken prisoner over 40,000 Germans in Breslau."

NEW WORK PLAN BEGINS

THE Government plan for the re-allocation of manpower will come into force to-day.

Members of the three services will not begin to be demobilised until six weeks after VE-Day. Then the first out will be those in Class A, Top 11 Groups, and the Class B. Top 12 Groups.

Men in industry aged 18 to 27 not needed in war factories are to be called up for military service.

Women in industry—married or single—will be allowed to leave their jobs, providing they have household responsibilities or wish to join their husbands on release from the Forces.

Where a factory closes altogether, men not in the 18 to 27 age groups will be transferred to other employment in the following order of priority:

Those needed for priority vacancies, including vacancies for skilled and experienced workers who are needed for re-establishing important industries and services; those who want to return home after working away for over a year but less than three years.

The major objective, the Government states, will be to return as many persons as possible to their homes, and those released will be sent to work as near to their home towns as possible.

The Essential Works Order will be lifted as soon as circumstances permit and replaced with the Control of Employment Order for women between 18 and 40 years of age and the Control of Engagement Order for men aged 18 to 50.

ADVERTISER'S ANNOUNCEMENT

FRY'S
COCOA
and all's well

THE FAMILY FOOD DRINK WITH THE REAL CHOCOLATE FLAVOUR
5ᴅ QTR LB • 9½ᴅ HALF LB

GEORGE YOUNGER'S ALLOA BEER

 Daily Record
and Mail.

EST. 1847—No. 30,669   1d   WEDNESDAY, MAY 9, 1945   A KEMSLEY NEWSPAPER

EDINBURGH WILL SEE THE KING

THE KING AND QUEEN, accompanied by Princess Elizabeth and Princess Margaret Rose, will visit Edinburgh on Wednesday, May 16, and will attend a service of thanksgiving in St. Giles' Cathedral.

The visit is for one day only.

London had its opportunity to cheer the King yesterday when crowds stood outside the Palace.

When Mr. Churchill had finished the King appeared smiling and radiantly happy.

Carnival Spirit For "Last All Clear"

On the balcony at the Palace, the Royal Family greets the cheering crowds.

Mr. Churchill

VE-NIGHT OF JOY IN GLASGOW

LIKE a European city on the eve of liberation, Glasgow went daft with joy last night. Victory celebrations were still in full swing in the early hours of this morning as thousands of happy citizens, hundreds left with no means of transport, made their way home.

Royal Family Hailed As They Bow From Palace Balcony

THE KING AND QUEEN, PRINCESS ELIZABETH and PRINCESS MARGARET stood in the sunshine on the balcony of Buckingham Palace yesterday. Beneath them were thousands upon thousands of their cheering people.

That picture was a symbol and emblem of the Empire's VE-Day rejoicings, which had culminated in the Prime Minister's broadcast of the end of the war in Europe.

Mr. Churchill had said, " We may allow ourselves a brief period of rejoicing "—the people were seeing to that already, " but let us not forget for a moment the toil and efforts that lie ahead," he warned.

Buckingham Palace and Whitehall were the magnets which drew multitudes of people.

They saw the Prime Minister go to lunch with Their Majesties at the Palace before making his historic pronouncement.

—And Again

They saw him again when, with the members of the War Cabinet and Chiefs of Staff, he was received by the King some hours later to receive his congratulations on victory.

All day Londoners, reinforced by many from the provinces, and by Service men and women of all nationalities had given a full rein to their rejoicing.

The King and Queen came on to the balcony again just before half-past midnight. A few minutes later the floodlights were switched off and gradually the crowds disappeared.

Police estimated that there were more than a quarter of a million people within a quarter mile of the Palace last night.

Garlanded with twinkling, coloured fairy lights, George Square was packed with crowds such as it has never seen before.

Nearly 100,000 people jostled, sang, danced, whistled, shouted, leapt on to passing buses, cars, taxicabs, tramcars, and formed " human chains " to guide them through the milling throng.

VE-NIGHT DELIGHT

Tramcars and buses were jammed. There were only inches to move around in. Men, women and children went delirious with pent-up VE-Night delight.

Almost one-tenth of Glasgow had come to George Square.

Young men and girls climbed on to statues to watch the historic scene. Gaily-clad in coloured paper hats, waving streamers, Union Jacks and Allied flags, the great Glasgow public " went to town " in real Victory spirit.

The police were not " killjoys." They warned a few people who were climbing dangerously high upon the Square's statues, but watched with benevolent eye two sailors on an air raid shelter throwing cigarettes with magnificent prodigality to the crowd beneath them.

And everywhere among the throng were the flag and favour sellers. Whatever else ran short in the city, their stocks seemed endless.

DANCE AND SONG

Where they could find room people danced eightsome reels and couples jitterbugged to the music that echoed through the square. Servicemen led rival groups in community singing.

A Dutch marine drew a large crowd in Exchange Square.

Perched on the equestrian statue in front of the Royal Exchange, he began with an imitation of Hitler, addressing a mob.

Then, in serious vein, he thanked the British people for all they had done for the Dutch, with a special tribute to Scots folk who had received them so kindly into their midst. He got a rousing cheer.

I watched the scene from a

Continued on Back Page, Col. 2

VICTORY, BUT JAPS REMAIN

IN their speeches yesterday both His Majesty the King and Mr. Churchill drew attention to the tasks that lie ahead.

The King said: " In the Far East we have yet to deal with the Japanese, a determined, cruel foe. To this we shall turn with the utmost resolve and with all our resources."

Mr. Churchill declared: " Japan remains unsubdued. The injury she has inflicted on Great Britain, the U.S. and other countries call for justice and retribution. We must now devote all our strength and resources to the completion of our task."

Much hard work awaits us, both in the restoration of our own country after the ravages of war, and in helping to restore peace and sanity to a shattered world.

This comes upon us at a time when we have all given of our best. For five long years and more, heart and brain, nerve and muscle, have been directed upon the overthrow of Nazi tyranny Now we turn, fortified by success, to deal with our last remaining foe.

King's Speech Page 2
Mr. Churchill Page 4

DANCING ON THE STREETS

Kemsley House The Mecca

KEMSLEY HOUSE, in Hope Street, Glasgow, was the Mecca of Glasgow's VE-Day celebrations, last night.

" The Daily Record " and " Evening News " provided the music from loud speakers wired along the gaily decorated and illuminated facade of the building, and the joyous crowd did the rest.

For hours they danced—not your master of ceremonied ballroom stuff, but real hard reeling and jigging on the tram lines. If the music was suitable, the crowd danced to it in rings or long wriggling lines; if it was not suitable, they just danced to their own yelling.

Pipe Music

But to see the crowd of sailors, soldiers, airmen, W.A.A.F.s, A.T.S., Wrens and 'civvies' of all types go really crackers you had to be there when the loud speakers gave out the pipe music, especially the reels.

Usually the dancers made way for the trams, buses and private vehicles good naturedly.

But not when there was an eightsome in the air. Glasgow, especially Hope Street, belonged to them so long as that music was on.

As the night went on the dancing became more and more hilarious.

Couples, especially sailors, even jumped on the drivers' platforms of cars and danced

No 'Daily Record' To-morrow

IN accordance with the expressed desire of the Government that workers generally should enjoy a VE-Day's holiday the " Daily Record " will not be published to-morrow, but will be out as usual on Friday.

The 'Evening News' has its holiday to-day but reappears to-morrow.

The 'Sunday Mail' will be published as usual.

A midnight flash: outside Kemsley House, and the cheering, dancing crowds are still there. Other pictures of scenes outside Kemsley House are on Pages 4 and 5.

Immaculate Dresswear
FOR ALL OCCASIONS.
Call, write or phone Central-
8527 for Brochure Price 1d
We do not buy second-hand
clothes, and offers of such
are only wasting our time
THE DORMIE
Menswear HIRE SERVICE
25-27 UNION ST., GLASGOW
37 Castle St, Edinburgh, and at Newcastle

Daily Record
and Mail

EST. 1895—No. 15,549   1d.   TUESDAY, AUGUST 7, 1945   A KEMSLEY NEWSPAPER

Ask by Name for—
George Webb
FOOTWEAR FOR MEN
MADE BY CRAFTSMEN IN NORTHAMPTON

"Greatest Scientific Gamble In History" Comes Off

ALLIES DROP FIRST ATOMIC BOMB ON JAPAN

Equal To 20,000 Tons Of T.N.T: Town Wiped Out At One Swoop

JAPAN HAS BEEN HIT WITH AN ATOMIC BOMB 2000 TIMES MORE POWERFUL THAN THE 10-TONNERS DROPPED BY THE R.A.F. ON GERMANY. PRESIDENT TRUMAN, DISCLOSING ITS USE YESTERDAY, SAID THAT EVEN MORE POWERFUL BOMBS ARE IN DEVELOPMENT

Sir Charles Darwin, one of the men who helped in the development of the Atomic Bomb. He was formerly Tait Professor of Natural Philosophy at Edinburgh University.

British and American scientists have been working on it for years out of reach of German long-range weapons. Hitler's V-1 and V-2 were the forerunners of the atomic bomb, but Germany lost the war before her scientists attained this goal.

President Truman described the bomb as "harnessing of the basic power of the universe The force from which the sun draws its power has been loosed against those who brought war to the Far East.

"**We have spent 2,000,000,000 dollars—about £500,000,000— on the greatest scientific gamble in history and we have won.**"

The first of the bombs which are to cast heavy shadows over the Land of the Rising Sun, was dropped 16 hours before the President's disclosure. It hit Hiroshima, the Jap army base west of Kobe.

MORE POWERFUL BOMBS COMING

President Truman said that two great plants and many lesser factories in the U.S. are devoted to the production of atomic power and have been working on it for more than 2½ years.

"**With this bomb we have now added a new and revolutionary increase in destruction to supplement the growing power of our armed forces,**" he said. "**In their present form these bombs are now in production and even more powerful forms are in development.**"

He also disclosed that Mr. Churchill and the late President Roosevelt agreed on the wisdom of carrying on atomic bomb manufacture in the U.S. out of reach of enemy bombing.

We Outpaced All German Efforts

BY God's mercy British and American science outpaced all German efforts, says Mr. Churchill's statement.

These were on a considerable scale, but far behind. The possession of these powers by the Germans at any time might have altered the result of the war, and profound anxiety was felt by those who were informed.

Every effort was made by our Intelligence Service and by the Air Force to locate in Germany anything resembling the plants which were being created in the U.S

100 Miles Of Devastation

EXPERIMENTS with the atomic bomb, one of which, according to Reuter, was dropped on Japan yesterday, were being carried out in Britain in August, 1941.

About the same time the Americans claimed an element had been developed which, if contained in a 10lb.-bomb, would wreck every structure within 100 miles.

The atomic bomb was to have been Hitler's V3 weapon, and but for a British and Norwegian paratroop raid on laboratories at Rjukan, Norway, in February, 1943, it would have been used.

ADVERTISER'S ANNOUNCEMENT.

Target Still Hid By Smoke

Washington, Monday.

ALLIED reconnaissance pilots were waiting to-day for an impenetrable cloud of smoke and dust to lift from Hiroshima to see the results of the first atomic bomb dropped on Japan this morning.

Many hours after the bomb was dropped the target area was still covered by the cloud, which alone indicates the bomb's incalculable destructive power.

Hiroshima, a town of 318,000 people, in south-west Honshu, is a big embarkation port and war supply depot. The town, with a congested port area, covers an area roughly four miles by three miles.

BOARDED-OUT BOY ARRESTED
Islay Farmer Shot

A SHOOTING incident took place at Ballychatrigan Farm, in the Oa district of the Island of Islay, just before midnight on Sunday, the injured man being Mr. Neil Sinclair, tenant of the farm.

In spite of his injuries, he was able to travel by car to a doctor in the village of Port Ellen, 5 miles away.

The police were called out and an 18-year-old boarded-out boy from Coatbridge, who came to the farm this year, was arrested.

HIS GUARDIAN

Mr. Sinclair was his guardian. He will make a first appearance before a Court at Bridgend, Islay, to-day.

Mr. Sinclair's injuries are not thought to be dangerous and he is at present at his father's farm, two miles from Ballychatrigan.

To-day's Weather
RAIN AT TIMES

Moderate northerly winds, cloudy with rain at times, rather cool.

Outlook:—Unsettled, showery weather.

With the atomic bomb in one sortie by one plane the same damage is expected to result as from five 1000-plane R.A.F. raids of the type levelled at Berlin, or from more than three raids by the great fleet of Super-Forts which dumped 6000 tons on Japan last week.

The "utter destruction" bombing thus begun will be added to the already great Continued on Back Page, Col. 1

Vital Metal

The vital radio-active metal needed in the making of the atom bomb was supplied by Canada—one of the world's richest s..ources of Uranium— to eke out American supplies of the material, it was disclosed last night.

The Canadian Government had taken over the Eldorado Mining and Smelting Company as part of the atom bomb programme.

"Before 1939 it was the accepted belief of scientists that it was theoretically possible to release atomic energy. But no one knew any practical method of doing it.

WE WON RACE

"By 1942, however, we knew the Germans were working feverishly to find a way to add atomic energy to other engines of war with which they hoped to enslave the world; but they failed.

"We may be grateful to Providence that the Germans got V1s and V2s late and in limited quantities, and even more grateful that they did not get the atomic bomb at all.

"The battle of the laboratories held fateful risks for us as well as the battle of the air, land and sea, and we have now won the battle of the laboratories as we have won other battles.

"Before Pearl Harbour, scientific knowledge useful in war was pooled between the U.S. and Britain and many priceless helps to our victories have come from the arrangement.

"£500,000,000 GAMBLE"

"Under that general policy, research on the atomic bomb was begun. With American and British scientists working together, we entered the race of discovery against the Germans."

Stating that more than 125,000 persons worked to construct atomic bomb factories in the U.S., the President said that over 65,000 individuals were now engaged at the operating plants.

"Many have worked there for 2½ years Few know what they have been producing. They see great quantities of materials going in and they see

Continued on Back Page, Col. 3

See
ATOMIC
"BRAINS TRUST"
AND OTHER STORIES
Page 3

SHE'S PROUD OF HIS
magnesia smile...

He's got that sparkling smile that mother loves to see! She makes sure that he keeps his teeth clean, healthy and free from discoloration by regular use of Phillips' Dental Magnesia, the one toothpaste containing 'Milk of Magnesia'*, which corrects mouth acid, so often the cause of dental trouble.

Children use Phillips' Dental Magnesia gladly because it leaves the mouth feeling clean, and they love its flavour. Sold everywhere. 1/1 & 1/10½d.

Phillips'
Dental Magnesia

* Milk of Magnesia' is the trade mark of Phillips' preparation of magnesia.

Wounded Service men and women from Hairmyres and Erskine Hospitals were recently entertained to a trip round the Three Lochs by girls of the Scottish Youths' Hostel Association. Here at Auchendennan Hostel, one of the girls serves tea.

'DORMIE'
Menswear
HIRE SERVICE.
Call write or phone
CENtral 4462/4463 for copy
of Illustrated Brochure
W. J. Thomson & Son
25-27 UNION ST
GLASGOW
37 Castle St. Edinburgh
13 Blackett St. Newcastle

Daily Record
and Mail

EST. 1895—No. 15,908   1d.   TUESDAY, OCTOBER 1, 1946   A KEMSLEY NEWSPAPER

Exclusively for Men
George Webb
FOOTWEAR
MADE BY CRAFTSMEN IN NORTHAMPTON

Goering Knows His Fate To-day

Jews Save Ship From 'Frogmen'

Jerusalem, Monday.

FRIENDLY Jews — whose identity will not be revealed by the police for fear of instant reprisals by terrorists —have foiled a plot to blow up a Royal Navy destroyer while refuelling at Haifa docks.

The Jews found an electric cable running from the quay into the sea and, after cutting the cable, warned the police.

FIVE ARRESTED

A diver followed the broken cable for 80 yards, and found it attached to a canister filled with explosives weighing 50lbs. and clamped to a pile of the jetty under water.

Five Jews, believed to be the crew of an oil barge moored a few yards from the jetty, have been arrested.

The police believe that Zionist "frogmen" who, using a limpet mine, recently attacked and holed the Empire Rival—used for transporting illegal immigrants to Cyprus— are responsible for the attempt.

Ellen Back

Miss Ellen Wilkinson, Minister of Education, returned to London from Prague, last night.

He Sums Up

Lord Justice Lawrence reading part of the judgment at yesterday's dramatic sitting of the court.

Judgment Day No. 2

Curtain Falls At Nuremberg

NUREMBERG, MONDAY.

AT 9.30 TO-MORROW MORNING HERMANN GOERING WILL STEP FOR THE LAST TIME INTO THE DOCK AT NUREMBERG AND HEAR THE WORDS THAT WILL DECIDE HIS FATE.

The finding on his guilt or innocence will be the first of the series the Judges will read dealing with the 21 individual Nazis in the dock, and absent Martin Bormann.

The verdicts are expected to take up the whole morning of Judgment Day Number Two. Then after a short recess the ten months old drama of Nuremberg will mount to its climax as one by one the defendants face the judges and hear sentence pronounced.

When the first of the two days of judgment ended to-night many of the men in the dock showed signs of strain.

All day in the packed, flood-lit courtroom—which maintained its dignity despite spectators sweeping its length with powerful binoculars — they had listened to the intoning of the judgment against Nazi organisations.

KEITEL AND JODL

They had heard the decision that the German High Command and General Staff would not be declared criminal.

But they had also heard— Wilhelm Keitel, once supreme armed forces commander, and Alfred Jodl, ex-Chief of Staff of the Wehrmacht, sitting poker-backed and emotionless the while—that evidence of criminality against many of the members was clear and convincing. That "they had been a disgrace to the honourable profession of arms."

The spotlight shone, too, on others in the dock as the judges intoned 55,000 words, product of painstaking research.

NAZI PARTY'S OBJECTIVE

The judgment declared that aggressive war had been established beyond all doubt as the Nazi Party's objective since its formation 25 years ago.

(See Page 5)

A-Bomb Can't Be Outlawed

"IF war on a global scale should come again, then the atomic bomb will undoubtedly be used whatever rules or laws have been made against it.

"If the atomic bomb is made and stored up so that countries can be ready for eventualities, then sooner or later somebody will pull the trigger and the atomic bomb war will begin."

This warning was given at Birmingham last night by atom expert Prof. M. L. E. Oliphant, who declared that one A-bomb on Birmingham would kill at least 50,000 people, while 100 atomic bombs would wipe out the productive capacity of Britain.

OUNCE OF NEW POISON COULD KILL MILLIONS

From a "Daily Record" Correspondent

Schenectady, New York. Monday.

A NEW "super poison"—so deadly that an ounce of it could kill 180 million people, or the entire populations of the United States and Canada — has been developed by the U.S. Chemical Warfare Service.

Announcement of the poison —the most potent known to man—was made by Dr. Gerald Wendt, of New York City.

He stated:—"If World War III comes, it will be a war in which most people may die from silent, insidious, anti-human weapons that make no sound, give no warning, destroy no ships or cities, but can wipe out human beings by the millions."

ONE OF MANY

The "super poison" is an innocent looking crystallised toxin prepared by the Special Projects Division of the Chemical Warfare Service during World War II.

Dr. Wendt classified the new poison as only one of many new biological weapons

£109 "SNATCHED"

Glasgow C.I.D. were early to-day investigating a complaint of a "snatch" from a customer in a Gorbals public-house last night. It was reported to them that the man had his pocket picked — and had lost £109

ADVERTISER'S ANNOUNCEMENT

FIGHT AGAINST SMOKE IN CITY BLAZE

EIGHT fire brigades were turned out early this morning to fight an outbreak in the laboratory workshops of Taylor's the chemists at 124 Trongate.

Smoke from the fire screened a large stretch of Argyle Street and firemen were at first unable to reach the seat of the blaze owing to thick choking fumes.

The outbreak was discovered by Joseph Duncan Halley, a passer-by, who noticed the first wreaths of smoke coming from the building shortly before three o'clock and broke a nearby alarm.

The premises are situated just off Argyle Street and are surrounded by high buildings on three sides.

Firemen eventually managed to get about a dozen lines of hose trained on the seat of the fire which, despite their efforts continued to grow quickly and fiercely.

"Jimmy" Finds His Father

LYING in hospital, a Greenock man yesterday identified a two-year-old boy who had travelled with the police from Glasgow, as his son. The child was found last week crawling out of a tenement close in Washington Street, Glasgow.

From there, he was removed to the Marine Police Office in Partick, and then to Cleveden Home, Kelvinside, where the little boy, temporarily christened "Jimmy"—the only name to which he would answer—was cared for.

Glasgow Police were at pains to trace the parents of the child, and the search led to Greenock where the boy's father claimed him.

British Quit The Lebanon

Last British troops in the Lebanon left yesterday for Egypt by way of Palestine.

A Lebanese Army detachment gave a farewell salute to the troops at the Palestine border.

Seven British representatives will later return to the Lebanon with civilian status to make certain payments to War Department employees.

TO-DAY'S WEATHER

Cold And Rain

S.E. and S.W. Scotland:— Light to moderate winds between south and east, fresh locally, occasional rain and showers, long fair periods, rather cold.

Outlook:— Unsettled, with occasional rain or showers.

Some Went Hiking—

The Sun Recorder Told Me

By a "Daily Record" Reporter

"AH'M fair burning up right now," remarked the sun-recorder on top of the water tower at Springburn Park, highest point in Glasgow.

"And it's rage, not heat that's making me smoulder," it added. "Imagine me working on a public holiday. It's a disgrace. Here Ah was, all set for a day off like the rest o' the Glasgow folk. With the rain belting down in the morning, it looked all set.

"But at five to three Old Sollie has to take it into his head that he wants to see Clyde beat Third Lanark. Out he comes and bang up the spout goes my holiday."

I had chosen a bad moment to interview it.

It was 4.40 p.m. The round shiny face of the recorder wore an unhappy beam. The sun was still out. Its rays, striking through the instrument's glass ball, was burning a thin brown line on the sensitised cardboard chart, marked off in hours and half-hours, which is daily changed, measured and logged. (Picture on right)

But the sun-recorder admits that it's not been working its passage this summer. "Lately I've been worried in case I'd find myself out of a job. Only four dry days this month, and 6¾in. of rain, not counting to-day."

I asked its opinion of the weather experts "Och them!"

—Others Worked

Back again

'CRUNCHIE,' the bar with a delicious flavour all its own. Crisp, golden honeycomb centre, double-covered with two fine blended chocolates.

price 3d. a bar
2 points

FRY'S for good chocolate

D662

Daily Record
and Mail.

EST. 1895.　No. 16,263　THURSDAY, NOVEMBER 20, 1947　A KEMSLEY NEWSPAPER　1d.

Wedding morning smiles from Princess Elizabeth and H.R.H. the Duke of Edinburgh. To-day they become husband and wife.

As Duke Of Edinburgh He Weds Elizabeth

IT will be as His Royal Highness the Duke of Edinburgh that Lieutenant Philip Mountbatten will drive to Westminster Abbey this morning to wed Princess Elizabeth.

In private at Buckingham Palace yesterday, the King gave his son-in-law to be the titles of Duke of Edinburgh, Earl of Merioneth, and Baron Greenwich.

After the wedding the designations will be "H.R.H. the Princess Elizabeth and H.R.H. The Duke of Edinburgh."

The King touched Lieut. Mountbatten on each shoulder with a naked sword, as he knelt before him in the ceremony of the Accolade of Knighthood, and invested him with the insignia of the Order of the Garter, the same great Order which he had given only a few days earlier to Princess Elizabeth.

EVERYONE DELIGHTED

Told of Lieut. Mountbatten's title, Lord Provost Murray of Edinburgh, who is in London, told the "Daily Record":—

"I am naturally delighted. It is what we have been hoping for —not only in Edinburgh, but in the whole of Scotland. I am sure that everyone will be delighted.

"This will strengthen further the ties between the whole of Scotland and the Royal House."

From this day forward

AT midday, they will be married. And history, written in the Abbey, will echo by radio across the world.

For to-day, the weather may be dull and foggy or rainy and cool. But no weather can damp the enthusiasm of London —or the world—on this romantic morning. Already, last night, a kind of happy frenzy was in the air in London's crowded streets.

CROWDS CHEER

The King and Queen with Princess Elizabeth and the Duke of Edinburgh (on left) appeared on the balcony of the floodlit Palace just before eight o'clock. The King and Queen and the two Princesses appeared again at 10.30 after thousands of people packed tightly outside the gates had shouted "We want the bride" and cheered for hours.

HAPPY

FAMILIES

HAVE THE

COCOA

HABIT

CADBURYS
BOURNVILLE COCOA

Bailey's
Quality Wine Merchants

GLASGOW. EDINBURGH
PAISLEY, GREENOCK.
HAMILTON. AYR.
IRVINE, TROON.

 # Daily ✸ Record *and Mail.*

ESTABLISHED 1895. No. 16,571   MONDAY, NOVEMBER 15, 1948   A KEMSLEY NEWSPAPER 1d.

Best known
—best liked
BIRD'S
CUSTARD

SON IS BORN TO PRINCESS

IT was officially announced from Buckingham Palace last night: "Her Royal Highness the Princess Elizabeth, Duchess of Edinburgh, was safely delivered of a Prince at 9.14 p.m. to-day.

"Her Royal Highness and her son are both doing well."

Sir Alan Lascelles at once telephoned the news to the Home Secretary. He filled the missing word on previously prepared telegrams which went at once from the Court Post Office in code to the Governors-General overseas.

And expectant Britain heard the joyful news of the birth of a child to the Princess and Prince, whose romance had thrilled the world.

(New baby second in succession, Page 2)

CROWD: "GOOD OLD PHILIP"

The other baby...

EIGHTEEN-YEAR-OLD Mrs Muriel Mathieson, 3 Union Glen, Aberdeen, gave birth to a baby boy at exactly the same time as Princess Elizabeth at Aberdeen Maternity Hospital. This was her first baby.

Mother and son are doing well. Mother and members of the staff were thrilled when they heard the announcement of the birth of the infant prince at the same time.

One other baby—a girl—was born 26 minutes later.

ANNOUNCEMENT of the birth was made to the crowds outside Buckingham Palace by a blue-liveried Royal page, who walked out from the Privy Purse door to the gates, where he told the police constable, who relayed the news to the crowds. At once there was a cheer and a great shout, "Good Old Philip."

Telephone calls went out immediately from the Palace to Queen Mary at Marlborough House and to Princess Margaret, who is spending the week-end with the Earl and Countess of Scarborough at Retford.

As soon as she received the news Queen Mary ordered her car to drive to Buckingham Palace to see her first great-grandchild.

ROYAL VIGIL

While the crowd waited outside Buckingham
Palace last night for the news of the Royal birth, the sentry on duty marched on im perturbably.

Queen Mary in an evening gown with a white fur wrap had a tremendous welcome from the crowds when she drove in through the Palace gates just after 10.30. She was at once shown up to the

Cont'd Back Page, Col. 1

"It's a son," Duke was told

THE DUKE OF EDINBURGH was told by the doctors that he had a son and he went in to see his wife before she had recovered from the anaesthetic.

Immediately afterwards he went in to see his son.

KING SHOOK HANDS

A few minutes later the Duke brought the King and Queen to see their grandson. The Queen embraced him and the King shook hands warmly with his son-in-law when he told them the news.

The Duke opened a bottle of champagne and with members of his staff drank to the health of the new Prince.

Bells Of Dundee

To-day the bells of Dundee's 300-year-old steeple will peal for half an hour.

"A leader of peace," is the Danish hope

"LET us hope the little child will lead a generation which will maintain peace in the world," said the Danish Prime Minister, Mr. Hans Hedtoft, when the birth was announced in Copenhagen.

Rumours were circulating that King Frederick would be invited to be the boy's godfather, but there was no confirmation.

Mrs. Fanny Jensen, officially Minister Without Portfolio but unofficially "Minister for housewives and children." and the only woman Cabinet Minister in Denmark, said, "I hope the child will be as loved by the English people as by his mother."

VERY HAPPY

Prince Viggo, of Denmark, second cousin to the Duke of Edinburgh, is abroad, but his American-born wife, Eleanor, said on receiving the news: "Oh, I am so glad. We are very happy."

New York radio stations broke into their programmes with the glad news.

EIRE LEADERS FOR PARIS

MR. SEAN MACBRIDE, Eire Minister for External Affairs; Mr Pat McGilligan, Minister for Finance; and Senator Cecil Lavery, Attorney-General, will meet members of the British, Australian, Canadian, and New Zealand Governments in Paris, to-day, for further discussions on questions arising in connection with the proposed Eire Bill to repeal the External Relations Act.

The Bill is down for first reading in the Dail on Wednesday.

The Eire leaders go to Paris on the invitation of the British Commonwealth representatives.

FURNISHING for XMAS ...

or Gift-hunting
for friends...
here's your answer!

FREE! *Post now for your copy of Smarts Special Christmas Catalogue showing how you can furnish in time for Xmas and find worthwhile gifts for yourself and friends. Magnificent suites, occasional furniture, radios, kitchen goods, mattresses, everything for the home and 24-month credit terms if you wish.*

Mr./Mrs./Miss _____

Address _____

A Smarts fireside chair de-luxe. New tension springing. Unbelievably comfortable £7.4.3

SMARTS 40/48 UNION STREET, GLASGOW, C.1
(Branches throughout Britain)
125M

BEAUTIFUL ballito STOCKINGS

Sunday Mail

Scotland's National Sunday Newspaper

No 2132.   JULY 31, 1949.   A KEMSLEY NEWSPAPER.   2d.

Ellis Island —The Facts
PAGE SEVEN

-improves all meals
HP SAUCE

"God Save The King" Flash To Admiralty

"AMETHYST" DASHES TO FREEDOM

The Signal

"Rejoined the fleet. No damage or casualties. God save the King."

This dramatic eleven words signal was flashed from the Amethyst to the Admiralty in London last night.

—And The Replies

LAST night Mr. Attlee radioed a message of congratulation to Amethyst's officers and men.

The message to the C-in-C Far Eastern station began: "Personal from Prime Minister. I will be grateful if you would pass the following to the Amethyst: 'My congratulations to Commanding Officer and crew of Amethyst for their gallant exploit.'"

Admiration

A signal was also sent from the Board of Admiralty to the commander-in-chief and to the Admiralty reading: "All our admiration goes to you and to Amethyst."

The Commander-in-Chief Far Eastern Station made this signal: "Welcome back to the Fleet.

"We are all extremely proud of your most gallant and skilful escape and that the endurance and fortitude displayed by everyone has been rewarded with such success.

"Your bearing in adversity and your daring passage will be an epic in the history of the Navy."

It was telegraphist Jack Leonard French, one of the Amethyst heroes — he was awarded the D.S.M. for outstanding devotion to duty in April when, single-handed, he kept the ship in touch with the rest of the world—who flashed to the Admiralty the dramatic news of the Amethyst's escape.

Record Crowds On Holiday

By "Sunday Mail" Reporter

SCOTTISH railway staffs will remember yesterday for a long time. As August holidaymakers packed the departing trains, returning July trippers arrived in crowded trains operating the biggest shuttle service between cities and holiday resorts.

Glasgow bore the brunt of the great holiday clash. Returning July holidaymakers had to battle their way through lengthy queues stretching from almost every station platform to the streets. And for every crowded train that arrived, an equally crowded one left.

Polish Consul Hit By Tomatoes

When Mr. Stanislaw Teliga, Polish Consul-General in Glasgow, visited a Polish boys' school in Glasgow, he was pelted with tomatoes by the students, according to Mr. John J. Campbell, Glasgow lawyer, who demanded in Edinburgh yesterday that Mr. Teliga should be recalled from Scotland.

Mr. Campbell, President of the Scottish Polish Society, said it was highly desirable that Mr. Teliga should be recalled.

Shelled Again, But Crew Safe

THE sloop Amethyst, captive of the Chinese Communists since April, broke away yesterday in the Yangtse under heavy shore battery fire and rejoined the Fleet.

The story was told in a naval statement issued in the name of Sir Patrick Brind, Commander-in-Chief in the Far East, who announced that the Amethyst had slipped her cables "in defiance of her jailers" and had escaped down river under heavy fire from the shore batteries.

She was fired upon again at the Kiangyin Forts, where she had to negotiate a boom and a treacherous part of the river.

A naval statement issued last night said the Amethyst was proceeding without the help of a pilot, and by skilful navigation was proceeding down the Yangtse.

It is believed in Hongkong that one or more British warships went to the mouth of the Yangtse to meet the Amethyst, but naval headquarters would give no information.

"Our Hopes Are High"

Earlier, the Commander-in-Chief's statement said:—"Our hopes are high, and all are indeed proud of her feat, she still has dangers to negotiate."

The Amethyst ran aground on April 20 after she was hit by shells from a Communist shore battery in the Yangtse River. She had been threatened by Communist guns ever since.

In the first attack 17 were killed and 20 wounded. When she was hit she was steaming upriver to Nanking from Shanghai to relieve the destroyer Consort.

During her three months isolation when the Amethyst was held by the Chinese Communists as a proof that the Royal Navy's power had waned, the courage and determination of the 60 officers and ratings never wavered.

After Lieut.-Commander Skinner, the commander, was killed in the first bombardment, Lieut.-Commander Kerans reached the ship from Nanking to take command and later Lieut. Geoffrey Weston, who was awarded the D.S.C. for taking command, although badly wounded after his captain's death, returned to the ship by train from Shanghai this month.

Battles With Reds

Attempts to reach the Amethyst by other naval craft resulted in major battles with the Communist shore batteries, and the cruiser London, the sloop Black Swan and the destroyer Consort brought British naval casualties to more than 40 dead.

While the ships attempting rescue were driven back by Communist fire the Amethyst was able to move further up river out of range of shore batteries and anchored off Chang Sang Chau Island.

All the badly wounded were landed, and on April 22 she was able to report that she believed herself capable of 17 knots.

Ten days ago the Communists guarding the sloop refused to free her from the trap until Britain "admitted responsibility" for the April shelling.

After a hold-up lasting several days the Communists allowed 17 cases of stores, including medical supplies, cigarettes and magazines to go aboard.

The Amethyst's crew had been on half rations since the beginning of July.

M.P.s Prepare T.V. Campaign

By J. D MARGACH

THE campaign by Scots M.P.s to compel the Government, the Post Office and the B.B.C. to give a square deal to Scotland in television, will be stepped-up in the autumn.

M.P.s are likely to convene a private meeting to consider how most effectively the agitation and pressure can be organised.

When Parliament reassembles. I understand the following moves will be considered:—

Ask the Government if the P.O. cannot speed up television for Scotland to allow commercial interests to develop a service for Scotland, or

Press the Government to increase the allocation of money to the B.B.C. for television development, so that a Scottish station and organisation can be developed much more rapidly.

They were angry and disappointed at the Assistant Postmaster-General's reply in the House of Commons yesterday when he said that priorities of expenditure must go to essential services, and vindicated the Government over any charge of television neglect by saying it was up to the B.B.C.

(Television Can Save The Highlands—Page Three.)

Sir Stafford May Be Home Sooner

Sir Stafford Cripps is progressing so favourably that his treatment may not take the six weeks expected, says Dr. Dagmar Liechti, senior woman physician of the Bircher-Benner clinic.

The camouflaged Amethyst which slipped her cables "in defiance of her jailers" and has now rejoined the Far East fleet.

19 HURT WHEN HOLIDAY TRAIN HITS BUFFERS

A ROTHESAY boat train, loaded with returning holidaymakers, skidded on the wet lines and crashed into the buffers at Platform 13 in the Central Station, Glasgow, yesterday. Five ambulances took 19 people to Glasgow Royal Infirmary.

Passengers, preparing to leave the train, were thrown across compartments, and many were struck by heavy luggage jerked off the racks.

Many passengers received treatment for shock, bruises and slight cuts at a first-aid station set up on the platform by ambulance men.

The driver and fireman were uninjured.

Only two of the 19 injured were detained at the infirmary and neither is seriously hurt. They are:—Mrs. Ina Grey, 5 Leubeggs Crescent, Bonnybridge (head injuries), and Mrs. Knowles, 15 Clyde Street, Port-Glasgow (head injuries).

"Screaming With Fright"

The train involved was the 4.30 p.m. from Gourock.

One of the passengers, Mrs Betty Pellow, 34 Greenside Cres., Millerston, who was returning from holiday with her two children, told a "Sunday Mail" reporter:—

"I was just rising to get the luggage from the rack when there was a terrific jolt.

"We could hear passengers in other compartments screaming with fright.

Speedway Fans Hurt In Smash

SPEEDWAY fans were among the 15 injured passengers taken to Edinburgh Royal Infirmary late last night after a bus in which they were travelling back from the Meadowbank track turned over in a crash with another bus at Cameron. Toll Dalkeith, Road, Edinburgh. No one, it is believed, was badly hurt.

"No Fear"—Attlee

"We have a fine policy which we can put out without fear to the country and that is a continuation of the work that has been done." said Mr. Attlee, replying to Mr. Churchill's address last Saturday, in a speech at Walthamstow. London, yesterday. *(Speech—Page 3.)*

Wot, No Sun?

NO beach-wear for the holiday-makers to-day. Rain is forecast for most areas of Scotland, with fresh to strong winds as an additional discomfort. Temperatures will be around 55 to 60.

Jet Wins By A Second

SQUADRON-LEADER NEVILLE DUKE, piloting one of Britain's latest hush-hush jet warplanes, the Hawker P1040, yesterday snatched a thrilling second victory in the air race for the Kemsley Trophy at Elmdon, Birmingham.

With a tremendous burst of speed he screamed down to the finishing line, flashed past the six other competitors, and just beat Group-Captain J. Cunningham in a De Havilland Vampire, the other jet entry.

Harry Drake's Report—Page 2

VOLCANO MENACE

A new crater, throwing up thick masses of lava at a great rate, opened yesterday on the Canary Island of Palma, Madrid radio reported.

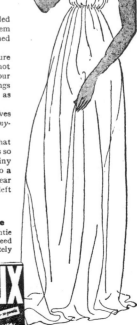
"The Lux look is enchanting!" say the under-25's

THE younger generation are thrilled by the Lux Look. It's new to them —they'd never used Lux till it returned after the war.

Now they say: "We're making sure we wash the Lux way every time, not just any old way. Lux is safe for all our fine things—precious undies, stockings and woollies stay fresh and dainty as new for ages.

"Lux is safe for hands too, leaves them beautifully soft and white. Anything safe in water is safe in Lux."

Besides, they have found out that Lux makes the washing of fine things so easy! Even in lukewarm water the tiny Lux diamonds dissolve instantly into a rich creamy lather. And there's no fear of undissolved particles being left behind.

Bewitching at Bedtime

This dainty, new nylon-mesh nightie doesn't need ironing—but it does need delicate Lux care. The exquisitely feminine frills and gossamer material call for the safe, gentle action of Lux. Lux suds—rich, pure, penetrating—can be relied on to remove every trace of dirt, from precious fabrics.

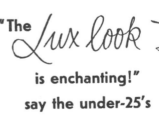
LUX

A LEVER PRODUCT

BEAUTIFUL ballito STOCKINGS

Sunday Mail

Scotland's National Sunday Newspaper

No. 2146. NOVEMBER 6, 1949   A KEMSLEY NEWSPAPER. 2d.

THE ANGRY HIGHLANDERS
Page Seven

-improves all meals.
HP SAUCE

Gardener, aged 61, Saved zoo's head keeper

HE BEAT OFF TIGRESS WITH A SHOVEL

A BENGAL tigeress escaped from her cage at Calderpark Zoo, Glasgow, yesterday, after severely mauling the head keeper, who was reported by Glasgow Royal Infirmary early this morning to be "as well as could be expected."

The man who beat off the tigress is a 61-year-old gardener who twice attacked the animal with a shovel.

The tigress, 10-year-old Sheila, was eventually shot by the Director of the Zoo and his assistant.

Fortunately, no visitors were near the cages when the animal broke loose. Thirty children with a teacher were 100 yards away, and were unaware of any incident until they heard the rifle shots.

Dum-dum bullets

The keeper, 30-year-old John Duffy, of 146 Second Avenue, Birkenshaw, Uddingston, was working in an exercise cage. The tigress came through from her adjoining cage by a communicating door and leapt on Duffy's back.

The keeper scrambled to his feet, but was mauled about the face and head. He escaped through the small doorway into a safety corridor, but the tigress bounded after him.

Duffy's cries and the animal's snarls were heard by gardener Alex. Innes, of Uddingston.

He ran to the safety fence, grabbing up a shovel.

"I brought it down heavily on the beast's head," Innes told a "Sunday Mail" reporter.

"It reeled slightly, but retained its hold on Duffy. As I struck again Duffy pulled himself free and scrambled across the safety fence into the courtyard."

Duffy stumbled and fell. The tigress leapt towards him.

"I crossed the fence and struck the animal repeatedly on the head with the shovel," said Innes.

The tigress rolled over on her side. Innes stood over her with shovel upraised until two men with rifles approached. He backed away, and Sheila was shot dead.

The marksmen were Mr. S. H. Benson, the Zoo director, and Overseer John Crawford, who had run from the Zoo office when they heard the roaring of other animals.

Both had rifles filled with dum dum bullets. Their first two shots—from about 15 yards—hit the tigress. They closed in until seven bullets had found their mark.

Duffy is being treated at the Royal Infirmary for multiple wounds to the head, face and shoulders and for severe shock.

Sheila, the only tigress in

Tigress Came Through Here To Attack

Keeper Left Here With Tigress In Pursuit

Where Innes Leapt Over Safety Fence To Assist

Alec Innes with the shovel with which he tackled the tigress (top right).

Scotland, was worth over £400. She was gifted to the zoo 18 months ago by Glasgow Corporation.

Circus Cry of Dread—Page Nine.

Falkirk murder: Clothing find

C.I.D. men investigating the Falkirk brickworks murder are checking on clothing, stained apparently with blood, which was uncovered last night in a Falkirk backyard.

A minute examination is being made of a jacket, a pair of trousers and a cap.

A man feeding his hens noticed part of a garment protruding from a hole in the ground. He discovered the clothing and immediately notified Falkirk police headquarters.

The hen-run, although in the back garden, is easily accessible. It adjoins a field and is separated only by a low fence.

Detectives have been working night and day since the murder three weeks ago of Miss Mary Terris in the office of the isolated Rough Castle brickworks near Camelon.

Their main clue, so far, is an iron bar, known as a "pit-jumper," which was the murder weapon.

Manhunt after car crash

Police from radio-equipped patrol cars were searching waste land near Dalmarnock Bridge, Glasgow, early this morning, for three occupants of a shooting brake which had somersaulted into a sand quarry.

Police cars had been seeking a stolen shooting brake seen near the scene of a burglary at a shop in Cleveden Road, Glasgow.

It was last seen near Dalmarnock Bridge, and Lanarkshire patrol cars continued the search from Glasgow boundary.

LADY IRENE ESCAPES POACHER'S BULLET

LADY IRENE HELEN CRAWFURD of Foich, Lochbroom, Wester Ross, yesterday missed death by inches when a bullet, believed to have been fired by a poacher, passed through the windscreen of her car on the main Garve-Ullapool road.

Scotland Yard have been called in.

The shooting took place when Lady Crawfurd, her husband, Captain C. C. Crawfurd, and owners of other estates in the area set out on an early-morning patrol, to look for poachers who have been troublesome.

Lady Crawfurd last night told the "Sunday Mail": "As we drove up the road, my husband thought he saw a man on the skyline 500 yards away. I was driving, and he told me to pull up."

Lady Crawfurd said that they were accompanied in the car by their stalker and two others.

"As I stopped the car, the men made off up the hill in pursuit of this figure. I drove on about half a mile along the narrow road to turn the car at a quarry.

"When turning I heard a

shot and a bullet passed through the windscreen six inches from my head.

"I jumped out as the windscreen collapsed, and hid behind the car thinking another shot might be fired."

Describing events leading up to the incident, Captain Crawfurd said that for weeks past estate owners in the area had been banding together to patrol their properties because of organised big-scale poaching.

"Deer and sheep have been disappearing and recently a sheep was found shot. How many have been taken away we cannot estimate, but one farmer has lost fifty," Capt. Crawfurd said.

"Well over a dozen poachers, armed with rifles are operating almost every day of the week and removing their kill in cars."

Ross-shire C.I.D. are searching the district.

A-blast to end Siberia desert

RUSSIA is to blast a channel between two mountain ranges in Siberia and reverse the direction of two rivers by means of atomic energy to create a new fertile "garden" territory, the size of France, it was announced yesterday in "Nacht Express," a Soviet-licensed publication in Berlin.

It will be located 1500 miles from Moscow between the Urals and the Kazak mountains.

The plan will turn the Karakum desert and the Siberian depression into gardens which will "show the world what a peace-loving people can do with atomic energy."

Pension "Insult"

Swansea branch of the British Legion is to take up the complaint of Mrs. Edith Thomas, a widow, of Landore, Glamorgan, who described as an insult the 5s pension given to her for the loss of her son, Ordinary Seaman Glyn Thomas, who was killed in the Amethyst.

S O S Cancelled

The 7000-ton British motor vessel Scottish Prince, built at Burntisland, radioed from mid-Atlantic last night cancelling a six-hours-old urgent distress call made when her engines broke down. The 34,000-ton Cunard White Star liner Caronia was on her way to the crippled ship.

Cut Off By Gale

A gale in North-West Scotland has cut off several lighthouses. Attempts to reach the lighthouses have been abandoned until the seas moderate. Inland, there was considerable flooding.

"I'm the cheery Welgar Boy
Who stands for Shredded Wheat
When I'm on view,
I promise you,
There's something good to eat!"

"Try this two-in-one breakfast treat!"

COLD CEREAL Welgar Shredded Wheat makes a wonderful all-weather breakfast. In mild weather, serve Welgar with cold milk and sugar. You'll love its golden crispness and all-wheat flavour.

HOT CEREAL Crumble two Welgar biscuits into a saucepan, add a pinch of salt, and enough water to cover the bottom of the pan. Boil, and stir till thick. Serve with sugar and a little milk.

WELGAR SHREDDED WHEAT
12 extra-large biscuits for 8d.

Free Recipe Booklet! Send to:— Dept. M.5, The Shredded Wheat Company Limited, Welwyn Garden City, Herts.

BEAUTIFUL
ballito
STOCKINGS

Sunday Mail

Scotland's National Sunday Newspaper

No. 2153.   DECEMBER 25, 1949   A KEMSLEY NEWSPAPER.   2d.

A Merry
Christmas
To You!

Pluto
SOUTH AFRICAN
SHERRY
Perfect for the Festive
Season!

Oh, What A Wonderful Morning!

Photograph by Robert Campbell, "Sunday Mail" Staff photographer.

They SHARE THE £350

MRS MOLLY ROSS, 21 Latta Crescent, Cumnock, joint winner of last week's "Sunday Mail" Fashion Contest, very nearly did not enter.

With her mother, Mrs Jacobina Bryce, she has been competing for over a year, but last Sunday she had been away for the day and did not come home until late evening. It was only when her mother reminded her that she decided to fill in her entry.

"The best Christmas I could have had," was Mrs Ross's comment when told of her good fortune yesterday.

This is the first prize she has ever won in a competition.

Her husband, Mr. Archie Ross, is a Western S.M.T. bus driver.

The prize money will be banked.

A "Sunday Mail" reporter who told Miss E. McLaughlin, c/o Wavy, 85 Holmscross Street, Greenock, that she had won £175, was welcomed as a real Santa Claus.

Miss McLaughlin is an assistant in a Greenock draper's shop.

May is nobody's baby—but Santa didn't forget to call...

By A "Sunday Mail" Reporter

THIS is the story of May Queen. May is only eight months old so she could hardly be expected to know about Santa Claus. She woke up this morning ready to announce to the world that she was hungry.

Then something caught her eye. Eager baby hands reached out and a cuddly doll was clasped tightly to her. The urgent cry did not come. Instead, there was a contented gurgle.

Story In A Name

No different from the scene in thousands of homes? Maybe not—except that May IS different.

Take a look at her name again—May Queen. A nice name for a pretty golden-haired baby, but more than that, it really tells May's short life-story.

It was on a dark, dirty morning last May that a railway cleaner opened the door of a train compartment in sooty Queen Street Station, Glasgow, and found a newly-born child lying on the cushions.

Her parents were never found.

Doctors saved her life, and she was handed over to Glasgow Corporation Children's Department.

To-day she is in Castlemilk Residential Home, the house where Mary Queen of Scots spent the night after the Battle of Langside.

Her first Christmas Day will be as merry as any child's in Britain. She will be dressed in a new suit of woollies sent by an anonymous donor, and, weather permitting, will be taken for a long ride in her pram by a nurse.

May is one of 400 orphans, foundlings and cast-off children. Each one represents a tragic human story. But they are all happy to-day.

They have toys, books, games, parties, lots to eat and kindly folk to care for them.

They have been deprived of a mother's care, but everything that can be done to make it up to them is all in a day's work to the workers at 266 George Street, headquarters of the Children's Department.

A Grubby Letter

What could be more touching than the faith of this little boy, who was recently sent to a private home in the East of Scotland after being brought up in Glasgow by the Department.

A week or so ago a grubby envelope was handed in to Mr. R. Brough, Glasgow Children's Officer.

It was addressed:—Mr. Santa Claus, George Street 266, Glasgow.

The letter inside, written in wavering print nearly an inch high, read:—"Please send me a train set. I am 6. Thank you. Donald ——." Below were neatly inscribed 10 "X's."

To-day Donald will be playing with his new train set. Perhaps 266 George Street is not a bad address for Santa Claus...

YOUR NE'ERDAY SUNDAY MAIL

THE "Sunday Mail" will be published on New Year's Day.

Special features will include:—

RT. HON. THOMAS JOHNSTON, ex-Secretary of State for Scotland, will answer the question: "Have we really progressed in the past 50 years?"

F. SHERWOOD TAYLOR, Curator of the Museum of the History of Science, Oxford, forecasts the life we will lead fifty years from now.

JOHN ALLAN, the famous Scottish sports writer, looks back over 50 years of football in Scotland.

Always mellow
Always the same

Grant's
STAND FAST
Scotch Whisky

Grant's
Stand Fast
Whisky

WILLIAM GRANT & SONS LTD
Distillers   Scotland

Maximum Retail Price (as fixed by the
Scotch Whisky Assoc.) bot. 33/4; ½ bot. 17/5

IT'LL BE A DRIZZLY DAY

There's no hope of a white Christmas. It will be mainly cloudy with some rain or drizzle in most areas of Scotland, say Met. men, with mild mid-day temperatures around 47 degrees.

BEAUTIFUL ballito STOCKINGS

Sunday Mail
Scotland's National Sunday Newspaper
No. 2157. JANUARY 22, 1950. A KEMSLEY NEWSPAPER. 2d.

ROMMEL—the story of an enemy's hero
Page Eight

—improves all meals
HP SAUCE

'PERIL UPON US: BEWARE CLASS WAR'

... World is watching

MR. CHURCHILL, broadcasting to the nation last night, said no nation of equal size, no society of equal civilisation had ever been in time of peace in the economic peril in which we stood If we acted wisely we could make our way through our dangers, but if we made serious mistakes and consumed our strength in domestic quarrels and class war, consequences might descend upon us the like of which we had never yet suffered or even imagined.

The Empire, the English-speaking world, all Europe, outside the Iron Curtain, are once again looking to us in curiosity and in anxiety, said Mr. Churchill.

Not to vote—or to vote in a way which wastes your vote—on what is now at stake for our country would be a failure to rise to the level of events.

At this moment, everyone ought to consider very carefully what is his duty towards his country, towards the causes he believes in, towards his home and family and to his own personal rights and responsibilities.

The practical question we have to settle now is whether we shall take another deep plunge into State ownership and State control or whether we shall restore a great measure of freedom of choice and action to our people and of productive fertility and variety to our industry

★

ON unemployment, Mr. Churchill said, "We are all agreed that American aid has prevented the kind of unemployment which appeared after the last war and rose again to hideous heights under the Socialist Government of 20 years ago .. The Conservative and National Liberal Parties regard the prevention of mass unemployment as the most solemn duty of government.

Britain alone

Mr. Attlee, at this moment, is the head of the only Socialist Government to be found anywhere in the whole English-speaking world, the birthplace and the home of Parliamentary democracy.

New Zealand and Australia, which have given a prolonged trial to Socialist Government, though not, of course, to Socialism in its complete form have recently shaken themselves free.

A young nation like the Australian, dwelling in a Continent growing ample food for itself and for export, may try experiments in Socialism without the risk of fatal injury.

But the 50 millions gathered together in this small island are in a very different position. We are a highly artificial community balanced precariously at a level of well-being which before the war was superior to anything in Europe but whose means of existence have been seriously, though not yet irreparably, undermined by changes in the surrounding world, and also by the actions of our own government during these last critical and difficult years

The main reason why we are unable to earn our living and make our way in the world is because we are not allowed to do so.

The whole enterprise, contrivance and genius of the British nation is being increasingly paralysed by the war-time restrictions from which all other free peoples have shaken themselves clear, but which are still imposed upon our people in the name of a mistaken political philosophy and a largely obsolete mode of thought

Our Government is the only one glorying in controls for controls sake. I am sure that a Parliament resolved to set the nation free would soon enable it to earn its own living in the world

Cast off controls

I am sure, on the other hand, that the Socialist policy of equalising misery and organising scarcity instead of allowing diligence, self-reliance and ingenuity to produce abundance, has only to be prolonged to be fatal to our British island.

The scheme of society for which Conservatives and National Liberals stand is the establishment and maintenance of a basic standard of life and labour, below which a man or woman, however old or weak, shall not be allowed to fall.

The food they receive, the prices they have to pay for basic necessities, the homes they live in, their employment, must be the first care of the State and must have priority over all other peace-time requirements.

Once we have made that standard secure, we propose to set the nation free as quickly as possible from the controls and restrictions which now beset our daily life.

Above the basic standard there will be free opportunities to rise

16s 4d worth

The Socialist Government has spent every penny which it could lay its hands on, or which it could beg or borrow

They have spent in their term of office over £17,000 million, including the enormous sums given or loaned us from abroad. They have exacted from us the heaviest taxation in the world

At the same time they have cut down the buying power of every £1 we earn in wages, salaries or trading with one another

The British £1 has fallen since the war stopped by no less than 3s 8d This has struck a heavy blow at the social services, at pensions of every

Continued on Page 4

HEIL, HEIL ... BUT NO FUEHRER!

THERE were more than 120 of them, all extremist right-wing German politicians. They were wearing Wehrmacht-style boots and riding-breeches — AND THEY CARRIED WHIPS.

They were meeting in the Nordic Hotel (chosen because of its name) at Kassel, in the U.S. Zone of Germany. And they voted to amalgamate the main Neo-Nazi parties under the title "GERMAN REICH PARTY."

Between them they represent 1,000,000 voters. They agreed on a political programme, which bears similarities to that OF THE NAZIS.

Communists get back their 600 rooms

By ANTONY TERRY, Our Berlin Correspondent

WEST BERLIN police yesterday handed back to armed East Zone police the Communist railway administration's empty 600-room H.Q. in the U.S. sector of the city in an attempt to remove the Soviet blockade threat to the Capital.

The U.S. Commandant of Berlin, Major-General Maxwell D. Taylor, after secret talks with British officials, announced that, "Falling over backwards to be reasonable," he had ordered the withdrawal of the Western police from the building, which had been taken over by the city of Berlin on Tuesday.

"It was in American interests to put this space to use for the benefit of badly-bombed Berlin," said Major-General Taylor

"Unfortunately, the unreasonable and provocative attitude of the Soviet makes it appear probable that the hardships which they intended to impose outweigh the benefits."

Armed Russian frontier guards, who last night tried to board the British inter-zonal train when it arrived at Helmstedt, on the zonal frontier, to interrogate five Soviet officers who were on board, were told "hands off" by the British train escort,

T.V. for Scotland in 18 months

By "Sunday Mail" Reporter

SCOTLAND will have television by the autumn of next year. From Dumfries to Dundee there will be a complete service from a "temporary" transmitter at Harthill. A second transmitter, near Aberdeen, will be working in 1952. In both cases, this is some two years earlier than the previous official estimates.

This is a complete change of policy by the G.P.O., the B.B.C and the Government and is a victory for the Television Emergency Committees whose members have fought strenuously for many months on Scotland's behalf.

An official statement is likely to be made soon by Mr Paling, the P.M.G.

When the new plan was worked out just before the New Year, only a handful of people were taken into the confidence of the B.B.C. Director-General, Sir William Haley The secret was well kept.

RADIO INDUSTRY GETS ITS CHANCE

The previous official programme (announced by Herbert Morrison at Radiolympia in September) gave no date for the first Scottish transmitter, but said that it was hoped—no promise given—that the programme would be completed in 1954.

This was taken to mean that 1954 was the year in which the radio link would reach Aberdeen, and that 1953 would be the probable opening date for Harthill. Even this was years earlier than previous Government estimates.

The radio industry said at once that it could cut the plan in half; and, with the help of the Emergency Committees and a committee of M.P.'s (in which Glasgow's Colonel Hutchison was prominent), kept on saying this to all officials concerned and offered figures to prove it

The industry is now being given its chance, and has said that the first Scottish transmitter can be in action in the autumn of 1951

FINAL WORD TO COME

Only one thing is holding up the new announcement and the start of work on the Scottish transmitter at Harthill. A Government planning committee in London has still to give final approval

This is the Plowden Committee on expenditure. They had previously applied the Cripps axe to expenditure on new transmitters (other than Huddersfield) this year. But, as the new plan is to reduce greatly the outlay on both Yorkshire and Lanarkshire transmitters, it seems unlikely that any objection can be raised to their being completed simultaneously

The plan is that two "utility" transmitters could be built for north England and south Scotland for the price of one non-utility Sutton Coldfield model.

RIGHT POLICY FOR BRITAIN

This is the right policy for Britain, for, apart from the pleasures it will take into millions of British homes, it will enable the manufacturers (who have so far *lost* money on T.V. through expensive research) to go ahead with mass production and capture overseas markets from competitor America.

Although they had no real reason to expect this sudden change of plan, the radio trade in Scotland has been getting into gear, preparing to give the best possible service.

During the past fortnight, T.V classes have started in Glasgow and Aberdeen. And, although enrolment was restricted to men already expert in radio, the organisers have been swamped with applications. Glasgow had to close the list at 200 (and run an extra class); Aberdeen at 100 (and find a bigger school).

THE MEN WE SHOULD THANK

The two men Scotland has to thank most for the T.V. speed-up are eloquent Irishman, C. O. Stanley, C.B.E., chairman of a famous English radio concern, who was making speeches in favour of an immediate Scottish transmitter in 1936, and James Robertson, M.B.E., J.P., well known Glasgow businessman.

They have been the prime movers in the demand for a fair deal for Scotland

And, in the case of Aberdeen, but for the activities of the North Committee under A. Ernest Buchan, there would have been no North-East Scotland transmitter in the Morrison Plan

The site and the evidence: a small boy in an empty field at North Hirst Farm, near Harthill, finds an old insulator left behind after the tests which fixed Harthill as Scotland's future TV site.

SEEING IS BELIEVING

Have YOU seen the truth yet?

MORE than half the housewives in the country have discovered the truth about washing-powders. They've seen with their own eyes that one washes whiter than the others. Which one?

Persil!

A nation-wide poll revealed this amazing fact. It indicated that as many as 7 million women plump for Persil every time.

Soap rationing really did it. Women were forced to use any soap powder they could get. So they've proved for themselves that Persil washes whiter.

The Magic

The magic is in Persil's amazing oxygen bubbles. They're tirelessly active against deep dirt, go on working till it's shifted clean away. Persil's whiteness is *cleanness*. That's why Persil brings up all your coloured things so beautifully, too!

Already, more than half the housewives in the country know

PERSIL WASHES WHITER!

PER 1185A-152-55

Bailey's
Quality Wine Merchants
GLASGOW   EDINBURGH
PAISLEY   GREENOCK
HAMILTON   AYR
IRVINE   TROON

Daily Record
and Mail.

ESTABLISHED 1895. No. 16,971.   MONDAY, FEBRUARY 27, 1950.   A KEMSLEY NEWSPAPER.   1d.

Sir Harry in picture and story, Page 7

With a tradition of over 80 years of Quality!
LANG'S Gold Medal
BANANA RUM
GUARANTEED PURE JAMAICA

End Of The Road

SIR HARRY LAUDER IS DEAD

Relatives were at bedside

Pitboy who rose to world fame

A 'phone message at 11.30 on Friday night invited Miss Florence Horsbrugh to stand for Moss Side, Manchester.

SIR HARRY LAUDER, the greatest Scots comedian of all time, died peacefully at his home, Lauder Ha', Strathaven, at 8.20 last night, after being ill since last August. He was 79.

At his bedside when he passed away were Miss Greta Lauder, his niece; Mrs. Alec Lauder, his brother's widow; and Mrs. Wardrop, his sister.

Ever since he took ill Sir Harry had been confined to bed. From the early bulletins, which revealed the gravity of his condition, the world that knew him as a great minstrel, was prepared then for news of his passing.

From time to time, however, he rallied slightly, though it was apparent to his family and close friends that he was nearing the end of the road.

At Christmas, messages from all parts of the world which reached Lauder Ha' could not be conveyed to him because of his critical condition.

A fortnight ago, he was not fit enough to receive a message from Mr. Churchill, during the Conservative leader's visit to Edinburgh.

FUNERAL ON THURSDAY

Mr. Churchill had instructed his secretary to telephone Sir Harry's home and inquire for him.

Miss Greta Lauder, who answered the telephone, thanked Mr. Churchill for his gesture, but explained that Sir Harry was not well enough to acknowledge his message.

Sir Harry's funeral will take place on Thursday to Bent Cemetery, Hamilton—the town where he began life as a pithead boy after his family had moved from Portobello.

Superb artist

By HARRY GORDON

THE grand old minstrel has taken his final call, but he has left a legacy not only to Scotland but to the world in the melodies and Scottish sentiments forever associated with the magic name of Lauder.

In the passing of this supreme artist, whose magnetic personality and clean homely humour, wedded to lilting tunes and infinite artistry, bar any successor to his crown, the world's variety stage has lost its most precious star.

MISS HORSBRUGH TO FIGHT MOSS SIDE

By A "Daily Record" Reporter

AFTER a two-hour meeting last night, Miss Florence Horsbrugh, a Minister in the Coalition and Caretaker Governments, was announced as Conservative candidate for Moss Side, Manchester.

This election was postponed through the death of the Tory candidate, Squadn.-Ldr. E. L. Fleming, Conservative M.P. for Withington, Manchester.

Miss Horsbrugh will be formally adopted to-night and will start immediately on a campaign until polling day, March 9.

Miss Horsbrugh was formerly M.P. for Dundee from 1931 to 1945.

Miss Horsbrugh met the Executive shortly after a seven-hour journey from Scotland, where she had only one day's respite after an exhausting campaign in Midlothian and Peebles, which she failed to win by 7188 votes.

A telephone message inviting her to stand for Moss Side reached her at 11.30 on Friday night as she was "crawling into bed"

Tall and spare, grey-haired and middle-aged, Miss Horsbrugh stepped briskly to Conservative ward headquarters to meet the executive last night.

FLEMING HALL

She met them—about 50 men and women—in the Fleming Hall, named within the last few days after Squadron Leader Fleming, whose sudden death on February 17 caused the election to be postponed.

Earlier in the day the executive had interviewed three local "possibles," Mr. Roy Jamieson, who failed by 42 votes at Blackley, and Councillors Harold Bentley and Clyde Hewlett.

Figures at Moss Side in 1945 were:—
Griffiths (Lab.) 10,201
Duckworth (C.) 7,423
Moore (L.) 2,525
Edwards (Ind.) 446
Lab. majority 2,778
Labour gain from Conservative.

Honours list—of 2 names

Mr. J. J. Lawson

A DISSOLUTION Honours List containing only two names is issued to-day. It is probably the shortest on record. The statement from 10 Downing Street says:

"The King has been pleased to approve the conferment of the following honours arising out of the recent dissolution of Parliament:—

"Baronies: Sir Francis Campbell Ross Douglas, K.C.M.G., M.P. for Battersea 1940-46, Governor and C.i.C. Malta 1946-1949. For political and public services.

"The Right Hon. John James Lawson, M.P. for the Chester-le-Street division of Co. Durham 1919-1949. For political and public services."

He began work in a Durham coal mine at the age of 12, and later sold his home so that he could study at Ruskin College, Oxford.

Sir Harry Lauder as he appeared in the film, "The End of The Road."

Leopard loose and they're loving it

Oklahoma City, Sunday.

A 175-POUND killer leopard, fresh from the jungle and very hungry, is loose somewhere in Oklahoma City—but the place is almost like a circus. Everyone wants to see it.

The leopard has been loose since yesterday, when it sprang to freedom from a 20-foot pit in a local zoo.

The roads are crowded with people. Cars are cruising around. Overhead a private plane is swooping.

A safari of 21 U.S. marines equipped with rifles and walkie-talkies is stalking through the suburbs.

Marooned on Dead Man's Isle

AFTER being marooned all night on Dead Man's Isle, an isolated piece of marshland in the River Medway, during the height of a 50 m.p.h. gale and in a temperature of 32 degrees, Albert Rotherham and his two schoolboy sons were rescued yesterday by the Southend lifeboat.

They had slept in a gully among the skulls and bones of French prisoners of the Napoleonic war.

"A gale suddenly sprang up," Mr. Rotherham said, "and our rowing boat was tossed about like a cork.

"Peter — eight years old— was washed overboard. I grabbed him and hauled him aboard.

"When I again attempted to row, one of my oars snapped and we were buffeted on to the mud flats.

"No craft were in sight. I searched for a likely spot to settle down, and the gully sheltered us a bit."

Verdict on wage claims

DECISIONS on wage claims affecting about 3,000,000 workers in the railway, engineering and shipbuilding industries, upon which the future of the wage restraint policy of the Government and the T.U.C. may depend, will be taken at meetings in London this week.

To-day the Railway Executive will tell the N.U.R. of their decision on the demand of the £5 a week minimum for about 200,000 adult workers in the lower paid grades. Employees in the nationalised docks, canal, railway catering and railway workshop services have already had a similar wage claim rejected.

A special general meeting of the N.U.R. will be held in London on Thursday and Friday.

SHIPBUILDING DEMAND

On Wednesday, shipbuilding and repairing employers reply to the demand of £1 a week increase.

The Confederation of Engineering and Shipbuilding Trade Unions has already received the rejection by the engineering employers of a similar claim.

On Thursday the A.E.U. will hold a special meeting of its National Committee to discuss the employers' decision.

The Edinburgh branch yesterday instructed shop stewards to hold workshop meetings this week to explain the claim. A mass meeting will be held in Edinburgh on March 12.

SCOTS MINERS' CLAIM

There are also wage moves pending in other industries — 160,000 men in the car repair industry are asking for a substantial increase, and the miners' bid for an increase in the cost of living bonus is awaiting arbitration.

The Scottish miners propose reviving the claim for two weeks' holiday with pay.

MISSING TRAWLER IS SAFE

A RADIO message received last night at the Humber radio station dispelled anxiety concerning the 580-ton steam trawler Isernia.

The trawler had been out of radio contact since Tuesday, and was over 30 hours overdue at Grimsby on a voyage from Norway.

On Wednesday morning rough seas were reported off the Norwegian coast.

The message, signed by Skipper Farmery, read:—

"Arrive river about midnight. Bridge, chartroom, and wireless room smashed up; steering unreliable; request assistance tug for docking."

It is believed that as her wireless room was smashed the Isernia sent a message by lamp to another vessel, which forwarded it by radio.

The Isernia, built in 1943 and one of Grimsby's most modern trawlers, carried a crew of 24.

Earlier yesterday, Mr. W. A. Butt, manager of the Great Grimsby and East-Coast Steam Fishing Co., the owners of the trawler, said that a ship, which left 24 hours after the Isernia, arrived at Grimsby without sighting her.

Look your best in *Windsmoor*
Most Windsmoor Clothes are lined throughout with SYLMYRA crepe
COATS • SUITS • SKIRTS

CLOUDY.—Rain at times; becoming milder, but cold in the East; fresh Southerly winds.

Sunday Mail

Scotland's National Sunday Newspaper

No. 2173. MAY 14, 1950.   A KEMSLEY NEWSPAPER. 2d.

BEAUTIFUL **ballito** STOCKINGS

REX ON THE HARRY LIME TRAIL — *Page Nine*

—improves all meals HP SAUCE

"THERE THEY ARE— AND WE THOUGHT THEY WERE ROCKS"

THE BIG 3 UNITE AGAINST THE REDS

AT the end of their three-day conference in London yesterday, the Foreign Ministers of Britain, the U.S. and France issued a joint communique pledging closer co-ordination in using their joint resources to maintain social and material standards, as well as adequate development of "the necessary measures" to establish lasting peace.

The statement expressed confidence that the peoples of the free world could achieve both these aims, and declared: "The strength of the free world will never be used for aggressive purposes.

"The Ministers find it necessary to re-state this fundamental truth in the face of the calculated campaign of misrepresentation of our purposes and policies conducted by the only militaristic and aggressive power in the world.

"Faith in freedom should not be taken for granted, but should be built into a dynamic force, and steps should be taken to increase public understanding of the exact nature, methods and dangers of the threat to its existence.

The communique disclosed that a general declaration on policy regarding Germany was being sent to the German Federal Government immediately

Switching to the Far East, the communique spoke of the "advance of Communist imperialism" to the borders of South-East Asia. It expressed the "firm intention" of encouraging and supporting the new governments of a number of countries there which have now emerged as independent nations.

"They consider," said the announcement, "that the region as a whole is economically under-developed and that it is desirable that all the governments in the region should collaborate to intensify measures of development designed to raise the general standard of living."

The Foreign Ministers decided to take every opportunity of "exposing the aims and methods of Communist imperialism which, whilst pretending to encourage nationalist movements, is, in fact, seeking only to control and exploit them for expansionist policies"

Brothers John and James McCallum proudly stand by their "find" on the beach near Dunbar.

147 whales stranded on the beach

THEIR death roars gradually weakening, 147 bottle-nosed whales lay on the sandy beach at Thornton Loch, four miles south of Dunbar, last night, only a few feet away from the life-giving sea.

The whales ranged in length from 18ft. bulls to 4ft. babies. They had swum ashore on the early morning tide and later they threshed the receding water into white foam in their efforts to reach the open sea.

The roaring of the adults and the shrill cries of the babies could be heard for some distance. A crowd of nearly 200 people gathered on the beach, and several times men tried to lift smaller whales out to sea. Each time they had to give up as the panic-stricken monsters struggled out of their grasp.

The discovery of the whales was made at 9 a.m. yesterday by 13-year-old local boy, John McCallum, and his young brother, James.

Playing on the beach, one of the boys spotted "black rocks" about a quarter of a mile away. Both ran along and found the "rocks" were whales—scattered over a 150-foot stretch of the bay.

To sea again?

East Lothian County Council officials and police stood by late last night helplessly watching the slowly-lessening struggles of the whales. Although they had been ashore for hours under a blazing sun, most of the animals were still living.

County officials are hoping that at the next tide, early to-day, the whales will be waterborne again and swim out to sea.

But—just in case—a firm of horse slaughterers and chemical manufacturers have been asked to prepare to remove the carcases if the need arises.

Why they do it?

Dr. A. C. Stephen, the foremost authority in Scotland, told the "Sunday Mail" last night that there was no single explanation of the mystery. "They may have been caught by a sandbank when the tide suddenly receded," he said. "Then they would panic."

RAID ON SAFE STARTED FIRE

GLASGOW C.I.D. officers were last night inspecting a safe found apparently blown open in the wreckage of a fire which swept through a Buchanan Street hair stylist's premises.

The safe was found on the ground floor, from which the flames had spread rapidly to the floor above. It was not known if anything had been stolen.

"Quick Ones"

Within minutes of the fire being spotted on the floor above the main entrance to James Stewart's, hair specialists at 78 Buchanan Street, flames were roaring up inside, and smoke poured out from every part of the building.

When a fire officer ordered evacuation of the crowded smoke-filled Rogano, some people finished their meals and nearly all "knocked back" their drinks before they left.

Within 15 minutes firemen had gained control, and prevented the blaze spreading from the badly-damaged first floor.

ABLAZE AGAIN

Earlier in the day flames swept over the gorseland around Gartloch Hospital, near Glasgow, for the second time in a week.

Throughout the afternoon an increasing cloud of smoke poured up from the blackened stretch where last Saturday firemen and scores of helpers hosed and beat at a 20-acres "bush fire."

Mystery man's gift

A man handed a parcel to a maid at Hesley Hall Home for Crippled Children, near Doncaster, yesterday, and walked off without giving his name.

It contained £100 and a note asking that the money be used for the children.

SCOTS SPLASHING IN THE SUN

THE MAY HEATWAVE is expected to last for a few days yet. Yesterday's temperatures were well over the 70 mark. And the "cast a clout" dirge was well and truly scotched. May wasn't out. But the women had on their light print frocks and the men their open-necked shirts. The coats were left at home.

Highest temperature of the day in Scotland yesterday was 76 degrees, recorded at Springburn Park, Glasgow. Sunshine duration reached the year's peak of 15 hours. And as the sun shone, Glasgow flocked to the seaside—and the public baths.

SEASIDE DIPPERS needed extra buses to the Clyde coast and five special trains to Gourock, Wemyss Bay and Largs.

STAY-AT-HOMES were queueing outside Glasgow's public baths from shortly after noon. By closing time it was estimated that 45,000 had been in the swim.

Tragedy at the loch

THREE LITTLE COUSINS were among the thousands of bathers yesterday. They chose Forfar Loch. But their day ended in tragedy.

David Walker, of Padnaram, and Sandra Bennie, of Drumgley, both aged nine, were drowned.

James Deas, also aged nine, of 220 East High Street, Forfar, was the third member of the tragic little party. A collie dog was the fourth. And the collie saved James' life.

David ventured too far from the edge. Sandra splashed towards him. But she too got out of her depth. James went to help. He went under as well.

But, as he struggled to the surface, the dog swam past. James clutched it, and was dragged back to shallow water.

Police recovered the bodies of David and Sandra after dragging.

Just big A-bombs

There is no truth in the story that the United States has atom bombs small enough to be carried in a jet fighter-bomber, a U.S. military official said in Washington last night.

ALL-IN BATTLE IN CITY BUS STATION

WOMEN and children screamed in terror as scores of men struggled in a packed free-for-all in Killermont Street bus station, Glasgow, last night.

An argument developed among a number of young men, and within minutes one side of the crowded bus station was a mass of fighting, struggling men.

Trapped women, children and elderly people scrambled aboard stationary buses or bolted out into the street for safety as the battle swayed right across the bus station.

At one stage the fight carried out into Germiston Street and back among the bus stances into Buchanan Street, with drivers and bus inspectors powerless to interfere.

Strong police forces arrived in squad cars, patrol wagons and on foot, and found what one senior officer described as "the worst Saturday night brawl scene in Glasgow for many years." They quickly restored order.

Ambulances were called and four men were taken to the Royal Infirmary with head injuries.

Police inquiries were still going on early this morning.

The Siamese twins

Surgeons hope to give Mrs. E. A. Townsend, of Edmonton, Alberta, two normal children to-day after a delicate operation to separate her Siamese twin daughters, born face to face on November 17. Mrs. Townsend is 20.

Doctors and nurses rehearsed for the operation with dolls earlier last week while the plump, healthy babies gurgled in a cot in the hospital nursery.

This is the Gin

Gordon's Special Dry London Gin

Quality Incomparable **Gordon's Stands Supreme**

Maximum Prices: Per Bottle 32/4
Half-Bottle 16/11; Quarter-Bottle 8/10;
Miniature, 3/5.   U.K. only

Rely on the Quality
ballito Stockings

Daily Record and Mail.

Christmas in Korea
Page 5

GRANITE HOUSE
FAMOUS
DRAPERY DEPT.
OFFERS
UTILITY CURTAIN MATERIAL
in Rust, Gold and Sand Colours. 36ins. wide. Yard.... 7/6
TRONGATE STOCKWELL STREET CORNER.

ESTABLISHED 1895. No. 17,230   TUESDAY, DECEMBER 26, 1950   A KEMSLEY NEWSPAPER.   1d.

Police check-up on Scots-bound cars

YARD DIRECTS SEARCH FOR STONE OF DESTINY

The Stone of Destiny below the Coronation Chair.

"Daily Record" Reporter

POLICE road blocks were established yesterday on main roads from England to Scotland following the removal earlier in the day of the Stone of Destiny from Westminster Abbey.

The stone, on which the ancient Scottish Kings were crowned, weighs about three hundredweights. Police, searching for a Ford Anglia car seen near the Abbey yesterday, received reports last night that a similar car had been seen heading north near Birmingham.

In the car are stated to be two men and a woman, who have Scottish accents. They called at a service station in Hockley Heath yesterday morning and drove off towards Birmingham.

A Scotland Yard description of the woman was that she was about 25 years of age, had long dark hair, long, pointing nose, dark eyes, fresh complexion, thin lips, and wore a green checked coat with long collar.

One of the men was between 26 and 29 years of age, had a snub nose and fresh complexion. He was of medium build and had fair hair which had not been combed.

It is certain that the plot to remove the Stone of Destiny was planned in Scotland and was carried out by a raiding party.

But leaders of the chief home rule movements, the Scottish National Party and Scottish Convention, last night promptly disowned any part in the scheme.

Prominent independent home rulers would not reveal whether they knew of the plot. Said one of them in Glasgow—
" Obviously at this stage we are not going to give a hint of who might be involved.

" But it will probably appear at some Scottish national monument — the Wallace Monument at Stirling for instance."

None of the thousands who attended the Christmas Day services in the Abbey conducted

The fake stone plot that failed—see Page 7.

by the Dean of Westminster, Scottish-born Dr. A. C. Don, knew that the stone had been stolen.

Afterwards Dr. Don said:
" The Stone was stolen in the early hours of this morning but we hope Scotland Yard will lay their hands on it."

McNEIL HORRIFIED

Secretary of State for Scotland Hector McNeil was horrified when he heard.
" I think it is mean and atrocious," he stated last night.
Referring to the possibility of Scottish Nationalists having organised the "removal," he said, " I cannot see how it furthers any argument."
Immediately it was discovered the Stone was missing Scotland Yard sent out a terse message to all police forces in Midland and Northern England: "Coronation Stone stolen from Westminster Abbey. Suspect work of Scottish Nationalists. Stop and search all cars heading north."
Special road blocks were set up on the main roads in Lancashire. All cars driving through the county towards Scotland were stopped while police searched them.
Chief Inspector Owen
Continued on Back Page, Col. 1.

THE DUKE OF MONTROSE said last night that if the Stone was on its way back to Scotland, he did not regret it. "Our old Scottish charters are now being returned to Edinburgh and everyone agrees that that is right and as it should be."
" I fail to see why the Scone Stone should be treated differently. It is part of our early Celtic history.
" England has plenty of good solid history to her credit and to be proud of, and she has no reason to weep if the Scone Stone should come again to Scotland and be restored to the old capital, which it should never have left."
"King" John MacCormick, chairman of the Scottish Covenant, whose petition for a greater measure of Home Rule was signed by nearly two million Scots last year, said that "whatever the outcome of the present adventure," he hoped the Stone would ultimately be kept in Scotland except on Coronation occasions.
"The Stone of Destiny properly belongs to the people of Scotland," he said. "Under the terms of the Treaty

The Duke of Montrose.

Duke says "it should be here"

of Northampton, in 1328, the Stone, which is the ancient symbol of Scottish nationality, was to be returned to Scotland, but the clause was never observed."
Mr. Nigel Tranter, one of the leaders of Scottish Covenant, said: "We in that movement stick to constitutional methods, but as an individual I would be the last to deplore initiative and enterprise shown by any person in Scotland—even if it is misplaced as this is—if it will waken people up to the feeling in Scotland.
" It takes a lot to get any news of Scotlands' national existence into the English press and this sort of thing is the only type of Home Rule story that gets a break in the English newspapers."

Reds send out 'probe' patrols

From RICHARD HUGHES
Tokio, Monday.

INCREASED Chinese activity was reported to-night by battlefront officers on the left, or Yellow Sea flank, of the United Nations forces.

There was, however, no development of the anticipated all-out Communist offensive during the second night of the full moon. Action by Chinese spearheads which have crossed the Parallel is described as " probing."

Fifth Airforce fighter-bombers hurled a Christmas Day offensive against all sectors in North Korea, but significantly concentrated their heaviest attack on the Chorwon-Pyongyang-Kumhwa area, where the strongest massings of Chinese troops have been reported.

16 MILES SOUTH

Reports have been received of 'enemy movement' as far as 16 miles south of the 38th Parallel, and 14 miles south of Kaesong, but these groups may be North Korean guerrillas.

With traditional efficiency the U.S. Navy has rung down the curtain on one of the most tragic and wasteful offensives in U.S. military history.

Evacuation of the Hungnam area on the north-eastern coast has been satisfactorily and officially completed.

The successful withdrawal of 105,000 troops and 100,000 refugees under the covering fire of a crushing naval bombardment and unchallenged air cover was described in grim talks as " re-deployment."

DR. A. C. DON
The Dean of Westminster.
A native of Broughty Ferry, Dr. Don was educated at Rugby School and Magdalen College, Oxford, and from 1908-1909 was in business in Dundee. He entered the Church and became a curate in 1912. From 1936-46 he was Chaplain to the Speaker of the House of Commons. He is a member of the R and A. St. Andrews.

Fog halts buses, ships and planes

GLASGOW was "blacked-out" by fog yesterday, which reduced visibility over most of the city to only a few yards.

Roads in many places were icy, and there were a number of crashes. Transport services were disorganised and buses were running as much as two hours behind schedule.

By early evening all shipping on the Clyde was brought to a standstill.

Renfrew airport had to close down and all services were diverted to fog-free Prestwick.

Full story—Page 7

Bells brought lost Clyde ferry to safety

By "Daily Record" Reporter

FIFTEEN passengers and the crew of two aboard Glasgow's small Linthouse-Whiteinch ferry will never forget Christmas Day, 1950. For an hour and a quarter they were lost on the Clyde in thick impenetrable fog on a journey which normally would have taken only a few minutes.

At last, with handbells clanging and whistles blowing to let them know they were near safety, they came to the river bank a mile from the landing place. In the fog the ferry had to move very slowly, constantly at the mercy of the swift current of the ebbing tide.

Almost as soon as it left Linthouse, the ferry was in trouble. Passengers heard the clatter of riveters at work and discovered they were going down stream past Stephens' yard instead of across the river

The ferrymen headed out into the river, but the swift current carried the boat down stream again and it landed close to Connell's shipyard on the north side. Out of Connell's they steamed, narrowly escaping the stern of a ship under construction.

"ALMOST HIT BANK"

" Once or twice in the search for the landing place we almost hit the bank," said 21-year-old John McKillen, 1090 Dumbarton Road, Glasgow, who had boarded the ferry on his way home from the abandoned football match at Hampden. "We were gathered round the wheel house, but could see absolutely nothing for a long time.

" When we came to the bank again, one of the passengers jumped ashore, saying he was going to get help. After that we went upstream, and soon we heard the bells and whistles from the north bank signalling to us to come in. We found we were at Mechan's works, where the men passed out a plank on which we walked ashore."

SHIP GROUNDS AGAIN

THE 7242-ton British steamer Domingo de Larrinaga, refloated from Redcar sands yesterday, went aground two hours later at the entrance to the Tees.

MALT VINEGAR
must be
BREWERY BOTTLED

● TO STAY BRIGHT AND USABLE TO THE LAST DROP

● TO BE FREE FROM SEDIMENT

● TO STAND UP TO ANY TEST

GRIMBLE'S GOLD MEDAL SCOTTISH DISTILLED MALT VINEGAR LEITH

Always insist on the name

GRIMBLE'S
OF LEITH

THE ONLY MALT VINEGAR BREWED IN SCOTLAND

SHOWERS—Light northerly winds; scattered showers and bright intervals; keen frost early and late.

Beautiful **ballito** Stockings

Sunday Mail

Scotland's National Sunday Newspaper

No. 2239.   AUGUST 19, 1951.   A KEMSLEY NEWSPAPER.   2½d.

THE SMILING PRINCESS
Page Nine

improves all meals
HP SAUCE

THIS IS WHY THE CLAN MARCH FLOPPED

Engulfed by the biggest crowds Edinburgh has ever seen, the march of the 1000 pipers is jostled to a dismal end. The kilted procession should have marched 16-abreast along Princes Street, but, as the crowds spilled into the road, the lane through which the pipers had to pass grew steadily narrower. Then finally, there was no way through at all.

500,000 crowd surged into Princes St.

THE march of 1000 pipers and 500 drummers through Edinburgh yesterday was an inglorious flop. The great spectacle didn't materialise—because the crowds that poured into Edinburgh wouldn't let it.

The worst dreams of the organisers could never have surpassed the utter chaos that resulted from their well-meant effort.

Never in Edinburgh's thousand years of history have such crowds been seen in the Capital. It was not thousands nor tens of thousands, but hundreds of thousands who came to see the sights.

It is estimated that 500,000 people were crammed into Princes Street and its environs. And in the seething mass struggling first for a view and later for breathing space hundreds fainted.

JOSTLED OUT OF EXISTENCE

The march literally disintegrated — jostled out of existence by the crowds that came to see it.

Half the pipers never started at all. Those who did get through went in three lots — never sixteen abreast as was intended — sometimes only three abreast.

Appeals by traffic and mounted police failed to clear the path as the crowds pressed inexorably forward.

Most of them had waited for a long time. From 10 o'clock in the morning the first arrivals were bagging vantage points in Princes Street,

(Continued on Page 4)

AT 2 am THEY WERE STILL TRUDGING IN

AT two o'clock this morning the rearguard of Glasgow's thousands of Clan Gathering trippers were still arriving weary-eyed and exhausted in the city.

That they did get back at all was a triumph of hectic organisation by the bus and rail companies.

Early this morning a bus official at Killermont Street station estimated that nearly 100 bus-loads of travellers had returned to Glasgow from Edinburgh between 5 p.m. and 1 a.m.

In Queen Street station at 1 a.m., railway inspectors and police heaved a sigh of relief as the last train from the capital pulled in with about 50 passengers, including a woman carrying a baby, and the news: "Everyone got away."

Corporation Transport officials waiting at the stations, cheered the late arrivals with the news that a special service of all-night buses was waiting

Storm ordeal for Clyde trippers

A 40-MILE-AN-HOUR gale howled up the Firth of Clyde yesterday. It battered shipping and overturned a yacht off Toward Point. Huge waves smashed in the dining saloon windows of the Duchess of Hamilton near Campbeltown and flooded the saloon, crowded with diners.

Early this morning a 6000-ton liner was cruising round the open Firth after the winds had dragged her from her moorings at the Tail o' the Bank.

A score of people were hurt and drenched when the seas cascaded into the saloon of the Duchess of Hamilton.

Mr. Alexander Tennent, 163 Braidcroft Road, Pollok, who
CONTINUED ON PAGE 3, COL. 4

POLICE MADE A WRONG DECISION

AN outcry about the closing of streets before the Orange Walk a few weeks ago led Edinburgh police to a decision to keep traffic going until the last minute yesterday.

"We know now that this should not have happened," a police official said last night.

"The crowds far exceeded our expectations. More than half-a-million people were jammed from the edge of the pavement to the shop fronts. The result was that the people who came off trams and buses between the West End and the Mound could do nothing but stand in the middle of the road. They were blocked by impassable crowds on every side."

CHAMPION PIPERS

The City of Glasgow Police Band, with 96¼ points, won the world pipe band championship at Edinburg yesterday.

Muirhead and Sons, Grangemouth, were second with 95.2 points. Other placings were: 3, Edinburgh City Police (94.8); 4, Shotts and Dykehead (94.5); 5, Clan Macrae Society, Glasgow (94.4)

MEN IN THE MINES

drink **GUINNESS** for strength

When a man comes off shift with the feeling that a good drink would be the very thing — Guinness is the very drink. Any man who does a good day's work deserves a Guinness. It's the drink for *natural* strength. That grand creamy head and deep, clear colour show you ... the clean taste tells you that Guinness is goodness itself.

It does you good to have a GUINNESS

G.E.1616.B GUINNESS SCOTTISH OFFICE, 85, CLYDE FERRY STREET, GLASGOW, C.3

ROSS'S LIQUEURS
Sloe Gin
Cherry Whisky

DAILY Record
and Mail.

ESTABLISHED 1895. No. 17,610. SATURDAY, MARCH 15, 1952. A KEMSLEY NEWSPAPER. 1½d.

CALCUTTA CUP Page 6

Ask for 'Red Tape' THE WHISKY you may be fortunate
Maximum Retail Prices as fixed by the Scotch Whisky Association Small sizes available

The tartan on television

TV "HELLO" TO SCOTLAND

...and it's rather awe-inspiring

Shop window displays attract crowds

● *Members of the Royal Scottish Country Dance Society in the Duke of Edinburgh Reel on last night's television programme from Edinburgh. Watching from the platform are Mr. James Stuart, Secretary of State for Scotland; Lord Provost James Miller of Edinburgh, Lord Tedder and the Very Rev. Charles L. Warr. Below, in the studio, Miss Mary Malcolm and Alistair MacIntyre, the announcers, maintain the tartan motif for Scotland's big night.*

"DAILY RECORD" REPORTER

SCOTLAND faced the television cameras —shyly and timidly—for the first time last night and home Scots seemed to find the experience awe-inspiring.

There was something uncanny about it all. Mr. James Stuart, Secretary of State for Scotland, nervously fingered his tie; Lord Tedder smoothed his jacket, and the subdued breathing of over 200 people could be heard in the deathly silence.

Suddenly a voice said—"Thirty seconds to go" and the breathing seemed to stop.

The man who had spoken—a technician with earphones over his head, raised his hand and then pointed to the far corner of the room. A woman's voice said—"This is the B.B.C. television programme" — and Scotland's television service was on the air.

Another page had been added to Scotland's history and the new medium had reached the land of J. Logie Baird—one of television's pioneers.

The scene was set in the B.B.C. headquarters in Scotland. The colourful evening dresses of the women showed up against the sombre black of the men.

At a table in the back of the studio were Lord Tedder, vice-chairman of the Board of Governors of the B.B.C.; Mr Stuart, Lord Provost James Miller of Edinburgh, and the Very Rev. Charles L. Warr, Dean of Thistle.

Fixed on those four men from different parts of the room were the large triple-lensed TV cameras, red lights flicking on and off as each one in turn took note of the scene.

BURST OF APPLAUSE

Everyone was excited. It could be seen in the nervous fingers of Mr. Stuart, the tapping of the Lord Provost, and restless hands and feet of the audience.

Exactly at 7.45 p.m. when Mr. Stuart officially declared the Kirk O' Shotts station open, the atmosphere, which had been so strained it could almost be felt, suddenly broke, and the nervousness dissolved in a burst of applause.

Mr Stuart sat down, obviously relieved that the nerve-shattering eye of the camera had now moved to the chief Scottish announcer, Mr. Alistair McIntyre.

For the whole gathering it was a memorable event, from the notabilities who overflowed into the foyer, to the Pressmen in the galleries, and the technicians behind the cameras.

Mr. Stuart condensed all our thoughts with his words: "One can imagine the scene and the visible restlessness of the

Continued on Back Page

Touch of brilliance

IT was a brilliant touch to make Scotland's first presentation the graceful dances which followed the speech making. Those gently swaying kilts, and charming figures, made a handsome picture at the close of "Rouken Glen."

Scots viewers will see so many red-nosed comedians and hard-boiled tap-dancers in future that they will be glad to think that their country's contribution was first offered in so happy an example of national grace and skill. Many will hope to see more of these dancers.

Alastair Sim's talk would have been a triumph at any time, but last night it came as a happy Scots contribution to a usually-serious feature.

Car crashed Through Vestibule

WHILE a motorist stood window-gazing in Stirling last night at Scotland's first TV show, his car ran off down a hill and crashed into the vestibule of the Regal Cinema in Maxwell Place.

It smashed through the swing doors after running up three steps leading to the cinema and finished up with its nose resting against the pay-box, where Mr. Edward Kelly, of 25 Cowan Street, Stirling, was buying a ticket.

FRIGHT OF LIFE

Mr. Kelly and the 19-year-old cashier, Barbara McLaren, of Tullibody, were showered with broken glass and wood as the car ripped through the entrance.

Miss McLaren escaped injury, but Mr. Kelly was taken to Stirling Royal Infirmary suffering from shock.

Miss McLaren, who sits with her back to the door, told the "Daily Record"—" I didn't see a thing.

"When I looked round, I got the fright of my life to find the car with its headlamps inches from me."

Inside, the audience were watching "Home to Danger"

Reception was near perfect, says expert

THROUGHOUT Central and South Scotland TV's opening programmes last night from the Kirk o' Shotts transmitter were reported generally as "very clear reception and sound good."

Summing-up, an engineer attached to a large firm of manufacturers, which was getting first-hand reports by phone from its representatives throughout the country, said in Glasgow: reception was as near perfect as we could possibly have expected. Most areas within a 30-mile radius of the transmitting station were getting first-class images.

"We're not greatly concerned at the moment about places farther afield. Their reception might not be a hundred per cent. at present, but when more power is added to the Kirk o' Shotts transmitter sometime in July they will see a marked improvement."

In some outlying districts viewers reported fading an interference.

Freak reception

There was freak reception at Aberdeen, which is outwith the transmission area, but it was fading badly.

Belfast viewers who have been unable to tune into Holme Moss, received the Kirk o' Shotts transmission with only slight fading.

Over on the east coast of Scotland reception was almost perfect. A Kirkcaldy report stated there was no fading and very little interference. Dundee viewers also said it was nearly perfect.

Crowds gathered at shop windows in many towns where firms had sets operating. There was slight interference at some of these shows, probably due to passing traffic.

In Oban last night reception was surprisingly good notwithstanding the surrounding mountains.

Reports from other parts—

Kelso — Interference and slight fading.

Berwick—Fading at times.

Ayr — Good reception but some interference.

Greenock—Perfect reception.

Rothesay—Fair reception subject to slight fading.

BREAD DEARER FROM TO-MORROW

THE price of bread in Scotland will be increased by 1½d a 1lb 12oz loaf from to-morrow.

The Wholesale and Retail Bakers of Scotland decided this at a meeting in Glasgow yesterday when the Budget proposals on the bread subsidy were discussed.

A sliced and wrapped pan loaf is to cost 9d, unwrapped a penny cheaper. Plain batch loaves, sliced and wrapped, will be priced at 8½d and unwrapped at 7½d.

The 14 oz. pan or fancy loaf is to cost 4½d.

The bakers have also recommended price increases for morning rolls in the Glasgow area. Cost is to be raised from to-morrow by threepence to one shilling a dozen. Plain tea-bread, which used to sell at four for threepence, goes up to four for fivepence.

CLOUDY—Moderate or fresh south-easterly winds; mainly cloudy and dry with bright periods.

for SPEED— ACTION— SAFETY— TAKE 'ASPRO'

There are plenty of colds about—particularly feverish ones. To arrest them at the onset you need a medicine which acts with MAXIMUM speed—and dispels the first shivery, uneasy symptoms as soon as they appear. That means you need 'ASPRO'. You can take 'ASPRO' at any time, anywhere—and directly you take it 'ASPRO' combats the cold in three different ways—it acts as an anti-pyretic, quickly reducing feverishness—it soothes away the aches and pains—it promotes the action of the skin, too, helping you to get rid of the cold through the pores.

DON'T TOLERATE SORE THROAT— Gargle with— 'ASPRO'

Mix two 'ASPRO' tablets in half a glass of water, and gargle with the mixture. Myriads of tiny 'ASPRO' particles cling to the lining of the throat—thereby exerting a LASTING, SOOTHING EFFECT. It is a good idea to sip some of the mixture afterwards.

Made by ASPRO LIMITED, Slough, Bucks.

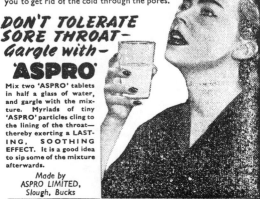

ballito Mirrasilk

SHEER AS NYLONS

NOW AVAILABLE · 12/6 A PAIR

Sunday Mail

Scotland's National Sunday Newspaper

No. 2274. APRIL 20. 1952.   A KEMSLEY NEWSPAPER. 2½d.

—improves all meals

HP SAUCE

GATHER ROUND JOHN—IT'S HERE!

At last, at long last!   The Cup comes home to Fir Park and to old John Hunter, the man who, perhaps, has done more than any other to bring Motherwell to the top of Scottish football.   None of the thousands waiting in Motherwell last night for the team's return knew that, before the general celebrations, eleven men with a cup had paid a private call to the old friend who missed the game.

Mr. Hunter (left), manager, team skipper and friends hold the Cup.

Life will never be sweeter ... champagne was never so fine. Face inside the cup is Old John's, taking the first sip.

'Well making whoopee at last

ELEVEN jubilant footballers took the Scottish Cup home to Motherwell for the first time for 48 years yesterday—and almost the entire population, men, women and children, turned out to welcome them.

Within minutes of the finish of the Scottish Cup Final at Hampden Park, Glasgow, the news that Motherwell had won the Cup for the first time in their history had flashed round Lanarkshire. From every direction, buses, motor cars, cycles and pedestrians converged on Motherwell Cross and every bus had a choir singing lustily.

Adding to the confusion, buses loaded with wildly excited supporters came nose to tail along the main roads from Glasgow. The whole town of Motherwell was quivering with excitement. But the majority of the happy people missed the most poignant moment in the Motherwell team's triumphant homecoming.

The team bus, with the 11 players perched on the roof, passed the Cross to the accompaniment of ear-splitting roars from the crowd.

It made straight for Fir Park. Waiting at the main entrance of the park was the man who means football to Motherwell—the man who has seen the team through many anxious moments. He was the man who did not see his team win the Cup

COULDN'T SPEAK

As he stood waiting for the players to come home, there were tears in the eyes of 74-year-old Mr. John Hunter, secretary of Motherwell Football Club, who, for health reasons, had been unable to travel with them.

No man had done more to bring the Cup home, but he could not be at Hampden to see it being done.

Less than 30 people were

Continued on Page Five

SIR STAFFORD: "EXTREMELY SERIOUS"

SIR STAFFORD CRIPPS is "drifting into unconsciousness," the Bircher-Benner clinic in Zurich reported late last night.

Earlier, yesterday, Dr. Dagmar Liechti, the specialist who has been attending the former Chancellor of the Exchequer, said that her patient's condition had become "extremely serious."

Sir Stafford will be 63 next Thursday.

"His heart and circulation are beginning to feel the strain as the disease spreads to various parts of the body. Any further changes in the patient's condition will be reported," said Dr. Liechti.

Lady Cripps is spending the whole time with her husband

Last were first in drama

IT was a case of the last being first when the Scottish Community Drama Finals concluded in Inverness last night.

The winners and recipients of the *Daily Record* Trophy were the Glasgow Jewish Institute players, who produced "Lucrezia Borgia's Little Party," by A. J. Talbot. Of the nine teams taking part in the three-day festival they were the last to perform.

They will now represent Scotland at the all-British finals. Runners-up were the Kirkintilloch Players, with "Hangman's Noose," by T. M. Watson, a Glasgow journalist, while in third place were Edinburgh City Police with "Gentle Like a Dove," also written by a journalist, Mr. Albert Mackie of Edinburgh.

In his adjudication on the winning play, Mr. Andre van Gysegham praised in particular the work of producer, Mr. Avrom Greenbaum. "There have been, I think, better individual performances in one or two plays during the festival, but here we had an ensemble at its very best," he said.

Her choice won £500, TV

"THIS is the best birthday present I have ever had." So said Mrs. Margaret Kay, of 5 G'ebe Park, Kirkcaldy, when told that she had won £500 and a £75 TV set in last week's Sunday Mail Fashion Contest —once she had got over the shock.

Mrs. Kay, who celebrates her sixty-fourth birthday to-morrow, has been a widow for 18 years, and to help the family budget along (she lives with an unmarried daughter) she works as a school cleaner.

A competitor in the Fashion Contest since its inception, she is truly pleased at her success.

Within minutes of being told of her good luck, she was planning just where the TV set would sit. On the question of the money she showed true Fife caution and said: "I won't waste it, that's one thing."

First use of her money prize will be for birthday presents in reverse to her immediate relatives. Then the rest will go into the bank — "for ma auld age."

LIGHTNING KILLS A BOY, BURNS TRAM

A BOY playing on a common was struck dead by lightning and 16 people were taken to hospital when lightning struck a tram during a brief but violent thunderstorm which ended the heat-wave in Birmingham yesterday afternoon.

The boy, 15-year-old Michael Edward Lowe of Alum Rock, Birmingham, was riding his bicycle when the lightning struck.

The tram was struck at the height of the storm as it stood at a stop near the city centre. There was an explosion and women passengers screamed as they rushed from the vehicle. The lower deck caught fire but this was quickly extinguished.

Sixteen passengers in all were taken to Birmingham Accident Hospital. Eleven were suffering from shock, five had burns. One 18-year-old girl had severe leg burns.

The storm, which lasted about half an hour, followed a maximum temperature of over 72 degrees at 2 p.m. Torrential rain followed the lightning

DID YOU REMEMBER?

Did YOU remember to put the clock FORWARD one hour before going to bed last night? Summer Time officially began at 2 a.m. to-day.

"You're right...it's GOOD HONEST FOOD

because it contains only the **PURE, NOURISHING ENERGY-GIVING WHOLE WHEAT**

With milk, and a little sugar, honey, syrup or jam **IT'S BRITAIN'S GREAT BODY-BUILDING BREAKFAST"**

Welgar Shredded Wheat is a favourite with the family right from the first spoonful. It's not only good for them — it's *all* food, remember — but it's tasty and satisfying. Take home a packet of Welgar Shredded Wheat today—only 1/0½d.

THE ALL-WEATHER CEREAL

WELGAR SHREDDED WHEAT

ballito
Mirrasilk
SHEER AS NYLONS

NOW AVAILABLE - 12/6 A PAIR

Daily Record
and Mail.

Air fare
cut
Page 6

MEN'S 30'-
for 16'11
With 2 Trubenised Collars
In all sizes. Beautiful
designs and patterns.
Were 30/-.
OUR PRICE.. **16'11**
GRANITE HOUSE
TRONGATE STOCKWELL STREET
CORNER. GLASGOW

ESTABLISHED 1895. No. 17,780. TUESDAY, SEPTEMBER 30, 1952. A KEMSLEY NEWSPAPER. 1½d.

Speed king's wife saw Crusader boat blow up

COBB DIED FASTEST MAN ON WATER

The last journey starts . . . Cobb adjusts his goggles and a member of his radio team points over to the mirror-calm waters of Loch Ness.

But his 206 m.p.h. can't be official world record

"Daily Record" Reporter

JOHN COBB—the fastest man on land—at the age of 52 yesterday travelled faster than any other man on water and was killed in doing so.

For on Loch Ness he was clocked at 206 m.p.h. —28 m.p.h. faster than the world's record, held by Stanley Sayers, an American.

At one time Cobb must have reached a speed of over 240 m.p.h., but there is no possibility of his run being entered as an official record.

He did the first run at 206.89 m.p.h., but did not complete the second run as essential for a new record. Lieut.-Commander Arthur Bray, chief observer at Loch Ness with John Cobb's party, said this last night.

But less than one minute before his supreme triumph—the reverse run along the measured mile on Loch Ness—the birch and alloy 4000-h.p. jet boat Crusader, blew up a hundred yards after the end of the first run.

Hundreds of people were standing stock still on the shores of the mirrored-calm waters breathless with admiration at the speed of this gleaming streak when suddenly there was a huge splash of spray, a

Continued on Back Page

12 saved from Atlantic

A RADIO message received at the Hague last night asked ships to help search for survivors of the 80 crew of a Portuguese motor fishing vessel, which went down in mid-Atlantic six days ago.

The message from Land's End radio said the American steamer Compass (7200 tons) had reported picking up three boats with 12 men aboard, near the Azores yesterday afternoon and was searching for others of the crew of the Portuguese vessel Joao Costa (773 tons).

STEAMER "TOO SLOW"

The Compass said she was "too slow for effective search" and asked all ships in the area to help.

She said survivors revealed that their ship went down at 9 p.m. on September 23, when bound for Portugal from Newfoundland.

Later, the Compass said she was forced to discontinue the search for further survivors due an engine breakdown.

Missing man found buried

Dublin, Monday.

AN elderly Co. Wicklow labourer, James Byrne, of Talbotstown, Kiltegan, who had been missing since Friday, was yesterday found dead, buried in a crude grave near his home.

The police had been searching for him since he was reported missing, and yesterday discovered the grave in a garden of the cottage in which he lived with his brother, Patrick, also a labourer.

A pathologist performed a post-mortem examination last night.

Bevan's damp squib

"Daily Record" Industrial Correspondent

Morecambe, Monday.

BEVANITES proved more royalist than their king when the Labour Party Conference opened here at the Winter Gardens to-day. Tension began to mount after a quiet and thoughtful presidential adress from mild-mannered conference chairman Mr. Harry Earnshaw.

Restlessly the Bevanites sat through a denationalisation motion couched in familiar terms—then burst into angry protest at the card vote defeat of an alternative resolution demanding expropriation of profits and no compensation if some future Labour Government re-nationalises industries restored to private hands.

This hypothetical retribution was outvoted by 2,386,000 to 1,652,000.

Then the undercurrent of antipathy between the five-million strong union delegates and the one-million strong constituency vote burst into a naked explosion of spleen.

VIOLENT BARRACKING

Shouts, boos and catcalls greeted T.U.C. vice-chairman Mr. Arthur Deakin who, with miners leader Sir William Law-

Continued on Back Page

"I think I'd like

a White Horse

better than anything"

CHURCHILL FOR BALMORAL

By IAN G FRASER

MR. CHURCHILL is to fly to Balmoral Castle to-morrow for an audience of the Queen.

After presiding over a Cabinet meeting at 10 Downing Street in the morning Mr. Churchill will leave London in a Viking of the Queen's Flight for Dyce Aerodrome, near Aberdeen. He will complete the journey to Balmoral by car.

He will stay at the Castle until Friday, when he will return to London by the Viking.

No special political signifi- cance is attached to the visit, it was emphasised in London last night. The meeting will be one of the customary series in which Mr. Churchill, as Prime Minister, has been keeping the Queen informed of the political situation at home and abroad.

AND THE LAST RUN ENDS . . .

The loch is still calm : : . but Crusader has gone and at Temple Pier they bring Cobb's body ashore.

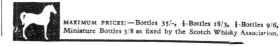

MAXIMUM PRICES:—Bottles 35/-, ½-Bottles 18/3, ¼-Bottles 9/6, Miniature Bottles 3/8 as fixed by the Scotch Whisky Association.

Bedding
Double Bed Size Interior Spring
Mattresses—Fully guaranteed.
Usual Price £8.3.4. Our Price £5.15.0
On easy terms — only 3/- Weekly
Interior Spring with pre-built Border.
Usual Price £10.10.0. Our Price £7.3.4
On easy terms 3/6 Weekly
NO DEPOSIT
CLYDESDALE SUPPLY Co. Ltd.
37 JAMAICA ST., GLASGOW
6 BRANCHES

Sunday Mail

Scotland's National Sunday Newspaper

No. 2315. FEBRUARY 1, 1953.   A KEMSLEY NEWSPAPER. 2½d.

SIX MEN *write about* WOMEN PAGE TEN

Not just a name but a guarantee
Culmak
SHAVING BRUSHES

Bangor — IRELAND — Lt. Ho. — Mew Isd — Copeland Isd — Donaghadee — TO LARNE — BLOWN OFF COURSE. SUNK HERE — N — Portpatrick — STRANRAER — Loch Ryan — SCOTLAND

IRISH BOAT DISASTER

132 PERISH: NO WOMEN OR CHILDREN SURVIVED

AS DARKNESS FELL ON THE RAGING IRISH SEA YESTERDAY AFTERNOON ONLY 45 SURVIVORS HAD BEEN PICKED UP OF THE 177 MEN, WOMEN AND CHILDREN ABOARD THE BRITISH RAILWAYS STEAMER PRINCESS VICTORIA, WHICH LEFT STRANRAER YESTERDAY MORNING BOUND FOR LARNE. NO WOMEN OR CHILDREN SURVIVORS HAVE LANDED AT DONAGHADEE SO FAR.

The Princess Victoria, within an hour of leaving Stranraer, ran into the full force of the 110 m.p.h. hurricane which has battered Scotland for the last 36 hours, and was blown 20 miles off her course before she capsized.

Desperate

The desperate search was being carried on last night by searchlight in mountainous seas, but there is only the faintest hope that the total number of survivors will be more than 50.

The scenes aboard the five - year - old Clyde-built ship, before she sank were among the grimmest in the long story of shipwrecks at sea.

As the water poured over her, doors at the stern were smashed and the seas swept through. She listed badly and the order was given to abandon ship.

Many were drowned, or crushed to death, as they jumped over the side to rafts in the heavy, boiling seas.

All last night searchlights tried to pierce the darkness, and all round the area the

Continued on Back Page, Column 1

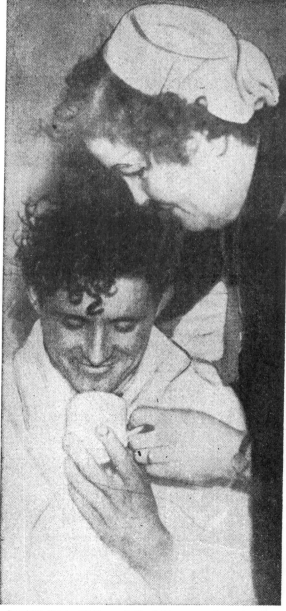

Survivor James Wallace, of Carrickfergus, receives attention after being brought ashore at Donaghadee.

Capt. James Ferguson, commander of the lost vessel.

More strong winds

To-day's weather forecast is that there will be strong winds decreasing slowly. Showers of rain, sleet or snow, will be broken by a few bright periods. It will be cold.

For only 4ᴰ

You can stop the pain of

ACID STOMACH

Refused invitations because of flatulence

The meal is over—then comes that persistent pain of flatulence. All the previous enjoyment ruined. Never again. Perhaps you know this feeling from experience. Wouldn't it be worth 4d. to avoid this source of such discomfort — that's all it would cost you for a trial packet of Rennies.

A trial size of Rennies costs 4d. It contains 10 tablets. Suck Rennies slowly, like sweets, allowing the antacids to trickle into your stomach, drip by drip. At once they begin to neutralise the excess acid which is the cause of your trouble. Soon you realise that the pain is gone. Rennies are obtainable at all chemists at 4d., 10d., 1/7. and 2/10. If Rennies don't relieve your indigestion, it's high time you saw a doctor.

DIGESTIF **Rennies** FOR INDIGESTION, ACIDITY, ETC.

NO BOOKING FEE
— NO DEPOSIT
with the
'DORMIE'
MENSWEAR
HIRE SERVICE
Call Write or Phone:
CENtral 4462 for
Illustrated Brochure
W. L. THOMSON
& SON LTD
25-27 UNION ST
219a ARGYLE ST
GLASGOW
Edinburgh & Newcastle

Daily Record
and Mail.

ESTABLISHED 1895.   No. 17,989.   TUESDAY, JUNE 2, 1953.   A KEMSLEY NEWSPAPER.   1½d.

Queen's
gown
Page 13

"Walters'
Palm"
Toffee
The best that
Mummy can buy!

CORONATION WEATHER

London—Winds northerly, fresh or strong and gusty; some sunny intervals; occasional showers, heavy at times, perhaps with hail and thunder here and there; very cool—midday temperatures 50 to 59 degrees.

Scotland—Sunny periods, with scattered showers. It will be rather cool, with midday temperatures 50 to 55 degrees. Winds will be northerly, moderate in the west to strong in the east.

AFTER IT'S ALL OVER . . .

TO-DAY, the Coronation; to-morrow, our memories of this great day of dedication . . . the solemn pageantry in London, the historic drama in Westminster Abbey as our young Queen is crowned, the gay crowd scenes outside and rejoicings throughout the land at this consecration of a new Elizabethan Age.

To-morrow's 32-page edition of the "Daily Record," partly in glowing colour, will be a store-house of these memories, a souvenir of the day's events for yourself, and friends abroad, to treasure.

The Coronation offers a splendid challenge to the newspaper world, one which Scotland's national paper has met with months of careful planning.

The "Daily Record" will have the finest coverage in the country of the whole colourful

Continued on Back Page

From a Palace window . . .

. . . Prince Charles and Princess Anne have a peep at the crowds.

AT LAST — IT'S THE GREAT DAY

On eve of crowning

The Queen at the Palace yesterday with Prime Ministers Churchill and Menzies.

By STANLEY BONNETT

THE lights in the first-floor bedroom went out early last night, but outside Buckingham Palace the Coronation crowd still roared excitedly, and swirled and grew.

Inside, in the quiet behind the double-frame windows, the Queen had already retired, and was peacefully sleeping.

"Bobo" was due to call her at 8 a.m. This shy, painstaking Inverness-born servant has been personal maid to the Queen since the Queen's childhood, as the nickname testifies.

The honour of awakening the Queen on a great day has belonged to "Bobo" before.

And as Margaret McKay drew the tapestry curtains tehn, on the day of the Royal wedding, murmured a soft "Good morning, Ma'am," and

Continued on Back Page

EVEREST IS CONQUERED

NEWS of the successful bid of the British expedition in reaching the summit of Mount Everest was given by announcers who broke into United States radio and television programmes to-day.

Graphic first details hit the first evening radio programmes broadcast to the American public.

Opening Time is Guinness Time

IT'S A GRAND DRINK, Guinness, when you really need reviving; wonderfully invigorating when you wilt in warm weather—and goodness, how refreshing! Guinness goes on doing you good even when it's finished. You stay invigorated. Your thirst stays quenched. That's what makes Guinness such wonderful value.

GUINNESS DOES MORE THAN QUENCH YOUR THIRST

GUINNESS SCOTTISH OFFICE, 85 CLYDE FERRY ST., GLASGOW, C.3   G.E.2093.14

Scotland celebrates Coronation Day
A TOAST FROM THE CHILDREN

First to be born in Glasgow's Maternity Hospital at Rottenrow, after the crowning of the Queen was Linda Elizabeth Youngman, here seen with Nurse Lorna Stephen, who delivered her. Linda weighed 7 lbs.

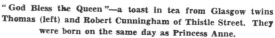

"God Bless the Queen"—a toast in tea from Glasgow twins Thomas (left) and Robert Cunningham of Thistle Street. They were born on the same day as Princess Anne.

Not official

There was a bonfire yesterday at at a farm at **BANTON**, Stirlingshire, which was not part of the celebrations. Fire swept from the stackyard into a hay shed and destroyed it. Damage is estimated at £450.

And at **STEVENSTON** a children's choir sang a Coronation hymn written by a local man, Mr. James Sinclair.

His unlucky day

Coronation Day proved unlucky for Joseph Banner, 14 Killearn Street, Possilpark, Glasgow— a day-tripper to **GIRVAN**.

While playing football at Victory Park, he fell and broke his leg and was removed to Ayr County Hospital.

He was not entirely unlucky, however, for he chose to have his accident outside a house where **Girvan's** part-time ambulance driver was viewing the Coronation on TV.

Trip on loch

Nearly 1000 old folks from the Vale of Leven were taken on an evening's cruise on Loch Lomond on board the new B.R. steamer Maid of the Loch last night.

At **DUNOON** there was a Coronation ball and dance, and a firework display rounded off the day's festivities.

Prison bonfire

The Queen Victoria School band played at **STIRLING** in the morning. In the evening two dance bands played in the King's Park.

One of the bonfires was lit in a tower of the old military prison. The local boating and swimming club staged a youth regatta on the Forth.

First claimant for the Stirling bounty for a Coronation Day baby is Mrs. Veronica Cullen, 13 Douglas Street, who gave birth to a baby boy at five minutes past eight.

Three kittens

The Smith family had no difficulty in finding names for three kittens born in their home at 55 Annick Street, Shettleston. Their choice: Red, Snowy and Bluey.

Castle floodlit

At **DUMBARTON**, the famous castle was floodlit last night.

First ceremony of the day was the planting of a commemorative British oak tree in Levengrove Park. Later a new rest garden on the west side of Dumbarton Bridge was opened and dedicated.

And while the local folk were huddled round their TV and radio sets, burgh officials delivered presents to the young patients of Crosslet Home.

Loyal Address

A large crowd attended the united service in **DUNBLANE** Cathedral which opened the local celebrations. A Loyal Address was later sent to Her Majesty.

The programme at **ABERFELDY** included football finals, a fancy dress parade and a carnival dance.

Their reminder

They will have a permanent reminder of the Coronation at **PAXTON**.

A playing field and a children's play park in the centre of the village were presented yesterday for the use of the villagers by Mrs. Home-Robertson, of Paxton House.

Bonfire too early

WESTFIELD village, West Lothian, had an earlier bonfire yesterday than was expected when a wing of the school was burned out.

The cause is thought to have been a spark from a bonfire or a firework at the children's gala day on Monday.

500 short

Children of **HAWICK** walking in the local procession yesterday were promised half-a-crown, and 2200 coins were held in readiness.

But the procession was the biggest ever known in the town and the supply of half crowns ran out with nearly 500 children still to be paid. Girls outnumbered boys in the procession by nearly 3-1.

While the children were running their races at the Volunteer Park a frantic search was being conducted for more half crowns and all claims were duly honoured.

Mail coach star

An 18th century mail coach which plied between Moffat and Edinburgh was the star at a fancy dress parade held at **GALASHIELS** yesterday afternoon.

Celebrations started with a united service in Old and St. Paul's Church. The evening was taken up with open-air dancing and a Coronation Revue in the Pavilion Theatre.

"Queen" on tour

Thirteen-year-old Christina Anderson was crowned Coronation Queen at celebrations in **BLACKBURN**, West Lothian, and afterwards toured the district in an open carriage drawn by two grey horses.

The procession was led by the Whitrigg Colliery pipe band and the Stoneyburn silver band.

Fleet review

Throughout yesterday the jubilations in the north had to contend with a cold northerly wind, and there were heavy rain showers in some places.

At **HELMSDALE** a review of the port's gaily-bedecked fishing fleet was held. Golspie celebrated with a race for men to the top of Ben Bhraggie (1293 feet) and a women's race to Dunrobin

Lairg had a fancy-dress parade, and even at lonely Suleskerry out in the Atlantic 35 miles west of the Orkneys the three lightkeepers hoisted flags and celebrated.

Largs watch

Police were keeping an eye on the decorations at **LARGS** municipal chambers last night following a partially successful attempt to deface them by cutting out the numeral II from an EIIR display.

Provost Andrew Montgomery was listening at home to the broadcast when he received a telephone call from a man who said he was a member of the "Scottish Republican Army." "The decorations at the municipal chambers have been damaged, and more damage will be done," said the caller and hung up.

It was found that "II" in the Royal cipher had been cut out of a banner hanging from the wall of the municipal chambers. A similar banner on a side wall, which was not so easy to reach, remained untouched.

Provost Montgomery said the telephone caller sounded like a young man.

And chalked along the promenade at **SALTCOATS** when townspeople wakened yesterday were many Scottish Nationalist slogans. Stencilled on litter bins was E II R.

"Kiddievee" to benefit

Ayrshire and Lanarkshire referees play their charity game at Meadow Park, Irvine on Friday

On this occasion the proceeds will go towards our "Kiddievee" Fund. The kick-off is 7.30.

DRAUGHTSMEN
and
STRESS ENGINEERS
(OF ALL CLASSES AIRCRAFT EXPERIENCE NOT ESSENTIAL)

Join a progressive and expanding organisation. Work on an intensive programme of research and development on advanced types of Super and Sub Sonic aircraft. Be employed on work of national importance. Live in the warmer, healthier climate of the Isle of Wight. Housing facilities available. Good opportunities for technical training. First class recreational facilities.

Arrangements will be made to interview applicants in their home area and for selected personnel to visit the Isle of Wight with expenses paid. Apply stating age qualifications experience salary. etc. to:

The Personnel Office (Dept. G.D.R.2)
SAUNDERS ROE LIMITED
COWES ISLE OF WIGHT

Daily Record and Mail, Friday, May 7, 1954.

Safe, Speedy Demolition ?
There's only ONE
Sam B. Allison Ltd.

Daily Record

ESTABLISHED 1895.　No. 18,279.　FRIDAY, MAY 7, 1954.　A KEMSLEY NEWSPAPER, 1½d.

VP wine with TV

Out the window went £150

SOMEWHERE among the long grass of a quiet roadside in South Ayrshire a diamond and sapphire ring, valued at £150, was lying hidden last night.

It belonged to Mrs. G. W. Dunn, of Bloomfield, Arbroath, who, along with her husband, was motoring to Portpatrick yesterday afternoon.

As the car neared the entrance to Culzean Castle on the Maybole-Maidens road, Mrs. Dunn, who had been eating a banana, threw the skin out of the window of the car.

HAD GONE

When she drew her hand into the car again she discovered that the valuable ring she had been wearing had gone.

Her husband stopped the car and the couple began a search, in which they were later joined by the village policeman from Maidens.

They failed to find any trace of the ring, however, and after more than an hour Mr. and Mrs. Dunn continued on their journey to Portpatrick, where they will be staying for a few days.

Mrs. Dunn, who has had the ring for less than a year, said last night that she had arranged with the police at Maidens to have some of the local children search for it.

"I shall most certainly reward the finder," she said.

SHOWERS.—Fresh northerly winds, cold.

The world was astounded at the news

FORTY minutes after Bannister had collapsed on the tapes after shattering the world record for the mile, tributes began to reach him. Here are some of them :

Mr. Avery Brundage, president of the International Olympic Committee (from Lausanne) : "Wonderful. My hearty congratulations." He appeared to be astounded at the news.

M. Rene Mourlon, training director of French Athletics Federation (from Paris) : "Britain can look forward to keeping the four-minute laurels for a long time yet."

Arthur Daley, "New York Times" sports columnist : "This is as historic as breaking the sound barrier."

M. Armand Nassard, French vice-president of the International Olympic Committee : "It is magnificent."

Mr. Dan Ferris, secretary of the U.S. Amateur Athletic Union: "He's a great athlete. We congratulate him on being the first to achieve what so many athletes have been trying for."

4-MINUTE MILE BANNISTER DOES IT

ROGER BANNISTER is the fastest miler in the world. At Oxford last night he ran the mile in 3 mins. 59.4secs.

To the 24-year-old St. Mary's Hospital, London, medical student went the honour of being the first man in athletic history to run a mile in less than four minutes.

Bannister made his world shattering record in unfavourable conditions. A 15 m.p.h. cross wind was gusting to 25 m.p.h. just before the race.

An expert stated that if it had been calm, Bannister's time would have been in the region of 3 minutes 58 seconds.

Collapsed

Ever since Gundar Haegg did 4 min. 1.4 secs. in 1942, every middle distance champion has set his eye on the four-minute mile, but the A.A.A. champion has beaten the world to it.

Bannister's time was taken at 1500 metres at which point he clocked three minutes 43 seconds to equal the world record at that distance.

After his brilliant performance, Bannister, surrounded by a mob of seething people as he breasted the tape, collapsed through exhaustion and had to be assisted off the track by officials.

Bannister and Chataway, his team mate and former A.A.A. three-mile champion, expressed their determination to go for a fast time right from the start even though Bannister remarked: "The conditions are stupid."

Chataway was suffering from slight stomach trouble, but he, too, was full of confidence.

Chataway decided to make all the running and strode out boldly followed by Bannister and Chris Brasher.

Brasher set up a cracking pace and at the end of the first lap he led. Bannister's time was 57.7 secs.

There was no alteration in the running at the end of the second lap, which Bannister reached in 1 min. 58.3 secs.

CROSS WIND

Shortly after the start of the third lap Chataway took up the running, with Bannister just behind him.

Hampered by the cross wind, they plugged along manfully, with the auburn-haired Chataway just ahead of Bannister at the end of the third lap (3mins. 0.5 secs.).

Murder: Eire move

"Record" Reporter

A GREY-HAIRED "Mr. Smith" with a bowler hat, tweed coat and pipe, and a tall, distinguished looking "Mr. Brown," with felt hat and raincoat, left Stratford-on-Avon secretly for Dublin yesterday.

And, dramatically, the hunt for the strangler of Olive Bennet, 45-year-old midwife, had switched to Eire.

In reality, "Mr. Smith" was Supt. John Capstick, of Scotland Yard. With him, as "Mr. Brown," was Det.-Insp. Eric Jenkins, of Warwickshire C.I.D.

They are to make secret inquiries in many counties in Eire as the result of information they received in Stratford.

The decision was made after Supt. Capstick telephoned Scotland Yard from Warwick.

He used a secret telephone line from the Warwickshire police H.Q. at Leekwootton.

THE STORM MOVES EAST

THE May gale—the worst for 20 years—which struck the Firth of Clyde area on Wednesday has now moved across Scotland and is raging in the North Sea.

But last night the storm, though slowly abating, still lashed the North East coast.

JAIL FOR DAWN'S PRINCE

Leghorn, Thursday.

ITALIAN Prince Vittorio Massimo — who married British film actress Dawn Addams last week — was sentenced to four months imprisonment for insulting a traffic policeman.

The charge alleged that the Prince had an altercation with a Leghorn traffic policeman on October 10 and used insulting language.

Rome police headquarters informed the Leghorn court that the Prince immediately gave notice of appeal.

The Prince had received a suspended sentence of seven months' imprisonment on a similar charge in 1940.

The Prince's lawyer, Signor Giovanni Funaro, said his client's words at the time attacked the Fascist regime, not the policeman.

Individually MADE TO MEASURE that's the point!

At HEPWORTHS a *Made-to-Measure* suit means precisely what it implies. First you select style and material ; then your chosen length of cloth is carefully cut by hand to your individual measurements and tailored by skilled craftsmen. It is this *individual* attention to each and every bespoke order that creates the noticeable distinction of HEPWORTHS tailoring ...

... such suits—perfect in every detail—are easily today's best value at

£8.15 　 £10.15 　 £12.15

Hepworths
Where the *GOOD CLOTHES* come from

H192

Branches at ABERDEEN · AIRDRIE · ALLOA · ARBROATH · AYR · BATHGATE · BUCKIE · CUPAR · COATBRIDGE · DINGWALL · DUNDEE · DUNFERMLINE · DUMFRIES · EDINBURGH (SOUTH BRIDGE AND TOLLCROSS) · ELGIN · FALKIRK · FORRES · FORT WILLIAM · GREENOCK · HAMILTON · HAWICK · INVERNESS · KEITH · KILMARNOCK · KIRKCALDY · KIRKWALL · LEITH · LERWICK · LEVEN · PERTH · THURSO · MOTHERWELL · PAISLEY · PETERHEAD · ST. ANDREWS · STIRLING · STORNOWAY

SUNDAY MAIL

Scotland's National Sunday Newspaper.

No. 2417. JANUARY 16, 1955. A KEMSLEY NEWSPAPER 2½d.

SNOW SOS: 'FOOD FOR CHILDREN'

WE DID IT AGAIN ...BY 20,000

ABOUT this time last year, the "Sunday Mail" announced that it had won and retained many new readers in the previous 12 months. To-day, it has much pleasure in making a similar announcement.

The average net sale of the "Sunday Mail" for the six months ending December, 1954, as certified by the Audit Bureau of Circulation, was ...

645,118

That means that the paper's total number of readers has increased over the same period of the previous year by ...

20,414

The understanding between us and our readers is something which also grows. It is always alive and thriving. For instance, do you know that....

1—*We could fill the entire paper with readers' letters every Sunday? (The Answers Man alone received 3400 this week, by the way.)*

2—*We are always surprised at the number of readers, many anonymous, who send us money to pass on in cases of misfortune reported in the "Sunday Mail?"*

3—*No complaint or protest in the "Sunday Mail" regarding a public grievance is ignored by the authorities concerned?*

4—*All sorts of public bodies ask us for permission to publish reprints of "Sunday Mail" special articles, especially those with a strong human appeal?*

And the future ?

Our immediate plans include several outstanding new features and special articles which are certain to be widely and keenly discussed. Watch for the announcements.

Now, many thanks to all the newsagents and news vendors who have done such a good job for us, often in bad weather.

Here's wishing all of you sunny days and still bigger sales of the "Sunday Mail."

Scotland's most controversial story is still ...

THE LOVES OF ROBERT BURNS

ON PAGE 12

And still it snows

Heavy snowdrifts surround the tiny Sutherland hamlet of Invershin on the main railway line from Inverness to Wick.

"**H**ELP us . . . we're almost af starvation level . . . there's not enough for the kids to eat."

These words, spoken over the telephone from a snow-blitzed Caithness hamlet, emphasise the plight of the people in the North of Scotland. . . .

. . . Now in their fifth day of trial by snow and ice, with a fresh blizzard raging and food and fuel stocks running low.

Darkness yesterday halted the "mercy mission" air-drops of supplies by the R.A.F. At dawn to-day, however, naval helicopters joined the air-lift to relieve the stricken communities, some of whom reported :

"Our need is desperate — the children are our main concern."

Hardest hit seemed to be the remote hamlet of Braemore, near Berriedale, Caithness. It was over Braemore's only line to the outside world that crofter Hugh Reid yesterday phoned his S O S for help, for food for "the kids."

SMOKE PILLAR

Soon an R.A.F. Coastal Command Shackleton was on its way: and as it droned across the snow the villagers of Braemore marked out a "dropping" zone by setting fire to diesel oil in a field.

The plane "ran in" on the pillar of smoke and, going down to 400 feet, parachuted canis—

(Continued on Back Page)

Other blizzard stories—page 3

FROST TO-DAY

There will be no let-up in Scotland's weather to-day. Throughout the country the weather will be very cold and frosty with snow at times.

MERCY LIFT

AS the great snow-storm gradually closed up the North of Scotland last night, desperate plans were made to rescue several cases of illness from their snow-locked hamlets by helicopters.

At first light to-day, two of these machines are due to leave from Wick

One of these two naval helicopters is to attempt to land on the snow-caked field beside her cottage and take an expectant mother to hospital at Thurso.

The second helicopter will try to bring out an appendicitis case from a croft not far from Wick.

It is understood that if the machines cannot land owing to drifts, a member of the crew will, in each case, be lowered by winding rope after which the patients, lashed to specially prepared harness, will be hoisted aloft, and flown to hospital.

She's the winner, in nick of time

MRS. CISSIE MEIKLE, of 47 Kilmarnock Road, Shawlands, Glasgow, who has just won outright, subject to rescrutiny, the prize of £250 and a TV set in "Sunday Mail" Crossword Contest No. 117, very nearly didn't submit her entry-form.

"I missed the post, and I was not going to send it in," she told a "Sunday Mail" reporter who called to give her the good news.

"I suddenly decided that it would be a pity not to send it in. I put my coat on, caught a bus into town, and handed the envelope into Kemsley House just before the entries closed."

Relaxation

Mrs. Meikle, when she had regained her breath after the excitement of the good news, said, "I get a great kick out of filling in the 'Sunday Mail' crossword. I have been sending in coupons for some time, but this is my first prize."

Mrs. Meikle, by winning the contest outright, also receives, in addition to the sum of £250, a TV set valued at £75.

Mrs. Cissie Meikle

Porter's bid to save man who slipped

BOARDING a train in Port Glasgow railway station last night, 61-year-old William Dick, of 61 Balloch Road, Greenock, slipped and fell between the train and the platform.

He was taken to Greenock Royal Infirmary and detained with severe injuries.

A young porter at the station, 19-year-old Joseph Kelly, of 19 Bridgend Avenue, Port Glasgow, tried to save Mr. Dick, but as the train gathered speed he had to let go.

He, too, fell between the train and the platform and was taken to hospital. He was allowed home after treatment for bruises and shock.

RADIO—Page 11

For COUNTLESS THOUSANDS throughout the world OVALTINE is the 'Goodnight' Drink

P950a

No other Beverage can give you better sleep

SUNDAY MAIL

Scotland's National Sunday Newspaper.

No. 2426. MARCH 20, 1955. A KEMSLEY NEWSPAPER 2½d.

Scotland can give a lead to the whole world but...

DO NOT LOOK FOR MIRACLES, SAYS BILLY

"The problem isn't the hydrogen bomb or the Communists ..." Billy Graham talking to the Press yesterday.

WITH his Bible in one hand and his hat in the other, Billy Graham acknowledged his enthusiastic welcome to Scotland yesterday with the message: "The eyes of the world are on you. You can be the start of a religious revival that will sweep the world."

But he counselled: "DON'T EXPECT MIRACLES. DON'T EXPECT TOO MUCH FROM US."

Billy Graham—"Call me plain mister. I haven't earned my degree of doctor"—obviously wasn't expecting the tremendous welcome that awaited when he arrived in Glasgow for the start of his six-week All-Scotland Crusade.

Certainly, he didn't expect the reception he got en route—at Dumfries, time 7 a.m.

In fact he was almost caught napping by the hymn singing crowds who had gathered to see him pass.

"I was still in bed when I heard them singing outside," he told reporters. "I decided if they had got up that early to greet me, I could get up to speak to them. I did, flinging my overcoat on top of my pyjamas. But it became rather difficult when they wanted me to pose for pictures ... I had to explain my position."

WELCOME HYMN

In Glasgow, over 3000 people crowded St. Enoch Station to welcome the tall, sun-tanned, wavy-haired preacher with the film-star looks. As he stepped from the train they started to sing a hymn. A man with a Salvation Army hat played a cornet, while another accompanied the singing with a concertina.

A diminutive, grimy-faced porter elbowed his way through the official reception party on the platform to grab Mr. Graham's hand and pump it up and down with great gusto. And a woman with a little girl broke from the crowd and put her arm round his waist. She accompanied the smiling evangelist as he

ALL-NIGHT PRAYERS

As Billy Graham was travelling to Scotland, an all-night prayer meeting for the success of his campaign was held in Aberdeen Gilcomston South Church.

When it began at 10 p.m. on Friday, there was a congregation of about 400. At the conclusion at 6 a.m. yesterday about 50 people were in the church.

There were sessions of hymn singing, scripture reading, and prayers.

pushed his way through the cheering, singing throng.

Before leaving to meet almost 100 reporters in a hotel, he told the crowd from a balcony window overlooking the station: "We have been praying all the way across the Atlantic that God may start a spiritual revival here in Glasgow."

And to reporters he said: "This mission to Glasgow is all-important. The eyes of the Christian world are on us. I believe we will have the start of a religious revival that will sweep the whole world.

Continued on Back Page

ANOTHER COAL SHOCK

By J. D. MARGACH

BIG increases in coal prices are coming. They'll be the biggest since the war, with drastic increases in the prices of coal for major industries and nationalised industries like the railways.

And the cost of the stiff increases in industry's overheads will have to be passed on to the ordinary coal consumers.

Facing a total deficit of £17M., the National Coal Board have decided big price rises are necessary to put their finances on a healthier level.

Wage rises

The Board also have an eye on the proposed new wage increases which will cost them £13M. extra a year.

But all the increased prices will be concentrated almost wholly on coal for industrial users, to relieve domestic and household coal of any additional burden.

Tanker got stop order

The crew of the Finnish tanker Aruba, carrying 13,000 tons of jet fuel for Communist China, have agreed to sail her into the Indian Ocean and wait in international waters between Ceylon and Malaya for further orders.

The decision was announced in Helsinki to-day by the Finnish Seamen's Union, which has authorised the crew to refuse to sail in "dangerous waters."

Singapore Port authorities will refuse bunkering facilities to the Aruba if she calls there. The Western powers have claimed that she is breaking a ban on strategic exports to China imposed by the United Nations, of which Finland is not a member.

In Peking, the official People's Daily accused the United States to-day of sending five warships to Singapore to interfere with the tanker's voyage to Whampoa, the port of Canton.

Report in Hong Kong say that the "Aruba" is operating under a contract which is valid only if the tanker reaches Communist China.

Nehru's war fears

The dangers of war were increasing, Mr. Nehru, the Indian Premier, told a rally at Chandigarh, yesterday. In the event of war, he said, India would stay away from it.

Baby in pram disappeared

LEAVING their four-month-old baby girl asleep in her pram outside yesterday, a young couple went into the new house they had bought in Garfield Street, Dennistoun, Glasgow. Minutes later the mother looked from a window and was horrified to see that the baby and pram had disappeared.

After a frantic search of the area the baby was found—still sleeping in her pram—being wheeled through a busy shopping area by a six-year-old toddler.

The baby, Fiona Anderson, is the daughter of Sergeant George Anderson, a 25-year-old national serviceman in the R.E.M.E., and his wife, Georgina.

When Mrs. Anderson saw that the pram had disappeared, she almost collapsed. Sergeant Anderson and his father, Mr. George Anderson, raced downstairs, but the street was deserted. Running in opposite directions, they scoured the area while a "999" call was sent to police headquarters.

Began to cry

It was Sergeant Anderson who spotted the pram—being wheeled along Bellfield Street by a small girl.

"I asked the toddler why she had taken the baby," said Sergeant Anderson afterwards, "and she just started crying and ran off through a close."

And the mystery girl? She disappeared leaving only one clue behind—a green, imitation crocodile handbag.

He broke siege of Leningrad

MARSHAL Leonid Govorov, who broke the siege of Leningrad in the last war, died yesterday after a long illness, Moscow Radio announced.

Marshal Govorov was Deputy Defence Minister.

The early stages of the war saw Marshal Govorov in command of artillery on one of the sectors of the Soviet-German front. When the Germans closed in on Leningrad he was chosen to command that front and the skill with which he conducted operations there led to the smashing of the blockade of Leningrad.

36,360 new cars

Cars registered for the first time in January numbered 36,360. New motor cycles totalled 11,264.

BOY (15) SWORE AT HEAD

WHEN the father of a 15-year-old Caithness boy was summoned because of the boy's irregular attendance at school, the boy went to his headmaster's house to get an explanation, the procurator-fiscal, Mr. C. J. H. Campbell, told Wick Juvenile Court yesterday.

The headmaster refused to discuss the matter and said that he would see the boy at school. And when the boy was ordered out of the house, he started shouting and swearing at the headmaster.

Mr. Campbell said the boy thought that he was being blamed for non-attendance on August 31, whereas he was actually at school on that date.

Later in the day, the boy went to see the headmaster in the school staffroom and again demanded an explanation about the date.

A policeman who was on premises was attracted by the noise of the boy shouting. The boy then calmed down and went away.

The warning ...

The boy was charged with having: (1) Within the schoolhouse occupied by the headmaster conducted himself in a disorderly manner and committed a breach of the peace. (2) Within the headmaster's staff room threatened the headmaster and conducted himself in a disorderly manner.

Sheriff Peter Thomson, in admonishing him, warned the boy that if he appeared in court again he would have to be disciplined.

"We cannot tolerate behaviour like this towards a headmaster," he said.

JAMAICAN INVASION

OFFICIALS of Salvation Army and Y.M.C.A. hostels and borough councils in London's coloured communities are planning emergency measures this week-end to meet an invasion by Jamaicans.

One thousand are due to land at Plymouth.

Look out for rain

It will be fine, despite fog patches, over most of the country early to-day. Rain or sleet possible later.

In the west and south-west it will be mainly cloudy with a chance of rain.

AFTER 16 YEARS MRS. NOIMA SEES DAUGHTER

FROM Communist China, 76-year-old Mrs. Sura Noima arrived at London Airport yesterday to meet her daughter and son-in-law for the first time in 16 years.

Her son-in-law, Mr. Arnold Thompson, of Peel Grove, Longsight, Manchester, said that he was married while serving with the Lancashire Fusiliers in China in 1938.

His mother-in-law was a White Russian and for the past four years he had been trying to get her to join him.

"But we had some difficulties with the authorities in China and finally, through the international Committee for European Migration, we were Ur... faiom faiom faiaoa advised that my mother-in-law would be joining us."

Mrs. Noima was flown from Hong Kong by the I.C.F.M., together with a number of European refugees.

Her three grandchildren—Arnold (14), Raymond (eight) and Ellie (six) were at the airport to greet her.

It is the **Quality** *of your* **Sleep** *which counts*

That *is why countless thousands drink delicious* **Ovaltine** *The World's Best Nightcap*

1/6, 2/6 and 4/6 per tin.

No other beverage can give you better sleep

SUNDAY MAIL

Scotland's National Sunday Newspaper.

No. 2432. MAY 29, 1955. A KEMSLEY NEWSPAPER 2½d.

3 DIE, 42 HURT, IN SUNDAY SCHOOL TRIP TRAIN CRASH

They sang—and then came this

The twisted wreckage of the picnic special litters the line at Wormit Station.

THREE people—two men and a 10-year-old boy—were killed and nearly 42 injured when a Sunday school excursion train loaded with children from two Dundee churches ploughed into the platform at Wormit Station, at the south end of the Tay Bridge, Fife, last night.

Ambulances from several hospitals dashed to the crash with doctors and nurses and casualties were rushed to Adamson Cottage Hospital, Cupar, Dundee Royal Infirmary, Bridge of Earn Hospital and the hospital at R.A.F. station, Leuchars.

Fire brigades from Cupar and St. Andrews were called to the scene.

Plunged into platform

The train was carrying 600 people—300 adults and 300 children from St. Ninian's and Morrison Churches, Dundee. The 600 had been spending the afternoon at Tayport Beach and were returning—happy but tired—to Dundee.

At 7.10 p.m., as the train emerged from the tunnel leading to Wormit Station, the engine and tender came off the rails and plunged into the platform.

FIREMAN TRAPPED

The engine struck the edge of the platform and reared up in the air. Then with a tremendous crash it fell back on the tender. The fireman was trapped in the wreckage.

The first three coaches—packed with singing children—rammed into the wrecked engine and telescoped. Then the whole mass of twisted, tangled metal and woodwork fell on its side

Station workers jumped from the platform and tore at the wreckage with their bare hands to get at the screaming children lying in the carriages.

Within a few seconds children and adults staggered out of the

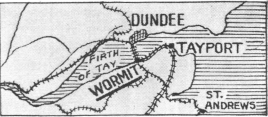

THE DEAD

Fireman John Cowie, of 84 Blackscroft, Dundee.

Ian Shaw, aged 10, of 247 Blackness Road.

Charles Harrower, aged 42, of Strathmartin Road, Dundee.

tunnel to stop, stunned and weeping, as they saw the shambles before them.

Within a few minutes of the crash word spread across the river to Dundee. Distracted parents and relatives rushed to the scene.

Among them was the Rev. John Macdonald, minister of St. Ninian's, whose wife and three young children were on the train.

Mr. Macdonald, of 20 Coupar-Angus Road, Dundee, had been with the trippers, but had returned home earlier by car.

His wife, Eileen, with her three children aged 10, seven and three, gave the "Sunday Mail" a dramatic eye-witness picture of the scene.

" We were just coming out of the tunnel when the train seemed to leap forward.

" Then came the terrible crash. We were thrown in a heap and the lights went out. Then the whole carriage seemed to slip sideways.

" Railwaymen ran along the track in the darkness and lifted us out of the carriages.

STUMBLED ON

" Then we stumbled towards the circle of light at the end of the tunnel.

" A terrible sight met our eyes. Everywhere people were crawling up the railway embankment.

" I saw many women and children being carried out of the wrecked carriages. It looked to me as if several of them were dead.

" Some of the children were

Continued on Back Page

Seconds—then help came

WITHIN a few seconds of the crash emergency calls were flashed to police stations, hospitals, and local doctors.

Over a score of ambulances—from as far away as St. Andrews—raced to Wormit. Fire brigades turned out from Cupar and St. Andrews.

The firemen immediately set about trying to raise the shattered engine and tender

PREMIER TO BROADCAST ON RAILWAY STRIKE

THE rail strike is on. Last ditch talks to avert it broke down last night only 20 minutes before the stoppage was due to begin. This afternoon at one o'clock, Sir Anthony Eden, the Prime Minister, will broadcast to the nation on the Home Service.

In a last dramatic bid to avert the strike the Ministry of Labour invited leaders of the Associated Society of Locomotive Engineers and Firemen and the National Union of Railwaymen to eleventh-hour talks.

The A.S.L.E.F. leaders—who had called the strike of their 70,000 members — went first. The time was 7.30 p.m.

Forty - five minutes later, representatives of the T.U.C. General Purposes Committee, who had been in session for much of the day, arrived.

Minutes to go

The Minister of Labour, Sir Walter Monckton, was there, too. So was the Minister of Transport, Mr. J. Boyd-Carpenter.

N.U.R. leaders also went to the Ministry.

Then, with only 20 minutes to go, came this blow to the hopes of those who had hoped for peace on the nation's railways: " Talks broken down."

The position was summed up in a Ministry of Labour statement issued four minutes before midnight. It said:

" The Chief Industrial Commissioner, Sir Wilfred Neden, has to-night held meetings at the Ministry of Labour with representatives of the A.S.L.E.F. and of the N.U.R. He was also in touch with the B.T.C.

" The discussions continued until 11.30 p.m., but did not succeed in finding a basis for averting the threatened strike on the railways."

Unwilling

Mr. J. S. Campbell, the N.U.R. secretary, said that Sir Wilfred's formula had been put to the Transport Commission, who had replied that they had not been aware of any proposals for the footplate staff which they were willing to accept

Independently of this, the Commission understood that any settlement which could be made for footplate staff at present would lead to counterclaims for other staff which they also would be unwilling to accept.

Mr. Campbell said that the formula put forward was that there should be an increase of 4s a week for drivers in their first, second and third years, nothing at all for cleaners or firemen in their first year, but 1s for firemen in their second and third year.

Neither of the unions had committed themselves to the formula, but it had not been accepted by the B.T.C.

His union executive would meet to-day to consider the strike position.

4 MINUTE MILE BROKEN—3 TIMES

THE greatest moment in the history of athletics occurred on the rain-sodden track of the White City, London, yesterday afternoon, when three men broke the four-minute mile in one race.

In the British Games International One Mile I. Tabori a 24-year-old Hungarian soldier won in 3 mins. 59 secs., only one second outside the world record of John Landy, of Australia.

Britain's Chris Chataway. was second in 3 mins. 59.8 secs., and Brian Hewson, of Britain, third with the same time.

See Page 22

YOUR NEW FEATURES GUIDE

£600 TO BE WON

SEE PAGE 6

SHELL WITH ICA

Summer Blend the most powerful petrol you can buy

THAT'S SHELL — THAT WAS!

Daily Record

FRI APR 20 1956

2ᴰ   SCOTLAND'S NATIONAL NEWSPAPER

No. 18,867

MILLIONS WERE AT HER WEDDING

THE girl with the proud and radiant look is Her Serene Highness Gracia of Monaco—known to all the world as Grace Kelly.

Yesterday television took millions of women to Grace's Cathedral wedding to Prince Rainier, an enchanting finale to two amazing days of romance and colour.

Last night, the couple stayed at the Prince's villa on the French Riviera. A Mediterranean storm halted the royal yacht's honeymoon cruise.

Mr. K. beams as London LOOKS

WITH 18 motor-cyclists escorting, and security boss Zakharov trailing, Marshal Bulganin and Mr. Kruschev zoomed around London yesterday.

It was a hectic day—taking in three visits to 10 Downing Street, a trip to Buckingham Palace, a chicken-and-vodka Embassy lunch and a Cenotaph ceremony.

London's traffic stopped several times, to let the Russian convoy whisk past. But the crowds raised little in the way of cheers—and hardly any boos.

Mostly they were just silent—and smiling.

The talks and lunches were described as "very, very happy." Mr. Kruschev beamed broadly. Mr. Bulganin looked pleased and dignified.

And last night Mr. Eden gave a dinner at Number 10 for B. and K. Sir Winston Churchill was there.

For most folk, the sensation was the SPEED of B. and K.'s journey to Downing Street. They took 21 motor-cyclists this time, and touched 50 m.p.h.

Not much time for looking OR booing!

PICTURES OF B. & K.: PAGE 3 AND BACK PAGE.

CUP FINAL SPECIAL

Don't miss tomorrow's issue of the "Daily Record"

Grace takes her poodle

It's the happy, happy ending. At the rails of the Royal yacht they stand. Princess Gracia wears a grey, shot silk costume with a white, close-fitting hat. Rainier has changed into dark grey flannels and a navy blue yachting blazer. With them goes Monaco's best wishes—and Grace's poodle.

WONDERFUL WEDDING PICTURES—centre pages

ON SALE TOMORROW
Shoe Bargains
ALL 9 A.M SPECIALS

LADIES CASUALS	LADIES SLIPPERS	LADIES SLIPPERS
In black, beige, yellow and blue linen. All sizes. Pair	"Mule" Slippers in variety of colours. Limited quantity. Pair	Paisley Pattern Slippers with wedge heel. Few only. Pair
10/-	5/-	2/6

COURT, CASUAL & TIE SHOES
Ladies high-grade Shoes in all sizes. Variety of colours. Were 69/11d to 75/-. Now, pair **39/11**

SPORTS AND CASUALS
Ladies Shoes in variety of styles and colours. Were 65/-. Now, pair **35/-**

BLACK SUEDE CASUALS
Ladies Casuals with wedge heels, Neo-Lite soles. Were 35/-. Now, pair **10/-**

CHILDREN'S SHOE ODDMENTS
Collection of oddments, in broken sizes. Black and brown. Limited quantity. From, pair .. **5/-**

WOOD & SELBY
ST GEORGES CROSS GLASGOW

Daily Record

MON JUNE 4 1956

2ᴰ SCOTLAND'S NATIONAL NEWSPAPER

No. 18,905

HEAT ROCKED A PLANE 2000 ft. ABOVE THE INFERNO

Bride, groom die in crash

A BEAUTIFUL young bride died yesterday with her husband hours after their wedding.

They were killed, these newly-weds, as the bride sat on her husband's knee, his arms around her.

Head-on

SHE still wore her white wedding gown, she still carried her bouquet of red roses. HE was still in his blue wedding suit.

And with them died seven of their wedding guests—including the bridegroom's mother, grandmother and uncle.

They were all in a van which was in head-on collision with a motor coach.

The bride was Florence Wilkinson, 21. Her husband was steel-worker John Curbishley, 23.

Watches tell

They were married at 3 p.m. on Saturday in the parish church at the Yorkshire village of Wales Bar, Florence's home.

The time of the crash that killed them and their seven guests

A guest took this snap of the bride and groom at their wedding on Saturday. They had nine hours to live....

was recorded by the watches found on the bodies.

THEY HAD ALL STOPPED SHORTLY AFTER MIDNIGHT.

Between the time of the wedding and the crash Florence and John, who had courted for four years, celebrated with their relatives and friends.

Sang, danced

They went to the home of Florence's parents in East Terrace, Wales Bar for the wedding breakfast.

Then they joined the 60 guests in a hotel across the road. Every-

Continued on Back Page

They pray for rain as forests blaze

THIS dramatic picture was taken yesterday by a " Daily Record " cameraman from a plane as it flew over one of the worst forest fires Scotland has ever had.

Isolated houses like the one arrowed above were ringed by the flames.

The fire raged through 10 square miles of valuable timber-land. Last night 50 firemen and over 100 volunteers prayed for rain.

They had the fire in check. But they said: "We can't put it out unless it rains."

A reporter who saw the fire from the air writes:

Long before the plane was over the Glentanar Estate, Aboyne, Aberdeenshire, we saw the first column of smoke spiralling 2000 feet into the overcast sky.

Soon we were over the outer edge of the fire —an awe-inspiring scene which made the blood jump in our veins.

Hot air rising from the inferno tossed the four-engine plane violently about. An acrid smell of burning wood penetrated the cabin.

Within minutes the air inside got hotter and hotter and we were glad to take our coats off.

More than 30 hours

Down below, fire-fighting units from Banchory, Kincardineshire, Aboyne, Ballater and Aberdeen—there were nine of them at one time —were being helped by every available estate and forestry worker.

For more than 30 hours the flames spread over the tinder-dry ground, the fire being fanned by a strong wind with gusts of up to 30 to 40 m.p.h.

The dirty grey smoke which hampered every step of the fire-fighters billowed up towards us from every side.

With each plunge of the plane, we caught glimpses of flaming patches on the ground. They twinkled through the smoke like pin-points of light.

Sometimes we caught a glimpse of scarred hillside where the flames had burned themselves out.

For every foot

And down below, mid the smoke and the flames, with every weapon at their disposal, making use of every ditch and burn, the fire-fighters fought for every foot of valuable timber.

Surrounded by the fire, almost isolated in the forest, one woman fought alone. She was Mrs. Margaret Fenton, wife of a gamekeeper who was himself helping the fire units.

Wrapping damp towels round her head, she kept soaking her furniture with the little water she had, as flames licked the outside and smoke seeped through the cracks into the house.

But she refused to leave and finally the fighters burst through to hose all round the cottage and save the Fentons' home.

'Gers beaten again

RANGERS were beaten in Valencia last night 4-1 in one of the roughest, toughest games of their tour. Inside-forward Sammy Baird was involved in an incident with a Spanish defender and was taken off by manager Scot Symon. He returned soon after.

On Saturday, Rangers were beaten 3-0 by Barcelona. Hungarian star, Kubala getting two goals. And last night Kubala, playing for Valencia, got another two.

(FULL REPORT—PAGE 15)

For a friendly Greeting...

You can offer your guests no friendlier welcome than a glass of "Black & White." Blended in a special way from the pick of Scotland's whiskies, "Black & White" is the outstanding example of just how good Scotch Whisky can be.

PRODUCT OF SCOTLAND

'BLACK & WHITE'

SPECIAL BLEND OF CHOICE OLD SCOTCH WHISKY

BUCHANAN'S

SCOTCH WHISKY

GLASGOW & LONDON

70° PROOF

'BLACK & WHITE'
SCOTCH WHISKY
"BUCHANAN'S"
The Secret is in the Blending

Max. Prices fixed by the Scotch Whisky Assn. (U.K.): 36/- Bot., 18/9½ Bot., 9/9 ½ Bot., 3/9 Min. Bot.

Daily Record

WED JULY 4 1956

2D SCOTLAND'S NATIONAL NEWSPAPER

No. 18,931

QUEEN AND DUKE IN THE LAND O' RABBIE BURNS

Cheers . . . cheers . . . all the way!

THE SUN BROKE THROUGH THE GREY CLOUDS AND THOUSANDS CHEERED AS YESTERDAY'S ROYAL TOUR OF AYRSHIRE BEGAN.

FOR THE QUEEN AND THE DUKE IT WAS A TRIUMPHANT TOUR, WITH CHEERING THOUSANDS LINING ALMOST EVERY YARD OF THE 70-MILE ROUTE.

Here are some of the other BRIGHT SPOTS of the visit . . .

- *THE TIME the Queen said: "I just could not rush past those lovely children."*

- *THE TIME the Royal car slowed down to walking pace so that children of a hospital could get a better view.*

- *THE TIME the Royal couple smiled as they saw children mounted on horseback to see over the heads of the crowd.*

- *THE TIME they chuckled on seeing the hole-in-the-wall bed at Burns's Cottage . . . where there was a . . .*
  NOT-SO-BRIGHT SPOT. That was . . .

- *THE TIME the Queen spotted tourists' names scratched on the cottage and turned, frowning, to the Duke and said: "Isn't it dreadful . . ."*

★ *FASHION NOTE: The Queen wore a fitting coat of hyacinth blue with an off-the-face petal hat in white and hyacinth blue. In her lapel she wore a diamond brooch and she had close-fitting pearl earrings.*

OPEN GOLF —SURPRISE FAILURES Page 18

FULL STORY AND MORE WONDERFUL PICTURES ON PAGES 10, 11 AND 20

" Ah, this is the famous Burns Cottage," the Duke of Edinburgh seems to be saying as he and the Queen step from their car into the sunshine on arriving at the museum home of the Bard.

Daily Record

FRI AUG 3 1956

2ᴰ SCOTLAND'S NATIONAL NEWSPAPER

No. 18,957

SUEZ ANSWER! WE USE FORCE IF IT IS NECESSARY

By MICHAEL KING

BRITAIN AND FRANCE WILL USE FORCE, IF NECESSARY, TO SET UP AN INTERNATIONAL CONTROL OF THE SUEZ CANAL.

That is the major result of the British, French and American conference in London following Colonel Nasser's grab of the canal.

America will not take military action herself, I understand, but will give all help short of it if force is used by Britain and France.

But the Big Three Western Powers hope to solve the Suez crisis, and keep the canal open for world shipping for all time, by a 24-nation conference to begin in London on August 16.

Britain sent out invitations last night to all these countries. They include Egypt and Russia.

Mr. Selwyn Lloyd, the Foreign Secretary, and Mr. Foster Dulles, the U.S. Secretary of State, described the London talks last night as "very satisfactory."

Reserves called up and troops move

BRITAIN IS ACTING SWIFTLY

Certain Army and Air Force units will go overseas.

Reservists in "A" category and some officers on the Regular Army Reserve will be re-called.

A limited number of Army "specialists" will have to re-enlist.

THESE WERE AMONG THE EMERGENCY MEASURES ANNOUNCED BY SIR ANTHONY EDEN, IN THE COMMONS, YESTERDAY.

He explained that the men required were in Section B of the Regular Army Reserve and A.E.R. (Army Emergency Reserve) category II.

A message from the Queen was read to M.P.s, stating her intention of signing a Royal Proclamation for the call-up of these groups.

R.A.F. leave is cut

LEAVE has been curtailed at a number of bomber stations in Britain.

It is understood that two of the stations are Marham, Norfolk, and Honington, Suffolk, two of the R.A.F.'s Canberra jet bomber stations.

The transfer of a number of Canberras to Malta within the next 24 hours is also being considered at a high level.

The 700 men of the 1st Battalion, **SOMERSET LIGHT INFANTRY** have been issued with tropical kit to "move overseas" from their barracks at Plymouth.

Ready to move

The 300 men of the **No. 42 COMMANDO, ROYAL MARINES**, are also ready to move from Plymouth.

Both the Admiralty and the Air Ministry announced yesterday that no reservists are to be called up.

The Admiralty repeated their statement of Wednesday saying: "There is no intention of calling up Naval Reservists."

The Air Ministry said: "So far as the R.A.F. is concerned, no Reservists will be called up."

The French Mediterranean Squadron, including

Turn to Back Page

Troops to leave from Scotland

DAILY RECORD REPORTER

TROOPS will move from Scotland "within the next few days" for the Middle East.

A War Office spokesman said that in London last night and added: "I cannot say what units are affected — but there are moves on the way and they affect some troops in Scotland.

"Where from? I can't say that either."

But at Maryhill Barracks, Glasgow, last night, it was stated: "We have not been told of any movements."

The tank landing craft Suvla was taken from her moorings in the Great Harbour, Greenock, yesterday, and towed to the Gareloch.

And speculation was rife that she was bound for the Middle East.

An Admiralty spokesman said in London: "We can't make any comment about the Suvla."

CARRIER, TOO

But the Clyde Reserve Fleet Headquarters in the Gareloch confirmed that the Suvla was being brought forward for "operational service."

Two tugs pulled the Suvla out of the harbour and took her across the Firth, and there was activity on two other tank landing craft in the Great Harbour.

And as well as that five tugs shifted the aircraft carrier Triumph from the middle of the Gareloch and berthed her alongside the quay at Faslane.

BATTLESHIPS

But an Admiralty spokesman said: "Any movement by the Triumph has nothing at all to do with any movements overseas. But the Suvla? No comment about that."

There are now 16 tank landing craft in the harbour, all in mothball.

And in the Gareloch there are two battleships and three aircraft carriers, all in mothball, all part of the reserve fleet.

'Lovely day for a GUINNESS'

*I feel so strong and fit today
I'm sure to win the Cup.
I put a Guinness down before
I picked the Caber up.*

Guinness does more than quench your thirst

GUINNESS SCOTTISH OFFICE, 85 CLYDE FERRY ST., GLASGOW, C.3

G.E.2747.B

A baby for Grace

● Lovely 26-year-old Grace Kelly is expecting a baby next February. And when husband Prince Rainier gave the news in a broadcast yesterday there was great rejoicing in Monaco....

Full story—Page 8.

Daily Record

TUES
SEP 18
1956

2ᴰ SCOTLAND'S NATIONAL NEWSPAPER

No. 18,996

TRIPLE MURDER AFTER 'TOP 20'

Gunman by moonlight kills mother, daughter and aunt

RIDDLE OF THREE 'SILENT' SHOTS

A KILLER BROKE INTO A BUNGALOW IN THE MOON-LIGHT EARLY YESTERDAY AND BRUTALLY MURDERED TWO WOMEN AND A 17-YEAR-OLD GIRL.

He shot them at close range in their bedrooms—BUT NO ONE IN THE QUIET RESIDENTIAL AREA HEARD THE SHOTS.

And last night the police faced these riddles . . .

VIVIENNE WATT
Music . . . then death.

WHY

did a girl next door who heard her murdered friend playing Radio Luxembourg's Top Twenty programme from her own house earlier, not hear the shots?

did a night watchman at a building site not hear the shots as he sat in his hut within calling distance of the murder house?

Husband was on holiday

The victims — Mrs. Marion Watt (40), her daughter Vivienne (17) and her sister, Mrs. Margaret Brown (30)—were found just before 9 a.m. yesterday in a detached bungalow at 5 Fennsbank Ave., High Burnside, Lanarkshire.

Mrs. Watt's husband, William Watt, who owns a chain of bakeries in nearby Glasgow, was on holiday in Argyll.

He returned last night and identified his wife in Glasgow mortuary.

Mr. Peter Collier, a postman, was delivering letters when Mrs. Helen Collinson, companion to Mrs. Watt, told him she could not get into the bungalow.

The door was locked **BUT A GLASS PANEL AT THE SIDE WAS BROKEN.**

Mr. Collier put his hand through and opened the door.

Curtains still drawn

Mrs. Collinson went in. In the front bedroom with the curtains still drawn she found . . .

MRS. WATT lying in bed, her head on a blood-soaked pillow . . .

MRS. BROWN lying by her side — also with severe head injuries — and . . .

VIVIENNE covered by sheets in the back bedroom which is separated from the front by a bathroom.

She too had been shot in the head. She moaned and she died as Mrs. Collinson looked down at her.

Mrs. Collinson told postman Collier. He phoned the police.

And within half-an-hour the murder hunt was on.

Squads of detectives and police,

under Chief Constable Thomas Renfrew and Detective-Superintendent James Hendry, both of Lanarkshire Police Force, arrived at the house of sudden death. They found:—

● That nothing had been taken from the death house;
● That another house had been broken into during the night farther along the avenue at number 18 . . . entry to the house was gained by smashing a pane of glass in the inner door;
● That a man's fairly new suede shoe was lying in the avenue outside the house at Number 28 . . . with two pieces of tissue paper lying alongside it;
● That there were footprints in the soft earth at the back of the house at Number 18, and;
● That sets of fingerprints were around the doors of both the death house and the house at Number 18.

Burglar — or maniac

The police are working on four theories. These are:

THEORY No. 1: The killer is either a burglar disturbed—OR A MANIAC.

THEORY No. 2: He is the same person who broke into the house at No. 18 and made himself soup.

THEORY No. 3: He knew his

Continued on Back Page

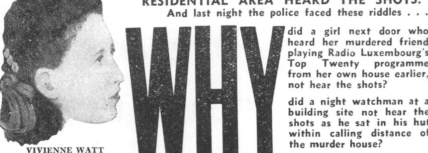

THE HOUSE (left) where the murdered women were found.

The house of death . . .

Doorway to murder

THE DOOR of No. 5, with broken panel on left.

DETECTIVE - SUPT. Hendry arrives at scene of the triple murder.

A HEARSE with a coffin leaves the murder house.

Sir Compton Mackenzie and Alan Melville discuss the pleasure of drinking good whisky

'Now Alan, you've given a great deal of pleasure to a great many people with your plays, revues and broadcasting. And this whisky we're discussing – Grants – is also a notable purveyor of pleasure. You two should get together!'

'But we do, Sir Compton! To me it is Utopia to pour myself out a very large Grants Stand Fast Whisky. Every evening that's a moment of bliss.'

'I must say Grants is a whisky that one can savour and enjoy in the real Scottish way.'

'Yes, it's the taste that I like. Grants is the friendliest, kindliest whisky.

when the clans gather, its

Grants STAND FAST

SUNDAY MAIL

SCOTLAND'S NATIONAL SUNDAY NEWSPAPER

No. 2506.   OCTOBER 28, 1956   3d.

Now it can all be told...

PUSKAS TRIED TO FLEE TO SCOTLAND

THE WONDER DRUGS THAT BEAT TB

Page 10

THE GREY HAIRS I HELPED TO SOW

My Mum and Dad

...he wanted to play for Celtic

"SUNDAY MAIL" EXCLUSIVE

FERENC PUSKAS, Hungary's wonder footballer reported killed in the Battle of Budapest, might have been playing for Celtic today ... if a secret escape plot had succeeded in Glasgow nearly two years ago.

It was disclosed in Glasgow yesterday that Puskas seriously thought about escaping from his team-mates — and the political watchers—while he was in Glasgow with the Hungarian football team in December, 1954.

The escape plot was tentatively laid. Puskas planned to go into hiding in a house in Dumbreck immediately after the Scotland-Hungary match.

He asked whether he would be allowed to play football in Scotland.

HE WANTED TO PLAY FOR CELTIC.

The Puskas escape plan has been kept secret for nearly two years by Polish-born Czeslaw Muchniewski, who lives in Dumbreck, Glasgow.

Having trouble

Now that Puskas is dead—killed in a bloody street battle—the full story can be told ... for the first time.

"It began on the Monday before the football match between Scotland and Hungary in December, 1954," said Muchniewski in his Glasgow home last night.

"I was in Marks and Spencers store in Sauchiehall Street when I noticed a man at the next counter having trouble making himself understood

"I thought he might be a Polish seaman so I walked across and asked in Polish if I could help him.

"He shook his head and said 'Not Polish . . . Hungarian.'

'No more'

"Finally we managed to carry on a conversation in Slovak, and I acted as interpreter while he bought two men's sweaters.

He had another man with him . . . I think he was also a player . . . but this man didn't understand any language but Hungarian.

Silent tribute

● Readers have suggested to Rex that at the Scottish League Cup final replay at Hampden on Wednesday, and at League games on Saturday a half-minute silence should be observed in memory of Puskas.

THIS is the Gin...

FOR THE POPULAR 'GIN AND ORANGE'

The popularity of this homely drink never wavers . . . and here's the simple recipe: Half fill shaker with ice and add ½ measure of Gordon's* Dry Gin and ¼ measure of Orange Squash ; shake well and strain into a cocktail glass. If preferred as a long drink— add soda or tonic water to taste.

*ASK FOR IT BY NAME

Gordon's
Stands Supreme

MAXIMUM PRICES: BOTTLE 34/5d. • ½ BOTTLE 18/-. • ¼ BOTTLE 9/5d • MINIATURE 3/3d • U.K. ONLY

★ **A** SON points to the grey hairs he helped to sow. His is the prize-winning letter on the subject: "My Mum and Dad." Here is his letter:—

I relish this opportunity of thanking my Mum and Dad for those grey hairs which I helped to sow.

I wish to apologise to them, most humbly, for all the anxiety I know they experienced because of their youngest son.

More especially, I wish to apologise for the misplaced grievances I nursed against them during those frustrating depression years, when Santa Claus 'forgot' to read my 'demand' notes placed so carefully over my well-darned stockings.

"I know now Mum why you didn't dress like the Lady you were."

My eyes always softly linger when I see a woman's toil-

hardened hands. To me they are the symbol of the tenderest love in this world. On a certain night next July our family will be gathered for a very special occasion, and each member will have a grateful prayer in their hearts when we toast Mum and Dad's health at their Golden Wedding Anniversary.

—ALEXR. McEWAN, 20 Kilcloy Ave., Glasgow, W.5.

More letters—Page 7

Continued on Back Page

Daily Record

WED NOV 21 1956

2ᴰ SCOTLAND'S NATIONAL NEWSPAPER

No. 19,051

RATION DAY IS DECEMBER 17

BACK TO BASIC

FUEL MINISTER JONES
Only a miracle can cancel it ...

PETROL rationing begins in Britain on December 17—and private motorists are to be restricted to a basic 200 miles a month.

Fuel Minister Mr. Aubrey Jones announced this yesterday and said that petrol coupons could be collected from tomorrow.

Buses, taxis, goods vehicles, farming, fishing—all are to be restricted in their use of fuel because of the Suez blockage.

But private motorists are to bear the brunt of the burden.

Private motorists can collect their coupons tomorrow from main post offices and local taxation offices.

Vehicle registration books must be produced.

The coupons should be drawn without delay—they will not be available at the post offices from December 8 until after Christmas.

They will cover a four-month period, but the motorist can use them how and when he pleases—all at once if he likes.

BIG CHANCE FOR RAILWAYS

Mr. Jones, answering questions at a Press conference last night, said: " I can cancel the scheme overnight if, by some miracle, the situation improves."

The Government's fuel cuts are a serious blow to industry.

Production will be hit, said the National Union of Manufacturers.

There will be a slow-down, too, in the transport and shipment of goods. In a plea to the railways, the union says:

" British Railways now have a unique opportunity of regaining the confidence which industry at one time placed in them."

A spokesman for the British motoring associations said: " This is a severe blow to the motoring public.

" But we will co-operate to the fullest extent in the hope of reducing individual hardship to a minimum."

A Farmers' Union spokesman commented: " Farmers will have to use a great deal of ingenuity if food production is not to suffer from the diesel oil cut."

● Late last night, Transport and Civil Aviation Minister appealed to firms to stagger working hours and for the public to avoid peak-hour travel.

● A leading Scots garage proprietor said last night: Although the bottom will fall out of the second-hand car market, I don't think the sale of new cars will be effected.

A 'dead' seaman WALKS home

DAILY RECORD REPORTER

FOUR hours after a wife was told that her husband had been washed overboard to his death at sea, her husband walked into his home.

While the man's boat was docked in the harbour, the crew were explaining how 43-year-old fisherman, John Craig, was swept overboard

As they talked, Craig lay unconscious beneath the small boat at the stern of the trawler.

Said Mr. Craig last night:—" I lay unconscious for four hours God knows how this has happened, but it's a miracle I'm alive."

Unseen

For more than two hours yesterday the crew of Mr. Craig's trawler, the Dorileen, three aeroplanes and a lifeboat, searched for the missing man . . . as he lay unseen under the small boat.

At 9 a.m. yesterday Craig, of Black's Buildings, Aberdeen, signed up with the Dorileen.

At 11 a.m. the boat sailed from Aberdeen for the Faroe fishing grounds.

At 2.15 p.m. Craig was seen—for the last time his mates thought — walking from the bridge to the forecastle.

Scared

Said skipper John Watson, of Dundee: " Jock came to the Continued on Back Page

JOHN CRAIG . . . " I don't remember a thing."

WAVERLEY *(Scotland's No. 1 football writer)* sums up Scotland's chances against Yugoslavia at Hampden today on Page 15.

Taxi, bus petrol is cut

PETROL for taxis will be cut by a third.

But taxi men in the West of Scotland do not think that rationing will hit them unduly.

" We shall still have the same number of taxis on the street," said Mr. William Rogers, manager of Paterson's Taxis, Glasgow, last night.

Glasgow taximan Bill Frame said: " It may even mean heavier calls on us. Many motorists who lay up their cars will turn to us for transport."

Bus services

The ten per cent. cut for buses will not affect the frequency of the bus services in Glasgow very much. " They are cut to the minimum at the moment," Mr. E. R. L. Fitzpayne, transport manager, said last night.

" It will not affect the frequency of the bus services in the city very much. They are cut to the minimum at the moment."

Production at Grangemouth's giant oil refinery which handles 2,500,000 tons of crude oil a year, is expected to drop by 30 per cent.

The last tankers to pass through the Suez Canal arrived in the Clyde a week ago.

This will mean a serious gap in deliveries. But there will be no pay-offs at the refinery or at the chemical works linked to it.

The oil shortage has given a definite boost to West Lothian's shale oil industry.

YOUR PETROL GUIDE

See Back Page

The Suite designed to meet Public Demand

This Craftsman-made QUALITY*

Cocktail 6 PCE. DINING SUITE 52½ GNS

QUALITY WORKMANSHIP

QUALITY MATERIAL

✱4ft. 6in Serpentine-front Cocktail Sideboard.
✱Fitted with interior light fitting as shown.
✱Full Size Extending Table.
✱4 Fully Upholstered Chairs. Sprung seats.
✱In rich Walnut veneers.

The 6-PCE SUITE Complete 52½ Gns

And also the Three Famous

FULL SIZE 3-PIECE BEDROOM SUITE, 4ft, dressing table, 4ft. 'robe, and 3-drawer chest in fine walnut veneer.
Complete 29½ Gns.

FULL SIZE 3-PIECE SUITE. In uncut moquette or " Florestine " covers. With walnut finished facings.
Complete 29½ Gns.

FULL SIZE 6-PIECE DINING SUITE. Oak or walnut veneer. Gateleg or draw-leaf table. Sideboard and four chairs.
Complete 29½ Gns.

29½ GNS SUITES

GRANITE HOUSE
OFFICIAL STOCKISTS OF REGISTERED TOP GRADE FURNITURE

STOCKWELL CORNER, GLASGOW, where Trongate meets Argyle St

Daily Record

TUES FEB 19 1957

2d   **No. 19,127**   SCOTLAND'S NATIONAL NEWSPAPER

IT'S THE HAPPIEST PICTURE OF THE QUEEN

This is the picture we give as the happiest yet taken of the Queen in 1957.

She laughs gaily with President Lopes of Portugal . . . She is watching a march past soon after her arrival in Lisbon with the Duke yesterday.

And the fashion-conscious women of the Portuguese capital are talking of the hats worn by the so-happy Queen.

They are velvet claw hats that sit neatly behind the hairline with mounts at the side to give width to the temples.

The one she wore for the parade yesterday had a diamante mount on the RIGHT temple.

But three days ago—for her reunion with the Duke—the Queen chose one with a rose mount in matching material at the LEFT temple (see below).

RENTS— TORIES CLIMB DOWN

THE TORIES HAVE CLIMBED DOWN ON THE RENTS BILL.

Mr. Henry Brooke, the Housing Minister, will today announce his concession for the 800,000 tenants whose homes become decontrolled.

He probably will agree to give these tenants FIFTEEN MONTHS after the passing of the Bill in which to reach agreement with their landlord or find another home.

As the Bill now stands tenants in decontrolled houses are protected for only seven months.

During that time their rent cannot be raised.

Under the new proposal the landlord is expected to get a limited increase in rent during the period that a tenant in a decontrolled house remains protected from eviction.

This would be on the same basis as in houses which stay under control —an increase of not more than 7s 6d a week at first, and, after ten months, a rent based on twice the gross rateable value of the house.

Back-benchers withdraw

When the long-awaited Government amendments were tabled late last night, 14 Tory backbenchers withdrew the amendment and new schedule they had put down.

This amendment had asked that tenants should be given five years' security of tenure in certain circumstances and that during this period their rents should not rise beyond a specified limit.

BASIC PETROL MAY GO UP BY ONE-HALF

AN increase in the basic petrol ration may be announced before the end of the present rationing period, on April 17. Stocks are believed to be high enough to allow the present 200-miles-a-month ration to be increased to 300 miles.

That is if there are no unforeseen circumstances and the Suez Canal is reopened for small tankers before the end of March.

Mr. Harold Watkinson, the Transport Minister, will tell the Commons that during the "holiday period" motor coach services will get threequarters the petrol they used before rationing.

Haley rock—two held

HUNDREDS of chanting teenagers struggled with police after the second-house Bill Haley show in Glasgow last night.

They gathered outside the Odeon Cinema in West Regent Street shouting . . . "We want Haley—We want Haley."

They did not know that Bill and his band had hurried off immediately after the show, leaving by a back lane, where a car was waiting.

When the mob of screaming youngsters looked like getting out of control, police reinforcements were rushed in by patrol car.

A large cardboard placard was thrown at a group of police as they took one violent youth into custody.

Sent home

Another man was arrested a few minutes later.

It looked ugly but the police handled the situation with tact and started ushering the chanting mob along West Regent Street into West Nile Street.

Singing and jiving, the crowd went up West Nile Street and into Bath Street, but getting thinner all the time as groups broke away and ran to the Central Station a couple of hundred yards away.

But the police re-grouped and formed up round the station.

Within five minutes the mobs of singing teenagers were broken up again and sent off home.

Sixteen-year-old Patricia Flynn of 1062 London Road, said: "I was waiting for Bill to come out. Suddenly people started milling round about me shouting.

"It was fun at first—but I got frightened."

Two have been charged with breach of the peace.

SEE BACK PAGE.

FLASHBACK—TO SATURDAY

STORY AND MORE GREAT PICTURES ON CENTRE PAGES

• IT'S FALKIRK'S CUP •

● Crack-shot Davie Curlett (above) gets the goal that put the Hampden final into extra time. Slater, arms outstretched and airborne, makes a despairing effort, while full-backs Parker and Rae watch, wait, and worry.

...and here's the winner

● Here it is (right), the goal that won the Cup. The glory goal . . . Doug. Moran scores . . . and for him it is an unforgettable moment. Jimmy Brown, beaten and helpless, watches in anguish as the ball goes past.

WHAT THEY SAID...

● Falkirk Manager Reggie Smith: " I am delighted with the boys' display. They all played with tremendous team spirit."

● George Merchant said: " This is the biggest thrill of my football career. I felt champion when I got that goal."

● Said Dougie Moran, the man who got the winner: " It was a real thrill to get that goal."

• ALL THE RESULTS •

Scottish Cup Final (replay) — Falkirk 2 (Merchant, Moran); Kilmarnock 1 (Curlett).

Scottish League Div. I—Aberdeen 2 (Glen, Davidson), Partick Thistle 0; Queen of the South 2 (Paterson 2), Motherwell 2 (Quinn, Baker).

Scottish League Div. II — Berwick Rangers 1 (McLeod) Brechin City 2 (Sprunt, Warrender) Forfar Ath. 4 (A. Craig 2, Martin, Dunn) Cowdenbeath 0. East Stirling 1 (Pulton) Arbroath 5 (McGrory, Kirkwood McKenzie). Morton 3 (Shaw, Gourlay Beaton), Alloa 1 (Newman). Stirling Albion 2 (Newman 2) Dundee United 1 (Coyle). St. Johnstone 0. Dumbarton 6 (H. Gallacher 3, Gibson 2, McKeown). Hamilton Acas 0, Clyde 0.

Scottish Reserve League—Partick Thistle 2 (McGill, Hogan), Aberdeen 5 (Yorston 3, Hay 2); Celtic 2 (Kennedy Divers), Airdrie 1 (Meechan, o.g.) Dunfermline Athletic 10 (McWilliams 4, Newman, Miller 3, Rattray Young) Queen's Park Strollers 0; Motherwell 2 (Junior, S Reid) Raith Rovers 0.

East of Scotland League—Peebles Rovs 3 (Sanderson 2, Russell), Edinburgh University 2 (Cavanan, Tat).

Edinburgh and District League — Easthouses Lily 1, Haddington Ath. 2; Armadale Thistle 1, Bathgate Thistle 3; Fauldhouse Un. 2, West Calder Un. 2; Rosewell Rosedale 3, Loanhead Mayflower 0.

Perth Half-Holiday P.A. Cup Final— R.A.S.C. 0, Half Holiday United 0.

East of Scotland Shield—Final— Hibs 2 (Fraser, Turnbull), Hearts 1 (Wardhaugh).

Perthshire League—Crieff Earngrove 2, Newburgh 1.

Football today

European Cup—Semi-final—Manchester Utd. v. Real Madrid.

Reserve League—Hearts Res. v. Kilmarnock Res. (k.o. 7 p.m.)

Fife and Stirling Cup—Third round —Nairn Thistle v. Thornton Hibs.

Angus League—Forfar Celtic v. Forfar West End.

Dundee Junior League—East Craigie v Osborne.

TOURNAMENT

Dennistoun Waverly — Shettleston Violet v. Elmvale Utd (Hagghill Park, 6.45 p.m.)

Football Specials

Saturday, 27th April

QUEEN OF THE SOUTH v. RANGERS

		p.m.
Glasgow (St. Enoch) ... dep.	12.05
Dumfries .... arr.	1.52

RETURN FARE

12/7 — 12/7

Return from Dumfries at 5.25 p.m.

REFRESHMENTS WILL BE AVAILABLE ON THE TRAIN TO AND FROM DUMFRIES.

CELTIC v. HIBERNIAN

	p.m.	Fare
Possil .... dep.	2.05	1/2
Maryhill (Cent.) ... ,,	2.09	1/2
Partick (West) .... ,,	2.17	1/2
Partick (Cent.) ... ,,	2.20	1/-
Glasgow (Cent.) ... ,,	2.27	7d
Glasgow Cross ..... ,,	2.30	6d
Parkhead Stad. ... arr.	2.39	

Return from Parkhead Stadium at 4.59 p.m.

Coatbridge

	p.m.	p.m.	Fare
(Cent.) ...... dep.	1.54	2.24	1/4
Langloan .... ,,	1.57	2.27	1/2
Drumpark .... ,,	2.00	2.30	10d
Parkhead Stad. arr.	2.14	2.42	

Return from Parkhead Stadium at 4.58 p.m.

BRITISH RAILWAYS

Daily Record

FRI FEB 7 1958

2½ SCOTLAND'S NATIONAL NEWSPAPER No. 19,429

21 die in disaster

BUSBY BABES AIR CRASH HORROR

MARK JONES
DEAD

ROGER BYRNE
DEAD

TOMMY TAYLOR
DEAD

EDDIE COLMAN
DEAD

DAVID PEGG
DEAD

GEOFF. BENT
DEAD

BILLY WHELAN
DEAD

SEVEN STARS KILLED: MATT IS 'CRITICAL'

SEVEN Manchester United players, three club officials and eight sports writers are among 21 feared dead in yesterday's Munich air disaster.

And early today doctors were battling to save Matt Busby, United's and Scotland's new team manager. He was one of the 23 survivors of the air crash that has shocked the world.

Four of the seven players who died in the holocaust played in Wednesday's European Cup tie against Red Star in Belgrade.

ENGLAND'S STAR CENTRE

They included England's star centre-forward **TOMMY TAYLOR** and international left-back **ROGER BYRNE**.

The other two were right-half **EDDIE COLMAN** and centre-half **MARK JONES**.

Two of the other three United players killed were internationalists — left-winger **DAVID PEGG**, for England. and inside - right **BILLY WHELAN**, for Eire.

The seventh was left-back **GEOFF BENT**.

Centre - half **JACKIE BLANCHFLOWER** is in hospital with badly broken arms, ribs and back.

Left - half **DUNCAN**
EDWARDS is in the same hospital with a broken right leg and broken ribs.

Inside-left **DENNIS VIOLLET** and outside - left **ALBERT SCANLON**, both have head injuries.

Club officials killed were secretary **WALTER CRICKMER**, coach **BERT WHALLEY**, and trainer **TOM CURRY**.

Former England goalkeeper **FRANK SWIFT** was among the sports writers who died.

The other writers were Archie Ledbrooke, of the Daily Mirror, Henry Rose, Eric Thompson, George Follows,
Alf Clarke, H. D. Davies and Tom Jackson.

One of the dead was a Manchester United supporter, Mr. W. Satinoff.

The other two were plane steward W. T. Cable and travel agent S. P. Miklos.

United's other injured players are goalkeeper **HARRY GREGG** and right-back **BILLY FOULKES** (both have left hospital) ;

Goalkeeper **RAY WOOD** (cuts and bruises), outside-right **KEN MORGANS** (concussion, suspected fractures) ;

Inside-right **BOBBY CHARLTON** (left hospital) and right winger **JOHNNY BERRY**.

MATT BUSBY . . . very ill in hospital.

FIGHT TO SAVE HIM

RECORD REPORTER

EARLY this morning Matt Busby was hovering between life and death.

He is in "Watch Room 457" in Munich's R e c h e s der Iser Hospital.

He has severe internal chest injuries.

A staff of young surgeons and German nurses are standing round him as he lies under a plastic oxygen tent.

He is being given regular blood transfusions.

Every now and again he has shown signs of life. and a nurse has called his name . . . "Mr. Busby . . . Mr. Busby."

He has never regained consciousness.

Surgeons believed at 3 o'clock this morning that his chances of survival were only fifty-fifty.

Dramatic pictures and story
—Pages 10, 11 and 20

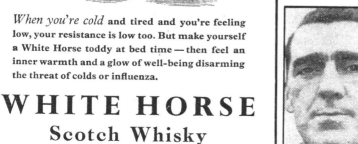

When you're cold and tired and you're feeling low, your resistance is low too. But make yourself a White Horse toddy at bed time — then feel an inner warmth and a glow of well-being disarming the threat of colds or influenza.

WHITE HORSE
Scotch Whisky

 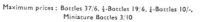Maximum prices: Bottles 37/6, ½-Bottles 19/6, ¼-Bottles 10/-, Miniature Bottles 3/10

FRANK SWIFT
DEAD

D. EDWARDS
BADLY INJURED

DENNIS VIOLLET
INJURED

KEN MORGANS
INJURED

BLANCHFLOWER
BADLY INJURED

SUNDAY MAIL

SCOTLAND'S NATIONAL SUNDAY NEWSPAPER

No. 2583   APRIL 20, 1958   4d

CRAZY!

Today you must meet DILLY The Sunday Mail's new sparkling cartoon girl

Just the CURE for those 4-0 BLUES

SHE'S ON THE CENTRE PAGES

Snatch by car

A GIRL returning from a dance last night had her handbag snatched — BY A MOTORIST.

The girl, Flora Long, 20, was only a few steps from her home at 41 Benview Street, Maryhill, Glasgow, when a car stopped beside her.

The driver jumped out, snatched her handbag and drove off.

She was able to give police part of the car's registration number.

There was a £1 in her handbag.

The ticket fiasco outside Hampden . . . it's 3 p.m. and there are NO takers.

TICKET FARCE!
A penny to see big game

'MAIL' REPORTER

THE big Hampden ticket shortage ended yesterday in a FARCE . . . with hundreds of tickets being sold for a PENNY!

And eventually the spivs could not even GIVE them away.

Fans who were also carrying one or two extra tickets found that just before the kick-off there were no bidders.

ONE MINUTE after the start of the game, the streets round Hampden were deserted—except for policemen, themselves laden with tickets they had been asked to give away and could not.

And last night the soccer bosses as well as the fans were seeking the answer to this riddle:

WHERE WERE THE MISSING 6000 SUPPORTERS.

Official attendance at the International was 127,857. Tickets distributed amounted to 134,000.

Thrown away

Did the missing 6000 guess Scotland s humiliation in advance? Or were they at home watching the 4-0 defeat on TV?

Whatever the reason, it was the leanest year ever for the ticket touts.

They finished up THROWING AWAY the precious briefs.

One vendor said: "I was in Central Station at five o'clock this morning . everyone was looking for tickets.

"I offered 10s 6d for 3s 6d tickets, hoping to sell them for more at the ground.

"But I couldn't get any.

"When I went to Hampden I picked up as many as I wanted for next to nothing."

And other vendors, a few minutes before the kick-off, shouted: "*Tickets . . . 1d each.*"

They had no sale.

This waste

A Sunday Mail reporter took four ground tickets. sent by readers in Stirling and Newcastle, to Hampden Park.

But they were not needed.

Most fans, who had great difficulty in getting tickets, were furious last night

Edward O'Donnell, of 49 Norman Street, Bridgeton, Glasgow, an official of the National Union of Seamen, said:

"Ticket matches should be abolished. We tried to get tickets for seamen and could not.

"Yet yesterday I find they are being sold half a mile away from the ground at black market prices.

"As I got nearer the prices became lower and lower until people were giving them away at the gate."

Next time?

The question thousands of people are now asking is:

"WILL TICKETS BE NEEDED AT ALL NEXT TIME?"

The sun shone during the game . . but it was not for Scotland

Four English goals ripped away the last remnants of Scottish football pride.

And at home, thousands of TV viewers saw a weak Scottish attack batter in vain against the might of England.

At 4.40 the referee blew his whistle and closed a game which may have marked the end of an era for Scotland.

DID YOU ?

★ Your clock should have been put forward one hour last night. Summer time began at 2 a.m. today.

Radio, TV—Page 16

TAKE HOME SOME WALL'S!

Wall's ICE CREAM

ICE 598-4824

SUNDAY MAIL

SCOTLAND'S NATIONAL SUNDAY NEWSPAPER

No. 2584   APRIL 27, 1958   4d.

JOY DAY!

... for Mattha

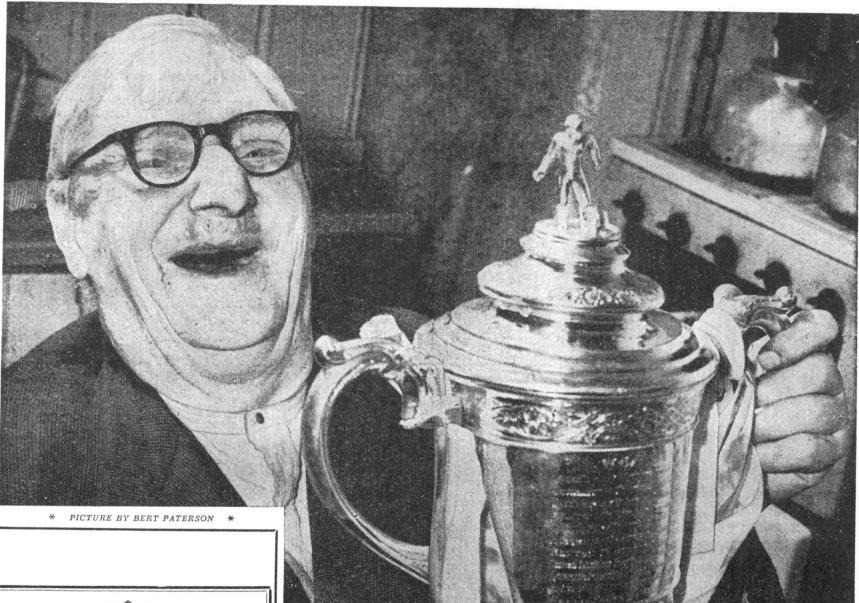

* PICTURE BY BERT PATERSON *

LLOYDS PERMANENT BUILDING SOCIETY

Stop Paying Half your Interest back in Tax.
Invest safely, Invest wisely.

Tax 4% Free

Ordinary Pre-Paid Investment Shares.

Equal to £6.19.1% at standard rate of tax

From 10/- to £5,000 accepted, with withdrawals on demand.

Tax 5% Free

Pre-Paid Contract Shares.

Equal to £8.13.11% at standard rate of tax

5% tax free interest paid from date of investment to 31st December and thereafter for each complete year. Interim withdrawals on demand subject to conditions contained in the Society's brochure.

Write for free explanatory brochure to Department G.S.M.5

34 GEORGE STREET, EDINBURGH, 2. Tel.: Caledonian 5130

Mortgages granted only on modern freehold properties for owner occupation.

★ Oh, the JOY of winning the Cup! And who better to portray the glorious, satisfying thrill of yesterday's VICTORY than Clyde's Wonderful Old Man of Football, MATTHA GEMMELL — 84-years-young and still goin' strong.

Clyde's jubilant players and officials didn't forget Old Mattha. They made a special journey to show him the Cup . . . And the Sunday Mail was there, too, to bring you this exclusive record . . . in a picture which captures the true spirit of VICTORY

THE COURAGE OF WEE ARCHIE

'MAIL' REPORTER

EXPERIENCED ambulance men talked last night of the COURAGE of little Archie McCuaig.

For as Archie — he's just seven—lay in a railway goods yard yesterday with his leg terribly injured, he SMILED as ambulance men gave him first aid.

When the pain was too much to bear he bit hard on a rolled bandage.

And during the agonising minutes he never made a sound . . .

'Bravest boy'

After a three-hour battle in the operating theatre, doctors told the little boy's mother: "We have had to amputate your son's leg."

Last night the ambulance man who took Archie to hospital said:

"He is the bravest boy I have ever met.

"NEVER ONCE did he cry out."

The railway drama happened at Gushetfaulds Goods Station, Gorbals, Glasgow.

Archie, of 323 Thistle Street, Gorbals, and his pal Peter Blair (7), of No. 317, went to the goods yard near their home and began playing football on a grass verge beside the rails.

When the ball bounced on to the rails, Archie ran to get it back.

His foot caught in one of the rails . . . and he struggled in terror as a heavy goods wagon trundled towards him.

Before Archie could escape the wagon wheels ran over his leg.

Only a few yards away, Peter watched helpless.

He said: "I saw the wagon and shouted to Archie — but he couldn't get away in time."

Archie was struck by a single wagon which was being shunted into a siding.

As he was taken to the Victoria Infirmary a railway official went with Peter to Archie's home and broke the news to his mother.

Mrs. Margaret McCuaig (27), rushed to the hospital in a taxi. Then her three-hour vigil began as doctors fought to save her son's leg.

Archie

Hello! Mr. Clyde

... Back Page ...

Queen better

THE Queen, who has a heavy cold, is slightly better, but is resting in bed.

Prince Philip takes the salute at the St. George's Day parade of Queen's Scouts at Windsor Castle today.

Princess flies

Princess Margaret flew from Trinidad to Tobago yesterday on the second stage of her West Indies tour.

The Princess will spend three days on this island, where Alexander Selkirk was marooned.

Radio, TV — Page 12

Daily Record

MON MAY 12 1958

2½d · SCOTLAND'S NATIONAL NEWSPAPER

No. 19,509

MANUEL ...goes on trial today

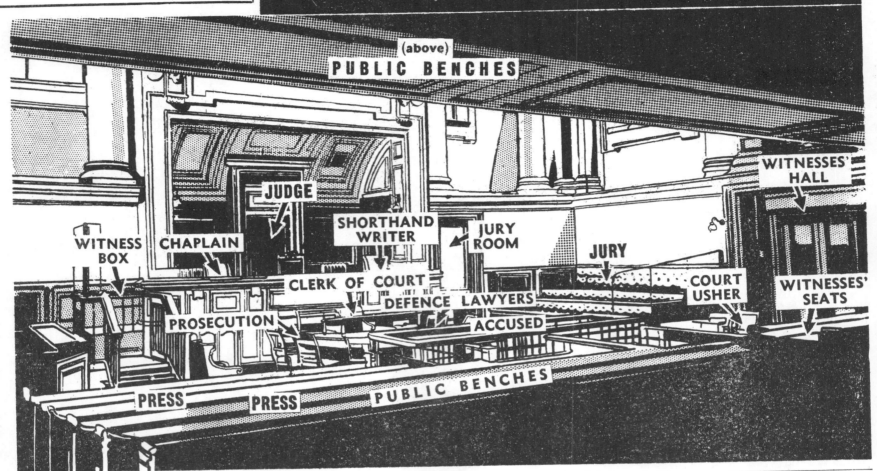

(above) **PUBLIC BENCHES**

JUDGE · **SHORTHAND WRITER** · **JURY ROOM** · **WITNESSES' HALL** · **JURY** · **COURT USHER** · **WITNESSES' SEATS** · **WITNESS BOX** · **CHAPLAIN** · **CLERK OF COURT** · **DEFENCE LAWYERS** · **PROSECUTION** · **ACCUSED** · **PRESS** · **PRESS** · **PUBLIC BENCHES**

● An artist's impression of the interior of the High Court in Glasgow.

Casual Clothes!

PRECISELY-Tailored Coat in cream summer velour 12½ Gns.

SUIT of cream "cable" weave all wool with ⅞th length Coat. 12½ Gns. In Other Colours

Bankok Breton, 49/11
Showerproof Felt Hat 42/-

Watt brothers

OF SAUCHIEHALL STREET, GLASGOW

He buys sports suit for court

AND COMPLETES DEFENCE NOTES

PETER MANUEL, wearing a natty new black blazer, will step into the dock of the North court at Glasgow High Court today — and the trial of the century will be on.

For the next three weeks world interest will be focussed on the man in the dock as his defence counsel fights for his life.

The trial of Manuel—accused of murdering eight people—will be long and dramatic.

He plays cards

DRAMA NO. 1 is certain this morning when Manuel's special defence—kept a tight secret—is made known.

It will be announced by Mr. Harald Leslie, Manuel's Q.C., after the list of charges has been read out.

Yesterday Manuel read in his cell in Barlinnie in the untried prisoners' block, played cards with warders, put the

DAILY RECORD REPORTER

last touches to the notes he has written neatly in exercise books for his defence.

A friend said: "He had written enough in the past three months to fill a novel."

TODAY Manuel will be up early, shaved, and ready for his trip by van to Glasgow High Court in the Saltmarket.

He will put on his new grey flannel trousers and his new black blazer, made specially for him by a Lanarkshire tailor, to his own measurements.

The 15 jurors

He will wear a white shirt and brown suede shoes.

TO-DAY, the 15 jurors will be chosen from 200 men and women who have been cited for jury service.

Their names, written on slips of paper—blue for women and white for men—will be drawn from two glass jars.

As the names are read out by the clerk of the court, the defence counsel can object. He is allowed five "peremptory objections" without giving reason.

For the length of the trial, the 15 jurors will be virtually cut off from the outside world.

The scene

They will stay at a hotel in the West End of Glasgow, and have occasional coach trips

They will not see their families until the trial finishes.

TODAY — at 10.30 a.m. — as Peter Manuel, 31, from Birkenshaw, Uddingston, climbs the stairs into the dock between

Continued on Back Page

THE OFFER ALL SLIMMERS HAVE BEEN WAITING FOR!

FREE DIET OFFER

PAGE 6

A MIDNIGHT BLAZE AT PAPER MILL

FIREMEN from Glasgow, Clydebank and Kirkintilloch were called out early this morning to fight a blaze at Milngavie paper mills.

Flames swept through a 40ft. high store, destroying thousands of pounds worth of esparto grass.

Firemen hosed water from the nearby River Allander into the building to put out the blaze.

Daily Record

TUES MAY 27 1958

2½ᴰ
SCOTLAND'S NATIONAL NEWSPAPER
No. 19,522

The SENSATION of the TRIAL

MANUEL

He tells his own story...

BARLINNIE
New poison drama
BACK PAGE

88 MINUTES—AND NO NOTES

By CHARLES SMITH

FOR 88 SENSATION-PACKED MINUTES PETER MANUEL TALKED NON-STOP IN THE HIGH COURT WITNESS-BOX YESTERDAY.

He talked without notes . . . He talked at a speed of between 180 and 200 words a minute . . . every minute. And this time the jury were there to hear him.

Seldom in his 17,000-word testimony did he falter for a phrase . . .

And when the court rose he had dealt with only FOUR of the EIGHT murders standing against him on the indictment.

Hands outstretched

During his marathon, Manuel, who was wearing his familiar dark blazer and flannels and a clean grey shirt and blue-patterned tie, stood erect in the box, his hands outstretched to grasp the sides . .

The court was packed—but completely still and utterly silent.

First, Manuel traced the investigations into the murder of Anne Kneilands at East Kilbride.

Then—still speaking rapidly —he turned to the Watt killings:

He sketched in the details of his association with Charles Tallis, a previous witness in the 13-day trial:

'Bunged away'

He revealed that he had found a .38 calibre revolver in his home AFTER the Watt killings . . . and he said it had been "planked" there.

He described how he had carried the gun—which was showing signs of having been fired — into Glasgow and "bunged it in the Clyde."

The gun, he said, contained five empty cartridge shells—and one live cartridge.

He talked about meetings he

'In fivers'

alleged he had with Mr. William Watt and Mr. Lawrence Dowdall—who have both given evidence . . .

He alleged Mr. Watt had told him he had killed his own wife and daughter:

He alleged Mr. Watt had told him someone must be arrested for the shooting:

He alleged Mr Watt had paid him £150 in £5 notes . .

Took oath

It was at five minutes to four in the afternoon of a day filled with tension that Manuel stood erect in the dock and told Lord Cameron.

"My Lord," he said, "I wish to testify on my own behalf."

He took the oath and then

Continued on Back Page

● DE GAULLE . . . to Paris by fast car

FRANCE: De Gaulle, Pflimlin in night talks

SEE BACK PAGE

That Casual Look!

Travel Coats in Wool and Camel Hair.

Belted Style .... **9 Gns**
Chrome Hide Shoulder Bag 58/11

Swagger Style, with Turn-down Collar .... **9½ Gns.**

From our Collection of Casual Coats in Coffee, Cream, Off-white & Camel

Watt brothers

OF SAUCHIEHALL STREET, GLASGOW

Daily Record

FRI MAY 30 1958

2½ᵈ SCOTLAND'S NATIONAL NEWSPAPER No. 19,525

SENTENCED TO DEATH

PETER ANTHONY MANUEL, WHOSE PICTURE IS ON RIGHT, WAS SENTENCED TO DEATH AT GLASGOW HIGH COURT

He was found:—

Not guilty

of the murder of Anne Kneilands.

GUILTY

of the capital murders of Marion Watt, Margaret Brown, and Vivienne Watt.

GUILTY

of the murder of Isabelle Cooke.

GUILTY

of the capital murders of the Smart family.

GUILTY

of stealing the Smarts' car.

GUILTY

of breaking into a house at Bothwell, and firing a gun into a mattress.

GUILTY

of breaking into a house at High Burnside, and stealing jewellery and other items.

Not proven

on a charge of breaking into a house at North Mount Vernon.

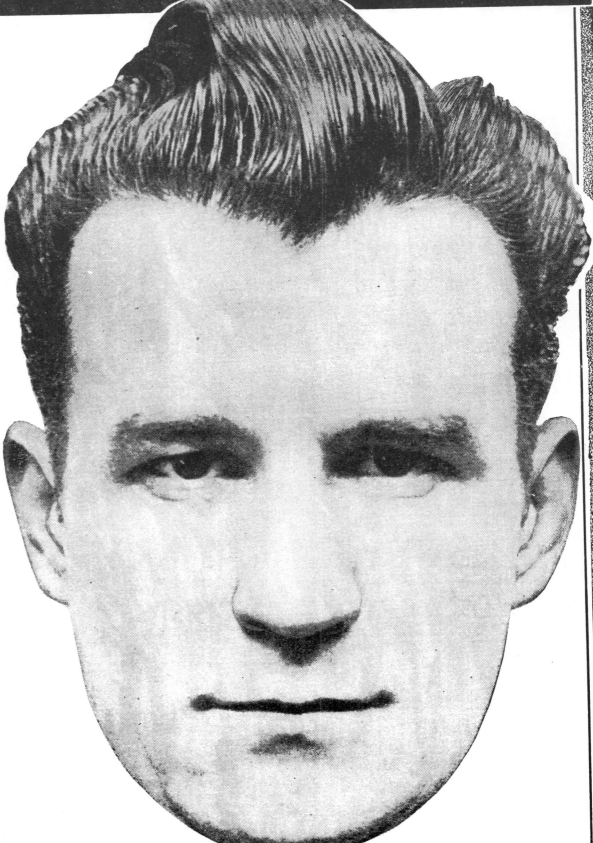

● PETER MANUEL . . . found guilty of seven murders

Daily Record

TUES NOV 11 1958

2½ SCOTLAND'S NATIONAL NEWSPAPER

No. 19,666

● THE BRIDE ... Theresa

WHY I LEFT MY BRIDE AT ALTAR...

WIN A TENNER!

★ See Page Six

WIN with GARRY OWEN!

His nap won at 100-8 yesterday (P.13)

WIN with the 'RECORD'!

SOS

DEATH 'PILL' STOLEN AT ATOM SHOW

TV warns the city...

TV and wireless programmes last night flashed out a warning to a man that he may be carrying in his pocket a capsule of DEATH. . . .

The warning was flashed specially to Glasgow's million-and-a-quarter inhabitants after a radio-active Cobalt 60 capsule dis-

● A drawing of the radio-active Cobalt 60 capsule.

appeared from an exhibition.

THE CAPSULE COULD WIPE OUT AN ENTIRE FAMILY.

And late last night—in CLAPHAM, LONDON—an English workman from the Kelvin Hall walked into a police station and said:

"I believe this may be the missing atom capsule."

Then he laid a tiny capsule on a desk

Investigations are going on.

'Don't touch'

All resources were mobilised to trace the man after the killer capsule was taken from a stand in the Kelvin Hall, Glasgow, between 7 p.m. Sunday and 9 a.m. yesterday.

It vanished from an exhibition being held by the Atomic Energy Commission and the South of Scotland Electricity Board.

Last night a police spokesman said:

"If the person who took it is carrying it about in his pocket—HE IS GOING TO DIE . . "

The grim warning continued:

"In no circumstances should the capsule be touched with the naked hand or closely looked at."

Inch long

And—as the men, women and children of the city poured into cinemas and dance halls, and on and off buses and trams and other transport —it continued

Listeners were warned:

"The capsule should not be thrown away as it will continue to be a source of danger INDEFINITELY."

The killer capsule is only

one-and-an-eighth inches long

It is like aluminium and is circular for quarter-of-an inch and flat the remainder.

And while the city carried on as normal, police discussed the theft at the highest level, with Chief Superintendent Robert Colquhoun, boss of Glasgow C.I.D., being kept informed.

In an all-out effort to get the capsule police said:

"We are more anxious to have the object TRACED than to find out who TOOK it."

Health check

The theft was discovered just before the opening ceremony of the exhibition by Mr. J. S. Maclay, the Scottish Secretary.

It was 11 a.m. and senior detectives of Glasgow Police, Marine Division, led by Chief Inspector John Johnston, began intensive inquiries immediately.

Police made a check of hospitals to find out if anyone had reported with a mysterious or unusual illness.

And late last night two detectives from the Marine Division toured the other police offices in the city, instructing them how to handle the capsule if they get any word of it.

Show quiz

In no circumstances should anyone touch the capsule if they know its whereabouts.

Leave it alone and report to the nearest police office at once. Police will arrange for its removal.

Any information should be sent to the Chief Constable, City of Glasgow Police—Telephone No. Bell 3500.

On the capsule is the serial number CKR-C2-60 RO11.

It was taken from a small lead container three inches long and shaped like a cylinder. The special container is being

Continued on Back Page

Groom blames a hangover

A VANISHING bridegroom, who left his bride at the altar on Saturday, turned up yesterday at his father's isolated Highland cottage.

He blamed a severe hangover for his disappearance and claimed he was unconscious for 28 hours.

THE BRIDEGROOM with a headache is 25-year-old Raymond MacPherson, of Loch Treig Farm, near Ben Nevis.

THE BRIDE with a heartache is 23-year-old London model, Theresa Heneghan, who was to have been married at Fort Augustus Abbey.

McPherson said yesterday: "I still want to marry Theresa . . . I am still very much in love with her."

'Excuse me'

On Saturday, as he and Theresa stood side by side at the altar, only seconds before the ceremony was due to start, MacPherson asked the priest: "Will you excuse me, father?"

Then he walked out of the abbey and vanished.

Yesterday he was back home in his father's whitewashed cottage, eight miles from the nearest road.

And he said it was a HANGOVER FROM HIS STAG PARTY that made him vanish.

For, he said, he passed out.

He added: "What has happened is nothing but a piece of bad luck. Anyone who says I ran out on Theresa is a liar."

Last night, MacPherson was waiting to hear from his lovely, lonely bride-to-be.

'Forgive me'

He said: "I pray that Theresa will forgive me.

"I suppose it is my own fault I had such a hangover. My stag party on Friday night was a fantastic affair. I could not help passing out on Saturday.

"My feelings have not changed in the least towards Theresa. Maybe she will feel differently about me after this. I am begging her to come back to me."

Yesterday he posted a letter

● Mr. HENAGHAN ... thunderstruck.

● THERESA ... on what should have been her wedding day.

to his fiancee, asking her forgiveness and promising never to drink again.

Then he told how he disappeared for two days.

'Terrible pains'

The tall, handsome shepherd said: "I was standing beside Theresa when I suddenly got terrible pains in my stomach. I just had to get outside.

"John Sutherland, my best man, took me into my father's car. A few minutes later I blacked out.

"The next thing I knew I woke up in a friend's house near Newtonmore, 50 miles away, at three p.m. on Sunday. I can't remember anything in between.

'I phoned'

"I am sure it was my rather wild stag party that brought on the black-out.

"I did not want to go to a doctor because, really, there was not much else wrong with me.

"When I came round my first thought was for Theresa. I got John to ring her at the hotel in Fort Augustus, but she could not get to the

Continued on Back Page

GINGER'S DIVORCE

Film actress Ginger Rogers, 47, got her final divorce decree yesterday from 31-year-old Jacques Bergerac, former Paris lawyer turned actor.

1000 Luxury Cashmeres!

TWIN SETS · LUMBERS · CARDIGANS DRESSMAKER-STYLE JUMPERS

all fully fashioned

Many of them made Exclusively for Watt Brothers

by

TOP CRAFTSMEN OF HAWICK

All the loveliest and most unusual Autumn Shades available only at Watt Brothers

TWIN SETS £7·19·6 CARDIGANS £5·5·0
LUMBERS £4·9·6 DRESSMAKER-STYLE JUMPERS £4·15·0

You will want one or two of these superb Garments for Christmas . . . at such new exciting prices!

Watt brothers

OF SAUCHIEHALL STREET, GLASGOW

Daily Record

THURS JAN 29 1959

SCOTLAND'S NATIONAL NEWSPAPER

2½d

No. 19,733

HERO DIES IN TRAM INFERNO

HOW IT HAPPENED

A SHEET of flame, sparked by 600 volts of electricity, set a tram ablaze seconds after it crashed into a lorry yesterday.

And in four minutes, the freak, 1000-to-1 accident killed three people.

The horror happened in the fog in Old Shettleston Road, Glasgow. The people who died were the tram-driver and two women.

Freak accident

And last night, Glasgow's Firemaster Martin Chadwick said:

"It was a freak accident — the point of impact was right on the tram's most vulnerable point . . .

". . . the electric resistance control gear panel, an area about 2 ft. by 6 ft. on one end of the tram.

"It is situated just behind the driver's seat. And in this case the driver was sitting there.

"The impact caused the shearing of wires which started arc-ing.

"This is the flash which jumps between two unprotected electric wires.

No doubt

"There is no doubt about what caused the fire. It was this 600-volt charge. It would be powerful enough to set fire to almost anything."

Firemaster Chadwick went on: "An accident like this could happen any time. It could even happen to a fire engine.

"But it was a chance in thousands.

"There is no reason why the trams cannot run as they normally do. You cannot take into account circumstances like this."

An inquiry

Mr E. R. L. Fitzpayne, the city's transport boss, said:

"I have been given no technical reason to suppose that there is any abnormal danger in continuing the service as usual tomorrow."

An inquiry under the direction of the Transport Ministry will begin this morning.

NO NEW TRAMS are being built for Glasgow. By the end of 1961, only the present 250 Coronation streamlined trams will be in operation.

By 1963 the city plans to abolish trams and complete the switchover to trolley buses and buses.

● WEAK POINT IN A TRAM'S ARMOUR and.

● DEAD HERO WAS TO HAVE WED TODAY—Page 3

● FULL STORY — Centre Pages

● WHAT THE RECORD SAYS—Page 2.

● At the very instant that this picture was taken, people were struggling for life . . . dark shapes which can be seen on the upper deck are passengers who eventually leapt to safety—most of them injured. Near the far end of the tram (as seen in this dramatic picture) died the driver.

MORE PICTURES on CENTRE PAGES

SUNDAY MAIL

SCOTLAND'S NATIONAL SUNDAY NEWSPAPER

No. 2636   APRIL 26, 1959   4d

The scene on the balcony above County Square as the Scottish Cup was held high to the thousands who celebrated St. Mirren's cup victory over Aberdeen.

TROOPS FALL OUT... PARADE IN A STORM

Saints go marching in with CUP

New Budget Terms

A LIMITED NUMBER OF THE NEW 17"

Starmaster IV

IMMEDIATELY AVAILABLE

Here is the latest 17" model on special Budget terms! Compare the value — and it's backed by the D.E.R. record of 21 years' good service.

Installed for first month's rental of 50/-

Reducing by 5/- a month every nine months to **30/-** a month

FREE SERVICE · REPAIRS AND REPLACEMENTS

Showrooms open for demonstrations 7-9 Friday evenings

356 SAUCHIEHALL ST., GLASGOW, C.2. Tel: Douglas 3025
554 LONDON RD., GLASGOW, S.E. Tel.: Bridgeton 7151/3
58 VICAR STREET, FALKIRK. Tel.: Falkirk 2436.

POST NOW

D·E·R

Est. 1938

Rent and Relax with D.E.R.

D.E.R. Ltd. Press Advertising
356 Sauchiehall St., Glasgow, C.2.
Please send details of Budget offer

Name _____

Address _____

GSM 26/4

ALSO SHOWROOMS THROUGHOUT ENGLAND AND WALES

THIRTEEN CAMERONIANS HAD TO BE HELPED FROM A PARADE GROUND YESTERDAY, DURING A CEREMONIAL REVIEW.

Some had fainted. Others showed signs of fainting as they fought to remain rigid in a biting wind and torrential rain.

The parade became an ordeal.

It SHOULD have been the proudest moment in the 100 years' history of the 6/7th Battalion of the Cameronians.

For they were receiving new Pipe Banners in recognition of a century of glory in battle.

A handful

But only a handful of people—most of them watching from cars—turned out to see the historic ceremony in their home town at Hamilton's Tower Park.

It was another "Wet Review."

For nearly an hour the soldiers stood rigid on the parade ground . . . already soaked to the skin.

Their ordeal had started nearly two hours previously when they assembled at Muirhall Barracks.

Bravely they marched to the parade, led by pipers and a brass band.

First casualty

The 90 part-time infantrymen lined up on the square with their backs to the driving wind which swept across the parade ground.

Then the first casualty collapsed to the ground.

Others followed one by one.

Senior N.C.O.'s scurried behind the ranks helping out the casualties.

Some were slung over N.C.Os' shoulders and carried to nearby trucks.

When Provost Gavin Cockburn

Radio, TV—Page 15

handed the pipe banners to Pipe Major Neil Reiley, the infantrymen had reformed ranks.

But only 77 remained to take part in the ceremony.

Provost Cockburn and Town Clerk James Kelly, in their ceremonial robes, tried to shelter

Back Page 👉

DARING RAID ON SAFE

OVER £100 was stolen in a daring safe-blowing raid in a Glasgow warehouse late last night.

The night watchman lay for two and a half hours bound and gagged before he managed to free himself and raise the alarm by phoning the police.

The watchman was doing his rounds in the premises of George MacLellan and Co., Ltd. in Shuna Street, Maryhill. When he reached the darkened office block he was suddenly attacked.

He was forced to the ground, gagged, and his hands tied while the raiders went next door and blew open the safe.

Davie Lapsley holds the Cup aloft for the cheering fans to see.   FULL STORY—PAGE 2

Daily Record

SAT AUG 29 1959

2½d

SCOTLAND'S NATIONAL NEWSPAPER

No. 19,915

The old friends meet

IKE NEARLY BLUSHED ON PARADE

● The FORMAL part of the visit (above) . . . President Eisenhower and the Queen inspect the guard of honour outside Balmoral. And the INFORMAL . . . Ike raises both his hands as he waves to the crowds

THE Queen left her private room at Balmoral yesterday and walked down a leafy lane to greet an old friend outside the castle gates.

THE FRIEND — President Eisenhower who made the 500-mile air trip from London to Aberdeen to see the Queen in her holiday castle on Deeside.

It was a gracious gesture which thrilled and delighted the President as much as it did the 5000 people who lined the quiet tree-lined road at Balmoral.

'How nice'

As Ike, in a grey suit and soft hat, stepped out of the Royal Daimler at the castle gates, his face lit up with surprise and pleasure when he saw the Queen and Princess Margaret standing by themselves in the road.

"How nice of you to reel me like this, ma'am," he said to the Queen.

And looking round at the ranks of the Royal Highland Fusiliers who formed the guard of honour, he added:

His 'clanger'

"They should have told me I was getting a reception like this."

Smiling, the Queen motioned him to inspect the guard.

"Right, ma'am," said the President—and then the ex-General walked to the WRONG end of the line.

The Queen told him: "You

DAILY RECORD REPORTER

start here " . . . and pointed to the other end of the line.

With just the faintest suspicion of a blush, the President turned and walked down the line of soldiers.

Surprise

The appearance of the Queen at the castle gates took the sightseers completely by surprise.

But when they recognised the Queen and Princess Margaret, a tremendous cheer

Continued on Back Page

echoed around the Deeside hills.

The Queen, who has been out of the castle grounds only once —to church—since she arrived three weeks ago, looked fit and happy.

And fashion-conscious women in the crowd noticed that the skirt of her powder-blue suit was two inches SHORTER than Princess Margaret's.

A minute before the President arrived the RHF's best-laid plans almost went agley.

And for Private Jimmy Laing, 23, of Glasgow, standing

WE'LL PAY YOUR BILLS

FIRST WINNERS ON MONDAY !

DAILY Record

TUES. MAR. 29 1960

2½D SCOTLAND'S NATIONAL NEWSPAPER

No. 20,096

Nineteen die as a whisky store explodes

INFERNO!

● High on a turntable ladder, a fireman fights the flames.

Death of Mr. C. B. Livingstone

WE regret to announce the death of Mr. C. B. Livingstone, Chairman of the Daily Record and Sunday Mail Ltd.

Mr. Livingstone had been seriously ill for some time. A week ago he underwent an operation in a Glasgow hospital and he died there early last night. He was 51.

Mr. Livingstone was a great newspaperman in the Scottish tradition. His personal success was remarkable.

He joined the Daily Record when he was 15. Before he had reached his 29th birthday he was editor.

Great 'scoop'

Among newspapermen his name will always be associated with the Record's great 'scoop' on the arrival in Scotland of Rudolph Hess.

His organising ability was outstanding and at one period he edited both the Sunday Mail and the Daily Record. In September, 1945, he became director and general manager.

In August, 1958, Mr. Livingstone was appointed Chairman of the company. He was a Justice of the Peace, and a past President of the Scottish Daily Newspaper Society.

Mr. Livingstone is survived by Mrs. Livingstone and their daughter and three sons.

TRIBUTES—SEE PAGE 5

ELECTRIC IRON KILLS A WOMAN

PRETTY Catherine Galloway, 23, offered to iron shirts for her young brothers last night . . . and was ELECTROCUTED.

Just after she started to iron in the living-room of her home at 110 Corsock Street, Dennistoun, Glasgow, her parents heard her scream.

And when Mr. Alex. Galloway, 51, and his wife, Jean, 41, rushed into the room, they found Catherine lying on the floor on top of the iron.

Plug out

Mr. Galloway said later: "The iron was warm but the plug had been pulled from the socket when Cathie fell. And the switch was turned off. We can't explain that.

"Cathie was moaning and I held her head in my arms. But she died before the ambulance arrived.

"We are stunned by the tragedy. She was a lovely girl and a great help in the house.

"Only a few minutes before this happened she offered to iron shirts for her brothers—Alex, 10, and Robert, 6—so that they would be tidy when they went to school in the morning."

● Flames envelop a fire engine buried in the rubble.

Crashing wall traps firemen

A FANTASTIC ERUPTION OF FLYING BRICKS AND LANCING FLAME LAST NIGHT TURNED A GLASGOW DOCKSIDE BLAZE INTO ONE OF SCOTLAND'S WORST-EVER FIRE DISASTERS.

For under the tons of broken masonry that was once the 60-foot wall of a warehouse NINETEEN FIREMEN WERE TRAPPED.

And early today it was officially stated

BLACKEST DAY

that there could be no hope for them.

Up until the time of the explosion—just after 7 p.m.—all that could be seen was smoke seeping from the building in Cheapside Street, Anderston.

Then came the blast. The

Continued on Back Page

For the Easter Bride!

In our Model Gown Salon we are showing

AN EXCLUSIVE COLLECTION
of
SUPERB BRIDAL GOWNS
20 Gns. to 48 Gns.

CHARMING BRIDESMAIDS' GOWNS
15 Gns. to 30 Gns.

In our Budget Dress Salon

LOVELY BRIDAL GOWNS
9 Gns. to 14 Gns.

SMART BRIDESMAIDS' GOWNS
8 Gns. to 12½ Gns.

* These attractive Gowns are available in all exquisite materials Short and Full-length Styles

Walt brothers

OF SAUCHIEHALL STREET, GLASGOW

Daily Record

THUR MAY 19 1960

2½d SCOTLAND'S NATIONAL NEWSPAPER
No. 20,140

ESTA MADRID!

WHICH IN ANYBODY'S LANGUAGE MEANS REAL MADRID WON... 7-3

KRUSCHEV SHOCKER!

ROAR upon roar surged down on the excited, jubilant men of Madrid as they trotted round Hampden Stadium last night . . . European Cup held aloft.

THIS WAS the salute of 127,000 fans for one of the most dazzling displays of soccer wizardry ever seen in Scotland.

THIS WAS the thunderous climax to 90 minutes of football extraordinary, which ended:

REAL MADRID 7, EINTRACHT 3.

Before the big game, Real Madrid were tipped as certain winners.

Sensation

But it was Frankfurt's Eintracht who gave the fans their first sensation of the game when outside-right Kress scored a brilliant goal.

Then relentlessly the Madrid football machine slicked into gear . . .

And before half-time the Eintracht net bulged ONE . . . TWO . . . THREE times.

In the second-half, never-say-die Eintracht wilted under the merciless onslaught of the magic men of Madrid.

Brilliantly led by Puskas and Di Stefano the Spaniards scored another four goals to Eintracht's two.

Glasgow was gay, glorious and hectic for this, the first-ever European Cup final to be staged in Scotland

In sparkling sunshine thousands mingled on the Hampden trek.

Accents from all over the globe mixed with the Glasgow burr as the good humoured crowd spilled across the city.

Ticket touts

Ticket touts were out early at the approaches to the stadium, and for a time business was brisk.

Then as zero hour came closer the touts began to panic

Hampden 127,000 salute magic men of football

as they were left with scores of unsold tickets.

One German supporter arrived with 44 spare 50s. tickets for the centre stand. He managed to sell many of them—but only at £1 a time.

INSIDE Hampden the Daily Record and Sunday Mail were right in the forefront of the big event as usual.

They presented a colourful pre-match display which opened with the mass pipe bands of the Argyll and Sutherland Highlanders.

There were also keep-fit

'RECORD' REPORTER

displays Scottish Country Dancing and an exhibition of the new "Kiki-Football Train-in Method" used by the Union of European Football Associations.

But the highlight of the pre-match show was a 5000 metres international race.

It was won by Frank Salvat, Finchley Harriers, who streaked past four-minute miler Derek Ibbotson.

● Three spectators collapsed and died in the Hampden crowd.

★ WAVERLEY'S REPORT—Pages 18 and 19

He shouts and raves at Press

MR. KRUSCHEV shook his fist yesterday at the Press of the world.

He ranted, raved and threatened at a fantastic Press conference in Paris.

And the man who wrecked the Summit was booed, jeered at and had his speech interrupted by some of the 2000 journalists.

Toned down

The loudest boos came when Mr. K. touched on the problem of Germany.

He said West German Chancellor Dr. Adenauer had sent "Hitlerites" to spoil his Press conference.

Much of the vulgarity and abuse he poured out was toned down by the official interpreters.

● FULL STORY AND MORE PICTURES ON BACK PAGE.

Someone isn't using Amplex

The coffee's hot—but the company's cool. Why? She's forgotten that in espresso bars conversations are conducted at close quarters. Don't *you* make the same mistake! To destroy offensive odours of breath and body at source–take an Amplex to keep you sweet all day!

AMPLEX
Breath and body deodorant tablets

Tablets 1/9

NEW!

AMPLEX FOOTFRESH

A morning spray and feet stay fresh for hours
Feet that feel hot and tired get a new lease of life with FOOTFRESH. This press-button freshener and deodoriser can be applied direct to bare feet, stockinged feet or the inside of shoes. Ask for FOOTFRESH now at your chemist. Price 7/6.

REAL HAPPY

● The game is over . . . and four happy Real Madrid players—Vidal, Pachin, Canario and goalkeeper Dominguez—run round the track with the European Cup.

And what a mighty cheer they got from the crowd.

★ More wonderful pictures on Centre Pages and Pages 18 and 19.

DAILY Record

SAT OCT 15 1960

2½ᴰ SCOTLAND'S NATIONAL NEWSPAPER

No. 20,268

LAST of the MANY

RAILWAY SHAKE-UP -TO MAKE 'EM PAY!

IT'S OFFICIAL—AN UP-TO-THE-MINUTE PLAN TO MAKE BRITISH RAILWAYS P-A-Y.

Secret Cabinet talks have been going on since April when Prime Minister Macmillan prophesied "radical changes."

And yesterday Mr. R. A. Butler dropped two bombshell hints that set the Tory Party conference at Scarborough buzzing with speculation.

Two key words

IN PUBLIC only two key words were mentioned—"commercialism" and "enterprise."

But, behind the scenes, it was being said that the Government had formed this three-point shake-up plan for the railways:

1 BREAK UP the rail system into regions — then let each manage its own cash and services.

2 SELL some subsidiary interests such as hotels, docks and ships — and put the rest

Secret talks

under separate management.

3 GIVE the railways a subsidy, either directly or indirectly.

All this, delegates were saying, could mean the abolition of the British Transport Commission—or its survival with very limited uses.

End of a joke

It could mean direct competition with road and air services.

It COULD mean that more of the country's uneconomic lines would be closed.

But it could also mean the

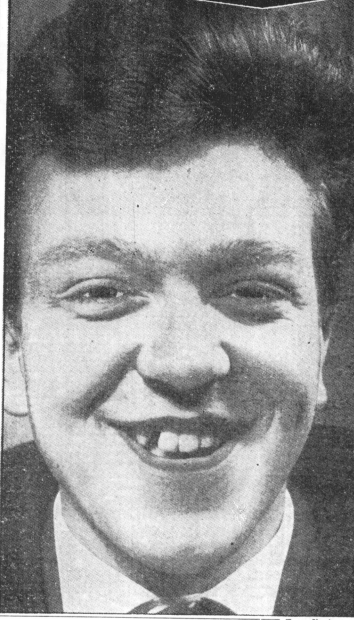

I KILLED A BOY, THEN WENT TO PICTURES

—alleged confession

A WOMAN said she pushed a three-year old boy to his death over a cliff, then had dinner and went to the pictures.

This was alleged yesterday at Lewes, Sussex, when barmaid Florence Owen, 44, appeared on a charge of murdering the boy.

A detective said he asked Miss Owen where the boy was. She replied: "He is in the sea."

The policeman added: "I said —'How did he get in the sea?' She said—'I knocked him in.'

"I cautioned her and she said: 'I went for a walk on the cliffs and pushed him in the water I don't know why I did it.

"'This nearly happened yesterday when I went out on the pier.'"

Week's stay

The boy, Barry Semple, was found dead below the 100-foot Telscombe Cliffs, near Brighton, on September 15, the court was told.

Barry's mother, Mrs. Eileen Semple, of Brighton, told the magistrates that she first met Miss Owen in July when the barmaid stayed for two weeks at her house.

After that Miss Owen called frequently and took Barry and his sister out. On September 13, Miss Owen arrived and told Mrs. Semple that she was staying in Brighton for a week.

Mrs. Semple whispered: "I made her a cup of tea and then she took Barry out to feed the pigeons. Next day she came again and took Barry out."

She said that they went out again on the third day at 2.20 p.m. and at 6 o'clock she reported the couple missing.

At this point Mrs. Semple broke down and sobbed, twisting her black gloves in her hands.

At the edge

Mr. David Walker, of The Esplanade, Telscombe Cliffs, said he saw a woman walking with a child and when he looked again the child was not there.

He saw the woman kneel at the edge of the cliff, look over it and then walk smartly away.

Miss Owen, of no fixed address, was sent for trial to the next sessions of Sussex Assizes.

RATES GO UP 1s.

Peebles County Council rates for the Landward Area are at 22s, an increase of 1s. There is also a water rate of 2s

Dandy loses battle No. 2

SAMUEL "DANDY" McKAY, alleged jailbreaker, alleged bank-raider, heard yesterday that the Crown won another trial postponement battle.

Postponement No. 1 was granted at the High Court in Glasgow last month, when certain necessary witnesses failed to turn up.

But yesterday the High Court in Edinburgh was asked to decide whether that covered both charges.

It was claimed on Dandy's behalf that the extension had been granted on the robbery charge only.

Nothing had been said to indicate that this was linked to the jail-breaking charge. it was said.

Mr. J. Irvine Smith sub-mitted that the Crown must either proceed against McKay on the prison-breaking charge beore October 22 . . .

. . . or free him from further proceedings on that charge.

But Lord Thomson granted the Crown's petition without comment.

Moss in car blaze but he will race

Stirling Moss was burned on the right arm yesterday when his Lotus Monte Carlo caught fire during practice at Riverside race track, California.

He was able to stop the burning car and emergency crews put out the fire.

Moss later said that both he and the car will be ready for the 200-mile sports car race at Riverside tomorrow.

...BUT NOT THE LEAST!

● You've probably never heard of David Bligh . . . but take a good look at him.

He is Britain's last National Serviceman—or so he believes.

David — a 22-year-old engineer of Eastleigh Hants —came out of his "medical" in London yesterday afternoon and sent this telegram:

"Mum, I'm the unluckiest man alive.

"I'm the last lad in the country to take his medical for National Service."

David said last night: "It was a real shock whe the clerk gave me my nine shillings travelling expenses and said, 'You're the last mate.'"

The Ministry of Labour and National Service—who control conscription—said: "He is probably right.

"Our medical boards throughout the country have completed their normal programmes."

● Anyone on deferment who has not heard from the Ministry has missed National Service.

The last conscriptions will be "on duty" by December 31.

Continued on Back Page

The proprietary wine ELDORADO

REGISTERED TRADE MARK

is a high duty **FULL STRENGTH** wine of character and quality and is undoubtedly todays best value at

10'6 bottle

5'9 half bottle **3'3** quarter bottle

Ask for it by name!

ELDORADO Old Tawny

TAWNY AND WHITE

Daily Record

WED NOV 2 1960

2½D SCOTLAND'S NATIONAL NEWSPAPER
No. 20,283

NUCLEAR SUBS ON CLYDE—IN 6 MONTHS

Angry M.P.s quiz Mac

IT'S official . . . nuclear submarines from America, armed with Polaris H-missiles, will be in the Clyde within six months.

And yesterday the Prime Minister revealed the base chosen for 1500 Americans and their subs—the Holy Loch, in Argyll, 30 miles from Glasgow.

He hoped M.P.s would see NO EXTRA RISKS in the move. But Scots Labourites protested in anger.

And last night a political storm was brewing over Britain's " lack of control."

No advance news

For Mr. Macmillan made it clear the subs will **NOT** be subject to the control arrangements which govern American planes here.

He will **NOT** know in advance of subs' movements in and out of the Holy Loch.

But the Premier also made it clear:

" I AM SATISFIED THESE MISSILES WILL NEVER BE USED WITHOUT THE FULLEST PREVIOUS CONSULTATION."

Spy promise

And later these official assurances were given:

1 There will be **NO SECRET MISSIONS** like the recent spy-plane embarrassment.

2 And there will be **NO FIRINGS** at all from British waters.

3 Accidental nuclear explosions and accidental firing of a Polaris missile are impossible.

4 There will be **NO DANGER** from nuclear leaks and no warheads or missiles will be stored ashore.

5 A Royal Navy monitoring team will be on constant duty testing for leakage and radioactivity.

Mr. Macmillan told the Commons that AT FIRST SIGHT the new base might seem to bring added anxiety.

"BUT ON REFLECTION I hope the House will feel that this does not add to the risks to which we are all inevitably exposed in this nuclear age."

The target

Up jumped Mr. Emrys Hughes, South Ayrshire There would be considerable resentment in the West of Scotland, he warned.

People believed a great industrial population was going to be exposed to destruction without any adequate means of defence

The Prime Minister replied that in the event of war, BOMBER BASES would be the natural target.

Within hours Moscow Radio was to boast that if the Clyde was used for aggression it

would suffer " an inevitable retaliatory blow."

But Mr. Macmillan seemed almost to anticipate the boast as he pointed out:

That the subs' home port will be in America. That they will use the Holy Loch only between patrols. . . .

. . . AND THAT IN THE EVENT OF A WAR THEY WILL BE AT SEA

" We have to accept danger," he added, " and the fact that we are all in it.

" I think the House and the country, on reflection, will agree we had NO OTHER CHOICE."

No interfering

The first of the U.S. vessels, the 18,500-ton submarine depot ship Proteus, will arrive in the Holy Loch in February.

It will be followed by a floating dock.

None of this, said senior Royal Navy officers in Glasgow last night, would interfere with normal Clyde shipping.

" It will not interfere with yachting or boating on the loch, either," they said.

And a liaison committee will be formed soon to work closely with all local authorities and organisations involved.

WILLIAMS & HUMBERT'S DRY SACK SHERRY

REGD.

For over 50 years DRY SACK — Spain's famous Medium Dry Sherry — has been a popular favourite throughout the world. Also available in half bottles and pocket flasks.

Shippers of the famous

WALNUT BROWN
PANDO
CANASTA CREAM
CARLITO and **CEDRO**

Sherries

BODEGAS : JEREZ DE LA FRONTERA · SPAIN
SCOTTISH AGENTS : Robertson & Baxter Ltd., 106 West Nile St., GLASGOW

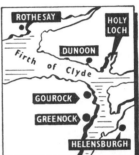

● THE PRINCESS . . . happy with her husband.

Margaret and Tony did not turn up

PRINCESS MARGARET and Mr. Antony Armstrong-Jones stayed away from yesterday's State opening of Parliament.

While the Queen opened the new Parliamentary session in the traditional glittering ceremony at the House of Lords, the Princess and her husband remained indoors at their home in Kensington Palace.

Both were invited to attend by the Lord Great Chamberlain, " but decided to decline."

Major Arthur Griffin, the Clarence House Press spokesman, said last night:

" I have no idea what is the reason for their decision The Princess had no official engagement.

" Perhaps they had some private engagement which they preferred to keep."

A surprise

Princess Margaret's absence surprised many of the distinguished guests.

Some thought she might have stayed away to save her husband from possible embarrassment.

Protocol is rigidly observed at the State Opening. And, it was thought, Mr Armstrong-Jones — a commoner — would have been unable to sit with his wife and other members of the Royal Family.

QUEEN'S SPEECH— CENTRE PAGES.

'RECORD' REPORTER

PROVOST FLETCHER . . For

PROVOST McPHAIL . . Against

'Big protest on the way'

A FORMER Lord Povost of Glasgow talked last night about a big attack building up on the " Polaris-on-the-Clyde " plan.

And, said Dr. Andrew Hood, it would gather momentum after to-day's meeting of Glasgow District Trades Council.

The Council, representing nearly 100,000 workers, yesterday expressed their " alarm " at the new plans for the Holy Loch.

They have invited Vale of Leven and Dumbarton Trades Council leaders to today's meeting

AND IT IS TO BE OPEN TO THE PRESS FOR THE FIRST TIME SINCE 1926

A march?

The Glasgow city treasurer. Councillor John Johnston who is also secretary of the Glasgow Trades Council. said:

" We might even have an Aldermaston-type march.

" To take no action is simply putting one's head in the sand " Bailie David Gibson, deputy

leader of the Labour group in Glasgow Corporation, said :

" I am quite opposed to the base being on the Clyde.

" AND I AM POSITIVE THIS IS THE GENERAL OPINION OF PEOPLE IN SCOTLAND "

No qualms

However, in Dunoon, the Argyll town with the shadow of an atom base on its doorstep, Provost Catherine McPhail said :

" I don't want the base myself . . but it is **UNLIKELY** the council will protest.

" There is no doubt that our economy will be improved."

Ex-Councillor Robert McArthur of Dunoon said : " I have no qualms at all.

" If an H-bomb came down, the whole country would be wiped out This area might as well get the financial benefit which the base will bring."

Ex-Provost E F Wyatt now

Continued on Back Page

SUNDAY MAIL

4D SCOTLAND'S NATIONAL SUNDAY NEWSPAPER

No. 2743   MAY 14, 1961

— GARY COOPER DEAD —

THE LAST OF THE GREATS

GARY COOPER, the last of the great film stars, died in his Hollywood home last night—six days after his 60th birthday.

His wife Veronica and his 21-year-old daughter Marie were at his bedside. He was suffering from cancer and had been under heavy sedatives for weeks to kill the pain. Just before he died his wife said: " It is the will of God."

A friend of the world...

● This is Gary Cooper as the world knew, and liked him—tall, lean and smiling.

Gary topped the world's film popularity polls for years—and off-screen he was just as popular.

He was the man who could always joke . . . even when he knew he faced death.

He never let down a friend and he was once called the " saint in spurs."

Gary and his wife once parted after 18 years of marriage.

The break-up brought no excuses from Gary—just a forthright warning to the curious to " quit meddling

In 1959 he and his wife were re-united. They took a Continental holiday. Then he made his last film.

'He was born a nice guy'

ALL over the world last night people mourned the death of the tall, drawling hero of 89 films.

Among those who had sent messages during his illness were the Queen and President Kennedy.

One of his best friends, **JOHN WAYNE**, said: " When Coop died, a part of our business died with him

" In this town, whenever a man moves on, they figure somebody else will take his place. But no one will ever replace Gary Cooper."

He joked

The last time they met was during a visit to London last November. Wayne went on:

" 'Coop' congratulated me on my apparent good condition. I told him, 'Coop, you don't have to take a back seat to anybody. I never saw you looking better.'

" Then 'Coop' said: ' Let's have a drink on that. Let's keep looking good to cover up what's going on inside.'

" I didn't know what he meant by that at the time," recalled Wayne. " I do now."

VITTORIO DE SICA, the Italian director and actor, said:

" Gary Cooper was the greatest actor the cinema has ever had. He never tired the public. He was a complete actor."

ACTOR RICHARD ARLEN said: " Some people are just born nice guys, and nothing—not even Hollywood—can change it. Coop just liked people. It was as simple as that."

Loved his home

Cooper loved his home, built round a terrace, swimming pool and tropical gardens.

He spent a lot of time during his illness on the terrace at one end of the pool, looking towards his favourite view of tropical ferns with a waterfall coming through them.

" A fella just can't ask for much more," he told his wife.

Gary, born in Montana, was the son of a Briton who emigrated to

● His wife Veronica

America and later became a justice in the Montana Supreme Court.

At the age of nine Gary was sent to England for schooling at Dunstable, Bedfordshire—his father's home district.

Then back to the States and to " Westerns."

Strangely enough Coop wanted to be an artist. He worked for five years as a cartoonist on a local paper.

Then a friend told him he could earn a few dollars falling off horses as a Hollywood stunt man.

Highest-paid star

" To tell the truth, my only thought was to become an artist," he explained years later. " Any money I earned from movies was to be put to this end."

That was his only idea, he said, until he found out that Tom Mix, the cowboy star, was earning 17,500 dollars (then about £4300) a week.

He decided to try to become a film star—and became a multi-millionaire.

In 1936 he commanded the highest salary in Hollywood, leaving behind Ronald Colman, Claudette Colbert, Mae West, Madeleine Carroll, Warner Baxter, Marlene Dietrich, Ruth Chatterton and Charles Boyer.

Cooper was still in the lead in 1954.

He married in 1933 and set something of a record for Hollywood by staying married to the same woman until his death.

He returned with his family in 1953 for a premiere in London when he was introduced to the Queen.

Two years later he was here again on holiday and " relaxing " from a strenuous film-making career.

The Royal favourite—Page 12

90,000 'missing children'

DOCTORS warned last night of the grave danger to 90,000 children who have not been immunised against polio.

After one of the sunniest spring weeks in memory, they warned: " If this means a long, hot summer the risk of polio is very much greater."

'Bad year' warning

Six cases have already been confirmed in Scotland.

And the battle has become a race against time.

Glasgow Medical Officer Dr. William Horne warned:

" Until now, every good winter like this year's has meant a bad year for polio

" If this is the start of a really warm summer, then the polio risk is much greater."

He stressed: " To have any protection at all, every man, woman and child should have two anti-polio injections before the end of June."

Experts say there are AT LEAST 90,000 children still unprotected in Scotland. Of these, 20,000 are Glasgow youngsters UNDER TWO.

In iron lung

Five cases of polio have been confirmed in Glasgow this year. ALL are children of six or under.

Dr. Horne said: " One boy is in an iron lung and is still very ill."

The sixth case of polio is in Renfrewshire. A boy of four is in hospital.

Tomorrow, 17,000 letters will be sent to county parents urging them to have their children vaccinated IMMEDIATELY.

IN LANARKSHIRE, nearly 25,000 children under 15 have no protection.

TV—PAGE 14   *WHAT EVERY WOMAN WANTS—A £500 PRIZE, IT'S ON PAGE 11*

ROYAL PICTURE bulletin

QUEEN OF THE GORBALS

● Massive as the hearts of its people is this amazing welcome for The Queen of the Gorbals.

The crowds roar, the ricketies clack, the bells ring, the flags fly from the gaily-painted windows with their spotless curtains.

For the Queen has come to No. 71 and, for the moment, Sunset Strip was never more famous than Sandyfaulds Street.

She's the captivating centre of this modern Miracle of the Gorbals, this amazing blend of slum and skyscraper.

And wherever she goes it's the same sunshine welcome.

From those toiling to keep tumbledown tenement together . . . to those lucky enough to have a shiny new maisonette.

Like the ones in Ballater Street where the Queen is seen (below) with Lord Provost Mrs. Jean Roberts.

Yes . . . a day never to be forgotten in this "little town" of warm hearts, this Gorbals of the heart of gold.

● **THE WELCOME THAT'S AS MASSIVE AS THE SCENE.**

S THERE...BY THE ROYAL CAR OR AT THEIR WINDOWS...TO GREET THE QUEEN WHO CAME TO OUR STREET

Daily Record

MON. AUG. 6 1962

3ᴰ SCOTLAND'S NATIONAL NEWSPAPER

No. 20,831

LIFE AND DEATH OF MARILYN

Fishers are saved

NINETEEN agony-filled hours of waiting, hoping and praying are over for the fishing port of Peterhead, Aberdeenshire.

NINETEEN HOURS which ended in tears of joy . . . with the news that the 10 men of the fishing boat Daisy were safe.

Full story and pictures—BACK PAGE.

STAR PRIZES FOR YOU

★ Another wonderful FREE holiday contest starts today. See Page 4.

STAR BETS FOR YOU

★ FOUR out of SIX . . . for GARRY OWEN at Thirsk.
★ FIVE out of SIX . . . for NEWSBOY at Leicester.
★ SIX meetings today . . . ALL the tips, Pages 12 and 13.

Fantastic VALUE *from* **Wilson's** OF BELFAST

SUMMER SALE

ENDS SATURDAY 1 P.M.

Excellent quality TURKISH HAND TOWELS and BATH TOWELS. Lovely Jacquard weave. Soft and absorbent. Pastel shades of Blue or Green only.
Size 20in. x 40in. Were 6/11. SALE PRICE, each **3/11**

TURKISH TOWELS in top grade quality. Jacquard weave in rainbow cross-stripe design with contrasting border at each end.
Size 20in. x 40in. Were 7/11. SALE PRICE, each **4/11**

Cambric reversible feather filled QUILTS. Small all-over floral cameo design. Nicely finished with frilled edge. In excellent shades of Red, Green, Turquoise, Rose or Lilac.
Single Bed Size. Were 69/6. SALE PRICE, each **45/-**

Completely washable QUILTS covered and filled with Tricel. Extremely light and warm. Self colours of Pink, Blue, Lilac or attractive small floral and square design in Rose or Lilac.
Single Bed Size. Were £6.19.6. SALE PRICE, each **75/-**

MAIL ORDERS despatched Post free over £5 or we will send C.O.D. Please state second colour choice if possible.

John Wilson & Son (Belfast) Ltd.

219 SAUCHIEHALL ST., GLASGOW
41 SHANDWICK PL., EDINBURGH
339 UNION STREET, ABERDEEN

Sleeping pills kill at 3 am...

From 'RECORD' REPORTER, LOS ANGELES, SUNDAY

MARILYN MONROE, the world's best-known sex-symbol is dead.

She was found in bed at her home in a Los Angeles suburb this morning.

She died from an overdose of sleeping tablets, and police are treating the case as "apparent suicide."

The tragedy was discovered by Marilyn's housekeeper, Mrs. Eunice Murray.

She told police in the actress's £25,000 home in Brentwood suburb, about ten miles from the centre of Hollywood, that she saw a light under the bedroom door about midnight.

When the light was still on three hours later (about 11 a.m. British time) she tried the door and found it locked.

Phoned doctor

She phoned Miss Monroe's doctor, Dr. Ralph Greenson, who called a colleague. They broke into the bedroom through a window.

They found the star lying on her bed, clutching a white telephone still on its hook.

On the bedside table, among 30 medicine bottle, was an empty bottle labled Nembutal — sleeping pills.

One doctor said he prescribed Nembutal for her on Saturday, but she did not say why she wanted it.

Marilyn's closest friend, attractive brunette Pat Newcomb, was the last person to see her alive.

She had dinner with Marilyn in her home last night, and the two girls had made plans for a " day out " today.

Called back to the house before dawn, Pat collapsed in tears. " Oh, my God, how could a thing like this happed ? " she sobbed.

Later, by telephone from her

Continued on Back Page

YACHT SAVED BY LIFEBOAT

A LIFEBOAT was last night towing into Arbroath, Angus, the yacht Myhaven, which had been wallowing in the heavy North Sea for two and a half hours after engine trouble.

On board the yacht were its owner Mr. Reginald Nash, of Harrowgate, Yorkshire, and Berwick Harbour Master Lieutenant Commander George Gibson, his wife and 19-year-old son, Murray. They had sent out an emergency call.

...THIS WAS A FILM WITH NO ENDING...

☆ This is how Marilyn Monroe appeared in the last film on which she worked . . . "Something's Got To Give." But the star was sacked by her studio for "wilful breaches of contract."

Daily Record

WED. SEPT. 5 1962

3ᴰ SCOTLAND'S NATIONAL NEWSPAPER
No. 20,857

250,000 take a...
SENTIMENTAL JOURNEY

TRAMCAR SOUVENIR

● The CAVALCADE of "CAURS" heads South over the Clyde at the Jamaica Street bridge.

AN AMAZING FAREWELL TO THE 'CAURS'

A QUARTER of a million people turned out last night to wave goodbye to Glasgow's last tram-car.

They HUNG OUT of tenement windows and JOSTLED on the pavements, even CROWDED out to the tramlines for a moment of history which touched every one of them.

CHEERED

And how they waved and cheered as a horse-drawn tram led the procession of 20 "caurs" of all ages.

Mobile patrols and squads of mounted police were drafted in to handle the huge crowds packing the city centre.

CLOUDBURST

And how the city's youngsters — who have seen only the modern trams — and the old folk cheered —

Not even a cloudburst could dampen their fond farewell as an era ended.

● FULL STORY and more amazing pictures on Centre Pages.

Cross-fire! As Reds get tough on U-2

THE Russians got tough again yesterday over America's foreign-based, high-flying U-2 "spy" planes. But almost immediately there were counter-blasts.

A Soviet Note, handed to an American envoy in Moscow, protested that a U-2 had "violated" Russian territory—Sakhalin Island, north of Japan. And the Note repeated the warning of possible "retaliation" against countries where U-2 planes are based.

Almost immediately, WEST GERMANY accused Russia of violating West German air space. Police at Helmstedt said two Russian jets crossed the border and stayed on the wrong side for about five minutes.

Later, a Western Allied spokesman said in Berlin that Russian M.I.G. fighters "flew near" three Western airliners in the Berlin air corridor. He said the fighters "accompanied for

YOUR MATTRESS RE-MADE **AT MUCH LESS COST**

IN ONLY 3 DAYS

Have your mattress re-made in the Stoddart Factory. Only finest materials used. A top quality job guaranteed at much less cost than a new mattress.

HAIR MATTRESSES RE-MADE OR CONVERTED INTO SPRING INTERIORS ● SPRING INTERIORS RE-MADE ● BASES OR OPEN TYPE SPRINGS RENOVATED ● QUILTS RE-COVERED

Write, or phone GLASGOW BEL 2897

Open all day Tuesdays

No matter how bad condition your present mattress is in, the Stoddart Re-making Service will return it to you as good as new.

Stoddart
FOR SERVICE & SATISFACTION

Our van has a regular collection and delivery service for Glasgow and a weekly service for certain Ayrshire, Renfrewshire and North Lanarkshire areas.

THOS. STODDART LTD., HUNTER ST., GLASGOW C.4. ● ESTAB. 1910

Daily Record

WED OCT. 24 1962

3ᴰ SCOTLAND'S NATIONAL NEWSPAPER
No. 20,899

BLOCKADE OFFICIAL TODAY—U.S. SHIPS HEAD TO INTERCEPT

TARGET No. 1

Alert for Soviet missile ship

From 'RECORD' CORRESPONDENT, New York, Tuesday

AMERICAN WARSHIPS, FANNING OUT INTO THE ATLANTIC TO ENFORCE THE U.S. BLOCKADE OF CUBA, TONIGHT MADE THEIR FIRST RADIO CONTACT WITH A CUBA-BOUND RUSSIAN VESSEL.

Television programmes here were interrupted for a flash report from the Task Force in contact. The name of the Russian ship was not revealed.

In Washington tonight, President Kennedy signed an official proclamation, ordering the blockade to start at 3 p.m. British time tomorrow.

25 Russian ships still sail on

It authorises the Defence Secretary to designate prohibited zones and routes "within a reasonable distance of Cuba."

Soon after the signing. Defence Secretary Robert McNamara told a Washington Press conference that about 25 Russian ships are believed to be continuing to sail on course to Cuba, undeterred by President Kennedy's search-or-sink orders.

IT WAS A FAIR PRESUMPTION, HE SAID, THAT SOME OF THEM WERE CARRYING OFFENSIVE WEAPONS.

Armed boarding parties, he added, would be ready to search the Russian ships when the blockade starts. But, there would be no effort to search any ships before the 3 p.m. dead-line.

Mr. McNamara also said he had ordered that all Navy and Marine personnel be held on active duty for up to a year beyond the end of their normal tours, to carry out the Cuba blockade and defend the American base there.

Late tonight, at least 40 American warships, with jet fighter escirts, were at their blockade stations.

Stop at all costs

They are lying in wait for the Soviet rocket - carrying frighter Polotavia—THEIR No. 1 TARGET.

She was specially designed to carry the 67ft.-long missiles which the Russians have been setting up in Cuba within range of Washington and U.S. bases.

The Polotavia has been running a regular service from Russian ports to Havana, Cuban dictator Castro's capital.

If she maintains her usual time-table, she should be making a westerly voyage across the Atlantic again within a few days.

The American ships have been ordered to intercept her at all costs.

And the next vital move rests with Kruschev. He can recall the Polotavia to Russian waters —or throw down the gauntlet by providing her with a naval convoy.

● Five British ships will be among the first to be intercepted—including one which is on a Russian charter.

Rocket site!
—THE FIRST PICTURE

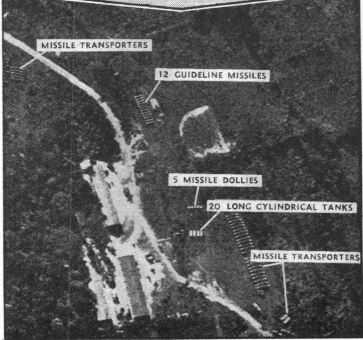

MISSILE TRANSPORTERS
12 GUIDELINE MISSILES
5 MISSILE DOLLIES
20 LONG CYLINDRICAL TANKS
MISSILE TRANSPORTERS

● This aerial picture of the Russian missile build-up in Cuba was issued in London last night.

Official American sources said pictures were taken about 48 hours earlier by U.S. spy planes. One picture was said to show a site containing 16 intermediate range missiles. Another showed seven medium range missiles. A third was of 39 Russian fighters on a newly-built air strip. Yet another revealed 21 Russian bombers, some still in crates. The medium range missiles were said to be operational. Work is believed to be still going on at the intermediate rocket sites.

The Russians appear to have made no attempt to camouflage the build-up. One top U.S. official said: "It seems they just don't care a damn."

KENNEDY MAKES IT OFFICIAL

● President Kennedy signs the proclamation formally putting into effect the arms blockade of Cuba from 3 p.m. today, British time.

The President, grim and unsmiling, made no comment during the signing.

Milletts FRONT PAGE BARGAINS

SHEEPSKIN JACKETS
FOR ALL THE FAMILY

Super natural top quality skins with luxurious white lambswool cosy linings

MEN'S	WOMEN'S
£18.10.0	**£16.10.0**

also **SIMULATED SHEEPSKIN JACKETS**
Super quality Tan Jackets: Men .... 99/11   Children's 67/6
R.A.F Flying Jackets, black or tan £6.6.0

BUY ONE PAIR, GET ANOTHER PAIR FREE—MEN'S SHOES

Men s black grain apron front welded sole SHOES. Each pair carries a written 6 months' guarantee. WELL-KNOWN 'REGAL' COMBAT BRAND ALL SIZES ONLY **49/11**

Remember! another pair FREE with each pair you buy

POSTAL ORDERS 3/- EXTRA
WOOL MELTON DONKEY JACKETS. All sizes 39/11

GUARANTEED ELECTRIC BLANKETS

Perfect quality with safety " On/Off " switch with 2 years' unconditional guarantee and 5 years' for old-age pensioners and invalids. Size 48 x 24. SENSATIONAL SELLING PRICE **39/11**
SUPER DOUBLE BED SIZE, 50 x 48. ONLY **79/6**
3-YEAR GUARANTEE

MILLETTS STORES (1928) LTD., 71 UNION ST., GLASGOW
TELEPHONE: CENTRAL 1678

Proteus sails out

SUBS GO—THEN 2 A.M. RIDDLE OF RENDEZVOUS

DRAMA flared at 2 a.m. today when the Polaris depot ship Proteus LEFT the Holy Loch, near Dunoon . . . for a mystery rendezvous.

This followed an evening of intense activity when all men on shore leave were recalled by U.S. Navy shore patrols..

Earlier in the day, all Polaris subs had left the Holy Loch . . . destination unknown.

First hint that Proteus might sail, apart from the re-call of the ship's company, was the cutting-off of the ship-to-shore telephone communication.

At the London headquarters of the United States Navy, a duty officer was taken by surprise to learn that the ship had sailed.

He agreed: "In a matter involving security, it is possible that the ship could sail first and then we might be informed afterwards."

Months at sea

Speculation about where Proteus might be headed was heightened by the fact that all Polaris submarines attached to her can stay at sea for months without having to return for supplies.

Daily Record

THURS. MAR. 28 1963

3ᴰ SCOTLAND'S NATIONAL NEWSPAPER

No. 21,031

Page One Sport

LAST NIGHT'S BIG GAMES

HEARTS	0	RANGERS	5
KILMARN'K.	6	CELTIC	0
FALKIRK	3	HIBS	1
CLYDE	4	RAITH R.	2

★ ★ ★

8 TO 1 DOUBLE | 3 OUT OF 6 !

● That was NEWSBOY'S score at Lincoln yesterday. Today's tips for Liverpool . . .

PAGES 19, 20

★ ★ ★

WIN WEMBLEY WINDFALL

● It's big-match time in the football world . . . and right with it is the 'Record' with a new football contest.

PAGE 17

Noble on railways:

I'LL FIGHT ALL THE WAY

Cuts only when roads improve

SCOTTISH Secretary Michael Noble gave a positive assurance in London last night that there would be NO rail cuts in Scotland until there were adequate roads and bus services.

He told me this—despite the fact that he had just heard Mr. Ernest Marples, Minister of Transport, say that he and the Cabinet were "at one" with Dr. Beeching's plan and hoped, subject to appeals, to push through closures by the end of next year.

Reminded that it takes time to build roads, Mr. Noble said: *"IF THE ROAD SYSTEM IS CONSIDERED BY ME TO BE INADEQUATE THE RAIL CLOSURES WILL NOT TAKE PLACE."*

By DOUGLAS MALONE

Hardest blow on Scots

As the details of the Beeching plan to reshape the railways were revealed yesterday, it quickly became obvious that Scotland has suffered grievously; has, in fact, been hardest hit.

The £24,000-a-year railway boss has scythed his way through the country.

Not only is he embarking on twentieth-century Highland clearances, he is denuding wide areas of Scotland in the North-East, the South-East and South-West of existing transport facilities.

Further cuts may come

HIS "AXE" is poised to fall on 435 stations and halts—including Glasgow's main line terminals, St. Enoch and Buchanan Street and Edinburgh's Princes Street — more than a third of the total now in operation.

HIS "AXE" is to lop off 51 complete passenger services—including all lines north and west of Inverness: all but one of the branch lines in Aberdeenshire and the North-East; the links from Ayr and Dumfries to the Stranraer Irish boats; and the main link from Edinburgh to Carlisle.

Of a total of 5000 routes miles and 2363 stations being abandoned in Britain, Scotland's share represents more than ONE-FIFTH—1100 miles and 435 stations.

And, bad as it is—this is not the end.

'What's left is adequate'

The Report, and members of the Railways Board, have made it perfectly clear that further cuts and closures may come if many of the "stopping trains" do not become economic.

Nationally, this could mean "hundreds" of stations being closed and Scotland, with its sparsely populated areas, could bear the brunt.

Dr. Beeching, who, from the outset made it clear that his job was to make the railways pay, leaving social problems to the Government, has done precisely that.

His report acknowledges the existence of social problems, of the need for alternative transport in remote areas, and Scotland's fight for new industries.

But that is all it does.

Many of the arguments which have been advanced against rail cuts have been dismissed.

According to the Report and members of the Board whom I questioned in London the attitude is this:

● **INDUSTRY:** If industry hasn't come to Scotland during the past 50 100 years while railways have been there, it won't come now.

"Scotland is being left with an adequate rail service for existing industry, and any that is likely to come."

Their future in doubt

● **TOURISM:** Most of Scotland's tourist traffic is by road and will continue to be.

● **STRANRAER** and **SKYE BOATS:** These will continue to run, but most of the passengers have come and will continue to come by road.

● **SCOTLAND** to **LONDON,** daylight services. Because of competition from the air their future is in doubt While they may be withdrawn, sleeper services will be increased

There will be no hold-up

● **SCOTTISH ROADS** and **BUS SERVICES:** It is conceded that in some areas in the North roads and bus services are inadequate.

But the planners say, the plan will NOT be held up until they are improved.

● **SNOWBOUND WINTER ROADS:** Better to have more snowploughs than unused or under-used railway services, is the attitude.

Services which are being "amputated" for passenger traffic may continue to carry

Continued on Back Page

ON OTHER PAGES...

TARGET SCOTLAND

WHAT

SAYS

FULL LIST OF AXED STATIONS AND SERVICES

WEAK after FLU?

This natural answer is sweeping Britain and may be YOUR solution

Has flu left you so weak and run down that you tire easily, lack concentration, are physically below par?

Perhaps also your digestion is impaired and your reserves of energy too low. This may mean that you need those natural vitamins so essential to maintain correct blood flow to the muscles of both body and brain.

Do as thousands of all ages and restore Nature to your diet by taking Doerenkamp's ACTIFS Capsules before your meals. New to Britain, tasteless ACTIFS Capsules, specially combine Wheat Germ—richest natural source of "growth" and "energy" Vitamins—with other natural vitamin-bearing concentrations. ACTIFS contain no drugs and are not habit-forming.

You will be amazed at the difference tasteless easy-to-take ACTIFS will make to your energy and whole well-being. You will feel stronger, younger and brighter in every way and you will look better. Clear skin, healthy hair and shining eyes will indicate your return to vital and positive health. Start taking ACTIFS now. From Retail, Multiple Chemists and Co-operatives, 8/6 for three weeks' course.

Actifs CAPSULES

VITAL POSITIVE HEALTH WITHOUT DRUGS

Daily Record

THURS. JUNE 6 1963

3ᴰ SCOTLAND'S NATIONAL NEWSPAPER

No. 21,091

Confession to Premier—then Profumo quits

● JOHN PROFUMO ... aged 48, he became War Minister three years ago.

'I LIED ABOUT CHRISTINE'

...to protect my wife and family

WAR MINISTER John Profumo last night resigned from the Government — after a sensational confession that he had lied to Parliament.

In a letter to the Prime Minister, Mr. Profumo admitted that he DID have an improper association with red-haired model Christine Keeler.

The hints . . .

This finally clears the cloud of rumour and suspicion which has hung over the political scene for more than three months.

The first public hint of a scandal building up around 48-year-old Mr. Profumo came during a Commons debate in the early hours of March 22.

Three Labour M.P.s referred to rumours surrounding 22-year-old Miss Keeler, who was then a missing witness in an Old Bailey shooting case.

A FEW HOURS LATER, MR. PROFUMO MADE A PERSONAL STATEMENT TO THE COMMONS IN WHICH HE DENIED THERE WAS ANYTHING IMPROPER IN HIS ASSOCIATION WITH MISS KEELER.

And he threatened to take legal action against anyone spreading these rumours.

Prime Minister Harold Macmillan and other senior Ministers were in the Commons and there were cheers as Mr. Profumo finished his statement

Also listening to him in the House was his wife, actress Valerie Hobson, who gave up the stage to support her husband's political career.

Now Mr. Profumo, Tory M.P. for Stratford-on-Avon, is also to give up his seat in the Commons.

'I misled you'

In his letter to the Prime Minister, Mr Profumo said: " I misled you, and my colleagues, and the House.'

He added that what he described as his " deception" was " to protect, as I thought, my wife and family, who were equally misled, as were my personal advisers."

Mr. Profumo opened his letter by recalling his statement to Parliament.

The letter went on: "At that time rumour had charged me with assisting in the disappearance of a witness and with being involved in some breach of security

" So serious were these charges that I allowed myself to think that my personal association with that witness, which had also

Continued on Back Page

● Dr. STEPHEN WARD . . . Profumo met Christine at his house.

The War Minister's resignation came after a letter from the doctor to the Home Secretary.

A SUNSHINE HOLIDAY — IN ARMCHAIR LUXURY

COTTER TOURS
FROM GLASGOW AND EDINBURGH

CAN STILL OFFER A FEW PEOPLE ACCOMMODATION ON THESE LUXURY TOURS :

8 DAY BELGIUM COAST	**27** GNS.	**13 DAY SWISS INTERLAKEN**	**43** GNS.
14 DAY AUSTRIA & RHINE VALLEY	**45** GNS.	**14 DAY SWISS & ITALIAN LAKES**	**59** GNS.

Popular 7-Day **Scottish Highlands**	*A glorious week-end at* **BLACKPOOL ILLUMINATIONS**
It includes day excursions to outstanding beauty spots from a really perfect centre. Huntly **13** GNS	Popular three-day tour leaving every Saturday from September 14 **£6.15/-**

Cotter Motor Tours Ltd., 192 BUCHANAN ST., GLASGOW, C.1.   DOU 7266

Daily Record

FRI. AUG. 9 1963

3ᴰ SCOTLAND'S NATIONAL NEWSPAPER

No. 21,146

The Brain Mr. Mac The Snout

GANG BOSS THEY CAN'T CATCH

TIP-OFF MAN IN SCOTLAND

UNDERWORLD INFORMER

WANTED MEN!

NAP AND DOUBLE

yesterday for
GARRY OWEN
and
HEATHBIRD
Today's tips
—PAGES 28 and 29.

* * *
HOLIDAY CONTEST WINNERS
The first list of lucky readers
—PAGE 19.

THEY WERE ATTACKED

● **DRIVER MILLS . . .** he was still in hospital last night with facial injuries.

● **CO-DRIVER WHITBY . . .** "A man grabbed me and said: 'I'll shoot if you shout.'"

Bow's SALE

SAVE £18 ON 3-PIECE SUITES
Delightful contemporary style. As illustrated, comprising 3-Seater Settee and 2 large Easy Chairs. Fully upholstered in uncut moquette, fitted with loose Marley Foam Cushions.
Regular value £57.10.0. Bow's Clearance Price **£39.19.6**

'VONO' CONVERTIBLE SUITES
These famous 3-Piece Convertible Suites at a greatly reduced price. Good quality moquette covers in various attractive designs. Regular value £76.10.0. Bow's Clearance Price **£58.10.0**

DEFERRED TERMS BEST OBTAINABLE

BOW'S OF HIGH STREET, GLASGOW

MAIL CROOKS' HAUL MAY BE TWO MILLION

A DRAGNET was cast for three key crooks last night . . . as the big train robbery haul was reported soaring towards TWO million pounds.

Scotland Yard was told that Britain's biggest-ever snatch was planned by a well-known London gang boss . . . The Brain.

The Brain was said to have escaped every trap for more than 15 years.

Other Yard detectives were concentrating on "The Snout"— the underworld informer who gave the gang the last vital pieces of information.

Police believe he may be a Post Office worker, because the railways are never told exactly what they are carrying.

Contact men

AND IN SCOTLAND, G.P.O. detectives were searching for "Mr. Mac," the Glasgow under-cover man who tipped off the bandits.

He is the man who knew exactly what the Aberdeen - Glasgow - London mail train was carrying.

With contact men in Carlisle and Crewe he reported on which night diamonds and used bank notes would be carried in bulk.

When the bandits pounced — between 3 a.m. and 3.30 a.m. yesterday— they were putting into operation a plan that had been prepared over many months.

Attacked

Near Cheddington, Buckinghamshire, the train was halted by a fake danger signal. The driver and his mate were overpowered and the two leading coaches uncoupled.

The driver was forced to take the two coaches almost a mile—to a bridge where the rest of the gang attacked.

Within minutes the bandits had loaded bulging mailbags into their get-away lorry and vanished.

SCOTS COUNT THEIR LOSSES

AS "Operation Dragnet" swung into action last night in the hunt for the big train robbers, two five-figure reward offers went out.

THE FIRST — one of £25,000 — came from a London firm of loss adjusters on behalf of the National Provincial and British Linen banks.

THE SECOND — for £10,000 — was made by Postmaster-General Reginald Bevins after he made a plane dash from Liverpool to London.

Scots banks

As police all over Britain joined the manhunt, officials said the total haul may be nearly TWO MILLION POUNDS.

"IT WILL BE DAYS BEFORE WE KNOW," THEY SAID.

"Reports from companies

Continued on Back Page

FIGHT FOR JACK'S SON

PRESIDENT Kennedy's day-old son was facing a life-or-death crisis in his Boston hospital early today.

Cardinal Richard Cushing, Bishop of Boston, issued a call for nation-wide prayers.

After doctors reported the baby finding it "increasingly difficult to breathe," the 46-year-old President rushed to Boston from his summer home at Squan Island, 65 miles away.

Soon after, he was told there had been a slight improvement.

This was after the baby—named Patrick Bouvier—was placed in a special apparatus to help his breathing.

Meantime, at Otis Air Base hospital—where Jackie Kennedy gave birth to the 4lb. 10½oz. baby by Caesarean section—doctors said the 34-year-old First Lady was "making a good recovery."

Nude-girl shocker

Continued from Page 1

part, 19-year-old blonde Anna Kesselaar, wasn't impressed by the stir.

AT HER HOME IN WINDSOR TERRACE, PORTOBELLO, EDINBURGH. SHE SAID: "I'D DO THE SAME AGAIN.

"I'm a model and I was paid for posing. I have no interest in drama past, present, or future."

Vulgarity

For her 30-second appearance on the balcony of Edinburgh's austere McEwan Hall, Anna got £4.

Now her brief venture into drama is to be the subject of a discussion by the Festival Society.

It's chairman, Lord Provost Duncan M. Weatherstone, said yesterday: "It was a piece of pointless vulgarity.

"It's a very great pity—indeed quite a tragedy—that three weeks of glorious Festival should have been smeared."

He is sending every member of the society a statement on the incident—"I expect it will be on the agenda for our next meeting."

Silly thing

In the audience on Saturday when Anna made her brief appearance, was the Festival's

● ANNA KESSELAAR . . . "I'd do it again."

artistic director, Lord Harewood, a cousin of the Queen.

Soon after, he said: "I think it was a very funny experiment. There's nothing more to be said."

But later, at his home in Yorkshire, Lord Harewood DID have more to say . . . this: "The whole thing was in completely bad taste . . . wildly silly. It was bound to offend a lot of people. I wish it hadn't happened."

Back in Edinburgh, kirk leader, the Rev. Dr. R. Leonard Small, called it "a form of sensationalism, which is part of the present attitude to sex generally."

Experiment

The man who organised the drama conference—he plans a poets' conference next year—was John Calder.

Of the incident, he said last

● CARROLL BAKER . . . "I was asked to strip."

night: "I'm quite prepared to stand by it."

American director Kenneth Dewey, 21, who "staged" the shock ending, said: "It was an experiment."

But as the big row boiled, the girl-in-the-middle, Anna Kesselaar had her last word.

"People say openly they don't like this sort of thing," she said. "Secretly I bet some wouldn't have missed it."

JIM CLARK—CHAMPION of the WORLD

● JIM CLARK . . . only the third Briton ever to win the championship title.

MONZA'S FLYING SCOT

SCOTS farmer Jim Clark yesterday won the Italian Grand Prix—and became world champion racing driver.

His win yesterday had seemed impossible. It sent the Monza crowd wild with delight.

His finest hour

THOUSANDS cheered as Jim Clark, the first Scot ever to become the world's top racing driver, took the chequered flag at Monza yesterday.

It meant the Berwickshire farmer had won five of this year's grand prix.

At Monaco in the first grand prix of the season he was leading when his V-8 works Lotus "packed up." In the German Grand Prix last month he came second to John Surtees.

Still to come are the American Grand Prix, the South African Grand Prix and, possibly, the Mexican Grand Prix.

Jim is only the third Briton to win the championship—the late Mike Hawthorn and Hill being the other two.

'Wonderful'

Seconds after yesterday's race, Jim said: "This is the most wonderful moment of my life.

"Yesterday I was so near to the world championship, yet so far from it.

"My car was not very well and John Surtees was going very fast in practice.

"We had to change the engine and the gearbox last night and it was touch and go whether everything would work.

"I put my foot down hard from the word 'go.' Fortunately for me it was the Ferrari that packed up after 17 laps and not the Lotus."

'Thrill'

Jim's mother, Mrs. Helen Clark, saw her son clinch the world championship as she watched a television news broadcast at her farmhouse home near Kelso.

She said later: "I am very pleased Jim has won and glad the race is over. We saw him win. It was a tremendous thrill."

Then Mrs. Clark, who has made no secret of the fact she doesn't like her son racing, said: "I hope he will give up at the end of the season."

In practice England's John Surtees had set the fastest lap. And in the early laps of the race he set the pace.

Before the race Jim had complained his Lotus was not producing maximum power and that it was jumping out of third gear.

But by superb driving he sat on Surtees' tail for the first seven laps of the 200-mile race.

Into lead

Then Surtees was forced to drive his Ferrari into the pits on the 17th lap—and the Flying Scot leapt into the lead.

FROM THEN ON THE REST OF THE FIELD SAW ONLY HIS EXHAUST SMOKE.

American Ritchie Ginther, in a B.R.M., finished second, a lap behind Clark. New Zealand's Bruce McLaren was third in a Cooper.

Jim, from Chirnside, Berwickshire, is the first Scot and the youngest British driver to become world champion.

Of the seven European Grand Prix races which count towards the championship Jim has won five—the Belgian, Dutch, French, British and Italian.

In the championship table he has 45 points. Ritchie Ginther has 24, John Surtees 22, and Graham Hill 17.

'Libel' snag for Lord D.

THE House of Lords may be recalled this month to solve a difficulty over publishing Lord Denning's report on the Profumo scandal.

The problem is: Will there be a spate of libel actions arising from the report?

If Parliament had set up the inquiry, it would have been covered by Parliamentary Privilege.

But the inquiry was ordered by the Prime Minister and there are doubts about whether the same immunity applies.

Way out

One way out is for either House of Parliament to authorise the report to be published, and it is easier to recall the Lords than the Commons.

Originally Parliament was due to reassemble on October 24.

GOOD SHOW!

Mr. John Garriock, of 44 Goodlad Crescent, Lerwick, Shetland, has won first prize for the town's best-kept council house garden.

HE FLIES TO FIGHT FOR JAILED MAN

LORD JOHN MANNERS flew to Spain last night to try to free jailed British businessman Anthony Greville-Bell.

The two have been friends since they were together in the Special Air Service during the war.

Alternative

War hero Greville-Bell has served nearly two weeks of a four-year sentence handed out in his absence 14 years ago for alleged smuggling.

In 1959 he won a divorce on the grounds of his wife's adultery with a former Spanish Ambassador.

A Spanish Embassy official in London said yesterday that the alternative to prison was a £7000 fine.

TODAY: Sunny periods, showers. Light-up—8.17 p.m. till 5.56 a.m. Phones: Dundee, 23461; Edinburgh, CAL 4275; Glasgow, CITY 7000.

STOP PRESS NEWS

IT'S QUINS FOR GRANNIE

A 35-YEAR-OLD grandmother gave birth to QUINS yesterday, and all are reported satisfactory.

The quins, five boys, weigh between 3lb. 11½ozs. to 4lb. 2½ ozs. and are in oxygen tents at Maracaibo, Venezuela.

The mother has five children by a previous marriage. The father has eight.

Step up into a HIGHER PAID JOB

It's no use waiting for something to turn up! Let ICS training develop your abilities, help you on to a higher-paid job. Training is individual. You learn at your own pace, in your own time. The fees are moderate and include all books.

TAKE THE RIGHT COURSE NOW

ADVERTISING & ART
Copywriting
Layout & Typography
Commercial Illustrating
Oil & Water Colour
Sign Painting

BUILDING & CIVIL ENG'NG
Architecture
Building Construction
Builders Draughtsmen
Bricklaying
Clerk of Works
Interior Decoration
Quantity Surveying
Air Conditioning
Heating & Ventilation
Carpentry & Joinery
Surveying & Mapping

COMMERCE
Book-keeping
Accountancy & Costing
Business Training
Letter Writing
Office Training
Purchasing
Secretaryship
Shorthand & Typing
Computer Programming
Small Business Owners
Storekeeping

DRAUGHTSMANSHIP
Architectural
Mechanical
Drawing Office Practice

ELECTRONICS
Computers & Maintenance
Electronic Technicians
Electronic Instrumentation
Industrial Electronics
Data Processing

FARMING
Arable & Livestock
Pig & Poultry Keeping
Rabbits & Chinchillas

FIRE ENGINEERING
Instn. of Fire Engrs.
Fire Service Promotion

GENERAL EDUCATION
G.C.E. Subjects at Ordinary or Advanced Level
Good English
Foreign Languages

HORTICULTURE
Home Gardening
Park Gardening
Market Gardening
R.H.S.

MANAGEMENT
Business Management
Hotel Management
Industrial Management
Office Management
Personnel Management
Sales Management
Works Management
Work Study
Foremanship

MECH. & MOTOR ENG'NG
Engineering Maths
Diesel Engines
Industrial Instrumentation
Workshop Practice
Welding
Refrigeration & Air Conditioning
Motor Mechanics
(many other subjects)

PHOTOGRAPHY
Practical Photography

POLICE
Police Entrance Exam.

RADIO T.V. & ELECTRICAL
Radio & TV Servicing
Radio & TV Engineering
Radio Construction
(with kits)
P.M.G. Certificates
Telecommunications
Electricians
Electrical Contractors
City & Guilds

SELLING
Company Reps.
Commercial Travellers
Retail Selling
Sales Management
Marketing

WRITING FOR PROFIT
Short Story Writing
Free-Lance Journalism

MANY OTHER SUBJECTS INCLUDE
Textile Technology
Ice Cream Technology
Small Boat Sailing
Dressmaking

INTENSIVE COACHING FOR ALL PRINCIPAL EXAMINATIONS
G.C.E., Secretaryship, Accountancy, Engineering, Work Study, Management, Radio, Architecture and Surveying.
EXAMINATION STUDENTS ARE COACHED UNTIL SUCCESSFUL

Member of the Association of British Correspondence Colleges

Dept. I.C.S., 51, Intertext House, Parkgate Road, London, S.W.11

Please send FREE book on ....

Name .... Age ....

Address ....

....

Occupation 9.63

INTERNATIONAL CORRESPONDENCE SCHOOLS

Ⓒ Scottish Daily Record and Sunday Mail, Ltd., 1963

Daily Record and Mail. Printed for and published by Scottish Daily Record and Sunday Mail, Ltd., 67 Hope Street, Glasgow, C.2. Telephone: City 7000.

SUNDAY MAIL

5ᴰ SCOTLAND'S NATIONAL SUNDAY NEWSPAPER
No. 2866   SEPTEMBER 22, 1963

DRIVER IN BUS CRASH DRAMA

THE BRAVEST MAN IN GLASGOW

That's what they're calling Joe after he saves sixty

SUNDAY MAIL REPORTER

BUS driver Joseph Leahy was being hailed as the bravest man in Glasgow last night after his split-second thinking stopped another bus toppling to disaster.

Twenty-eight-year-old Mr. Leahy had just turned his bus into busy Stirling Road, Glasgow, from Castle Street.

Suddenly he saw a bus in front of him collide with a van.

Saved

The bus, packed with passengers, was rocking wildly.

Mr. Leahy slammed on his brake. His ten passengers scrambled off.

Then he roared up to the other bus to prop it up.

His gamble paid off. The other bus didn't capsize. The passengers were saved . . .

Last night Joseph, who lives at 60 Priesthill Road, Priesthill, said:

"One minute I was on a routine tea-time run. The next there was chaos.

"I wouldn't like to live through it again."

Full load

Driver of the other bus was 23-year-old Pakistani, Anwar Haq, of 50 Burnbank Terrace, Kelvinbridge.

The van collided with the side of his cab.

Badly shaken, but unhurt, he said afterwards: "I was just coming up to Castle Street when I saw the green van coming towards me. I swerved to try and get out of the way

"But we collided and the bus began to rock.

"If it hadn't been for Driver Leahy I would have been right over.

"I had a full load of about 60 passengers. I hate to think of what might have happened if we had toppled over."

The conductress of Mr. Leahy's No. 4 bus, dark-haired Willemina MacKay, of 18 Hatton Drive, Crookston, said:

"Joe deserves a medal for what he did. The other bus could have fallen and crushed him in his cab."

Mr. William Thomson, of 25 Torryburn Road, Barmulloch, was standing at a bus stop.

34 hurt

He said: "The man who saved the day was Mr. Leahy.

"I have never seen anything as brave as what that man did."

A third busman, 34-year-old Bernard Harkin, of 203 Millburn Street, Garngad, drove his bus into the rear of the toppling bus to steady it after Mr. Leahy.

Four ambulances took 34 people to the Royal Infirmary with cuts, bruises and shock. No one was seriously injured

Crowds gather around the scene after the crash. Inset—Driver Leahy.

Labels on photo: CRASHED VAN — DRIVER LEAHY'S BUS — BUS READY TO TOPPLE — AMBULANCE

IT'S ALL IN THE MAIL

SPARE PART SURGEONS

Amazing story of the men who save lives.
—**PAGE 8**

THE GREAT CAR JUNGLE

THE JUDGE gives you all the facts.
—**PAGE 10**

Z-CARS AND ME

INSPECTOR BARLOW tells of his big break.
—**PAGE 13**

RANGERS v. REAL

A full-page special.
—**PAGE 24**

WOMAN STOPS RIOT

A WOMAN yesterday stopped a riot by hundreds of angry football fans.

It happened outside Pittodrie Park, Aberdeen, after the Dons had crashed to their fourth successive defeat.

Hundreds of shouting supporters gathered in the street outside the ground, yelling for Aberdeen's manager.

Moving from group to group grandmother Mrs. Jemima McFarlane.

Jeers

Facing the crowd, Mrs. McFarlane pleaded with them to go home.

As more than 30 police, led by Chief Superintendent Hugh McQueen, deputy chief constable of Aberdeen, rushed to clear the street, she stepped into the crowd.

Then up stepped 56-year-old Mrs. McFarlane, secretary of the Aberdeen Supporters' Club, pleaded: "This sort of thing will not help. Go home and be quiet."

The riot, outside the players entrance, happened after Aberdeen were beaten 2-0 by St. Mirren.

The dejected Aberdeen players left the field to the jeers of their fans.

Then, minutes later, more than 300 young supporters gathered outside the players' entrance chanting: "We want Pearson."

They were referring to Aberdeen manager Tommy Pearson, the former Newcastle and Aberdeen outside-left.

CHIEF SUPERINTENDENT McQUEEN SAID: "I HAVE NEVER SEEN SCENES LIKE THESE AT PITTODRIE BEFORE."

Discover for yourself the secret in the blending!

To enjoy Scotch Whisky at its best ask for "Black & White".

You'll discover at once that the special "Black & White" way of blending fine individual whiskies achieves a smoothness and satisfying character that makes this superb Scotch first favourite everywhere.

'BLACK & WHITE' SCOTCH WHISKY "BUCHANAN'S"

THE SECRET IS IN THE BLENDING

Retail Prices (U.K.): Bottle 41/6; Half Bottle 21/9; Quarter Bottle 11/2; Miniatures 4/3

Daily Record

SAT. OCT. 26 1963

3ᴰ SCOTLAND'S NATIONAL NEWSPAPER

No. 21,213

NEVER AGAIN SAYS BARDOT

BIG GAME

CAN Second Division Morton beat mighty Rangers in the League Cup Final? See:—

★ Sports Editor Hugh Taylor and Waverley on **PAGE 19**

★ Cup Final special on **CENTRE PAGES**

BIG TRANSFER

ST. MIRREN and Aberdeen shook the football world yesterday with a sensational player swop. Full story— **PAGE 18**

BIG BATTLE

LESTER PIGGOTT cancelled his Doncaster engagements yesterday because of a cold and Scobie Breasley caught him in the jockeys' championship. Scobie won on Atbara at Newbury. He and Lester now have 170 winners each.

BIG SERIES

JOHN McPHAIL starts next week an important new series on Celtic's chances in the European Cup-winners Cup.

He is just back from Austria where he saw Zagreb, Celtic's next opponents play Linz.

● IT'S NO GO! Brigitte packs up filming in Hampstead yesterday.

FANS RIOT AND FILM UNIT QUIT FOR PARIS

BRIGITTE BARDOT'S £500,000 film was abandoned in London last night—after police moved in.

The reason—hundreds of fans caused a near-riot in their eagerness to see Brigitte.

In her London hotel last night the disappointed French star said : " Why did it happen to me ?

" **HAVE YOU BRITISH NEVER SEEN A BEAUTIFUL GIRL BEFORE ? "**

Between sips of Scotch and puffs at a cigarette she said : " I'll never make another film here."

Yelled in French

The row began shortly after the " Adorable Idiot " film unit arrived to shoot street scenes in Hampstead.

● ARC LIGHTS were set up.

● CAMERAS taken into position.

● BRIGITTE, 30, who plays a British girl spy, approached in a car.

● THEN THE FANS went wild.

Cameramen fought with one another as the crowds struggled to see Brigitte.

Film extras playing soldiers tried to push the fans back with their imitation sten guns.

Michael Arden, producer of the " Adorable Idiot," waved his hands and yelled in French.

THEN BRIGITTE'S CAR REAPPEARED AND " RIOT SCENE, TAKE TWO," BEGAN.

Finally two police inspectors ordered the film executives to clear the street.

Angry

An angry M. Arden said last night : " Now we have to go back to Paris, build sets, and start work all over again.

" I will never film in London again."

Sir Alec flits in by moonlight

By Bill Robertson

PRIME MINISTER Sir Alec Douglas-Home made a moonlight arrival in Perthshire last night—to start his fight for a seat in Parliament.

He had been held up by trouble on the 120 mile drive from his estate at Coldstream.

His car, navigated by Sir Alec and driven by daughter Caroline, 26, went off the route once . . . ran into fog . . . and nearly ran out of petrol.

And in Edinburgh, where he made an unexpected stop, the Prime Minister met law trouble.

Brief nod

He parked unwittingly in a parking meter zone in the city centre.

He was about to walk away when officials pointed out his mistake—and moved him to a meter.

When the tweed - suited Premier arrived at Comrie, Perthshire, he gave a brief nod as a handful of villagers cheered.

Then, waving away three small boys with autograph books, he made it clear to 60 pressmen and photographers that there would be no talking in the dark.

Sir Alec quickly ducked inside the door of Easter Ross, his H.Q. in the fight for Kinross and West Perthshire.

Meanwhile, last night a new TV squabble broke out over his first campaign speech.

He will make it today from the sale ring at Perth Cattle Market . . . and TV news cameras will be there.

Both the Liberal and Labour camps in Crieff called this " unfair tactics."

Labour candidate Andrew Forrester said : " The Tory is using his position as Prime Minister to make an impact with this speech.

" William Rushton of TW3 is a candidate too.

" He is being barred from appearing on TV this week. I don't see why there should be one law for Rushton and apparently another for Sir Alec."

Shock

Liberal candidate Mr. Duncan Millar has already vetoed the possibility of all candidates appearing on a TV programme.

● Liberal leader Jo Grimond, who arrived in Crieff last night to help his Party's candidate, said :

" The Tories may be in for a shock. Our man is doing well enough to win."

WHEN DID IT START..?

SUMMER ends officially tomorrow at two o'clock in the morning.

That is the time the Home Office say all clocks must be put back one hour.

It means an extra hour in bed for anyone who wants a late breakfast.

Ask for it by name!

11/-

NO OTHER WINE CAN TAKE ITS PLACE

ELDORADO Rich White

FULL STRENGTH

HIGH GRADE WINE SELECTED WITH CARE AND SHIPPED UNCHANGED FOR OVER 20 YEARS

ELDORADO

SCOTLAND'S BEST SELLING PROPRIETARY WINE

Daily Record

SAT. NOV. 23 1963

3D SCOTLAND'S NATIONAL NEWSPAPER

No. 21,237

AS THE PRESIDENT, SLUMPS DYING—

OH, NO! cries Jackie

● A security man, a weeping wife . . . and the car where a President lies dying.

● Accused . . . 24-year-old Lee Oswald (right). charged with killing a Dallas policeman and questioned over the President's assassination.

THIS moment yesterday stunned the world.

President Kennedy lies dying in the back of a car—mown down by an assassin's bullets.

His wife, Jackie, screams "Oh No" and cradles her husband's head.

A security man leaps to the back of the car.

It happened in Dallas, Texas, before a crowd of 250,000. The Texan Governor was also hit.

Last night police were questioning a suspect—24-year-old Lee H. Oswald, an American who once lived in Russia.

(FULL STORY: Back Page)

BULLETS OF AN ASSASSIN KILL KENNEDY

Daily Record

WED. FEB. 26 1964

3p SCOTLAND'S NATIONAL NEWSPAPER
No. 21,317

It's the greatest boxing sensation

CLAY WINS!

Home faces M.P.s' mutiny

By VICTOR KNIGHT

A SENSATIONAL Tory back-bench revolt exploded last night after the Government published their Bill to abolish Resale Price Maintenance.

Eight Tory M.P.s threw the Cabinet into complete confusion by tabling a motion to reject the Bill.

This action is without precedent in post-war politics and is the most serious mutiny faced by the Government since they came to power in 1951.

Rushed

The complaint is that the Bill does little to prevent small shopkeepers being driven out of business by the big price-cutting supermarkets.

The critics argue that Mr. Edward Heath, President of the Board of Trade, has rushed the Bill through the Cabinet without securing adequate safeguards for small traders.

If the rebels force their motion to a vote Sir Alec Douglas-Home and his Tory Government will face a grave crisis of confidence.

They will have to choose between going into the election with a split party or suffering the humiliation of having to withdraw a major Bill.

Hostile

Mr. Heath was given a hostile reception when he went to a packed meeting of Tory M.P.s.

AFTERWARDS THE BILL WAS CRITICISED EVEN BY TORIES WHO FAVOUR THE ABOLITION OF PRICE FIXING.

Some were even openly laughing at Mr. Heath for bringing in a Bill which is so "watered down" as to satisfy nobody.

R.P.M. will be abolished as soon as the Bill comes into force. This will probably be in September or October.

● *THE RULES—PAGE 8*

● *Shouting insults Cassius was held back as he went for the champion at the weigh-in.*

Her gamble with death

LIFE-LOVING Mariona Munn took a 50-50 gamble with death . . . and lost. Hundreds of weeping schoolgirls lined a town's silent streets for her funeral yesterday.

They murmured a last goodbye to the girl they knew for her impish smile, for the love she seemed to have for the whole world. And, most of all for her fantastic courage.

From b i r t h, 14-year-old Mariona had endured a hole-in-the-heart condition which baffled surgeons at dozens of hospitals.

She missed half her schooling. The least nip in the air gave her a heavy cold.

Games and dancing tired her. A serious infection would have killed her.

Then, a month ago, came hope. Surgeons had perfected a technique to repair her faulty heart.

The risks were great. The chances of survival only 50-50 —and her parents were afraid.

'Loved her'

But Mariona calmly grasped the chance of a normal life. Quietly she told the doctors that she HAD to have the operation.

● *"Victory for me," Sonny hit back with his own prediction.*

BRAVE MARIONA LOST

Her mother, Mrs. Josephine Munn, of 186 Glasgow Road, Burnbank, Lanarkshire, said last night:

"Just before she went to the theatre last Thursday, Mariona told us not to worry.

"She was still smiling when they wheeled her away.

"It was the last time we saw

Continued on Back Page

By PETER WILSON

IT'S Cassius the Champion! And in Miami early this morning Cassius Clay caused the boxing sensation of the century. He beat Sonny Liston— against all the odds — to become the World's new heavyweight champion.

Ringsiders were as stunned as glowering Liston when boasting, arrogant Clay showed he could fight as well as talk.

From the start, Liston, intent on cruel revenge on the man who had heaped insults on him for months, bored in relentlessly.

Savage

He threw savage punches— and some of them had Clay flinching.

But a g i l e, dancing Clay escaped disaster and the dark

Nemesis who lumbered after him with dreadful menace at the start became flustered.

Clay, arms going as quickly as his lips had before the fight, weaved and ducked, flicked right and left with cobra-like venom.

And Liston, shaking his head mournfully, couldn't do much about it. Clay proved he was the better boxer.

Worried

The pattern started from the bell—Liston making the running Clay moving away, away. Jabs from the champion worried Cassius—and the challenger held on.

First blow to hurt Clay was a hook to the body—but then the champion grew wild and missed badly.

Excitement was intense and clever Clay boxing made Liston scowl.

Still Liston stalked like a

Continued on Back Page

NON-HOUSEHOLDERS *are invited to open a* **CREDIT ACCOUNT WITHOUT GUARANTOR** *for all their bridal requirements at*

SHELLEYS *of Glasgow* X

Bridal Gowns 7 gns. to 15 gns.
BRIDESMAIDS' DRESSES from 6 gns.

Easy Terms

2'6	Weekly for 42 weeks buys £5 of goods.
5'-	Weekly for 42 weeks buys £10 of goods.
10'-	Weekly for 52 weeks buys £25 of goods.

we give ● **GREEN SHIELD STAMPS**

COATS • SUITS • DRESSES
KNITWEAR • CASUALS
NYLONS • FOOTWEAR
UNDERWEAR

FUR COATS

20 SALTMARKET·GLASGOW X

Daily Record

FRID. MAY 1 1964

3ᴰ SCOTLAND'S NATIONAL NEWSPAPER

No. 21,373

● WHERE ARE THEY? . . . even policemen on guard steal a peep.

BEATLE RIOT NIGHT!

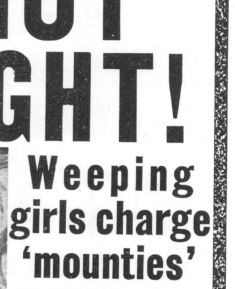

Weeping girls charge 'mounties'

THOUSANDS of Beatles fans went berserk last night outside a Glasgow cinema.

Mounted police were driven back by hordes of screaming, sobbing schoolgirls.

Frightened police horses shied as electric light bulbs, thrown from the crowd, shattered on the roadway.

It happened at the end of The Beatles' first house at the Odeon Cinema, Renfield Street.

Some of the 3000 fans around the theatre thought they caught a glimpse of one of their singing idols at a window . . .

Screaming girls tried to break through the 100-strong police cordon round the cinema.

Ambulancemen rushed forward to rescue fainting girls, in danger of being trampled underfoot.

Police horses backed away from the shrieks—but the cordon of foot policemen held.

Glasgow's Assistant Chief Constable Mr.

Continued on Back Page

BABY ANY MOMENT NOW

Margaret drama

EVERYTHING was set last night for the arrival of Royal baby number four.

Midwife Anne Thomson was waiting in Kensington Palace, where Princess Margaret was expecting her second child "any time now."

Sir John Peel, who will deliver the baby, was staying near a telephone.

The baby—who will be known as Lady . . . Armstrong-Jones or the Hon. . . . Armstrong-Jones — will be seventh in succession to the throne.

Progress

Princess Margaret's husband, Lord Snowdon, was waiting in Kensington Palace last night.

Their first child, three-year-old Viscount Linley, was born at Clarence House.

This child will be the last of this year's crop of Royal babies, following Princess Alexandra's on February 29, the Queen's on March 10, and the Duchess of Kent's on Tuesday.

The duchess and her daughter were said last night to be making "quite excellent" progress.

STARRED for sophistication, elegance and charm. Dress and Jacket, trimmed floral silk — edging and lining to tone.

20½ Gns.

CUT a dash for Spring in this smart Tailored Suit in novelty weave fabric.

12 Gns.

Watt
brothers

SCOTLAND'S LEADING FASHION HOUSE

OF SAUCHIEHALL STREET ● GLASGOW

I want to -er- tweak your nose

SHE REALLY wanted to hold his hand . . .

But this Beatle fan at Callander, Perthshire, yesterday couldn't get close enough to Paul McCartney.

SO SHE TWEAKED HIS NOSE INSTEAD.

Before the Beatles left their Callander hotel for last night's Glasgow concerts, news came to gladden DUNDEE and ABERDEEN fans.

"It is most likely The Beatles will visit these two cities in an autumn tour," said Derek Taylor, assistant to Brian Epstein.

"But as yet no bookings have been confirmed for Scotland."

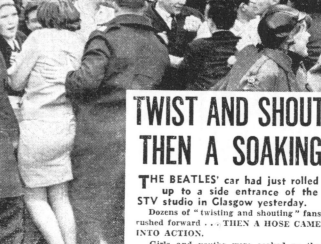

TWIST AND SHOUT THEN A SOAKING

THE BEATLES' car had just rolled up to a side entrance of the STV studio in Glasgow yesterday.

Dozens of "twisting and shouting" fans rushed forward . . . THEN A HOSE CAME INTO ACTION.

Girls and youths were soaked as the fab four ran into the building.

Anne Burnside, 16, of 79 Bruce Road, Paisley, said later : "My face and coat were drenched. It was unnecessary."

An STV spokesman said : "We knew nothing about this. It wasn't done with our permission."

Daily Record

SAT. SEPT. 5 1964

3ᴰ SCOTLAND'S NATIONAL NEWSPAPER
No. 21,482

SOUVENIR SPECIAL

Off on Royal trip then—

CRASH UNDER THE BRIDGE

PAGE ONE SPORT

JIM BAXTER SENSATION

ARSENAL TRANSFER MOVE

By JIM RODGER

ARSENAL manager Billy Wright flew into Glasgow last night on a gilt-edged mission.

He wants to buy Jim Baxter, Scotland's left-half Today Mr. Wright will watch Baxter play in the Celtic - Rangers game at Parkhead.

Baxter has been on the transfer list for almost two years since he asked Rangers for a transfer.

After that move Arsenal fans petitioned the club to buy Baxter.

Desperate

In the past year Arsenal have spent more than £100,000 to buy Ian Ure from Dundee and Don Howe from West Brom

At the same time they still have a lot of money from selling players . . .

THEY ARE EASILY ABLE TO TOP A £100,000 FEE FOR BAXTER!

Billy Wright has been desperate to sign a wing-half for some time. HE WANTS BAXTER.

● FULL STORY . . . Page 23.

19 TO 1

DOUBLE

THAT was the great performance by KLONDYKE at Epsom yesterday.

FIVE MEETINGS TODAY —including the big race at Lanark, the Silver Bell.

All the tips —Pages 20 and 21.

IT'S DERBY DAY . . .

● The biggest club day in Scottish soccer, with derby games throughout the country. Top news on today's programme. —Pages 22 and 23.

Columns of cars stream across the new bridge after the opening ceremony by the Queen pictured (inset) with the Duke.

THOUSANDS of cars poured bumper - to - bumper over the newly-opened Forth Road Bridge last night.

There were dozens of minor collisions on the approach roads.

One on the Fife side brought the first 999 call.

A woman passenger was taken to hospital with shock.

There was even a collision UNDER the bridge in mist.

The flagship of the Home Fleet, the cruiser Lion, was still at anchor after the bridge-opening ceremony by the Queen . . .

The frigate Lowestoft was getting under way.

Suddenly there was the crunch of tearing metal as the Lowestoft's bows bit into the Lion.

On board the Lion at the time was Vice-Admiral Twiss, Flag Officer Home Flotillas.

Damage was not serious but both ships are to go into Rosyth Dockyard for repairs.

★ THE QUEEN'S opening of the bridge: Full reports and sparkling pictures of Scotland's great day—

Pages 10 to 15

"An inquiry will be held," said a Navy spokesman.

The bridge opening brought a fantastic flood of cars—far more than expected. At one point 6000 an hour were crossing.

On the Edinburgh side queues were reported seven miles back on the approach roads.

On the Fife side there was a four-mile queue of 2000 cars.

After six hours "clearing" the bridge following the Royal opening, cars had started to roll at 5.50 p.m.

FIRST MAN to pay the 2s 6d toll on the Edinburgh side was Mr Jack Hamilton, resident engineer of the bridge project.

He handed over the cash then his dark green Jaguar

moved off . . . first across the bridge.

Next through the barrier were Mr. Charles Grimm and his wife from **Brechin,** Angus.

From the Fife side two motorists claimed a joint "first."

In one lane was Robert Morrison, 42, of 132 Balgillo Road, Broughty Ferry, **Dundee** with his wife Jemima and daughter Donna, four.

'Made it'

"I wanted to go across on the first day but I had no idea that I would be the first, or first equal," Mr. Morrison said.

Driving alongside him was 28-year-old Jimmy Archibald, a cigarette salesman, of 59 Wedderburn Crescent, **Dunfermline.**

"For a long time now I've had the idea of being first across the bridge," said Mr. Archibald. "Now I've finally made it."

At 10.30 p.m. with thick mist covering the bridge, the traffic eased off.

It is expected again today and tomorrow.

FINE NOTE: An extra £5 was added to the bridge receipts yesterday . . . fines from three motorists who broke down on the crossing.

FIRST ACROSS

● Jaguar driver, Mr. Jack Hamilton, resident engineer of the bridge project, hands over the first half-crown to a bridge toll-keeper.

SPECIAL EDITION

—TO KEEP, OR SEND TO FRIENDS ABROAD

● The gun carriage . . . with Sir Winston on his last journey.

● The last salute . . . from Prince Philip on the steps of St. Paul's. Beside him is the Queen. Behind are the Queen Mother and Prince Charles, Princess Margaret and Lord Snowdon. In the row behind them are (left to right) Prince Michael of Kent and the Duke of Kent, both saluting, the Duchess and the Duke of Gloucester. Behind them are President de Gaulle with Queen Juliana of the Netherlands beside him.

8 PAGE SPECIAL—SEE PAGE 13

SUNDAY MAIL

No 2982   DECEMBER 12, 1965

● Safe in the dry dock, the Queen Elizabeth towers over nearby buildings.

HOME AND DRY

● Tugs swing the Queen Elizabeth round to enter the dock, but her port side scraped the quay. On the right, nearest the dock, a new tanker is being fitted out.

Picture by ERIC CRAIG

FROM a thousand feet up in the air it looked as though the mighty Queen would never make it.

The 83,673-ton Queen Elizabeth, forward funnel belching smoke, took an hour to inch her way into Greenock dry dock.

But at the second attempt nine tugs managed to get her into the correct line and she nosed her way down the dock— with a 31ft. "V" cut into it to take the ship's 1030-feet length.

There was only one mishap. As the Queen squeezed through the dock entrance she nudged it with her port side. A 2ft. scrape appeared near her bow. The tugs quickly took the strain and eased her clear.

Dock masters used walkie talkie radios to direct the movement of the ship.

The final movement came when a dock master called: "Twelve inches forward." And 83,673 tons moved forward — exactly 12 inches.

About 1500 of John Brown's workers and 500 men from the Dockyard Company will be busy for the next three months giving the Queen a major £1,000,000 refit.

Greenock police will make special arrangements to cope with sightseers today. A spokesman said: " The best view of the Queen Elizabeth can be seen from the Gibbshill area.''

SHOCK FACTS ABOUT OUR NURSES
—Pages 4 and 5

Elvis Presley's secret

—Page 13

Rhodesia: SMITH SPEAKS OUT
—Page 2

Give while they live
—Page 2

● The Sunday Mail will be published as usual on Sunday, December 26.

No national Sunday newspapers will be published, and there will be a big demand for the Sunday Mail.

Make sure of your copy by placing a firm order with your newsagent NOW.

SUNDAY MAIL

6d   No. 3011   July 10, 1966

INSURANCE BOSS VANISHES

● Dr. Savundra.

DOCTOR EMIL SAVUNDRA, the man in the middle of the crash of Fire, Auto and Marine, the British insurance company, has vanished.

For months the Sunday Mail has been investigating the activities of Fire, Auto and Marine. Last week came the collapse of the company.

Savundra disappeared from a Swiss clinic, where he was receiving treatment for a heart attack, on Friday afternoon.

Three weeks before his company collapsed, Dr. Savundra had sold his controlling interest for only £4000.

As a result of the crash, more than 280,000 motorists had to pay out new premiums for insurance with other companies.

Since Dr. Savundra's disappearance it has been discovered that the company held £903,029 in "quoted securities"— invested in a little-known bank in the tiny state of Lichtenstein.

Dr. Savundra, whose big hobby is power-boat racing, has master-minded business deals in Ceylon, Belgium, Ghana, Costa Rica and other countries.

READ: The vital facts for Mr. and Mrs. Motorist by the Judge—Page 4.

● The winning moment . . . Nicklaus has just holed the last putt.

● Jack with his wife — and the trophy

JACK PUTTS TO VICTORY

JACK NICKLAUS, golf's "Golden Bear" from Ohio, completed a grand slam when he won a brilliant one-stroke victory in the Open Championship at Muirfield, East Lothian, yesterday.

The fair-haired golfing giant finished with a round of 70 over the bone-dry links for 72 holes aggregate of 282.

This was enough to give him the coveted title and gold trophy by a stroke from fellow-American Doug Sanders and the gallant Welshman, David Thomas.

Nicklaus, who claims the £2100 first prize

has now completed his great ambition of winning the United States Open and Masters titles and the British Open.

The new Open champion will not leave Scotland until the end of the week.

With Gary Player and Arnold Palmer, he plays at Gleneagles tomorrow, Carnoustie on Tuesday, and St. Andrews on Wednesday, in three 18-hole matches for B.B.C.-2's colour TV.

This series offers a first prize of 25,000 dollars, second prize of 15,000 dollars, and third prize of 10,000 dollars.

It is not yet known when the series will be seen in this country but it will be released throughout the world.

Nine other matches, including professionals from all over the world will also be televised shortly throughout Great Britain for TV.

— ALLAN HERRON'S FULL REPORT — Back Page

And this is how he does it!

● *Every week the Mail gives Jack Nicklaus's golfing tip. Here's how he holes those winning putts There's another on Page 3!*

● STAND FIRM for PUTTING ●

THE IDEAL PUTTING STANCE COMBINES COMFORT AND STABILITY

TO REMAIN RELAXED YET WELL-BALANCED AGAINST THE OCCASION OF STRONG WINDS, I FIND KEEPING MY WEIGHT ON THE INSIDE OF MY FEET WORKS BEST.

FORE AND AFT STABILITY IS BEST ACHIEVED BY DIVIDING WEIGHT EVENLY BETWEEN THE BALL AND HEEL OF EACH FOOT THIS IS THE AREA OF GREATEST SUPPORT

TAY BRIDGE SOUVENIR SPECIAL

IT'S OPENING TIME!

THE new Tay Road Bridge, soaring high, wide and handsome from Dundee to the Kingdom of Fife, will be opened today.

At 12.25 p.m. the Queen Mother's car will drive through a fluttering ribbon to "christen" the steel-and-concrete road link that has been dreamed of for a hundred years.

All Tayside will be there to cheer, for it is their greatest day this century . . . a jubilant climax to long years of effort, planning, frustration and determination that the bridge would be built.

VITAL LINK

Forgotten for the moment, in the excitement of today's opening ceremony, will be the vital trunk road to link the new bridge with the Forth Road Bridge.

Without it, the bridges

Fit for a Queen...

CANNOT work together to speed a two-way flow of commerce and prosperity across the Forth and Tay.

But the Tay Road Bridge, Scottish designed and built, is now a reality and the road must follow.

Today's pageantry should be worthy of the bridge that is Britain's longest road crossing over water and spans Scotland's longest river.

When the Queen Mother arrives at the Dundee terminal, she will be welcomed by Lord Provost Maurice McManus, chairman of the Tay Bridge Joint Board, and Scottish Secretary Mr. William Ross.

A guard of honour will be provided by the 4/5th Battalion The Black Watch (T.A.), and as Her Majesty declares the bridge open, a formation of R.A.F. planes will thunder overhead.

Before the Queen Mother drives over the bridge she will

be presented with a souvenir of the occasion—a silk stole embroidered with Tay pearls.

The widows of the five men who died during the construction of the Bridge have received special invitations to the opening ceremony.

At the Fife end, Her Majesty will be greeted by Lord Lieutenant of the County Mr. John McWilliam and other V.I.P.'s before driving back for a private lunch with members of the Tay Bridge Board.

THE TIMETABLE

Here is where and when to see her.

11.30 a.m.—arrives at Dundee city boundary and drives to the Bridge terminal via Coupar Angus Road, High Street, Lochee, Logie Street, Lochee Road, North Tay Street and Marketgait.

11.45 a.m.—arrives at terminal for opening ceremony.

12.25 p.m.—leaves by car across bridge.

12.35 p.m.—arrives at Fife terminal of bridge, for presentations.

12.42 p.m.—leaves Fife end of bridge for lunch at Angus Hotel, Dundee, going via Dock Street, Whitehall Crescent, Whitehall Street, Nethergate and Marketgait.

2.45 p.m.—Leaves hotel for Balmoral Castle, leaving Dundee by same route as on arrival.

The first private motorist across the bridge today will find himself driving behind a police car.

Dundee Chief Constable John Orr has taken care of this to avoid any racing across the bridge.

Special parking facilities in Dock Street and Riverside Drive, Dundee, will be allocated to motorists wanting to queue up before the opening.

Pedestrians will not cross the bridge as the footways will take about another two weeks to complete.

● Men dreamed of it, fought for it, planned for it and even died for it but at last the Tay Road Bridge is complete and IT'S OPENING TIME!

Yesterday 'Record' photographer Bert Paterson flew over the bridge to take this and other pictures.

Like a massive, slender piece of sculpture it pointed straight as an arrow to the Fife shore . . . and the future.

For its clean lines, which seem almost too fragile, hide a core of steel and concrete which will strengthen the whole economy of the east coast of Scotland.

DOOMED

Yesterday the tempo of work was gently slowing down Great yellow cranes and road-making machines were trundling back to land,

Carriageways, freshly painted road signs, and elegant street lamps made a sparkling summer picture.

At Newport cars lined up to board the ferries—the famous "Fifies" whose time is numbered in hours.

Above, a scarlet R.A.F. Jet Provost made dummy-runs over the bridge, practising for the salute and fly-past today.

The city of Dundee lay waiting . . . for the big leap into the seventies.

Daily Record

WED. AUG. 24 1966

4D   SCOTLAND'S NATIONAL NEWSPAPER

No. 22,095

Gaming club boss injured

CAR BOOBY TRAP MURDER

● SHATTERED by the blast, the death car in Provanmill Road . . . it travelled only 10 yards before the explosion.

● THE WOMAN who died, Mrs. Maggie Johnstone, 61—a chance passenger in her son-in-law's car.

90 ARRESTED AND P.C. HURT

RIOTS AFTER IBROX GAME

A POLICEMAN was in hospital and more than 90 people were under arrest following clashes between rival gangs after the Rangers - Celtic game last night.

Celtic beat Rangers 4-0 at Ibrox.

The injured policeman, Constable William Dow, 25, of Glasgow's Northern Division was on duty at the ame when he was hit by a flying bottle.

He was taken, unconscious and bleeding, to the Southern General Hospital.

Fourteen people were arrested during the game.

Afterwards, policemen on points duty stopped huge streams of traffic returning from the game to let squad

Continued on Back Page

ONLY minutes before a bomb exploded in a car yesterday, killing a woman and injuring a gambling club boss, his four - year - old daughter had pleaded with him:

"Please take me in the car as well, Daddy."

Arthur Thomson, part-owner of the Hanover Club in Frederick Lane, Glasgow, told his little girl: "Not this time."

I refused

Minutes later, his M.G. Magnette car blew up, killing his mother-in-law Mrs. Maggie Johnstone, 61, and injuring him.

Last night Thomson. 36, of 176 Provanmill Road, Glasgow,

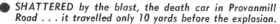

By BILL ROBERTSON, ROBIN KIDD and KEN STEIN

recovering in the Royal Infirmary told friends :

"The children always want runs in the car, but I told Margaret she couldn't come with us this time.

"I'M GLAD I REFUSED HER NOW . . ."

Thomson had driven just 10 yards when the bomb exploded killing Mrs. Johnstone —who was in the car only by chance.

She had gone to her son-in-law's yellow-painted home in Provanmill Road half-an-hour earlier to give her daughter

three 2s pieces for the gas meter.

She had wanted to walk the few hundred yards home to 62 Hogganfield Street.

But Mr. Thomson said: "Jump in the car, and I'll drive you home, hen."

My children

They stepped out into the street, into the car, Mrs. Johnstone to murder by bomb, Mr. Thomson to injury that required an operation.

Friends said last night: "It

Granny killed in blast

was only by chance she was at the house, and went into the car. That's what makes it so terrible."

They said that Thomson's children were always keen to go with him and often did.

Thomson had told them: "" It was because I was only giving my mother-in-law a lift of a few hundred yards that I said "No " to Margeret.

"On any other trip, the

Continued on Back Page

Daily Record

SAT. OCT. 22 1966

4D SCOTLAND'S NATIONAL NEWSPAPER

No. 22,146

Rescue teams fight the moving mountain

180 CHILDREN DIE

● THE AGONY OF ABERFAN . . . A policeman carries a five-year-old victim through the crowd. By his side walks a poor, weeping mother.

Toll could be 200

TWO HUNDRED . . . that is the final toll expected in yesterday's Aberfan disaster.

Of these, about 180 are feared to be children between seven and 11.

New risk

So far 44 bodies have been recovered from the rubble. Another 28 are lying injured in hospital.

Last night rescuers searching debris that was left after a coal waste tip engulfed a school and 14 homes were faced with a new danger.

No sleep

For the huge tip is still moving slowly. Special equipment was being used in an attempt to freeze the moving mass.

Nearly every home in the mining village has a relative feared lost.

No one slept last night.

Hours that Meant Death— Back Page. Five more pages inside, starting on Page 13.

Daily Record

THURS. JAN. 5 1967

4D SCOTLAND'S NATIONAL NEWSPAPER

No. 22,209

CAMPBELL'S WIFE HAD PREMONITION—

I KNEW HE WOULD DIE

● Campbell's lifelong friend and chief mechanic Leo Villa recovers Donald's mascot, " Mr. Whoppit," from the water.

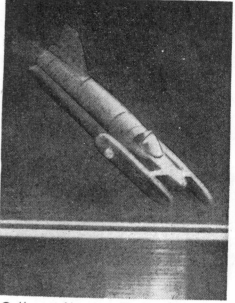

● Moment of impact . . . Bluebird dives into the water—to explode in a sea of spray.

I asked him to wait—he didn't

I KNEW Donald would kill himself on this one and I think he knew it too . . .

Fighting back tears, Tonia Bern, wife of Donald Campbell, said this last night as she told of her premonition about the record-breaking bid that ended in death.

Just hours before, 45-year-old Campbell died as his Bluebird jet boat back-somersaulted to disaster at more than 310 m.p.h. on Coniston Water in his bid to beat his own 1964 world water speed record of 276 m.p.h. on the same lake.

"I was never worried at any of his previous attempts," said Tonia. "But this one really worried me.

"I told Donald, but he said 'Why do you worry, poppet?' I said it was instinct. I just knew it would end in disaster. He felt it too."

Frogmen

Tonia, 36-year-old Belgian-born singer, was at home in her London flat when the tragedy she had feared came true. Immediately she flew to Coniston to stay by the lakeside until her husband's body is recovered from the depths.

A team of eight Navy frogmen from Rosyth, Fife, will start diving today to find the wreck of Bluebird, which went down with Campbell strapped in the cockpit.

Sadly Tonia said last night : " It was the first time since we were married eight years ago that I was not with Donald when he tried to break the record.

"I had arranged to go up to see him tomorrow He said I was his lucky mascot and I asked him to wait for me before making the attempt. But he said the water was calming down.
" I told him ' Wait I might bring you luck.' But he didn't . . ."

Wonderful man

Then Tonia spoke of the eight years she shared with the man whose whole life was danger. " They've been like living on top of a volcano," she said, " but, oh boy, it was fun.

" Donald was a wonderful man and a true patriot. He died for Britain. He only wanted this record for Britain.

"Now I can't believe I will be without him. He was always there when I needed him . . ."

On Sunday Tonia was due to begin a week's cabaret engagements in Scotland, with dates at Dunfermline, Perth and Callander. The bookings were postponed immediately.

She said last night : " I can't bear to be without Donald. I shall change my name to Tonia Bern-Campbell. I want his name to live forever. He was a truly great man."

As Tonia spoke, nearby lay a little bedraggled teddy bear— Mr. Whoppit, the mascot that went with Campbell on every record bid.

It was with him yesterday . . . and was recovered from the lake by Leo Villa, Campbell's chief mechanic.

Villa was also his life-long friend. When Donald's father Sir Malcolm Campbell was breaking records, Villa was chief mechanic

Continued on Back Page

Scots trawler has mast shot away

A DANISH coastguard ship shot the top off a Scots trawler's mast, it was claimed yesterday.

Danish marine authorities said in Copenhagen that the trawler, named as the Aberdeen Venturer had ignored a call by the Danish ship Vaedderen to halt.

The trawler was stopped by warning shots, off the Faroe Islands. One shot blasted the top off her mast, the authorities said.

Escaped

They claimed the Vaedderen caught the trawler fishing within the islands' four-mile territorial limits and immediately sent a helicopter which hovered above it.

A boatload of marines was sent from the Danish ship to board the Aberdeen Venturer after the shooting. But the trawler set sail again, the authorities said.

The Vaedderen fired several

more warning shots. But the trawler escaped while the coastguard ship was picking up the boarding party. The Danish authorities gave the Venturer's registration number as A-488.

The Aberdeen Venturer, port registration No. A488, arrived back in her home port last night with her crew of 13.

Early today, Mr. Alex Elder, trawler manager of Aberdeen Motor Trawlers, Ltd., said: " I know nothing of this incident.

' I shall interview the skipper in the morning and see the log book. Then I'll be prepared to comment."

Skipper Joe Glass, sen., would not comment.

A Ministry of Defence spokesman in London said no calls for assistance had been made by a British vessel in the Faroes area.

● TONIA BERN . . . " This one really worried me."

QUOTES

—by Donald Campbell, the man who lived with death as his co-driver :

I SHALL die with my boots on, but not for a long time yet.
—in hospital after a crash on Utah Salt Flats in 1960.

I BELIEVE that, in some way I don't understand, my father watches over me in these record-breaking seconds of danger.
—at Lake Coniston, after smashing the record in 1956.

YOU'VE just got to live it up, old boy. We have only one life each and we've got to make the most of it.
—at Lake Coniston last month while waiting to make his new record bid.

WELL, I reckon it should all be over tomorrow— one way or the other.
—at Coniston, late on Tuesday night.

SHE'S going, she's going . . .
—his last words yesterday as Bluebird crashed.

Daily Record

TUES. FEB. 21 1967

4D · SCOTLAND'S NATIONAL NEWSPAPER

No. 22,249

BREATH CHECK
—If you cross a white line or go too fast

DRINK TEST SWOOP ON MOTORISTS

WHEN the new Road Safety Bill becomes law, there WILL be random roadside breath tests —in fact, if not in name.

Transport Minister Barbara Castle made this clear in the Commons last night when the Bill was given a third reading.

She rejected moves by several Labour back-benchers to have wholesale random testing restored to the Bill—then pointed out that the Bill at present contained "a very important random element."

Mrs. Castle said: "The range of circumstances in which a driver can be required to take a breath test is extremely wide.

"He does not have to be driving dangerously before he is stopped.

"A motorist can be stopped for crossing a white line or exceeding a speed limit—then given a breath test."

ANYONE

She added: "There may be no signs of his having taken alcohol, but this does not matter.

"It simply means that a breath test can be given to anyone who commits a driving offence."

The Home Secretary, she said, would tell chief constables that in applying these tests, an element of random testing would be required.

"I have made it clear time and time again," she went on, "that the proposals now before Parliament contain a very important random element."

Wholesale random tests were originally in the new Road Safety Bill, but were discarded by Mrs. Castle when she moved the second reading late last year.

SEVERE

Last night she said that as the Bill now stood they were striking a balance between absolute random and tests based on suspicion.

She added: "I have given this matter a lot of serious thought and I think everyone will agree that our common aim is to deter.

"Under this Bill, tests are provided and once the specified limit of alcohol is exceeded, there can be no doubt at all.

"Penalties will be severe. I have stood by automatic disqualification for this offence."

Mr. Dick Taverne (Labour, Lincoln), moved an amendment to provide for a second breath test to be taken at a police station. It was accepted.

He said the second test would be offered to those who refused a roadside test as well as to those whose roadside test proved positive.

There would normally be a time lapse of about 20 minutes between the tests to safeguard against the effects of mouth alcohol.

Another amendment, by Mr. Mark Carlisle (Tory, Runcorn), was unsuccessful.

He wanted courts to have discretion to reduce or wipe out the automatic 12 months disqualification for first offenders.

Mrs. Castle said disqualification was the great deterrent.

"I cannot accept that one offender should be let off more easily than another," she said.

When Mr. Carlisle said the ban would hit most heavily at people who earn their living by driving, Mrs. Castle said: "They should be the last to plead mitigating circumstances."

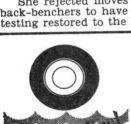

TWO SHIPS— 4-Sailings Weekly from each Port

IMMINGHAM · AMSTERDAM GOTHENBURG

Starting April 16th the MV 'TOR HOLLANDIA' joins the MV 'TOR ANGLIA'

7,500 tons fully stabilised, 23 knots, Drive on/Drive off Ferries. Fastest across the North Sea. Book Now for Europe and Scandinavia.

Only TOR-Line takes you and your car into Amsterdam, Gateway to Europe.

Your holiday starts on TOR-Line, enjoy all the wonderful amenities on board—

SPACIOUS PASSENGER ACCOMMODATION
FINE CUISINE ■ 2 BARS ■ 3 TAX FREE SHOPS
HAIRDRESSING SALON ■ CHILDREN'S NURSERY
SAUNA BATH ■ CASINO *(for those who like a flutter)*
DANCING TO CONTINENTAL BANDS

Send to us direct for the 'PLAN-A-TRIP' Wallet which will help you to plan your vacation or contact your Local Travel Agent for full details:
London Agents:
E. H. MUNDY & CO. (PASSENGER AGENCIES) LTD.
87 JERMYN STREET, LONDON, S.W.1.
Tel: Trafalgar 1321. Telex: 23129

TOR LINE

West Gate, King's Dock, Immingham (Lincs.)
Telephone Immingham 771 or South Humberside 321

Washday death

AN elderly woman was electrocuted yesterday as she started to use her washing machine.

Retired teacher Miss Maggie Calderhead, 75, was filling the machine in the back kitchen of her home at 1 Thornlie Gill, Wishaw.

Alone

It is believed she had her hands in the tub when she received the shock that killed her.

Miss Calderhead, who lived alone, had a heart condition. She was found by a neighbour.

THE MODEL Miss WORLD

SHE'S called the most beautiful girl in the world, and she's certainly one of the busiest.

She's been to Vietnam . . . she's passed her driving test.

But yesterday 23-year-old Reita Faria did something she's never done before. She modelled European dresses.

Later Reita denied rumours of a new romance, which began when she wore a diamond ring on her engagement finger.

She had it on at a party where the guests included wealthy American lawyer David Gorman.

Reita explained: "I bought the ring myself, David and I are just good friends."

SUNDAY MAIL

6d.   No. 3051   APRIL 16, 1967

SUPERMACS

THE GREATEST SIDE I'VE EVER SEEN WEARING DARK BLUE, says Allan Herron

THIS IS IT. Young Jim McCalliog, playing his first game for Scotland, scores the winner

"LANLIQ"

SOUTH AFRICAN WINE

FULL STRENGTH ...this is **THE** wine with **THAT SOMETHING EXTRA!**

enjoy it and take some home!

LANLIQ SOUTH AFRICAN WINE

LANG BROTHERS

FULL STRENGTH

THERE were fantastic scenes in London last night after Scotland had beaten England, the World Cup holders, 3-2.

Twenty thousand Scots went on a victory rampage. They poured into cafes, bars and Soho clubs.

Throughout the night the chant went up in Piccadilly Circus: "Sir Alf is on the dole." Meaning, of course, that with Scotland's sensational victory England's team boss Sir Alf Ramsey will have to think again.

Eros was boarded up and squads of extra police stood by as Scots chanted the new hit: "We all live in a tartan submarine!" But there was little trouble. "No major incidents," reported Scotland Yard. "They're all too happy."

And the most precious souvenir any Scot will be taking back home today . . . A PIECE OF THE WEMBLEY TURF. Swarms of fans raced on to the pitch and hauled up divots of the sacred sward.

Wild with joy

At Euston Station last night pieces of Wembley turf were being sold for up to 10s a time. Some tiny patches, said to be from the centre circle, were fetching up to a pound.

At the end of the game Scottish supporters went wild with delight. They made a dash for the dressing-room tunnel leading from the pitch, but police and attendants foiled the rush.

Waving banners, the Scots started a running, good-humoured "battle." For 10 minutes the officials held their own. Then the tam o'shantered Scots burst on to the pitch. They danced "Ring-o'-Roses." They hugged each other They danced round the Scottish flag.

The pitch was not cleared until almost half an hour after the finish and not before mounted police had arrived in the arena in case they were needed. Scottish soccer fans have never before enjoyed themselves so much at the expense of their Sassenach rivals !

Scots bookies were thumped as hard as the back of the England net by yesterday's result. The Sassenachs started off firm favourites with most firms offering odds of 4-1 against Scotland to win and 7-4 on England.

● Despite pleas by Scots football fans, STV have no intention of re-shuffling Sunday programmes to take in more of yesterday's thrilling game.

A spokesman for STV said last night: "There is no chance of any more film of the match being shown. I think we have given reasonable coverage. What's wrong with 40 minutes ?"

WE'VE DONE IT! Jim McCalliog and 'keeper Ronnie Simpson walk off with arms round each other's shoulders.

Full reports—Pages 29, 30, 31, 32

Daily Record

FRI. MAY 26 1967

4D SCOTLAND'S NATIONAL NEWSPAPER

No. 22,329

CHAMPIONS OF EUROPE

CELTIC
V-E NIGHT '67!

CUP SPECIAL

IT'S THE GREATEST MOMENT IN THE LIFE OF CELTIC'S MANAGER JOCK STEIN AS HE PROUDLY GRASPS THE EUROPEAN CUP IN LISBON LAST NIGHT. SHARING JOCK'S JOY IS RIGHT-HALF BOBBY MURDOCH.

CELTIC are champions of all Europe. The European Cup manager Jock Stein held last night will come to Britain for the first time.

Tonight it will be in Glasgow. The team are due to fly in from Lisbon about 6.30 p.m. following their wonderful European Cup victory over Inter Milan.

But the fans are advised NOT to go to Glasgow Airport.

As soon as the team touch down, they—and the Cup—will be driven to Parkhead where the big fan welcome is planned.

World match

Celtic will meet the champions of South America in a two-leg match for the title of World Champions.

Present world club champions are Penarol of Uruguay, who beat Real Madrid 4-0 in last season's decider.

In Lisbon about 10,000 Celtic fans — including some from America and Ireland — celebrated throughout the night.

At the end of the game there were fantastic scenes as hundreds jumped the moat to invade the pitch.

Some were hurt in the crush, but none seriously.

Liveliest

Chanting and cheering, the fans mobbed the players and hacked at the turf to carry off bits of grass as souvenirs.

Bar and cafe owners in the city braced themselves for one of the liveliest-ever nights. And what a night it was . .

DONALD BRUCE tells the Lisbon story on Page 19. Celtic's glory goals in pictures are on the Centre Pages and the full match report on Pages 38 and 39.

Wilson to see De Gaulle • Middle East crisis BACK PAGE

Daily Record

SAT MAY 27 1967

4D SCOTLAND'S NATIONAL NEWSPAPER

No. 22,330

The Cup is in Glasgow

FANFARE FOR THE CHAMPIONS

The European Cup with a good-luck mascot sitting inside.

Lorry on a lap of honour . . . the Parkhead scene last night as victorious Celtic show that Cup to thousands of cheering fans.

It's the city of 200,000 cheers

Congratulations to Celtic's chairman Bob Kelly (left) from Lord Provost Johnston of Glasgow and Rangers chairman John Lawrence.

SIXTY THOUSAND screaming, cheering chanting fans packed Parkhead last night to welcome home European Cup heroes Celtic.

And in the city streets, thousands more waited to cheer as team and Cup were driven in triumphant cavalcade from Glasgow Airport to the stadium.

It was a fantastic welcome, the biggest Glasgow has ever seen, dazzling and deafening.

Dazzling in the stadium as the terracings erupted in a blaze of green banners.

Deafening in the streets as thousands of car horns blared a victory fanfare when the cavalcade swept past.

Invaded

At Parkhead, hundreds of young fans invaded the pitch as the team climbed on to a lorry for a lap of honour.

Manager Jock Stein, clutching the Cup, was escorted from the lorry and

'RECORD' REPORTER

back down the tunnel by eight policemen.

For five minutes, while police cleared the pitch, the lap of honour was held up.

Then back came Jock and the Cup. Headed by an accordion band, the lorry crept round the track at snail's pace. Once round, twice and then again. And all the time the fans cheered. Jock thanked them all.

In a plane 1500 feet above Park-

Continued on Back Page

NASSER'S WARNING

•

RUSSIA'S PLEDGE

—Page 2

Daily Record

FRI.
JUNE 30
1967

4d SCOTLAND'S NATIONAL NEWSPAPER No. 22,359

Jagger and Richard will appeal

BID TO FREE TWO JAILED STONES

MAN SHOT DEAD IN BANK RAID
—Back Page

HIGHLAND ROW FLARES
—Page 3

RAILMEN SAY NO TO STRIKE
—Centre Pages

FAREWELL TO JAYNE MANSFIELD
—Centre Pages

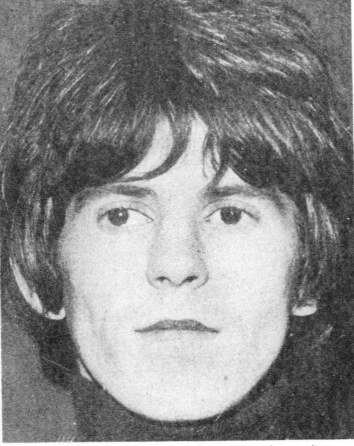

RICHARD . . . showed no emotion at the verdict.

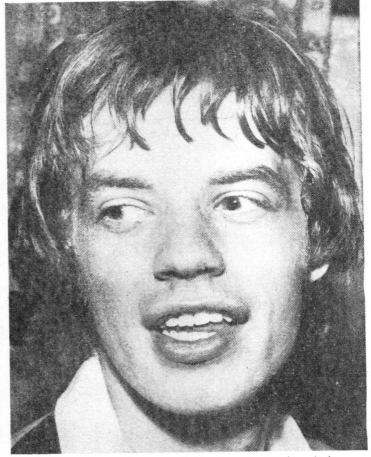

JAGGER . . . almost collapsed as the trial ended.

Why girl was wearing only a rug

ROLLING STONES Mick Jagger and Keith Richard, both 23, were in jail last night after being sentenced on drug charges.

Their legal advisers have said they will appeal.

Application will be made today to a judge in chambers for them to be freed on bail — the usual procedure when an appeal is pending.

In court at Chichester yesterday the sentences — three months for Jagger, a year for Richard — drew gasps from the public gallery.

A third man, London art dealer, Robert

'RECORD' REPORTER

Fraser, 29, was also jailed — for six months.

RICHARD was found guilty by a jury of allowing his Sussex farmhouse home to be used for the smoking of Indian hemp at a party.

Earlier this week **JAGGER** was found guilty of being in unauthorised possession of four Italian pep pills at the party, and **FRASER** pleaded guilty to unlawfully having 24 heroin tablets.

Yesterday, at the end of Richard's trial, all three stood in the dock awaiting sentence.

Richard, in a black regency-style jacket, showed no emotion as Judge Block jailed him for a year and ordered him to pay £500 costs

Next to be sentenced was Fraser—six months and £200 costs.

Jagger waited, a tense figure in green corduroy jacket, bright shirt and dark green trousers. He shuffled nervously and his face showed he sensed that he, too, was to be jailed.

Tears

Then the judge spoke. Three months and £100 costs. As the public gasped, Jagger swayed, almost collapsed, then turned to step down to the cells.

In the suddenly silent court papers rustled on the barristers' benches. Whispers grew: "Are they going to appeal?" Then lawyers said: "Yes, they are."

About 30 minutes after the end of the trial, singer

Marianne Faithfull arrived at the court building in a blue Bentley.

Tears streaming from behind dark glasses, she murmured "thank you" to a fan who wished her luck.

She was allowed into the cells to see boy friend Mick Jagger for 20 minutes.

Handcuffs

Later, when the three men left the court to travel to jail in a bus with other prisoners. Jagger was handcuffed to a prison officer. Richard and Fraser were handcuffed

Last night Richard was in Wormwood Scrubbs. Jagger was in Brixton Jail. He will not need to have his long hair cut, unless on medical advice.

In the witness box, yesterday, Richard was questioned by his counsel Mr. Michael Havers, Q.C., about the night police raided the party at his home.

He was asked about the girl who was found dressed only in a bearskin rug.

"As far as I understand," said Richard, "she had been upstairs to have a bath and must have taken off her dirty clothing, because we'd been in the country all day and she had not brought any fresh clothes

"She must have gone down-

ROBERT FRASER . . . jailed for six months.

stairs to get a cup of tea or something."

Mr. Havers: "Did she let fall that rug?—Absolutely no.

Later when asked by the prosecutor if he regarded the presence of a girl clad only in a rug to be quite normal. Richard said: "We are not old men. We are not worried about petty morals."

More than 200 chanting teenagers jammed Bouverie Street, off Fleet Street, last night, to protest against the prison sentences.

CAN THE STONES SURVIVE ?
—Page 17.

PETROL PRICES GO UP BY 2d.

PETROL is to go up by 2d a gallon. The oil price increase is "over the board" for Diesel fuel, and oil for industry and heating a r e all included.

Permission for the temporary surcharge, to cover the increased cost following the

Arab-Israeli war, was announced in t h e Commons yesterday.

B u t Minister of Power Richard Marsh said there is "no prospect" of rationing in the immediate future.

Cleveland, which is owned by Esso, is increasing prices at midnight tonight.

Esso is almost bound

to follow and the cut-price petrol brands of European petroleum and Olympic will go up by 2d.

Spokesmen for Shell Mex and B.P. Limited and Total Oil Products said announcements may be made today..

Bus fares are likely to rise because of the new petrol price.

Glasgow Corporation

Transport Department face an extra £40,000 a year on diesel costs.

And as they already estimate a £500,000 loss on next year's working, fares will almost certainly go up.

The Scottish Omnibus group facing an extra £65,000, are not meantime increasing fares.

Daily Record

THURS. SEPT. 21 1967

4d SCOTLAND'S NATIONAL NEWSPAPER No. 22,427

R.M.S. Queen Elizabeth II

THE HIGH AND MIGHTY QUEEN

DWARFED by HER SHIP . . . The Queen stands at the front of the launching platform, above a giant Union Jack.

She has just pressed the button to launch the Queen Elizabeth II at John Brown's shipyard yesterday.

The christening "toast" of champagne still drips down the 58,000-ton ship, the gasp that greeted the name still runs around the yard.

But men up on the ship look down, wondering why the ship has not moved. They waited for 55 long seconds.

Then there is a smile from the Queen, below, as the liner moves off, and Princess Margaret and Prince Philip step forward to join her as she gazes up in delight.

☆ "Beautiful," said the Queen—Back Page.

SIX SOUVENIR PAGES OF THE LAUNCHING INSIDE

A HUNDRED THOUSAI

From shipwright to scaler, dignitary to draughtsman's wife, all acclaim the Queen at John Bro

CHEERS

Even big John had it wrong

" I NAME this ship Queen Elizabeth the Second."

As the Queen revealed the long-kept secret, there was a hush, and then gasps before the 30,000-40,000 crowd gave three traditional cheers.

To some it was a surprise, to some a shock, and to others, the most natural choice of name.

What else but the name of the royal sponsor?

But the name Queen Elizabeth II was far from the thoughts of most people.

Most people were wrong—even the rigger on board the liner who, before the launch, shouted down to the Queen below. "Call it Prince Charles ! "

And big John Rannie, the Clydebank yard managing director, who wrote his choice of name on a piece of paper more than a year ago and put it in his safe until the big day. was wrong.

By Douglas Malone

WRONG

His choice . . The Queen. Not far out, but still wrong.

Many people felt the same way. They had been looking for something different, something to project the new liner into the 70's . . . the age of change.

But as Cunard boss Sir Basil Smallpeice, the man who chose the name, explained to the Queen and others after the launch:

" Change is a dominant feature of this new Elizabethan Age.

"The Queen Elizabeth the Second is nothing if not the product of change, a blending of new ideas and techniques with the best of our old maritime traditions and practice, in order to meet the challenge of new circumstances."

Earlier, in her speech after the launch, the Queen said:

" Every great enterprise has an element of risk and uncertainty about it, and I am sure that no one can predict the future career of the new Cunarder.

"However, I am equally certain that, in the experienced and capable hands of the Cunard Company, she will stand the very best chance of a happy and profitable lifetime."

WONDERFUL

Lord Aberconway, chairman of John Brown's, confessed that up to the very moment of the naming, that he had been "completely in the dark," and described the choice of name as "absolutely wonderful."

● Many small punters won at 10-1 when the name was announced, but the big money was on the names of Princess Margaret, Mauretania, Churchill, Prince Charles and Britannia.

As a result, Glasgow bookmaker John Banks cleared £383 15s, which will go to a nautical charity.

The women who cried with pride

(By JUNE HULBERT

IT was the men who built her, bless them, but when the Queen Elizabeth II faced the world yesterday, it was the women who cried with pride.

Princess Margaret, gorgeous in a sedate, creamy-coloured coat and a cheeky, hair-hiding pony-skin hat, had to borrow a hankie—large, white, obviously belonging to a man—and, mascara wiped, she handed it over to the Queen.

Most women needed a hankie just at that minute.

Flowered

The Queen, in singing, swinging, turquoise blue — a semi-fitting coat and a little matching hat that ran around in swathed circles—wiped her own eyes when it was all over.

Then she laughed . . . and the

microphones, still not cut off, carried her gaiety across to the crowds.

In the throng below the colours of the women would have made a rainbow look washed-out.

In the box behind the Queen flowered hats were so many and so real that one could almost smell them. There were bits of mink, too . . . impressive but stifling on a day like this.

Only one mini-skirt and it was worn by a gorgeous girl, all in blue, with a cowboy hat. So very mini that, when it showed itself first, all the TV lenses went zooming out in unison.

It was a woman's day, right enough. Every one there—from the Queen and Princess Margaret down to the last, little, tired, uncomprehending schoolgirl—had had a day from which the colours were not likely to fade.

PICTURE BY GEORGE McEWAN

Daily Record

TUES. JAN. 16 1968

4d SCOTLAND'S NATIONAL NEWSPAPER No. 22,525

20 KILLED BY HURRICANE

Picture by GEORGE McEWAN

THE PICTURE OF DESTRUCTION...

THIS dramatic picture is vivid witness of the force of the hurricane that wrenched homes apart and killed 20 people in Central Scotland yesterday.

It came in the night as families slept, a howling terror of destruction.

From this building in Maryhill, Glasgow, 12 families escaped . . . without time even to put out the lights. Their story is told on Page 16.

Elsewhere, in other buildings, other families were not so lucky. For this was the night when death was blowing in the wind.

NOW TURN TO BACK PAGE
Disaster Special: Pages 11-17

Daily Record

FRID. APRIL 5 1968

5d SCOTLAND'S NATIONAL NEWSPAPER No. 22,594

The boy who buried his girl alive ...

MICHAEL FINNIGAN ... aged 17.

Ambush by white man

LUTHER KING IS SHOT DEAD

Luther-King ... he won Nobel Peace Prize.

DR. MARTIN LUTHER KING was shot dead by a white man in Memphis, Tennessee, early today.

The man got away, dropping his gun as he ran.

A police ambulance, siren screaming, took Dr. King to the emergency entrance of St. Joseph's Hospital in the city.

The Negro leader was carried inside with his face covered by a bloodstained towel.

An emergency call went out for a team of surgeons, and Dr. King was said to be " critically ill."

Then, two hours later, came the

From TONY DELANO in NEW YORK

announcement that Dr. King had died of his wounds.

Later police said that two white men had been arrested after a car chase through the city, in which shots were fired.

Dr. King was sitting in his car outside a hotel when the assassin struck.

With Dr. King, one of America's most active Negro leaders, was the Rev. Hosea Williams, of the Southern Christian Leadership Conference, Dr. King's civil rights organisation.

Mr. Williams said: "The bullet hit in the right side of the face. It took away most of his jaw."

Dr. King, 39, a Nobel Peace Prize winner, had planned to lead a large-scale demonstration in Memphis on Monday.

Bomb

Early today the Memphis city authorities were preparing for an outraged uprising by Dr. King's Negro supporters.

And there is almost certain to be a wave of trouble throughout America.

Dr. King has been the subject of repeated assassination threats over the past 10 years. There have been at least two serious attempts on his life.

Two years ago a knife was hurled at him while he was speaking in Chicago. In January, 1957, a bomb placed on the porch at his home in Montgomery, Alabama, failed to explode.

The fuse burned out just before reaching the explosive— 12 sticks of dynamite bundled together.

THE smiling girl in the white dress, 18-year-old June Roy, was buried alive by her boyfriend after he tried to strangle her.

Her body was later found in a shallow grave at Motherwell, Lanarkshire.

Yesterday, 17-year-old Michael Finnigan admitted the murder. He was sent to the High Court for sentence.

The court heard that after the killing, Finnigan went to June's parents—then joined in the search for her.

THE KILLER WHO WENT TO TEA—Page Three

Ross to move in new Cabinet?

THE Prime Minister was believed last night to be on the eve of a major reshuffle of his Cabinet.

Speculation over changes began after the failure of the Cabinet to hold its normal Thursday meeting.

This is not a unique event but at a time when politicians are on edge, it is rare enough to set off rumours.

Reshuffle

The Premier himself triggered off the speculation when he authorised the speech last Friday by Mr. Crossman, calling for Government changes.

Mr. Crossman, Leader of the House, said it was time for a reshuffle to what he described

By JAMES CAMPBELL

as "Wilson's Mark II" Government.

In the Commons yesterday, Mr. Heath asked Mr. Crossman if he would make a statement about the composition of the "Mark II" Cabinet.

Amid laughter from M.P.s, Mr. Crossman replied: "It is not for me to make the statement."

Mr. Crossman added, amid further laughter: "I would not like to commit myself."

The belief is that most of the senior Cabinet posts will be unchanged.

But some Ministers seem certain to be moved.

Among them might be Mr.

William Ross, Scottish Secretary, who could be replaced by Commonwealth Secretary Mr. George Thomson, M.P. for Dundee East, whose department is to be shortly merged with the Foreign Office.

Popular

Mr. Thomson, one of the Government's most popular and successful Ministers, is reckoned by the bulk of Scots M.P.s of all parties as the man with the ability to halt the erosion of the Labour vote in Scotland.

Mr. Ross's proved ability as an administrator and skilful Parliamentarian is unlikely to be lost to the Party.

Mr. Wilson, in his reshuffle, would find a job for him, replacing some other Minister involved in the change-round.

Daily Record

MON. APRIL 8 1968

5d   SCOTLAND'S NATIONAL NEWSPAPER   No. 22,596

" Racing was Jim's life. We had to accept it and we were proud of him. Now it has ended. *"*

— Jim's father yesterday.

Mystery crash at 170 m.p.h.

JIM CLARK SOMERSAULTS TO HIS DEATH

THE LAST PICTURE . *Jim Clark seconds before the start of the race.*

JIM CLARK, the "Flying Scotsman" of the racing track, died in a mystery, somersaulting crash on Germany's Hockenheim circuit yesterday.

Clark, 32, World Champion Driver in 1963 and 1965, was driving a formula II Lotus-Ford in a race for the German national trophy.

He had roared away to a perfect start on a track which was wet and slippery.

Then, on the fifth lap when he was lying eighth, Clark, who earned £60,000 a year as Britain's top driver, lost control at 170 m.p.h. on a sweeping curve.

Disappeared

Eye witnessses said the rear of the car seemed to "break up". It slipped away to the right then disappeared over the rim of the track turning over and over.

Seconds later it smashed broadside on into a tree.

Clark's team-mate Graham Hill, who has raced with him all over the world, was also taking part in the race.

He telephoned Clark's parents in Berwickshire, with news of the tragedy.

Last night Jim's father Mr. James Clark said: "Racing was his life. We had to accept it and were proud of him. Now it has ended."

It was only by a grotesque twist of fate that Clark drove in the race at all.

He had originally intended to drive in yesterday's Brand Hatch meeting in England . . . then Lotus chief Colin Chapman changed the team plans and sent Clark to Germany.

Twisted

Rescue teams reached the wreckage of Clark's Lotus only seconds after the crash.

He was taken by ambulance to hospital in Heidelberg, where surgeons had been warned to stand by.

But when doctors examined Clark he was dead. He had been killed instantly with multiple skull fractures and a broken neck.

Today, Clark's body will be flown by chartered jet to Edinburgh's

Continued on Back Page

Where it all ended for the Scot who beat the world

Four wheels and an engine lie in the grass. The cockpit has been torn off a £15,000 car. And Jim Clark, "one of the safest drivers in the business," is dead.

★★★ ALLAN HERRON at HAMPDEN

THE KINGS OF FIFE!

No. 1 . . . and it's all eyes on the ball as Pat Gardner thumps it into the Hearts net in 56 minutes. Keeper Jim Cruickshank and wing-half George Miller look back in anguish . . .

No. 2 . . . as keeper Cruickshank fails to stop this low, well-directed penalty kick from Ian Lister in 59 minutes.

No. 3 . . . and it's that man Gardner again—with a snap shot which thundered high into the Hearts net past the startled Cruickshank.

DUNFERMLINE .... 3 HEARTS .... 1 (H.T. 0-0)

Scorers: Dunfermline—Gardner (56 and 73 mins.), Lister (pen., 59). Hearts—Lunn (o.g. 70).

THEY got rid of the rubbish in the first half, then they got down to winning the Scottish Cup in the second half—Dunfermline Athletic, who marched into Europe on the broad shoulders of Roy Barry and on the smart shooting of Pat Gardner.

I don't know what manager George Farm said to his men at the break, but I had the impression that if they did not come to the pavilion with the Cup at the end then they'd be well advised to head for the terracing steps! It was the fearless ferocity with which Dunfermline threw themselves at the Hearts defence on the restart which won this game. A sustained burst of all-out attack which ran for 14 minutes brought life to a game dying on its feet and pushed Hearts out of business.

Tynecastle skipper George Miller, a medal winner with the Pars seven years ago, desperately tried to marshal his troops as the Fifers gave this second half the works. It began with Ian Lister crashing a shot off a Hearts jersey for a corner .. then Paton smashed a shot off some poor soul for another corner. And in four minutes of this grim offensive, Jim Cruickshank clawed away a free-kick from Edwards which Sneddon booted to touch.

In seven and a half minutes Cruickshank just got his fingers to a Paton shot . . . and held it four yards from goal. This came after Paton had wormed his way past thre opponents at the edge of the box

★

Some 90 seconds later Miller actually kicked his own 'keeper a yard from the goal-line in the desperation to survive this tremendous pressure

A goal had to come—and it did in exactly 56 minutes. Dunfermline winger Ian Lister took a free-kick on the left. A good one. Cruickshank came out for it Arthur Thomson jumped for it and impeded his 'keeper.

Desperately Cruickshank tried to get some weight on his punch at the ball but only succeeded in deflecting it across the box.

Pat Gardner was on to it like a hawk, and smashed the ball high into the unprotected net with his right foot from some 10 yards

No easing up from the Fifers They kept their finger on the button Three minutes later Bert Paton swept through on a Hughie Robertson lob and found that he had no one to beat but Jim Cruickshank Cruickshank did the only possible thing left to him—he pulled Paton away from the ball and sent him flying to the turf IT COULD ONLY BE A PENALTY

Lister took it He hit the ball low with his right foot and beat Cruickshank easily on his right side.

Two goals in three minutes—the Scottish Cup was in the hands of Dunfermline for the second time in eight years. Or was it?

Hearts manager Johnny Harvey promptly pulled off Norwegian outside right Raold Jensen and pushed on Rene Moller Dunfermline appeared to ease off after their 14 minutes of fire and fury

★

Hearts now began to play like they can play They whipped the ball across field from man to man in a manner they found impossible in the first half They stretched Dunfermline and they reminded Bent Martin that he still had a part to play in this game.

In 70 minutes Moller who had added pace to the Hearts attack broke clear on the left He deliberately smashed the ball low in to the crowded goal area and leapt with delight when the ball hit Lunn on the body and flew high past Martin into the net!

What a transformation in a game which had limped unsteadily through an opening 45 minutes of mistakes, muddle and nervous debility.

★ Stars for merit

DUNFERMLINE		HEARTS	
Martin ...	***	Cruickshank	***
Callaghan	***	Sneddon ...	***
Lunn	***	Mann	***
McGarty ...	****	Anderson.	***
Barry	****	Thomson ..	***
Callaghan .	***	Miller ...	****
Lister	***	Jensen	*
Paton	****	Townsend	**
Gardner ...	****	Ford	***
Robertson	***	Irvine	**
Edwards ...	***	Trayner	**
Sub.: Thomson		Sub.: Moller	***

Referee—W Anderson *** (East Kilbride)

Attendance—56,365

But any hopes of a Hearts fight-back were killed stone dead three minutes later when Gardner scored his second goal for the Fifers. The type of goal which separates the true striker from the guy who runs about with a No. 9 on his jersey

The goal came following a throw-in on the left from Alex Edwards. After a bit of give and take between attack and defence, Edwards whipped the ball high across goal. In went Miller and Paton. The ball broke OUT—and there was Gardner to crash the ball high past the startled Cruickshank with a venom which almost lifted the net from the cross-bar

A SNAP SHOT WHICH HAD THE TYNECASTLE DEFENDERS SKINNED TO THE BONE

★

They could have finished the game right there—unfortunately for Jim Townsend, Ian Lister Rene Moller they didn't They were all booked in the closing two minutes of the game.

Townsend was booked for fouling Edwards on the right touch-line in 88 minutes after having been twice warned previously Lister was booked for deliberately kicking Moller from behind in the final minute . . . and Moller was booked for trying an arm-lock on Lister's neck which Mick McManus would have been proud of

While I thought the referee Willie Anderson of East Kilbride, had a very sound game, I thought he showed a fair bit of clemency here. Lister and Moller should have been sent off

Dunfermline won the Cup, as I said they would, because they managed to raise their game considerably in the second half

They made more scoring chances than Hearts and Pat Gardner took two of them gloriously Here was a real match-winner The type of player who does not look all that clever in the thick of the play—but give him a glimpse of the clay pigeon!

The inspiration of the Dunfermline success was the formidable figure of Roy Barry. He didn't make a mistake. Kept a tight grip on the middle of the field and roared himself hoarse trying to get more effort from the men around him.

JOHN McGARTY, WHO WINS A SCOTTISH CUP MEDAL IN ONLY HIS THIRD FIRST-TEAM APPEARANCE, WAS A BIG SUCCESS AS SWEEPER ALONGSIDE BARRY

With his trousers in the baggy mould of Alex James, John operated with all the poise of a player who has been around the scene for a long time

★

But the Fifers didn't have a weakness. They all played their part. This was a team effort from keeper Martin to outside-left Edwards. No-one was allowed to hide—and no one wanted to Manager George Farm said he could see no way of Hearts beating him and he was right.

Skipper George Miller, centre-forward Donald Ford, and full-backs Ian Sneddon and Arthur Mann were the players who did not deserve to be in a losing side.

There was always a flicker of hope for Hearts when any of these four got possession, but in the end this Edinburgh side didn't have enough fire or pace to overcome the power of Dunfermline.

Norwegian outside-right Jensen failed to make any impact. The close marking, and back-tracking had him in confusion throughout his stay on the field, and it was no surprise when he was substituted by Moller. who was more profitable in this type of game

I think the 56,365 crowd—the poorest Cup final attendance since the war—got their money's worth in the second half. The first half was a bit of a disaster when the game was heading for the record book as the worst Cup final of all time.

Strangely enough it was in this period that Hearts had their best scoring chances — an Irvine drive from 14 yards past the post in 12 minutes and a rather weak Irvine header which Martin held on the goal-line

★

It was a nervy, tortuous first half which no one enjoyed and which no one will remember. I will thus deal with it no further

So the bold effort of the young Hearts side has failed . . . BUT THE EXPERIENCE WILL DO THEM NO HARM IN THE NEW SEASON

For Dunfermline it means a place in the European Cup-Winners' Cup and a perfect finish to the season on Tuesday when they meet the Scottish League champions, Celtic.

IT GUARANTEES THEM THEIR BIGGEST HOME GATE OF THE SEASON. FRANKLY THEY DESERVE IT

THE MOMENT STEIN KNEW CELTIC WERE CHAMPIONS...

By IAN PEEBLES

THERE was drama at Hampden Park yesterday . . . but it didn't all happen on the field! At 4.49 Celtic manager Jock Stein stepped out the doors of the main entrance. Someone asked him the score at Ibrox and he shouted, with a smile: "Two-two." But a stranger behind him said: "No, No, it was 3-2." Jock looked at him, laughed, and said: "You're at the kidding."

The man behind was adamant, however, and in a flash the Parkhead boss turned, swept through the doors again, then rushed into the Queen's Park secretary's office where he grabbed a phone. He dialled the newspapers, failed to get through, dialled again, then after a few moments laid the phone down.

Nobody needed to ask him what he had been told. His face showed all too clearly that, at that moment, HE KNEW HIS TEAM WERE CHAMPIONS FOR THE THIRD YEAR IN SUCCESSION Back out of Hampden he came, a huge grin on his face and as a journalist approached him he called: "That's the best result I've heard at Hampden." Then he dashed off with his good news to the car park where his team were waiting to return to their seaside headquarters at Seamill.

Celtic's final League game against Dunfermline at East End Park on Tuesday is now a formality as the Parkhead men have won the League Flag on goal average.

If the Ibrox result made great news for Jock Stein, it came as no surprise to Parkhead chairman Bob Kelly. He heard the result in the Hampden boardroom and said later:

"I expected the Ibrox result. I told our players this morning that if Aberdeen played as well against Rangers as they did against us at Pittodrie then they would win"

S.F.A. president Tom Reid was quite frank about his views on the League championship He declared:

"I feel sorry for Rangers. I don't like to see any team beaten. But this is a good result for Scotland. Celtic are the best team and should be our representatives in the European Cup next season."

Reid's comment on the Cup Final was:

"It was a terrible first half. A great second half. And Dunfermline fully deserved to win."

Angry Farm hits out

DUNFERMLINE manager George Farm, despite his joy at the Scottish Cup victory, was also an angry man last night —because his team were not allowed to take the Cup out on to the field at Hampden after the formal presentations.

As captain Roy Barry and the rest of the players reached the end of the tunnel they were turned back by police officers and forced to return to their dressing room.

"I feel very strongly about this. said Farm.

"We've worked all season for this moment yet once we have the Cup we are not allowed to show it to our fans because some Old Firm supporters threw bottles in the past."

"It's the supporters who keep the game going Why should ours be denied this pleasure because of some hooligans? Surely nobody seriously thought there would be trouble if the Cup was paraded today."

"Highlights"

The Dunfermline boss went on: "One of the highlights of the English Cup final at Wembley is when the winning team runs round with the Cup. These are the things which help to make a final a special occasion."

Farm I suspect, is in the mood to make an issue of this point later, but yesterday he got no sympathy from S.F.A. officials

Secretary Willie Allan confirming that the police had acted on instructions from the Association, said: "The decision not to allow any lap of honour after a Cup Final was taken after a happening in a Rangers-Celtic game. If you once relax it . . ."

Mr Allan paused at that moment as if to indicate that a precedent would be dangerous, then he added finally: "You can never please everyone.

I asked S F A vice-president Hugh Nelson what his views were on the parading of the trophy and he answered: "I don't want to say anything

Words that worked wonders!

DUNFERMLINE manager George Farm admitted after the final: "Certain players got a dressing down at half-time." And boy, did it show!

Before the interval the Fifers attack was pathetically lacking in ideas and, more important, the urgency which wins any game. But from the first kick of the second half these same forwards certainly played as if they had had a tongue-lashing.

Indeed, they played as we know they can play. They were sharper, trickier than Hearts and, throughout those last 45 minutes, the Edinburgh fans must have known they were going to have a dismal journey home

Wingers Ian Lister and Alex Edwards became much busier and as they stretched the Hearts rearguard strikers Paton and Gardner began to get much more space

At the end of the day the Fifers had no failures. Everybody justified his place in the team, including the transfer-seeking Bent Martin, who made one or two vital saves before the interval when the game might easily have been lost.

Centre-half Roy Barry gave his usual no-nonsense performance and Tom Callaghan deserves a mention for his scoring efforts in the first half when nobody else seemed to care

Young John McGarty, despite the handicap of extra long pants still gave a very workmanlike performance and made a series of excellent tackles before the interval, when Hearts always threatened to break away and grab a goal

I felt sorry for centre Donald Ford, whose sharpness clearly worried the Dunfermline defence at times But I had little sympathy for Jim Townsend who was finally booked after umpteen lectures by the referee

I've seen players sent off with fewer warnings, and Messrs Moller and Lister were also fortunate to get away with a booking after their last-minute violent clash

George Miller was a terrific captain for Hearts, but I think most of us knew before the game that Dunfermline were a basically better team than Hearts And this was one of those days when form worked out although half the game had gone before form and the Fifers really started working!

That's my view anyway—and here are some other comments on the Final.

Manager **GEORGE FARM:**

"We went out to play football I don't know what they went out to do But the better team won"

Manager **JOHN HARVEY:**

"I'm very disappointed I thought we had a great chance at 2-1 but after their third goal we had too much to do. Dunfermline were good winners"

Dunfermline skipper **ROY BARRY:**

"I'm very pleased to win the Cup My transfer request? It still stands."

SUNDAY MAIL

7d   No. 3106   MAY 5, 1968

The odd aches and pains —but he's feeling fine

THUMBS UP FROM THE HEART MAN

Heart patient Mr. West at home before his operation.

FORTY-FIVE-YEAR-OLD Frederick West, Britain's first heart transplant patient, gave a smile and the thumbs-up sign yesterday, when asked how he felt after his operation.

A bulletin issued at the National Heart Hospital, London, last night said his condition was "entirely satisfactory" 24 hours after the operation.

Doctors said Mr. West had been asking after his wife. He felt "quite well," and mentioned "odd aches and pains," which was only natural.

Mrs. West was believed to have been at the hospital last night and to have seen her husband through the glass window overlooking the theatre.

Before the operation Mr. West, a father of two, of Leigh-on-Sea, Essex, had been given a month to live. Heart disease had been increasing for three years, and he was unable to walk across a room.

The crucial question now is whether Mr. West's body will accept the new heart tissues.

Dr. James Mowbray, an immunologist, said at the hospital that the tissues of the donor and Mr. West were fairly well matched.

The acute troubles ought to stop after about 50 days, he said.

Head of the heart-switch team Doctor Donald Ross said Mr. West would be able to have solid food today.

Brain damage

He is breathing normally and doesn't complain.

Last night Doctor Ross confirmed that the operation was done under the National Health Service.

It was revealed yesterday that Barbara Bushell, 18-year-old daughter of a London police sergeant,

● Delighted at the news . . . Mr. West's 12-year-old daughter Ann.

has received a kidney from the heart donor.

He was Irish labourer Peter Ryan, 26, who suffered fatal brain damage in a fall on Thursday.

The kidney operation was at Hammersmith Hospital, London.

Miss Bushell collapsed on Whit Monday, 1966, and since then has had kidney machine treatment at the hospital twice a week.

Yesterday the donor's widow, Mrs. Mitzi Ryan, 26, who is in Beckenham Hospital, Kent, said: "It is of some comfort to me

that someone should benefit from my tragedy. I hope the operation will be completely successful."

Mrs. Ryan, who is expecting her second baby, was taken to hospital when told of her husband's fall. There was a danger of miscarriage. Yesterday her condition was satisfactory.

Permission

In Leigh-on-Sea, the heart patient's wife, Mrs. Josephine West, also 45, stepped into the garden of her home to face a barrage of Press and TV cameras.

Wearing a powder blue dress, she stood arm-in-arm with her son Michael, 25.

She said: "I felt so happy when I heard the news of the operation. Fred was all for it. He even joked about it."

Neither she nor her son knew her husband had had the operation until they saw it on a newspaper board while travelling to the hospital.

In Ireland, Mrs. Mary Ryan, 55, told how she gave permission for her dead son's heart to be used.

Mrs. Ryan said another son Michael, 24, phoned to tell her about the accident.

She said: "Michael asked me was it all right if his heart were used and I said, well, if Peter was dead a heart is no good to him and if it can be of use to somebody else then that person should get it."

Last night Mr. and Mrs. Ryan flew from Ireland to attend their son's funeral at Beckenham, Kent.

THE MAN STILL ALIVE — PAGE FOUR.

At home yesterday . . . Mr. West's wife and son.

How to look younger—Pages 14 and 15 : Discover Scotland—Page 19

SUNDAY MAIL

7d   No. 3116   JULY 14, 1968

3 DUSTBINS FULL OF WEAPONS

The scene as youths handed in weapons last night, surrounded by onlookers and cameramen.

THERE were fantastic scenes in Easterhouse, Glasgow, last night as local gang members surrendered their weapons during an hour-long amnesty.

Hundreds of onlookers crowded a piece of waste-ground near St. Benedict's School to watch the gang members put their weapons into three large dustbins.

Five minutes before the amnesty began at 7 o'clock two uniformed policemen marched on to the field carrying the bins.

On the stroke of seven a youth, who said he was a member of the Pak, struggled through the crowd of cameramen and onlookers to drop in the first weapon.

It was a small sharpened spade.

A few minutes later about a dozen youths, most claiming to be gang leaders, arrived from the nearby adventure playground.

Each was carrying an armful of weapons—ranging from knives and cut-throat razors to a pick-axe !

To the whirring of film cameras—there was even a team there from the National Broadcasting Corporation of America — they fought through the crowds to drop their weapons in the bins.

Some of the youths were unable to reach the bins and ended up tossing their weapons over the heads of the crowd into the bins.

By the time the hour was up the bins were full of the hundreds of discarded weapons—many of them wrapped in brown paper.

There were many children in the 500 crowd. Mothers stood with babies in their arms. Toddlers held on to parents' hands.

Four ice cream vans and two mobile fish and chip shops did a roaring trade nearby.

During the afternoon, Frankie Vaughan—whose meeting with the leaders of the Toi, the Rebels the Pak and the Drummy last week sparked off the idea of the amnesty—made a surprise return visit to Glasgow.

He held a meeting with the gang leaders before flying back to Birmingham.

Only one of the gangs—the Drummy—boycotted the amnesty.

But some of the gang leaders arrived at the scene and one of them, who gave his name as Big Jim, said :

"We won't be handing any of our weapons over." There's too much to forgive and forget in one night."

Hugh Brown, M.P. for Provan, who watched

CONTINUED ON PAGE THREE

Daily Record

TUES. NOV. 19 1968

5d SCOTLAND'S NATIONAL NEWSPAPER No. 22,788
**

20 DIE

THE BIG FIRE
6 more pages inside
Dramatic pictures

TRAPPED BEHIND BARS

Their bodies were found behind a bolted fire door

FIREMEN play hoses on the barred windows of a Glasgow factory . . . the factory where 20 people died yesterday.

Steel bars over the windows prevented their escape, and later the bodies were found behind a steel padlocked fire exit.

Five women, including a mother and 15-year-old daughter, were among those killed. The victims also included three teenage boys— aged 16, 17 and 18.

Three people escaped, and one is still missing in the James Watt Street blaze.

Last night as a disaster probe was ordered, Bailie James Anderson, convener of the Corporation Fire Committee, said: "These poor people were trapped like rats and they were only a step from safety."

Scottish Secretary Mr. William Ross will make a statement in the Commons today.

My husband, my husband!

Barred windows!

Firemen with a giant foam hose are held back by barred windows . . . just like the people trapped inside.

The picture that explains the high death toll

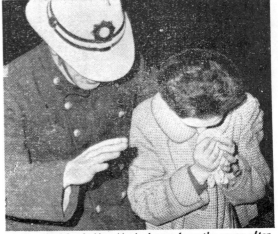

A fire chief leads Mrs. Masie Jesner from the scene after she tried to save her trapped husband.

FULL STORY OF THE DISASTER BEGINS ON PAGE 12

Daily Record

5d SCOTLAND'S NATIONAL NEWSPAPER No. 22,876
***

MON.
MAR. 3
1969

THE GIANT BIRD TAKES TO THE AIR

- SIX YEARS TO DEVELOP
- COST £300 MILLION
- POWERFUL AS THE QE2

The droop-nosed Concorde soars into the sky. "The handling was splendid," said test-pilot Andre Turcat.

From PETER HARRIS
Toulouse, Sunday

LIKE a giant bird of prey, Concorde took to the air for the first time today . . . after more than eight hours of cliff-hanging suspense.

And after her perfect 28-minute flight over the French countryside here, jubilant test-pilot Andre Turcat, 48, was delighted.

He told a huge international press conference: "Finally, the big bird flies. And I can say now she flies well."

"The take - off and landing were smooth, and the handling was splendid."

There were two big surprises in the flight of the Concorde, which has cost £300 million to date and has taken six years to develop.

Power

Her take-off run is fantastically short and her four Olympus turbo-jet engines, which develop as much power as the Q.E.2, make little noise.

The droop-nosed giant —designed to carry 140 passengers across the Atlantic in less than four hours—will work up to its cruising speed of 1450 m.p.h. towards the end of the year.

Watching the flight from a helicopter was British Aircraft Corporation test pilot Brian Trubshaw.

In about six weeks, he will pilot the British assembled "twin"

Commemorative stamps for the maiden flight will be on sale at all main Post Offices today.

BRIDE OF 19 IN ATTACK RIDDLE

Married for a day .. now in hospital

A YOUNG bride was in hospital last night only hours after her wedding.

The girl, 19-year-old Helen Keilloh married in Aberdeen's Registry office on Friday.

On Saturday she and her husband Alan, also 19, held a reception in a hotel on the outskirts of the city.

But instead of being on honeymoon yesterday Helen had an emergency operation in Aberdeen Royal Infirmary.

And later police announced: "The C.I.D. are investigating an assault on Mrs. Keilloh in a house at 23 Stonehaven Road, Aberdeen.

"A man is in custody on a serious charge and will appear at the Sheriff Court on Monday."

The bridesmaid at the wedding was hairdresser Marlene Brown, of 190 Garthdee Road, Aberdeen.

A relative said: "Marlene was at the wedding on Friday night and then at the reception on Saturday — but we don't know what happened."

Last night Helen had been transferred to Aberdeen's Woodend Hospital. Her condition was said to be "fairly comfortable."

HELEN KEILLOH

CHINESE KILLED OUR MEN, SAYS RUSSIA

RUSSIA protested sharply to China yesterday over a border gunfight in which, it was claimed, some Soviet guards were killed and others wounded.

The incident — promptly announced to the world by the Russian news agency, Tass, is thought to mean a worsening in relations between the two major Communist nations.

Russia has complained before about Chinese "provocation." But this was thought to be the first allegation of border bloodshed.

The shooting is said to have broken out yesterday, about 110 miles south of the Soviet far east city of Khabarovsk — on the Ussuri river, which divides part of Russia from China's Heilunkiang province.

Daily Record

5d SCOTLAND'S NATIONAL NEWSPAPER No. 22,977
****

WED.
JULY 2
1969

Shining through the Royal ceremonial .. the pride of a mother

THE Queen's eyes flash towards the newly-invested Prince, her son.

THAT'S MY BOY!

IT was a moment of pride and emotion. The moment the Queen stepped on to a balcony at Caernarvon Castle to present her son, the 21st Prince of Wales, to his people.

Throughout the world, 500 million viewers watched this climax to the investiture.

Presenting the Prince of Wales

But only a privileged 4000 were inside the castle walls to see the Queen clasp Charles's hand as a fanfare echoed through the ancient battlements.

An estimated 250,000 people thronged the decorated streets

Many of them had waited overnight . . . to catch a glimpse of the young man the Queen promised a decade ago would be the Welsh nation's Prince.

THE TOP WRITERS AND THE BEST PICTURES—PAGES 12, 13, 14, 15, 16, 17

Daily Record

WED JULY 16 1969

5d   SCOTLAND'S NATIONAL NEWSPAPER   No 22,988

**

A policeman: A boy: 2 women: 9 men

13 SHOT IN CITY STREETS

RECORD EXCLUSIVE

Cameraman Bob Hotchkiss had to dodge bullets to take this exclusive picture of the gunman in the attic.

The only picture of the sniper before he died

THIRTEEN people were wounded by a gunman during 105 minutes of terror in Glasgow yesterday.

They were a policeman, a seven-year-old boy, two women and nine men.

The gunman opened fire when police went to interview him in connection with the death of Mrs. Rachel Ross, 72, in Ayr.

From an attic window bullets rained down into Holyrood Crescent, Woodside, at the start of the running battle with police.

..GUNMAN AT THE WINDOW

Even ambulances arriving to take away the injured had to run the gauntlet of shots from the third-floor window.

The detectives—who had been looking for James Griffiths, a 34-year-old man from Rochdale, Lancs—called for reinforcements.

The battle went on through the streets of the city in a 60 m.p.h. car chase . . . even into a pub, where the gunman stopped for a drink of brandy.

It ended in a cul-de-sac five miles from Holyrood Crescent.

By then, 13 people had been shot.

The gunman himself was dead—shot as police cornered him in a block of flats.

POLICEMEN AT THE READY..

Policemen during the siege with .22 B.S.A. Martini International rifles . . . guns of the same calibre and similar to those used by American snipers in Vietnam.

Full story—Back Page ● more pictures—Pages 13, 14 and 15

SUNDAY MAIL

7d   3169   JULY 20, 1969

Senator in death drama

TEDDY KENNEDY IN CAR PLUNGE HORROR

Secretary dies as he swims to safety . . .

SENATOR Edward Kennedy—last of the four Kennedy brothers escaped death when the car he was driving plunged off a bridge into water yesterday.

But his woman passenger, 29-year-old secretary Mary Jo Kopechne of Washington was drowned.

The crash happened when Kennedy, 37, and Mary Jo were driving to catch a ferry to Chappaquidick Islands in Massachusetts.

Mary Jo was a former secretary to Kennedy's brother Robert.

Senator Kennedy told police later he repeatedly dived into a pond in a vain attempt to rescue her.

Exhausted

In a statement to police yesterday, some 12 hours after the accident, Senator Kennedy described how he was "exhausted and in a state of shock" immediately after the crash, and that he only reported it to police "when I fully realised what had happened this morning."

He went on: "I was unfamiliar with the road, and turned right instead of left.

"After half a mile I descended a hill and came upon a narrow bridge the car went off the side of the bridge.

"The car turned over and sank into the water and landed with the roof resting on the bottom.

"I attempted to open the door and window of the car, but had no recollection of how I got out of the car. I came to the surface, and then repeatedly dived down to the car in an attempt to see if the passenger was still in the car.

"I was unsuccessful.

"I was exhausted and in a state of shock. I recall walking back to where my friends were eating There was a car parked in front of the cottage and I climbed into the back seat.

"I then asked for someone to bring me back to Edgartown I remember walking around for a period of time and then going back to my hotel room.

"When I fully realised what had happened this morning, I immediately c o n t a c t e d the police."

Accidents and trouble seem to dog the footsteps of the young Kennedy.

Broken back

On June 19, 1964, he was flying to the Massachusetts Democratic Convention when his light plane crashed in an apple orchard, killing the pilot and the senator's aide, Edward Moss.

Kennedy's back was broken in the crash and he spent five months in a Massachusetts hospital. He still wears a brace.

The eldest Kennedy brother Joe was killed in a plane during the war. President John Kennedy was assassinated in 1963 and Senator Robert Kennedy was assassinated in June, 1968.

Ted Kennedy with his wife Joan.

All-night TV drama of walk on the moon

MILLIONS of viewers will have to stay up all night tonight if they want to be certain of seeing man take his first steps on the Moon.

Last night Apollo 11 reached the Moon and went into orbit around it. All is set for the touchdown on the Moon tonight at 9.14.

The two astronauts, Armstrong and Aldrin, were not due to come out of their "Moonbug" until 7.12 tomorrow morning.

To make sure you see it live both BBC and ITV will stay on the air all night tonight.

And to make certain that viewers don't miss the historic moment by falling asleep ITN have bought an alarm clock which they will ring when Neil Armstrong is due to step on the Moon.

Because the mysterious Russian craft Lunar 15 is still orbiting round the moon, the first walk on the moon may be speeded up and be as early as 3 a.m.

The Russians have promised America that Luna will not endanger the Apollo mission.

Last night, space commander Neil Armstrong gazed at the Moon and commented: "The view is worth the price of the trip."

At 6.42 today, Armstrong and Aldrin will cut the frail black, gold and silver moonbug, Eagle, adrift from the main ship to make ready to drop down to the surface of the Moon.

When Armstrong radios to mission

An artist's diagram showing how the space module Eagle will have to land with its spider - like legs straddled on the flat surface

control in Houston at 9.02 p.m. "We are go," Eagle will be nine miles above the surface of the Moon.

At eight miles from the Moon surface, Eagle will flip on to its back. Not until the moonbug is a few hundred feet from the surface of the Sea of Tranquility will Armstrong, peering through the triangular window, be able to see where he is going.

Armstrong said : "For the first two hours after touchdown, we'll have a very busy time verifying the integrity of the lunar module."

If all goes well the two will sleep in the module, have breakfast, then step out on to the Moon's surface.

There was a slight moment of

Continued on Page 2

HOLIDAY HEATWAVE ON WAY, SAY MET MEN—Page 2

Daily Record

MON. JULY 21 1969

5d Scotland's National Newspaper No 22,992

9.18 p.m. Sunday, July 20, 1969

**THE HISTORIC DAY
FOR WHICH THERE IS REALLY ONLY ONE HEADLINE..**

MAN ON THE MOON

From Arthur Smith at Mission Control in Houston

THEY'VE done it! AT 3.39 B.S.T. this morning, just five hours after lunar touch-down, astronauts Neil Armstrong and Edwin Aldrin opened the hatch of their spacecraft Eagle in the Sea of Tranquillity. And by 4 a.m. Armstrong was taking man's first steps on the Moon.

The astronauts, who had landed on the Moon at precisely 20 seconds before 9.18 B.S.T. last night, cut out a planned four-hour rest period and stepped out on the first real inter-planetary space spectacular.

The change in plan was fixed up in a dramatic early morning exchange of messages with Mission Control in Houston, Texas.

Armstrong said: "Our recommendation at this point is planning to start extra-vehicular activity at about 8 o'clock Houston time (2.15 B.S.T.), if you concur. We'll give you some time to think about it."

In two seconds flat, back flashed the answer from capsule communicator Charles Duke: "We thought about it. We will support it."

And with a flash of humour, he added: "You guys are getting prime TV time there."

Knock-out

Armstrong, referring to the £166,000 TV camera which was to record the Moon-walk, replied: "I hope that little TV set works, but we will see."

For the astronauts, the early walk solved a problem that could have been tricky.

After all the tremendous excitement of the landing, it is probable that if they had gone on with the planned rest period, they would have needed knock-out pills to cool them down enough to sleep.

And, in a chain reaction, they would possibly have had to take pep pills to shake off the effects of the first drug when the time eventually came to make their walk.

By going out early, they avoided all that and faced no risk that their judgment might be impaired by pills at a time when split-second reactions could be vital.

Finale

For President Nixon, the change of plans meant a quick up-timing of arrangements. Soon after the earlier walk was fixed, it was announced in Washington that he would speak to the Moon Men 55 minutes after they stepped on the lunar surface.

The walk was the grand finale to the greatest show in the universe, a show that began dramatically at 6.47 p.m. yesterday when Eagle, with Armstrong and Aldrin aboard, went into independent orbit.

As it parted from the command module, Columbia, piloted by Mike Collins, third man on

4 am..Armstrong takes the first steps outside

the mission, Armstrong said exultantly: "Eagle undocked. Eagle has wings." The great adventure was go.

Then, for hours as millions watched on TV, the long, tense ritual of orbit and descent was played out, until just before 9.18 p.m. history was made as Eagle touched down on a pock-marked lunar plain.

"The Eagle has landed," Armstrong said. And within minutes he and Aldrin were sending back man's first close-up, ground-level view of the Moon.

Mystery

Meantime, as America triumphed, their space rival, Russia, stole into the picture. From Moscow it was announced that the mystery Russian Moon-probe Luna 15 had swooped into a new orbit within 10 miles of the lunar surface.

As speculation grew about a possible Russian scene-stealer landing by Luna-15, the mystery deepened when the spacecraft signals ceased after 9 p.m.

And early today there was a new theory—that the Russian craft might have smashed into a mountain on the far side of the Moon. From Moscow, there was no comment.

But nothing could steal the glory of Armstrong and Aldrin as they flew their fragile Eagle to a frightening, but safe, touchdown, bringing true

Continued on Back Page

the centuries-old dream of men —to land in an alien world

From Houston, Texas, ground control told Eagle: "We're blue but we're breathing again."

Minutes after the landing Eagle was sending its signals back to Earth under the new proud call-sign Tranquillity Base.

Delicate

During the last few tense seconds of the descent to the lunar surface, reports flashed back and forth as Armstrong and Aldrin delicately jockeyed Eagle to a safe landing site— about four miles beyond the planned area because of rocks on the original site.

This was how it went:

From Control: "Eagle looking great. You're go."

From Eagle: "75 feet, looking good, 50 seconds, lights on, down 2½, forward, forward, picking up some dust . . . just move to the right a little . . ."

Then, dramatically: "The Eagle has landed."

Disaster

Mission control flashed congratulations: "Guys, that was one beautiful job. There are a lot of smiling faces in this room, all over the world."

Armstrong replied: "There are two of them here. . ."

Behind the breezy cross-talk lay the relief of safe touchdown after what Armstrong revealed could have been

● THIS was how the astronauts prepared for the great Moon walk . . . by practising the whole operation inside a Moon simulator at Houston. On the last test run, when this picture was taken, Edwin Aldrin (left) used a scoop for collecting samples while Neil Armstrong tested a camera. Today they know if the rehearsal matched the reality.

MEN OF THE MOONSHOT—Pages 9, 10 and 11

DOWN, DOWN TO TH

THE WORLD held its breath last night as one of the greatest adventures in its history unfolded.

The crucial stage began soon after lunch yesterday as American astronauts Neil Armstrong and Edwin "Buzz"

Aldrin climbed from the command module into their lunar landing module to check it over.

Then came the decision to undock from the command module and float slowly away, leaving Lt. Col. Michael

Collins to orbit the Moon 70 miles a its surface.

Just after 8 p.m. our time the lander module's main descent engine was on the far side of the Moon.

And a little after 9 p.m. the

The team who took a rocket-ri

ARMSTRONG

He got his pilot's licence before he could drive a car

NEIL ARMSTRONG . . . even as a boy was fascinated by the moon.

NEIL Armstrong was a fair-haired, quiet schoolboy of 14 when he got his first close-up look at the Moon.

He lined up with classmates to peer through a home-made but powerful telescope which amateur astronomer Jacob Zint had installed in a modest laboratory in his back garden in Wapakoneta, Ohio.

Two weeks later, Neil Armstrong was back for another look.

"He got his mother to phone and ask me if he could come along to study the Moon again," said Mr. Zint, a 58-year-old draughtsman.

"He was interested in the heavens. But it was always the Moon that particularly fascinated him.

"He would keep it in view for minutes at a time. Then he would turn away without saying anything, as though lost in his own thoughts."

Today that boy is Armstrong . . . the man in everyone's thoughts.

FLYING

Wapakoneta, Armstrong's home town, is a slice of grass roots Americana. Named after an Indian chief and his daughter, it slumbers amid flat acres of farmland.

Wapakoneta's 7000 population, many of German origin, are almost delirious with delight that their home town boy is about to write its name into the history books.

Already the town has declared two Neil Armstrong Days, and named a street and an airport after him. And it's here that they remember Armstrong as the quiet boy who was mad about flying.

He went for his first plane ride at the age of six when his father, Stephen, let him skip Sunday school and took him for a flip in an old crop-dusting biplane in which a local farmer used to give joyrides.

' Neil was absolutely fascinated with the flight," recalls his mother, Mrs. Viola Armstrong, as she sits in her comfortable home on Neil Armstrong Drive, Wapakoneta. "Mind you, I think his daddy was a bit scared."

By the time he was in high school, Armstrong was spending every moment of his spare time at a grass field airport about four miles from home.

Neil took flying lessons and, when he hadn't enough money, paid for them by helping mechanics and pilots tinker with aircraft engines in the ramshackle hangar.

"Just being around that airfield with the touch and the smell of the planes was enough," says Mrs. Armstrong.

He got his pilot's licence at 16—even before he had learned to drive a car.

At high school, Armstrong was never

much more than an average student, though he collected As in science and maths.

Neil made it clear his heart was set on aeronautical engineering. But his physics master, 78-year-old Mr. John Crites also remembers him as once standing on the porch, looking up at the Moon and saying : "One day I'd like to go up there."

At school Neil played the baritone horn in the band and sang in the glee club. But outside, his passion for flying never gave him much chance to go around with girls . Dudley Schuler, one of his former classmates, says : "He was never much of a lady's man.

"I guess when you think about him being an astronaut, there should be a dozen exciting stories one could tell. But, frankly, he was just a very average sort of person."

One double date Mr. Schuler does remember was the night he and Neil took two girls to a school dance. Neil had borrowed his father's car, and on the way home ran it into a ditch.

Mr. Schuler says: "Neil had quite a bit of explaining to do that night."

EMERGENCY

But getting out of tight corners has been a speciality for Armstrong. After winning a Navy air cadet scholarship at the age of 17, he went on to fly 78 combat missions in Korea.

On one mission over enemy territory his plane was hit by anti-aircraft fire. He ejected, parachuted down behind enemy lines but was picked up by an American rescue patrol.

Good luck—plus the icy nerve of a skilled pilot—pulled him through in March, 1966, when Armstrong piloted his Gemini 8 spacecraft back to an emergency splashdown in the Pacific.

Armstrong is married to the former Janet Shearon, a college beauty queen. They have two young sons. They live in Houston, Texas, the space centre of America.

And, like the folks back home in Wapakoneta, they think he's the greatest. Not just in the world—in the universe.

ALDRIN

'The plodding type who always seemed to have clammy hands!'

BUZZ ALDRIN . . . he became a brilliant cadet at West Point.

EDWIN "Buzz" Aldrin was determined to be the first man on the Moon. That's what he told friends after his spectacular walk in space nearly three years ago.

But the fact that he was chosen as No. 2 on the Moon won't worry him. For instant adaptability is something he's famous for.

At the age of 16, for instance, Buzz Aldrin was a twelve stone, curly haired halfback in the football team at the High School in his home town of Montclair, New Jersey.

The team was badly in need of a new centre. And coach Clary Anderson decided to experiment with Aldrin.

"He'd never played centre before, and I was a little anxious about how he'd make out," said Mr. Anderson.

He needn't have worried. Aldrin took over the centre spot as if he'd been playing there all his life.

He hardly put a pass wrong . . . and the team went on to win the State championship.

OUTSTANDING

At school, too, Aldrin was determined to succeed. He spent only one year in kindergarten, instead of the normal two. And he worked much harder than the normal child.

Aldrin's 73-year-old father, Colonel Edwin Aldrin, a distinguished American flyer and former World War One pilot, admits he was behind the plan to get Buzz working faster than the normal child.

"I don't believe in wasting time," he said in his businesslike, military manner. 'I knew Buzz could do it, and I'm sure he did."

Buzz was born in Montclair, a prosperous commuter dormitory town within an hour's train ride of New York City, on January 20, 1930.

Although they were the depression years his father had a good job as head of flying for the rich Standard Oil Company, of New Jersey, and the family—Buzz had two older sisters—lived comfortably with a cook and a coloured maid.

At High School, just like the other two apollo 11 astronauts, he wasn't remembered as one who chased the girls.

Even his position as a football hero and an excellent athlete who was an outstanding pole vaulter never made him a pin-up boy.

Mrs. Verity Webb, a Montclair housewife who went out with him occasionally in High School, recalls that he was "A solid

citizen." She added : "If you want the truth, I think you could say he was pretty dull company."

Another girl who knew him said he was "The plodding type who always seemed to have clammy hands."

Aldrin seemed to be more interested in study and athletics, and even his friends found it difficult to get close to him.

But his friends say it was obvious from an early stage at High School that Aldrin was headed for an Army career.

It was his love of athletics that finally attracted him to the Military College at West Point.

When Aldrin left Montclair High School in 1947 (he was voted the boy "most likely to succeed") he listed his ambition in the college newspaper as hoping he could become "A general in the Lower Slobovian Army."

In fact he went on to become a brilliant cadet at West Point, and later flew 66 fighter missions in Korea, where he shot down two Migs.

WHIRLWIND

Just before going to Korea, Aldrin met Joan Archer, a good looking blonde, at a party in New Jersey.

They never wrote to each other. But when he got back from Korea after a year he looked her up again.

It was a whirlwind courtship, rather untypical of the methodical Buzz. They had been out together less than half a dozen times when they married. They have three children.

Where does Aldrin get his nickname Buzz ? He acquired it from one of his sisters who, when she was small, used to tell everyone about her "baby buzzer."

No one in Montclair is really surprised that Buzz Aldrin has gone to the Moon ' Once Buzz made up his mind to do something, it got done," says football coach Clary Anderson.

"He always knew exactly where he was going."

CO

IT'S astro Com Arm the

A move who a chil his ow

It' steal ing M

He 1930, Gener Attac there

Hi Joe '' comm Staff, Army

B just so as his t

A kn fig on

W a Ho him ' Mic know abou

A which teasi any

H space " and cond ' just

E at a wher and

J decid want right says

wh T

DUST OF THE MOON

hazardous trip in modern history went into its 12-minute final stage.

Man's feet in the dust of an alien planet, a moment that ten years ago was only a science-fiction dream becomes reality. And a new era in history opens.

to history

ng Joe's

plays

Michael Collins . . . an Army background.

vitable that hould be the round in the Ship while rin land on

as been on the a military family t to Army post as ome town to call

ta'ly will try and under by claim- eir own.

on October 31, the late Major was the Military States Embassy

wton "Lightning World War Two Army Chief of her James is an

a home town, it's p quiet about it, hero's welcome will receive.

quietest of all "If you didn't aut, you'd never talking to him,"

lor, President of per, has known rs. He explains: fellow to get to about work or

y College, from 2, the Year Book hael Collins has "stay casual."

g the Gemini 10 a walk in space Houston that in space were

oint, Collins was ool, St. Albans, wrestling team. otball.

Armstrong, he just what he st Point in mind entered school."

d he knew just

or 1948 describes

his "characteristic glum and poutin; expression," but another master explained "That wasn't really true.

"Mike had a mobile face. He always wore an inscrutable expression and, when you were talking to him, you always wondered what he was really thinking and what mischief he was planning."

If Michael Collins was planning any mischief he must have got away with it No one can ever remember him being in serious trouble.

Even his mother, Mrs. Virginia Collins who sti'l lives in Washington, can't remember him getting into any real scrapes "He was a very ordinary little boy," she says

"I can't really remember him ever saying what he wanted to be when he grew up. But of course with the family's mili- tary background, it was no surprise when he went to West Point," she added.

RIPPED

His taciturn manner was still with him the day his jet got into trouble while he was taking part in a training exercise with the U.S. Air Force in France.

An explosion ripped a jagged hole in the side of his plane. He calmly ejected and parachuted down on to a field while the aircraft crashed in flames in a nearby wood.

"It was sort of an easy problem," Collins explained later, "because there was no doubt in your mind what to do. Bail out!"

He met his wife, Patricia Finnegan from Boston in the ifficers' club at Chambley. France.

She recalls that he came up to her "very serious looking" and introduced him- self. They were married a year later and now have three children.

Michael Collins is naturally disappointed that he's not going to be the first man on the moon, or even one of the astronauts who make the first landing.

But in his usual relaxed way he shrugs and says: "I'm going 99.9 per cent. of the way there. And that's good enough for me."

This time it's for real!

THIS is how the Apollo 10 lunar module looked as it began its descent towards the surface of the Moon. But last night—with Apollo 11—the descent did not end in an orbit nine miles above the surface. This time it was all the way. This time it was for real!

Alone, he rows 2,500 miles in just 72 days

'MOBY' BEATS THE ATLANTIC

LONE oarsman Tom "Moby" McClean stepped ashore on dry land yesterday . . . after rowing the Atlantic in 72 days.

As the weather-beaten 26-year-old soldier landed on the West coast of Ireland near Blacksod lighthouse, County Mayo, he claimed a new record for the crossing . . . and won a five-bob bet. Tom, from Dublin, set out in his 20ft. red and white boat Super Silver from St. John's, Newfoundland, on May 17. His fantastic time for the 2500 mile crossing beats by 20 days the previous record.

It was set up by Captain John Ridgeway and Sergeant Chay Blyth three years ago.

Determined

Tom — known as "Moby" to his friends — served in the same regiment, Special Air Services. And it was the feat of Ridgeway and Blyth that inspired him to make the crossing.

But Tom, who admitted: "I'd only ever rowed on a boating pool before," was determined to row alone.

Last night, stocky 5ft. 6in. Tom said: "It was pretty rough, but I've been in situations just as rough. But I was glad to see land."

He told how his voyage almost ended in disaster . . just yards from shore. His boat was driven on to jagged rocks, and for more than an hour he struggled to pull it clear.

"It was very tricky," he said. "I could have got off all right myself. But I did not want to lose the boat.

"A few times I thought I would be drowned."

Swamped

Bachelor Tom also told of his most frightening experience when he woke up in the early morning to find his boat swamped.

"Only the buoyancy compartment kept it afloat," he said. "But I managed to pump it out."

He spoke about the five-bob wager he had won from a friend in his regiment for making the crossing.

"But I didn't do it for the money," he went on. "I just wanted to prove that the journey could be done alone."

"I was quite happy by myself, and never thought once about giving up," he added.

Tom leaves the Army soon, and hopes to set up a small boat business. "I have a little knowledge of boats now," he said.

RIDDLE OF LONE YACHTS-MAN—Centre Pages.

Two days after daughter's wedding

Scotland's Army chief takes a bride

GENERAL Sir Derek Lang's secret has leaked out . . . the 55-year-old G.O.C. Scotland is to marry today.

His bride will be Mrs. Elizabeth Balfour, 52, Hungarian-born ex-wife of a wealthy Australian —and for years the companion of the late Earl of Balfour.

The wedding, in London's Caxton Hall Registry Office, will be the second involving the Lang family in three days.

On Saturday the general's 24 - year - old daughter Sarah married schoolteacher John Hunt in Edinburgh.

Mrs. Balfour came to Scotland in 1960. The Earl of Balfour, former N.C.B. chairman, announced that he planned to make her his second wife, but later found a divorce impossible.

She took his name by deed poll and was a constant companion at his Whittinghame, East Lothian, home until his death last year.

The general and his wife were divorced earlier this year. He retires from the Army at the end of September.

MRS. BALFOUR . . . was the Earl's constant companion.

The last can of food

Lone Atlantic rower TOM "MOBY" McCLEAN brings ashore his last can of food. In his 72 days afloat he lived on a diet mostly of curry . . . and special Army rations.

SUNDAY MAIL

8d   3220   JULY 12, 1970

'I may feel like a king tomorrow'

THE MILLION DOLLAR MISS

Rail chaos tomorrow say rebel signalmen

SERIOUS disruption of Central Scotland train services during the next two days, was forecast last night by a wildcat strike leader.

Signalmen in Glasgow and Dundee campaigning for an immediate £3-a-week pay bonus, are due to begin a one-day strike at midnight tonight.

Lanarkshire men are to come out 24 hours later.

Mr Albert Long, chairman of the strike committe which is defying official N U R policy, warned:

"We should achieve serious disruption of commuter services."

He said: "It's extremely unlikely all signalmen will obey the strike call.

"But we are hoping for a figure of 400 men to come out in the main city areas."

Upset

Mr Long said it was "unfortunate" that holidaymakers could suffer. 'It is just one of those things," he said. "We have no alternative."

Worst hit services are likely to be those from Glasgow to outlying districts — Balloch, Helensburgh and Airdrie and Blue trains within the city.

A British Rail spokesman said they would maintain as many services as possible but some trains to England could be affected, too.

On Wednesday the N U R decided to negotiate for a £5-a-week bonus, but the rebels' leader, Mr Long, said: "The increase would take too long to achieve."

Yesterday thousands of rail passengers on the Edinburgh-Newcastle-London line were unable to get anything to eat or drink because of a one-day strike by 800 dining-car staff.

The men are upset over suggestions that they have been offered pay rises to stop pilfering and waste.

The holiday island of Jersey was last in the grip of strikes—by dock workers, dustmen and airport maintenance men among others—for a £3 wage award.

The airport was kept open yesterday by supervisors, and B E A officials in Glasgow said they expected it would be open all week

THIS is how a wife feels when her husband just misses an easy chance to win the Open.

Mrs Scotty Sanders and one of Doug's friends hide their faces in their hands as that vital putt slips past.

Jack Nicklaus said afterwards: "I'm a darned lucky man to still be in tahe competition."

Live coverage of the play-off today will be screened by B B C-1. Full details on centre pages.

"TONIGHT my wife and I feel like sheep. Tomorrow if I win I'll feel like a king."

Doug Sanders, the Texan, who missed the vital last putt in the Open golf tournament at St. Andrews told me this last night as he left the world famous course.

That miss, watched by a record crowd as well as millions on TV, means there will be a play-off between Sanders and Jack Nicklaus today.

It could cost him a million dollars—the amount reckoned he could take in sponsorship fees and advertising by winning.

Clad in a magenta coloured outfit down to his shoes, the greying Doug made no excuses for not winning.

He said: "I could have missed that putt for a dollar just as easily as for this championship"

Asked if the clicking of cameras at the 18th green might have put him off he replied: "There were certainly plenty of them around and its not the best thing to have. But I am making no excuses."

Downing his second beer he told me: "A winner in big games like this has to live with tension."

Doug, when asked his age, quipped: "Why must you ask me that, because I have a few grey hairs. A man is as old as he feels and a woman as she looks. But seriously at the last count down I was 36."

Doug and Jack last took part in a play off in America in 1966 . . . and Doug won. Doug said: "The result is all that matters. After all, you don't have a box after each hole for explaining your score on that hole."

As he left the interview tent Doug was asked if he would be practising later that night.

Looking amazed, he shot back: "Pardon me, Sir, I think one day's play on that Old Course is a full day's work."

WARNING TO GIRLS GOING ABROAD ON HOLIDAY —Page 13

DAILY · RECORD · SPECIAL

The Scots girls in the uniforms that won the loudest applause—tartan mini skirts and waistcoats with tammies.

It's black hats and handbags for the girls of the

Save-As-You-Earn

...and get two whole years' savings as a tax-free bonus

Regular monthly saving (of any sum from £1 to £10) in the Halifax 'Save-As-You-Earn' scheme will bring you a *tax-free bonus* equivalent to one year's saving at the end of five years. After seven years this *tax-free bonus* is doubled! The bonus is equal to a compound rate of 7% per annum (approx.), representing a gross return of about 12% per annum to those paying the standard rate of tax of 8/3d: in the pound.
Ask for our brochure about S.A.Y.E. at your local Halifax office or agency.

Amount saved each month	Savings plus 5-year bonus	Total Savings after 5 years	Savings plus 7-year bonus
£	£	£	£
1	72	60	84
2	144	120	168
3	216	180	252
4	288	240	336
5	360	300	420
6	432	360	504
7	504	420	588
8	576	480	672
9	648	540	756
10	720	600	840

HALIFAX
BUILDING SOCIETY
Member of The Building Societies Association

District Offices:
FALKIRK 23 High Street. District Manager: L. C. Low. Tel: 25550
GLASGOW 119 St. Vincent Street, C.2. District Manager: E. L. Thompson A.C.I.S., A.B.S. Tel: 041-221 2025.
also at 12/13 Charing Cross Mansions, St. George's Road, C.3.
Manager: P. H. Brown, A.B.S. Tel: 041-332 1888
AYR 254 High Street. District Manager: W. Muir, A.C.I.S. A.B.S. Tel: 65181
KILMARNOCK 57/71 John Finnie Street. District Manager: A. W. Martin. Tel: 22978 & 22806
MOTHERWELL 51/55 Muir Street. District Manager: W. W. Halliday. Tel: 66531
PAISLEY 23/25 Moss Street. District Manager: D. A. Smith, A.C.I.S., F.B.S. Tel: 041-889 9231

THOSE lucky people who were in at the start of the Games yesterday saw more than just a crowd of runners and jumpers taking a walk.

They saw a parade. And, among other things, it was a fashion parade.

Naturally, the greatest appreciation was reserved for

Games girls

the favourite dish—the girls of the home team.

And with remarkable foresight, not to mention protocol, the Scots were kept till the end.

Then on they matching mini kil specially designed topped off in neat t

But the cheers th

CEUD MIL

WHICH, FOR THOSE WHO DO NOT HAVE THE GAELIC

AND so let battle commence. The Ninth Commonwealth Games are on.

They whirled into splendid momentum yesterday in a gay merging of pageant and precision, music and marching.

It happened in Edinburgh ... under grey, windless skies, with the sun occasionally coming out.

TRIUMPHANT

Around the tiered perimeter women in summer dresses added a final bold colour splash to the assorted mass of bandsmen's tartans and athletes' striking uniforms.

The athletic armada, flags steaming, brightly blazered, walked in and out of the stadium in what started as a moderate impersonation of Her Majesty's brigade of guards and ended for most of them in loping strides and half-hops.

THEY ENTERED to tremendous cheers and sharply contrasting reactions to their eye-catching get-ups.

THEY WENT OUT to roars of "England, England" from a group of sailors off HMS Londonderry lying in Leith docks with the added imploring cry "Save our tots."

The Duke of Edinburgh was in the stadium for one hour and 50 minutes after driving

By ALEX

triumphantly around the ar in an open Rolls-Royce.

As he performed the ce monial, I couldn't help feel that he was fighting a petitor's instinct to leap down join the athletes and upset alphabetical orderliness.

Polo, however, is not am the events.

SPLENDOUR

The superb opening unforgettable. It always is course. But this was just t little bit better.

Old Edinburgh rose up in background in rugged splend

And the best of British luck, says the Re

TO every one of the 1959 athletes of the Commonwealth who today begin competing in the Ninth Games the Daily Record wishes the very best of British luck.

As the Queen pointed out in her message yesterday: Scotland is one of the founder members of the Commonwealth Games and, for the first time, the host.

Host to the largest number of competitors and countries ever to take part.

The burghers of Edinburgh deserve the highest praise for what is obviously going to be an outstanding staging of a very great occasion.

So today we say:

To the devil with the griping, money-pinching critics who've been snapping for so long at the Games organisers' heels.

To the devil with scribblers from that south of Berwick who of our biased cheers.

Of course we're b
Of course we'll b our tartan heads off.

As we've already

The best of Britis every competitor — the English.

But may the best

A striking touch to set off their red costumes.

The English girls parade in their smart green uniforms—showing obvious signs of mini-hems improvised at the last minute.

h the height of fashion

them had been matched minutes earlier, when the English girls appeared.

Maybe it was because the "Auld Enemy" had just won their battle—over the mini-hem.

Despite a team order NOT to hitch their skirts more than the official three inches above the knee, the English roses rebelled — with the aid of a few last-minute pins.

By way of contrast—except in the leg department—the New Zealand girls wore striking red costumes, with black hats and handbags.

And the outfits were more than matched by the attractiveness of their wearers.

There were lots and lots more—girls of every size, shape and shade.

And all deserving medals for sheer chic and charm.

FAILTE!

HUNDRED THOUSAND WELCOMES'

ERON

rthur's Seat gave no ntment at having one C's 20 colour cameras i it to gobble up the below as a dozen ors struggled for s.

openings are old hat ike Keino of Kenya, Australia, Jones of d Fairbrother of

e they will not forget. ted with a booming uns fired in Holyrood reet the Duke, and a f Lightnings and from Leuchars.

The Duke, accompanied by eut. General Sir Henry Leask, O C Scotland, inspected his ard of honour from the een's Own Highlanders.

BRIGHT

There was a respectful air out the place. And the wait r the big parade was livened by Highland country ncing and the music of the assed bands.

The splendid colour of pipes d drums of the Royal Scots, ack Watch, Queen's Own ghlanders, 52nd Lowland lunteers, and the police nds of Aberdeen, Dundee, inburgh and Glasgow was a agnificent sight.

It was even more so when ey massed with the military

bands of the Royal Marines, the Scots Guards and the Royal Air Force.

Then came the moment everyone had waited for so patiently.

With the Duke on a velvet-covered dais, the teams began to troop out . . . Jamaica first, their girls in mini skirts and canary-coloured jackets.

Australia, all 132 of them, were only a place away with their girls in yellow so bright that it looked luminous.

There was a tremendous cheer for Canada in bright red blazers and their girls with white hats and red dotted shoulder bags.

MESSAGE

And then, assured even before the parade began of the greatest reception of all, came the small figure of Kuhanda Badru, carrying a streaming flag of Ceylon.

Miss Badru, a sprinter, was a one girl team, and the Duke himself appeared to check an impulse to give her a cheery wave.

Behind her came Horatia Ignatius Scotland, a fencer who is the only competitor for Dominica.

England's girls brought out a "Oh" with their turquoise rigouts. Their team was the biggest, 244.

Gibraltar sneaked in an ape mascot. And one coloured competitor wore a kilt.

Swaziland caused a minor sensation . . . they boosted a leader who was bare to the waist in a loin cloth and carrying a ceremonial axe.

The Scots, carrying their giant teddy bear, were grandly

received in their final host position.

Then the great assembly of athletes, nearly 2000 of them, waited on the Queen's message, which had been handed over in Yellowknife, North-west Canada, taken on its final lap by lone runner Jim Alder, 30-year-old gold medal winner of Scotland in Jamaica

It said: "The founders of the Games described their intentions in these words: 'They shall be merrier and less stern and will substitute the stimulus of a novel adventure for the pressure of international rivalry.'

"These words should be remembered. I hope that all who have come together in Edinburgh from all parts of the world will first and foremost enjoy themselves.

"I hope too, that both the competitions and the social events will encourage new friendships and a better understanding of the Commonwealth as a free association of people of goodwill."

FLAG

Led by the pipes and drums, the Commonwealth flag was trooped into the arena.

Crawford Fairbrother, the veteran high-jumper raised his right hand and pronounced the oath of the Games on behalf of all the competitors.

And it was time for the athletes to go and prepare for the earnest business of competing for medals in "these friendly Games."

The tone and the spirit have been set . . . amidst the loudest, the matiest, the most colourful setting the Games have seen in 40 exciting years.

The most colourful member in the parade Swaziland's team manager, David Nsibandze. Barefooted and dressed in antelope skin, he carries his country's ceremonial axe.

Daily Record

6d   Tuesday, July 21, 1970   ★★   No. 23,303

3 AM NEWS   IAIN MACLEOD DEAD

THE Chancellor of the Exchequer, Iain Macleod, died early today. He was 56.

He was taken to hospital two weeks ago for an emergency appendicitis operation and when he came out two days ago his condition was said to be satisfactory.

Mr Macleod's illness was a closely guarded secret. Few who watched him take part in the Commons economic debate on the night he went into hospital knew about it.

During the debate he battled against "considerable pain" to deliver his speech.

Mr Macleod died suddenly late last night at 11 Downing Street, his official residence.

As he was preparing to go to bed at about 11.20 he suffered a heart attack and died at 11.30.

Mr Macleod's death was announced by Prime Minister Edward Heath at 3 a.m. in an official statement from 10 Downing Street.

It said: 'The Prime Minister has learned with deep regret that the Rt. Hon. Iain Macleod, Chancellor of the Exchequer, died suddenly last night, 11 Downing Street."

Mr Macleod leaves a wife and a son and daughter, both married.

The Chancellor, who had been Tory MP for Enfield West since 1950, was a Scot, the son of a doctor. He was educated at Fettes College, Edinburgh.

PILOT'S ORDEAL

FOR three hours last night a critically injured pilot lay trapped in this wrecked jet at Turnhouse Airport, Edinburgh.

As a surgeon tended him constantly in a desperate bid to save him, rescuers hacked at the wreckage.

Then, when he was finally freed, the fight for life went on as an ambulance rushed him to hospital.

But the long battle was in vain. For after his ordeal, Captain Brian Ianson died before reaching the hospital.

Flames

The drama began when the plane, a Hawker Siddeley HS 125 executive jet, owned by the Imperial Tobacco Company, crashed on take-off and burst into flames on Turnhouse's Runway 13.

As fire engines raced out to smother the plane in foam, an off-duty surgeon from

Death trap battle in Turnhouse jet crash

Edinburgh Royal Infirmary, waiting to catch a flight south, rushed from the terminal building.

He tended the plane's two occupants—pilot and co-pilot—while ambulances sped out from the city with a police escort.

One man, Imperial Tobacco's chief pilot Captain Peter Nethercourt from Bristol, escaped with face injuries. Early today he was "fairly satisfactory" in hospital.

But co-pilot Captain Ianson from Weston-Super-Mare—known to his friends as "Chunky"—was trapped and badly hurt.

The crash happened just half an hour after Prince Charles had landed at the airport on a visit to the Commonwealth Games. The Queen and Princess Anne had flown in an hour earlier.

Minutes before the accident, the crash jet had flown in from Bristol to land several Imperial Tobacco executives at Turnhouse. Then, after a quick turn-round, it was taking off for Newcastle.

It had just got airborne when the port wing dipped and the plane slewed on to the runway, swung round in a circle and burst into flames.

Insurance company executive Mr Joseph Crocker, of Northwood, Bridge of Earn, Perthshire, who was driving to the airport, described what happened next.

"At first I thought it was the sunset," he said. "Then I realised it was flame coming from the plane. I saw one fireball, then another and a huge pall of smoke."

Another eye-witness, Mr Jim Reid, of Barnton Crescent, Edinburgh, who was watching from a window of nearby Turnhouse clubhouse, said: "The plane's nose seemed to come off."

Problem

Last night Mr G. M. MacIntosh, Board of Trade Aviation Controller for Scotland, said an inquiry had already been started.

At the weekend, the British Air Line Pilots' Association named Turnhouse Airport among nine it is to check for safety.

But last night BALPA pointed out that the problem they were concerned with was approach and landing aids.

A spokesman said: "This crash had nothing to do with what we were talking about. This aircraft was taking off."

Story by IAN METCALFE: Pictures by BILL FRASER

SUNDAY MAIL

8d   3222   JULY 26, 1970

PANIC BUYING EMPTIES SHOPS

SUNDAY MAIL REPORTER

SCOTTISH housewives felt the first effects of the dock strike yesterday when panic buying left scores of shops without sugar, tinned fruit or bacon. As the "sold-out" signs went up, rationing started in two Scots cities and there was talk of it spreading.

Wholesalers and suppliers are likely to impose indirect rationing for in many cases stocks are low and some shops are being told: "Sorry. No more deliveries meantime."

Shops were packed yesterday as canny housewives stocked up—afraid of a prices explosion later in the week.

The manager of one big chain of shops in the **FALKIRK** area said: "People are panic buying. Some bought as much as 28lb of sugar.

"We're sold out and other shops are in the same position. And my suppliers have told me they cannot guarantee further deliveries.

"Danish bacon is the same. I have been told to expect no more meantime."

Prices are holding steady meantime, but Mr Thomas Brechin, head of one of Scotland's largest meat businesses, said: 'There MUST be an increase by the end of this week."

Bulk ban

Mr David Campbell, manager of Woolworth's store in **STIRLING**, ran out of sugar and had to turn away local shop owners who had gone to him for supplies.

Mr Campbell said suppliers seemed to be holding back stocks and that he had received only a third of his weekly order.

In **ALLOA**, Clackmannanshire, one store manager said he would not allow people with money to buy in bulk "leaving none for folk who couldn't afford to do that."

In **EDINBURGH** a spokesman for the Edinburgh and Dumfriess-shire Dairy Co. said his firm was low on sugar, but that rationing was not being considered yet.

Sugar shoppers in **GREENOCK** were disappointed yesterday. Supplies that should have reached Massey's on Friday never arrived.

A spokesman said: "We don't know when our next load of sugar will arrive."

Where rationing has already started — in Glasgow and Dundee—some big stores are

(Continued on Page 2)

Double Scotch!

IAN AND ROSEMARY GRAB TWO MORE GOLDS

THIS was the moment that sent all Scotland wild with excitement yesterday — Ian Stewart winning the Commonwealth Games 5000 metres, with fellow-Scot Ian McCafferty second and Kenya's Kip Keino trailing third.

Making it a "double Scotch" gold medal finale, Ian's girl-friend, Rosemary Stirling, surged to victory in the womens' 800 metres.

Immediately Ian crossed the finishing line, Rosemary rushed forward (right) to congratulate him with a hug.

What an end to the biggest and friendliest Games in the history of the event.

The climax came as 2000 athletes flooded into the Meadowbank arena in a display of international friendship.

After the Queen's closing speech the athletes and officials danced and dined the night away at a farewell party at Murrayfield Ice Rink.

Games Special—See Pages 30, 32.

The Secret Of A Perfect Complexion

BY TOP SWEDISH MODEL GUNILLA KNUTSON
—PAGE 22

Home Truths About Council Houses

SUNDAY MAIL SPECIAL REPORT —PAGES 4 AND 5

SUNDAY MAIL

9d 3238 November 15, 1970

31 crashes on the Kingston

SAFETY SCANDAL HITS NEW BRIDGE

An A A patrolman stands beside crashed cars stranded on the bridge.

DOZENS of cars spun out of control on Scotland's newest bridge yesterday as frost turned it into a skating rink.

And as angry motorists counted the cost of trying to cross Glasgow's £11.5 million Kingston bridge, the Mail uncovered a scandalous reason for the smashes:

Because of a year-long wrangle between the Corporation and the Electricity Board, **NO POWER** is going through the heating system designed to keep the bridge ice-free.

The heat generating pads and wiring were installed in all the bridge approach roads when it was being built.

Only the "safe" 470ft. centre span had no under-road heating because it is straight with no camber.

Last night a major row was brewing because of the Mail's disclosures.

The A A expressed "grave concern." An official said: "It was the first cold snap of the year and motorists were caught completely unawares by black ice on the bridge.

"We dealt with 31 accidents on the bridge and approach roads and motorists sorted out many others themselves."

Most of the accidents happened on the approach roads and caused absolute chaos. At times the bridge was jammed with cars as harassed AA men and police tried to get the lane exits clear.

One motorist, Mr Michael Begg, of 1004 Pollokshaws Road, Pollokshaws, Glasgow, said: "The bridge was like glass.

"Cars were sliding and spinning all over the place. I was in a bump myself. It was absolute chaos."

At one time, on the Stobcross approach lane, there were nine crashes within five minutes. On the south side there were multiple pile-ups.

The reason for the year-long delay is because the Highways Committee thought the cost of electricity too high.

The Board wanted a guaranteed 800 hours of power used annually. But the committee was prepared to offer them only 400 hours.

The Highways Committee even considered buying their own generators.

Eventually at their meeting last month—they agreed to accept the board's price of £6575 to install the necessary plant to supply the electricity.

This got Corporation approval on October 29—and the board started work.

Heat pads on the south approach roads to the bridge should be ready within a week.

But work on the north side of the bridge is behind because it is a bigger job.

Another complaint by motorists is the difficulty of being able to define lane markings at night when it's raining.

Because of poor lighting the white lines which mark the lanes don't show up.

The A A said: "Cat's eyes would have been better."

YIPPIES FLY HOME

Jerry Rubin gives the Black Power salute from steps of the plane.

THE two leaders of the Yippie movement were flown out of Britain yesterday on a BOAC flight from Prestwick.

The two, Jerry Rubin and Stan Albert had been detained in Belfast.

They dodged deportation by deciding to leave of their own free will.

They were first flown from Belfast to Prestwick—then to New York.

As they left Belfast, Rubin gave the Black Power salute from the steps of the plane. The flight to Prestwick was without incident and the two yippies stayed at the rear of the plane, kept apart by two escorts.

Security measures at Prestwick included Ayrshire C I D men on the tarmac and a Special Branch escort for the yippies.

Can you judge fashion?

WIN
£2,000
PLUS
colour TV
—*PAGE 12*

Where you can move into a council house NOW

Pages 4 & 5

SUNDAY MAIL

9d   3245   JANUARY 3, 1971

108 injured, and boys are among the dead

66 KILLED IN IBROX DISASTER

SIXTY-SIX spectators were killed and another 108 injured—three critically —in Britain's biggest-ever football tragedy at Ibrox Park, Glasgow, yesterday.

It came at the end of a trouble-free match between Rangers and Celtic watched by 80,000 spectators.

Just before the end of the match, Rangers fans on their way out heard the roar of the crowd when Rangers scored a last seconds equalising goal.

They tried to get back up the steps to the terracing but were engulfed by hundreds of jubilant fans swarming down after the final whistle.

Crash barriers on the stairway were broken by the crowds . . . and fans fell on top of one another.

Lord Provost Sir Donald Liddle, weeping at a press conference, said: "It is quite clear a great number died of suffocation."

The Chief Constable, Sir James Robertson, said it was clear that barricades had burst and people had piled on top of each other.

Fans help injured

Ambulances, fire engines and police cars were rushed to the stadium. Some had difficulty in reaching the scene because home-going crowds leaving the match were unaware of the tragedy.

As well as the official figures, many more were treated on the spot by first aid men and volunteers from among the spectators.

Police appealed to spectators who had escaped the disaster to help in carrying stretchers.

Many friends, still wearing their club colours, helped to carry dead and injured to the pavilion.

Club officials worked in their shirt sleeves, giving help to injured spectators.

The first bodies were extricated and brought

Continued on Page Two

Shrouded bodies lie in rows on the Ibrox turf.

POLICE NAME THE DEAD—SEE BACK PAGE

PICTURES PAGES 3, 4, 5, 7, 9

SUNDAY MAIL

4p   3268   JUNE 13, 1971

Here's another great exclusive!

32000 JOBS AT STAKE IN UCS CRISIS

UPPER Clyde Shipbuilders may not even be able to pay this week's wages.

This was the fresh bombshell last night as chairman Anthony Hepper flew to London for a face-to-face meeting with Government ministers.

More than 32,000 jobs are at stake, after the shock news that the company needs £6m by tomorrow to avoid going into liquidation.

U C S itself employs 7500, but 25,000 more work for smaller firms which rely entirely on supplying the U C S yards.

Desperate

As top management ended an emergency five-hour meeting yesterday —without issuing a statement — it seemed likely that the first news would come in the Commons tomorrow.

But before then:

● Chairman Hepper will have talks in London today with John Davies, Minister for Industry, about the need to save these 32,000 jobs.

● Scottish Secretary Gordon Campbell will consider a telegram sent to him last night by the Scottish Trades Union Congress;

Even this week's pay is doubtful

MAIL REPORTER

● And UCS managing director Ken Douglas will address a mass meeting of the workers today.

The crisis came to a head after a series of desperate "Help us" phone calls from Mr Hepper to senior Government ministers early yesterday

And it was revealed that U C S and the Government, its principal shareholder, have been talking all week in an attempt to save the consortium.

Twice the Cabinet have held secret meetings.

Yesterday a U C S spokesman said:

"The money will have to be in the pipeline by early next week or we close down.

"It is no secret that we've suffered from a lack of working capital for the last six months. We have been living hand-to-mouth.

"Creditors have been pressing us. We had to pay cash for everything. Because of this we have not been able to do business in normal terms."

Will the workers be paid this week? The spokesman declined to give a specific answer. "Financially things are very tight, but I don't think they're as desperate as that."

Melting-pot

"We must wait for the Government's decision. The future of U-C S is in the melting-pot."

Could the Government make this another Rolls-Royce ?

Mr Tam Dalyell, Labour M P for West Lothian, said yesterday: "If Mr Davies announces a liquidation of U C S in the House on Monday we will create pandemonium.

"A closure would be unthinkable in present economic circumstances."

BIGGS POLICE HUNT IN SCOTLAND?

TWO top Australian detectives have flown 10,000 miles to Scotland . . . to hunt down an international criminal.

And last night, as a massive clampdown was made on their movements, the big question was:

Are they hot on the trail of Ronald Biggs, the only Great Train Robber still at large?

The secret mission of Detective Sergeants Noel Morey and Matthew Carmody is to probe possible links between three separate robberies—two in Australia, one in England—totalling almost £906,500.

It is thought that one man who evaded capture in one of the Australian raids may have been a crime mogul who flits from country to country organising big robberies.

And Ronald Biggs has been suggested by a former Scotland Yard man as a possible leader behind one of the daring crimes . . . the Qantas airline bomb hoax which cost the company £233,000 last month.

The detectives flew to Britain from Sydney about 10 days ago. This week they stayed in Scotland, following up clues.

Then, last night, the security blackout went up.

EVERY major police force in the country said they did not know them.

THE SCOTTISH Regional Crime Squad, the country's special task force, said the detectives had never contacted them.

GLASGOW'S C I D boss, Detective Chief Superintendent James Binnie, said neither he nor his assistant had been approached by them.

The detectives stayed at the city's Royal Stuart Hotel . a few hundred yards from police H Q. When the Mail called on Friday a receptionist said: "They have just checked out. They are going on a bus trip, then to the Ivanhoe Hotel."

But the Ivanhoe, in Buchanan Street, said they never booked in.

Later the Royal Stuart's manager

Continued on Page 3

SIBELLA DORMAN
Gay and impulsive.

ALEXANDRA GALITZINE
Swinging girl.

ARABELLA CHURCHILL
Charity worker.

BETTINA LINDSAY
"A bit beatnicky."

CHARLOTTE PONSONBY
Twiggy-type.

Could one of these girls be the next Queen?

WHO WILL marry Prince Charles, the world's most eligible bachelor? "She will have to be pretty special," says Charles . . . could she be one of the girls on the left? For the full fascinating story turn to

—PAGE 11

PLUS

JOHN BURROWES

reports from Belgium on why are the Second-class Citizens of Europe.

—PAGES 4 AND 5

PLUS

Win £1100 and colour TV in fashion contest

—PAGE 22

Daily Record

2½p   Tuesday, June 15, 1971   *   No. 23,582

IT'S ALL IN THE GO-AHEAD RECORD

JOIN THE GIRD GAME

☆ Rally drivers, councillors, TV stars . . . they're all getting into the gird game. The Record looks in on the amazing comeback of Dad's childhood sport on Page 3.

A BABY AT 40

☆ What happens when you are over 40 and you find you are pregnant? Readers who know tell us about the enjoyment of being a parent at 40 plus in the Record tomorrow.

JOHN BROWN'S FACES THE AXE

3000 JOBS FIRST TO GO IN UCS CRISIS

By DOUGLAS MALONE, Record Industrial Editor

THE Government is letting Upper Clyde Shipbuilders sink — but providing a lifeboat to salvage as much as possible of the group and its 8500 jobs.

Last night on Clydeside, however, the speculation was that at least one UCS yard will die.

And the most likely to be axed is Clydebank—the famous John Brown's—which employs more than 3000.

Viable

For purely on the basis of performance the yard that built the Queens is the least successful of the UCS undertakings.

The decision to scuttle UCS was announced in the Commons yesterday by Trade and Industry Minister John Davies amid an uproar of protest from Labour MPs.

He turned down the group's plea for £6 million immediate aid, but at the same time promised Government support in reorganising "whatever groupings may prove to be most expedient."

The final decision on how much can be saved rests with the liquidator who will be appointed today—and on how much cash the Government gives him to do the job.

Last night no one at Westminster would make any guesses, but one estimate was that 60 per cent of the group could be considered viable.

This supports the belief that at least one yard will go and, in terms of productivity and profitability, John Brown's is the most likely.

The outcome will not be known until the liquidator has been able to make a cool assessment of the tangled situation.

It is his job to look after the interests of creditors and shareholders and to save what is worth saving

Halt

The Government, as a major shareholder, has already indicated its wish to see the profitable parts of UCS survive.

So the scene could be set for a salvage job along the lines of that which followed the recent Rolls-Royce crash.

In that operation a new company was formed to continue some of the firm's activities and buyers are still being sought to take over other sections.

Meanwhile, the most immediate effects of the Government decision not to stake the £6 million UCS needed will be:

LOSS of orders in the pipeline, estimated to be worth up to £100 million.

CANCELLATION of many contracts in the current £90 million order book.

POSSIBLE removal of ships from UCS yards for completion elsewhere; and

WITHDRAWAL of supplies to UCS by outside contractors. The clampdown on supplies has already started. Yesterday the British Steel Corporation stopped further deliveries to UCS "until the position is clarified.'

Tough

If the ban is maintained, work at the yards will come to a halt when existing steel stocks are exhausted

For British Steel workers at the Clyde Bridge works, too, the ban will mean short-time working. Almost a third of their output went to UCS

Union reaction to the Government's tough line on the crisis was predictably bitter last night.

But at UCS, workers who earlier threatened to "take over" the yards if faced with closure are now expected to work normally while the liquidator assesses the situation.

For them—and for all Scotland—it is the beginning of an agonising wait to see just how much can be salvaged from the wreckage.

ANDY DOWNIE . . . cheerful, as his parents pray for a miracle.

Lung-swop hope for boy who drank poison

By BRIAN SWANSON

A LUNG transplant may be considered to try to save a little boy's life.

Five-year-old Andy Downie swallowed a deadly weedkiller.

But it is slow-acting, and yesterday he played cheerfully with his toys in Edinburgh's Royal Hospital for Sick Children.

Chirpy

His heartbroken parents hid their tears and prayed for a miracle.

Doctors have told them: "Don't hold out much hope."

Andy swallowed the paraquat weedkiller during a "pretence" birthday party in the garden of neighbour Eddie Holmes, at 6 Hillwood Avenue, Ratho Station, near Newbridge, Midlothian.

He spotted a pop bottle hidden under a shed and thought the reddish-brown liquid was lemonade.

Andy spat it out because of the taste but a poisons expert warned yesterday: "One mouthful can be fatal."

Mr Holmes, who had apparently planned to use the poison in his garden, was too shocked to talk about the incident, which he did not see.

Mrs. Anne Downie, 31, of 8 Hillwood Avenue, said: "I would do anything to see my Andy well again."

She added: "He is quite chirpy. The only thing worrying him is his sore throat."

She and her husband Jack have moved into Edinburgh to be near their son and visited him again last night.

"He was looking very well," said Mrs Downie. "You wouldn't know how serious things were."

Paraquat weedkiller caused the death of 15-year-old Lewis boy Alex Dan Smith in Edinburgh Royal Infirmary, despite a lung transplant.

A hospital spokesman said yesterday: "In general the boy's condition is satisfactory.

"Different methods of treatment which have been used in the past in cases of paraquat poisoning are under constant consideration — including a transplant. But this depends on his condition and progress."

The poison ultimately solidifies the lungs. ICI say they make two paraquats— Gramoxone for farmers and the much weaker Weedol for domestic use. Gramoxone liquid is reddish brown.

THEY'LL RUE THE DAY - Page Two
20 VITAL QUESTIONS - Centre Pages

Daily Record

2½p   Thursday, June 24, 1971   ✳   No. 23,590

THE WAKE FOR JOHN BROWN'S BODY

APOSTOLIC CHURCH

Scotland's workers march in anger. Their fear . . . what does the future hold?

But it was more than a funeral for UCS.. the workers of Scotland had gathered together to ask: What of the future.. what of our jobs?

WHAT THE RECORD SAYS —PAGE 2

THE GREAT MARCH —PAGES 4 & 5

Daily Record

3p   Friday, October 22, 1971   ★   No. 23,691

12 KILLED

52 INJURED

DEATH AT THE SHOPS

‘ Don't move please .. this is the police. Don't smoke. Don't move an inch. Firemen are trying to listen for sounds from the injured who may be crying for help ’

Nurses and ambulance teams continue the search for buried survivors after the police loud-hailer appeal for silence.

THE CLARKSTON TOLL DISASTER — Back Page, Pages 2, 3, 5 and Centre Pages

SET FOR EUROPE ..

● Thistle 'keeper Alan Rough gives Celtic one of their many frustrating moments at Hampden with this save, at the feet of Harry Hood. Bobby Murdoch backs away, while Lou Macari throws his arms in the air. Defenders Hugh Strachan, Jackie Campbell and Alex Forsyth move out to aid their young 'keeper.

Jags' cup victory may open door

By DON MORRISON

PARTICK THISTLE — as far as their fans are concerned they are the marvellous, magnificent Jags — carried the League Cup back to Firhill in triumph last night.

And with them went the good news that the Scottish League are to fight hard to have Thistle included in next season's UEFA Cup competition.

"The League Management Committee met on Saturday morning," said secretary Tom Maule. "They decided to do everything in their power to have the League Cup winners included in the two teams definitely in the tournament.

"And we still have not given up hope that Scotland will again have three teams playing in the UEFA Cup."

Played well

Not that Partick needed much of a boost after their 4-1 win over Celtic.

"I'm delighted for the players and the fans," said a calm manager Davie McParland.

"We came here to play well and we did — particularly in the first half.

As he hugged the gleaming silver trophy, Jags skipper Alex Rae, scorer of a wonderful opening goal, said: "I've thought about a day like this since I was a wee boy.

"I thought we could do it but never thought we'd do it so well."

Celtic have appeared in the past eight finals winning five of them.

The defeat yesterday was the heaviest they have suffered in any competition since they lost 5-1 to Dunfermline in the League in season 1964-65.

"We made mistakes, missed chances but good luck to Thistle," said manager Jock Stein. "They deserved to win and it won't do the game any harm."

Celtic outside right Jimmy Johnstone, injured after only 16 minutes of the final, had four stitches inserted in a knee wound and will miss the midweek League game against Dunfermline.

● Smiles all round from the scorers who swept Partick Thistle into the history books—skipper Alex Rae, Jimmy Bone, Denis McQuade and Bobby Lawrie—as they pose with the trophy they won so magnificently before 62,740 at Hampden.

Glasgow	Edinburgh	Ayr	Aberdeen	Dundee	Inverness
041-248 7000	031-225 4275	0292-62765	0224-52361	0382-27481	0463-33334

Printed and published by Scottish Daily Record and Sunday Mail Ltd., Anderston Quay, Glasgow, C.3, for I.P.C. Newspapers Ltd., Holborn Circus, London, E.C.1 Registered at the Post Office as a newspaper.
© Sunday Mail, 1971

Daily Record

INTO EUROPE

3p   Friday, October 29, 1971   ★★   No. 23,697

YES BY 112 VOTES

IT'S "Yes" to Europe—by a massive and decisive Commons majority of 112.

The momentous decision to join the Common Market was taken by MPs last night in one of the most dramatic scenes ever witnessed in Parliament's long history. The result was 356 votes to 244.

The unexpected size of the Government's majority will give them all the authority they need to carry through their plan for getting Britain into the Market by January, 1973.

Unhappy

When the figures were announced there was a tremendous roar of triumph from the pro-Marketeers.

Tory MPs stood cheering and waving their order papers as Premier Edward Heath, smiling broadly, walked out of the House.

Many of the Labour pro-Market rebels listened to the result with mixed

By JAMES CAMPBELL

feelings. Though they were pleased with the size of the majority, they were clearly unhappy about voting against their own Party line.

For many of them it was the first time they had ever rebelled against their Whips.

The Government's morale was given a further boost when the House of Lords voted with an overwhelming 8-1 majority in favour of the Market.

Proud

Last night a jubilant Mr Heath said: "Today's decision has been reached by a clear majority of the elected representatives of the people—men and women who, irrespective of party political differences, share the conviction that this decision is for their country.

"Now we stand ready to take our first step into a new world full of new opportunities.

"Let us show ourselves to that new world as we would wish it to see us—confident, proud and strong."

Mr George Thomas, Shadow Welsh Secretary and Labour MP for Cardiff West, said: "This is a sorry day for the areas of traditionally high unemployment. The people of Scotland, Wales, Ulster, the North, Merseyside and Cornwall have been sold down the river.

"I believe that the British people will look back upon this day as a time of great betrayal."

Major

Labour MP Fred Peart, former leader of the House, said: "This is only the beginning of a major Parliamentary battle on the essential legislation which will be needed."

Mr George Thomson, MP for Dundee East who was the Labour Government's negotiator on the Market, voted for entry.

Thirty-six Scots MPs came out **AGAINST** joining the Market—32 of them **FOR**.

Two, Mr Wm Hamilton (Labour, Fife West) and Mr Patrick Wolridge Gordon (Tory, Aberdeen East), abstained from voting.

Senior

Other Shadow Cabinet members who voted with the Government were Mrs Shirley Williams, Mr Douglas Houghton and Mr Harold Lever.

Mr Michael Stewart, Mr Ray Gunter, and Mr Patrick Gordon Walker —all former senior ministers—also voted for the terms.

Conservative backbenchers exercising a free vote and voting against the Government

> Now we stand ready to take our first step into a new world full of new opportunities.
>
> —EDWARD HEATH LAST NIGHT

totalled 38. They were headed by Mr Enoch Powell. Others included Sir Derek Walker Smith, Sir Gerald Nabarro, Mr Angus Mude and Mr Edward Taylor.

When Mr Heath wound up the big debate, he said that any Premier who recommended that we should reject this opportunity of going into Europe would be taking a terrible gamble with the livelihood of the British people.

Before the historic vote, Opposition Leader Harold Wilson warned of the possibility of Britain leaving the Market under a Labour Government.

He said they would renegotiate the terms of entry.

"The Six might accept that—and they might agree that we should part," he said.

Gt. BRITAIN for the EUROPEAN CUP and SCOTLAND

Turnbull.

"Oh stop girnin'—we should win easy!"

The rocky road ahead —PAGE 2

How your MP voted —PAGE 9

ANNE SEES WHAT GOES ON..
BEHIND THE

THE Press Princess . . . that was Princess Anne yesterday when she literally made the headlines.

The Sportswoman of The Year became the Newspaperwoman of The Year when she opened our new £7 million home at Anderston Quay, Glasgow.

Fascinated, Princess Anne swept into the rhythm of the world's most modern newspaper plant and briefly took over the jobs of . . .

A PHOTO COMPOSITOR, by tapping out with one finger this heading: *"THE PRINCESS SET THIS HEADLINE."*

A TELEPHOTO OPERATOR, pushing a button to send a photograph of her taken the previous evening at the Clyde submarine base at Faslane to 150 newspapers throughout the country.

A COMPOSING-ROOM MANAGER, pressing another button to send a reporter's news story along a conveyor belt to a photo compositor.

TREMENDOUS

And after a two-hour tour of all the departments—seeing how a story is born and ends in print—the Princess said:

"It is tremendous to see Scotland leading the way in this highly competitive field, and I wish the Daily Record all good fortune in its new home."

At the gala opening lunch, Mr Don Ryder, chairman of Reed International Ltd., the Daily Record's parent company, thanked Princess Anne for setting "such a gracious seal on the years of planning and research which have come to fruition here today."

Scottish Secretary Gordon Campbell sent a telegram of congratulations, saying the £7 million investment demonstrated confidence in Scotland's future.

Earlier, Princess Anne smiled and waved to cheering schoolchildren when she arrived at the Record plant on the Clyde.

She was welcomed by Mr A. Fraser Anderson, chairman of the Scottish Daily Record and Sunday Mail, and presented to company directors, including Mr Hugh Cudlipp, chairman

The power of those mighty presses

THE power of the presses . . . Princess Anne watches fascinated as special editions of the Daily Record thunder past her on the giant web-offset machines.

Seconds later, she is shown a copy (right) by Deputy Night Production Manager Ken Humphries.

ADLINES

Getting the picture

THE process that amazed Princess Anne—the working of the telephoto machine, explained here by telecommunications manager James Yates.

Beside the Princess, right, is Mr A. Fraser Anderson, chairman of the Scottish Daily Record and Sunday Mail.

ef Reporter
Airs.
am Thornton
amilton.

onal Publishing

ut what makes the
h its space-age

HQ of the Press
fourth floor of the
she operated the
ephoto machine,
to of herself to
Britain.

the Record's tele-
department she
the same picture
hoto receiver after
on.

almost unbelieving
e process.

"Surely that's not the same picture?" she asked telecommunications manager James Yates.

"It's no trick," he replied. "You've done a first-class wiring job."

In the Record's giant editorial floor, where up-to-the-minute news is gathered and planned for publication, she saw again the speed of a modern newspaper.

A photograph of herself being welcomed at Queen Street Station by Lord Provost Sir Donald Liddle lay on the art desk. It had been taken only minutes before.

In the computer-keyboard composing room, she pressed a button to send a news story along a conveyor belt to a compositor.

"I hope it doesn't go sailing past. I am not very good at these things," she said.

But as it reached the right destination she smiled: "Oh good, it got there."

Then she saw the computers that produce the photographic reproductions of stories for the pages.

The day a Princess became a press girl for a day was ending.

And appropriately with her own words: "I have been very impressed . . . "

Fashion note

SHE may not wear tiaras all the time, but Princess Anne still has a pretty regal way with a bouquet—even in what you might call her working clothes.

Yesterday, they consisted of a beautifully tailored single breasted coat, with side panels split to the thigh, and a little pom-pommed cap.

And her favourite pearl and gold ear-rings, worn with a matching brooch, were her only concessions to opulence.

Anyhow, when you look like a princess who needs the crown jewels?

Princess Anne's bouquet was presented by eight-year-old Sarah Jane Nisbet-Smith.

Johnston, Stein clinch Cup for Ibrox men

'Gers do it the hard way

From
Ken Gallacher
Barcelona,
Wednesday.

RANGERS won the European trophy they have searched for for so long—but the glory that should have been theirs was tarnished by the behaviour of their fans.

It was a night that no-one in European football will ever forget, a night of shame for the Scots who invaded the field at Barcelona at the end of the game.

But these same fans also robbed Rangers captain John Greig of the chance of being handed publicly the European Cup-Winners

Cup which he and his team mates had earned.

They had earned it the hard way—just as they have had to do everything the hard way in this tournament.

Sparkling

In a sparkling first half they looked as if they had the game won when they scored twice.

The first goal was a magnificent shot from centre-forward Colin Stein in 24 minutes.

And the second in 40

RANGERS........3, MOSCOW DYNAMO........2

Scorers: Rangers—Stein, Johnston (2). Moscow Dynamo—Estrokov, Makovikov.

minutes came from a Willie Johnston header after a magnificent cross from Dave Smith.

And when Johnston added a third goal, and his own second, just three minutes after half-time, the game seemed won.

The fans—there must have been almost 25,000 in the ground—celebrated

wildly on the terracing.

They waved their banners, their Union Jacks. and their Scottish standards—but their celebrations had come too soon.

Trouble

For the redoubtable Russians refused to acknowledge defeat.

Two minutes from the end, as the Russians

Desperately they made two substitutes, each time bringing on an attacking player.

Estrokov came on first in 55 minutes—and five minutes afterwards he had scored the goal which suddenly put Rangers in trouble.

forced relentless pressure on Rangers defence, Makovikov scored a second goal for Dynamo.

It was an astonishing fight-back. Rangers, who had looked so certain to win, had seemed almost invincible, were suddenly in trouble.

But the main thing remained—Rangers have won the European Cup Winners Cup on their third appearance in the final.

Nothing can change that —although the hooligan fans certainly tarnished the victory by their behaviour.

It was not a night to pick out individual stars.

In that first half Rangers were magnificent—every single one of them—and after half-time they fought desperately against a Russian team which played with as much courage as any side I can remember in Europe.

Cool

In that spell when Rangers were in so much trouble, the coolness of Derek Johnston and Dave Smith and the brilliant goalkeeping of Peter McCloy have to be mentioned.

Just as earlier in the game the goal scorers, Colin Stein and Willie Johnstone, were the heroes.

But it was a tragedy that

this night of trial should have been spoiled by the fans.

For this should have been a night of celebration, it should have been a night of joy.

It should have been a celebration carnival for the Rangers fans who had waited so long for this European victory.

For the game, though, there can be nothing but praise.

Praise for the way the goals were scored, and praise too, for the way they refused to give in under that tremendous Russian fightback.

They lived dangerously to win this trophy—but they have won it.

At last the Ibrox trophy room will hold the European Cup Winners Cup.

And even the second half worries cannot take away the glory which was earned indeed in the epic battle across Europe.

It was just a tragedy for the thousands of decent fans who stayed in the stand and on the terracing that they could not see John Greag, that great Rangers captain, hold aloft the trophy that had eluded him for so long.

In a game of tremendous tension John Greig and Alex MacDonald were both booked by the Spanish referee.

But although the match was tough, it was not a dirty one.

Rangers—McCloy, Jardine, Mathieson; Greig, D. Johnstone, Smith; McLean, Conn, Stein, MacDonald, W. Johnston.

Dynamo—Pilgui; Basalaev, Dolmatov; Zhykov, Dolbanasov, Zhukov; Daidahyi, Jakubik, Sabo, Makovikov, Evruzhikin.

Referee—Jose Ortiz de Mendibil, Spain.

No. 1 for Rangers in Barcelona last night—and it's Colin Stein (left) evading a tackle to blast the ball past Dynamo 'keeper Pilgui.

The first of two goals for Willie Johnston as he rises between two Russian defenders to head in No. 2 for Rangers. Alex MacDonald (right) looks on.

Don wins title shot

SCOTTISH champion Don McMillan, 35-year-old Glasgow middleweight boxer, earned a crack at the British title with a fifth round win over Kevin Finnegan at the Bedfordshire Sporting Club last night.

Finnegan, younger brother of British and European light-heavyweight champion, Chris Finnegan, was odds-on favourite to win this final eliminator.

But the durable McMillan, who had won his previous

eight fights, seized what could be his last chance of a British title fight.

McMillan should now get a crack at champion Bunny Sterling for the British title.

The turning point came midway through the thrd third round when Finnegan was caught with a hard right hook. The punch opened a cut at the side of Finnegan's left eye.

Good work by his corner man repaired the damage but in the fifth round the cut was opened once more. At the end of the round referee Sid Nathan examined the cut and stopped the fight.

Daily Record

3p Friday, May 26, 1972 No. 23,878

20,000 FANS HAIL IBROX HEROES

REVELS IN THE RAIN!

THIS was it! The moment Rangers brought the European Cup-winners' Cup home to Ibrox—with 20,000 fans revelling in the rain.

On a red, white and blue-decked lorry, captain John Greig, his team-mates clustered around him, held the Cup aloft.

And slowly, proudly, the triumphant progress began—two circuits of the stadium,

STORY BY KEN STEIN.   PICTURES BY ERIC CRAIG

with cheering, cheering, all the way.

Many of the fans, just back from Barcelona, were still wearing souvenir sombreros.

They waved them and their banners and their scarves—and yelled themselves hoarse

Before the team appeared, a loudspeaker announcement had warned that "stringent action" would be taken

against anyone who invaded the rain-soaked pitch.

But, warnings or weather, nothing could dampen the good-natured enthusiasm of the crowd.

Earlier, Glasgow's Lord Provost John Mains had met Rangers chairman John Lawrence and the team when they flew into Prestwick Airport.

But all of that was just the curtain-raiser to the fantastic welcome at the stadium.

This was an Ibrox night of nights, a time to stand up and cheer.

And they did, 20,000 of them, like cheering had just been invented.

Police said later: "There was no trouble at the ground. Only two arrests were made —outside the stadium."

Willie's hat-trick —Back Page   **Follow, Follow—See Centre Pages**

Daily Record

3p Monday, May 29, 1972 No. 23,880

Death of the Royal Exile

BOAT FIRE KILLS TWO

CUSTOMERS at a lochside restaurant watched helplessly as two teenagers died aboard a blazing speedboat.

Would-be rescuers scrambled into boats and raced towards the burning motor boat . . .

By CHARLES BEATON

But the fierce heat from the flames kept them at bay—and they could only circle desperately as the 16-foot speedboat sank.

The drama happened as late-night customers left the Duck Bay Marina on Loch Lomondside.

There was a loud explosion—and flames lit the gale-swept loch.

In the boat were 19-year-old Hugh Moore, of 38 Cables Drive, Bonhill, and Phillip Graham, 19, of 5 Back Street, Renton, both Dunbartonshire.

Search

A third youth, 18-year-old Robert Dunn, flung himself overboard as flames ripped through the boat—and swam to safety on the shoreside.

Torch-light searchers found him early yesterday lying semi-conscious on a stretch of shingle.

An ambulance rushed Robert to the Vale of Leven Hospital—and after treatment for shock and exposure he was allowed to return to his home at 34 Cables Drive, Bonhill.

The search for the survivors was restarted at first light yesterday. But later a police spokesman said:

"We have found neither the boat nor the boys.

Drinks

Hugh's parents, William and Mary Moore were given sedatives after police broke the news of the tragedy.

And Phillip's 20-year-old sister, Rosemary, said: "He was all set to go to England for a new job. He said he was going out with his pals for a few drinks."

Last night a police spokesman said: "A man has been charged in connection with this incident.

"He will appear at Dumbarton Sheriff court tomorrow on theft charges."

The Duke and Duchess together, in exile . . . with one of the pet pugs they loved.

THE QUEEN INVITES DUCHESS TO BUCKINGHAM PALACE

THE Queen invited the Duchess of Windsor to stay at Buckingham Palace for the first time yesterday . . . the day her husband died.

The Duke, who was 77, died of cancer at his home in Paris.

And last night, a Buckingham Palace spokesman announced that his body will be flown to Britain by the R A F on Wednesday, accompanied by the Duchess.

He will lie in state at St. George's Chapel, Windsor, on Friday and Saturday.

On Monday, after a funeral service in the chapel, he will be buried, at his own wish, at Frogton Mausoleum, half a mile from Windsor Castle. The burial will be private.

The 75-year-old Duchess is expected to stay at Buckingham Palace at least until the day after the funeral.

In 1936, the Duke abdicated as Edward VIII to marry American divorcee Mrs Wallis Simpson, as the Duchess then was.

Shunned

After their marriage, the Duchess was never accepted by the Royal family, who until recently virtually shunned her.

The first real move towards any recognition came only 10 days ago when the Queen visited the Duke and Duchess during her State visit to France.

After months of illness, the end for the Duke came swiftly. He fell into a deep coma on Saturday night, with the Duchess at his bedside, and died at 2.30 a.m.

The Queen, who was told by phone, sent a telegram to the Duchess. In it, she said:

"I am so grieved to hear of the death of my uncle. Philip joins me in sending you our heartfelt sympathy.

"I know that my people will always remember him with gratitude and great affection.

"I am so glad that I was able to see him in Paris 10 days ago."

Westminster Hall, London, is traditionally where British monarchs lie in state, and last night there were protests over the choice of St. George's Chapel, Windsor, for the Duke.

Protests

Labour MP Geoffrey Rhodes, in a personal protest to the Queen and Mr Heath, said:

"It will be a matter of regret for many who have a deep personal regard for the Duke and Duchess, that he will be the first king who has not had a lying-in-

Continued on Back Page.

THE WORLD'S GREATEST LOVE STORY Centre Pages

Daily Record

3p   Wednesday, September 6, 1972   No. 23,963

4am: Germans admit airport bloodbath

HOSTAGES ALL DEAD

ALL eight Israeli Olympic hostages held by Arab terrorists were killed late last night as police gambled on a desperate bid to save them.

They died amid a hail of bullets while the Arabs and West German police and snipers fought a pitched battle on a darkened airfield.

Three of their Arab captors were also shot down and a fourth blew himself up with a

From ALEX CAMERON in the Olympic Village, Munich

grenade. Unconfirmed reports said that three others were in custody. One policeman was killed.

So the total death roll in the Olympics horror, which began early yesterday with the murder of two Israelis as the Arabs invaded their team quarters at the Games village, is now 15.

All day, after the Arabs' first shock moves

at dawn, the German authorities plotted and planned to defeat them.

And the master-plan was conceived—to let the terrorists believe they'd be allowed to fly out with their Israeli hostages.

But late last night, when that plan went into action, it all went tragically wrong.

Exploded

From the Games village, the Arabs and the hostages were flown by helicopter to Furstenfeldbruck military airfield where a Lufthansa jet was waiting to fly them to the Middle East.

As the helicopters, a fleet of three, landed guerillas got out to inspect the jet.

Police snipers, in hiding behind the aircraft, waited until the terrorists had gone back to the helicopter to get the hostages out.

Then they opened up, killing three of the Arabs and a police helicopter pilot who had been forced to stand in front of them as a shield.

All hell broke loose. Another Arab, seeing it was all up, committed suicide by exploding a grenade.

In the blast, one of the helicopters caught fire trapping people who were sheltering beneath it.

Horror

At first, the German authorities were exultant about the apparent success of their ambush.

"It was a military operation," they said. "We planned it hours in advance and it has gone very well."

But by early today the first dreadful doubts were being voiced.

An Olympic spokesman said: "We cannot yet say what the position is about the hostages. The situation is very confused."

It became much less confused . . . . more agonisingly clear when at 3.30 a.m., the official Olympic

A coffin with the body of one of the Israelis shot dead at the start of the Arab terrorist raid early yesterday is carried from the team quarters last night.

Continued on Back Page

THE FULL DRAMA— Pages 2 and 3, Centre Pages

Just One Big Happy Family

AND COUSIN PATRICK TOOK THE PICTURES

THIS is a picture of the most exclusive family in the world, taken to commemorate the Royal Silver Wedding anniversary.

Every inch has the regal touch, from the splendour of the Windsor backdrop to the photographer—the Earl of Lichfield, second cousin to the Queen.

The informality of this family group contrasts strongly with the stiff portraits behind of ancestors King George III and his wife, Queen Charlotte, who, 200 years ago, looked dignified for the artist.

Here's your guide to the royal line-up:

BACK row standing left to right—Lord Snowdon, the Duke of Kent, Prince Michael of Kent, Prince Philip, the Earl of St. Andrews (elder son of the Duke of Kent), Prince Charles, Prince Andrew, Angus Ogilvy and his son James.

SEATED on chairs, left to right—Princess Margaret, the Duchess of Kent (holding Lord Nicholas Windsor, her younger son), the Queen Mother, the Queen, Princess Anne, Marina Ogilvy, and her mother, Princess Alexandra.

SEATED on floor, left to right—Lady Sarah Armstrong-Jones, Viscount Linley (Princess Margaret's children), Prince Edward, Lady Helen Windsor (daughter of the Duke of Kent).

Today the Record takes you into a family occasion with the Royals.

FOUR PAGE SILVER WEDDING PULL-OUT
—PAGES 7, 8, 25, 26

Printed and published by Scottish Daily Record and Sunday Mail Ltd., Anderston Quay, Glasgow, G3 8DA, for I P C Newspapers Ltd., Holborn Circus, London, E.C.1. Registered at the Post

Daily Record

3p Tuesday, October 31, 1972 ★★★★ No. 24,010

SILVER WEDDING SPECIAL

Daily Record

SCOTLAND'S BIGGEST DAILY SALE

4p Friday, August 9, 1974 No. 24,557

'I shall resign as President at noon'

THE END

SO Richard Nixon has gone. And a great sigh of relief is heard throughout the land.

He held on to his mighty office with the tenacity of a dying man.

And all who still honour democracy are well rid of him.

HE GOES, deserted by his friends. Despised by his enemies.

HE GOES, condemned out of his own mouth by the tape-recordings which—by terrible irony—he once intended as part of his memoirs.

SHAMED

HE GOES, labelled a liar and a cynical traitor to the constitution he had sworn to preserve and defend.

And yet even from this, the sorriest episode in nearly 200 years of American independence, it is possible to take comfort.

If the most powerful nation

PAGE ONE COMMENT

on earth was shamed by her leader, she did not lose her self-respect.

For the fall of Richard Nixon was set in motion by men who fearlessly sought the truth—within a social system which eventually put truth above all else.

The White House was dirtied. But the dirt was not permitted to stay under the carpet.

It is also worth remembering that many other countries have had to tolerate heads of state who, by comparison, made Richard Nixon seem a paragon of virtue.

And if the presidency of Nixon is dead, unmourned, it may still be said—'' Long Live America.''

● **THE HAND-OVER**
PAGES 2 and 3

● **THE FALL OF TRICKY DICKY**
CENTRE PAGES

Daily Record

SCOTLAND'S BIGGEST DAILY SALE

5p Saturday, November 9, 1974 No. 24,635

Murder squad issue picture

FIND THIS EARL

LORD LUCAN . . separated from his wife a year ago.

UNION BOSS SCANLON DEFIES PICKETS

ENGINEERING union boss Hugh Scanlon defied pickets from his OWN staff yesterday as "blacklegs" fought to enter his OWN headquarters.

Police were called after scuffles broke out between the strikers—members of the office workers' union APEX—and their AUEW colleagues who tried to get into the HQ in Peckham, London.

Mr. Scanlon drove through amid shouts of "traitor to the trade union movement."

Conscience

Three other AUEW executive members, Bob Wright, Bill Johns and Les Dickson, also pushed their way through the pickets.

A spokesman for the "blacklegs" said the AUEW executive had left a return to work to the conscience of each member after a meeting last night.

After the clashes it was decided by the AUEW members to hold an emergency meeting to decide what further action they should take.

Official

Mr. Bill Knight, APEX branch chairman, said: "It's a disgusting situation against all trade union principles.

"A week last Friday when the strike was made official, the AUEW members assured us they would not cross our picket lines.

"They did not until they were ordered to come in at the meeting last night."

APEX is striking for more money.

NANNY DEAD.. WIFE FIGHTING FOR LIFE

THE COUNTESS

She ran screaming into pub.

MURDER squad detectives were hunting for the Seventh Earl of Lucan last night after his children's nanny was found brutally battered to death.

And as photographs of debonair, 39-year-old Lord Lucan were issued, his estranged wife fought for her life in hospital.

She had severe head injuries.

A special watch was being kept on several plush London clubs frequented by the playboy peer, who was once considered for the film role of James Bond.

The drama began late on Thursday night, when Lord Lucan's wife, Countess Veronica, fled screaming from her Victorian home in London's posh Belgravia.

Her face was covered in blood. She staggered into a pub 100

By JACK McEACHRAN

yards from her home, and collapsed in the arms of barman Derrick Whitehouse, 44.

He said last night: "She was screaming: 'I think my neck is broken.'

"She kept murmuring: 'My children, my children'."

Police raced to the house and forced the door.

Eton

In a blood-spattered basement room, they found a canvas tent-bag.

Inside it was stuffed the body of 29-year-old nanny Mrs Sandra Rivett.

Police took away a blood-stained piece of lead pipe.

Detectives went to Lord Lucan's home 100 yards away in Eaton Row.

But he was not at home.

Relatives later arrived at the Countess's home and took away her children, seven-year-old Lord Bingham, heir to his father's title, and his sisters, Lady Frances, 10, and Lady Camilla, four.

Lord Lucan, who is dark-haired and moustached, married his wife in 1963.

When the couple separated last year, the three children were made Wards of Court.

Lord Lucan's title dates back to the first baronet, Henry Bingham, who was made a Peer of Ireland in 1634.

He is a former lieutenant in the Coldstream Guards and was educated at Eton.

His great-great grandfather, the third Lord Lucan, was in charge of a cavalry detachment during the Crimean War.

He had a heated argument about the advisability of the Charge of the Light Brigade—but obeyed orders and sent the gallant 600 into "the valley of death."

At one stage, because of his looks and debonair appearance, the present Lord Lucan was considered for the James Bond film role.

And in 1966, film director Vittorio Da Sica spotted him playing baccarat in France's Deauville Casino and gave the peer a Paris screen test for a starring role opposite actress Shirley Maclaine in a film called "Woman Times Seven."

| **INSIDE TODAY** | **LAWYERS PROBE MERCY KILLING** —Page 3 | **SISTERS FIGHT FOR HAPPINESS** —Page 5 | **MILHENCH THE FORGER** —Page 11 |

Daily Record

SCOTLAND'S BIGGEST DAILY SALE

6p   Wednesday, March 17, 1976   No. 25,052

Queen says Yes to shock break-up

MARGARET AND TONY DIVORCE

After Harold

quits the bets are on Big Jim

FULL STORY —BACK PAGE

DIVORCE proceedings have begun between Princess Margaret and Lord Snowdon, I am reliably informed.

The Queen is expected to make this shock announcement shortly.

The news follows rumours linking Margaret with 28-year-old Roddy Llewellyn, son of former top show jumper Colonel Harry Llewellyn.

Since Princess Margaret, who is 45, went on her latest holiday to her bungalow on the Caribbean island of Mustique—which belongs to Scottish landowner Colin Tennant—the rumours have flared again.

Distress

There were pictures of Margaret and Roddy together in swimsuits on the island, sipping cool drinks in the tropical sun.

Roddy was described as a "close companion."

It was later reported legal discussions on the marriage had been taking place—culminating in a conference of senior counsel last Saturday.

Last night a Palace official told me: "Everything possible has been done to make the couple patch up their differences.

"But the situation has become untenable—not only for the Snowdons. It has also become a cause of great distress for the Queen.

"It has been obvious for several months that the Snowdon household has been far from

Lawyers in secret meeting at Palace

By AUDREY WHITING

happy, and no one in Palace circles will be in the least surprised to learn that the marriage has foundered."

I am told that in the event of a divorce the two children of the marriage, David, Viscount Linley, and Lady Sarah Armstrong-Jones, will divide their time between both parents.

Duty

A close friend of the Royal Family said last night: "It will not come as a surprise to anyone close to the Queen if Tony and Margaret decide to divorce.

"It would certainly be on the grounds of mutual incompatability."

It is likely that Lord Snowdon, who is 46, will soon move out of the apartment where he and

Princess Margaret now live in Kensington Palace.

For some years now they have gone their separate ways. They have had a different circle of friends and have often taken separate holidays.

Margaret, fifth in line to the succession, was only 25 when she first had to make the choice between duty and love—and decided on duty.

The man she wanted to marry was Battle of Britain hero Group Captain Peter Townsend.

But Court, Church and State saw a bar to marriage. Townsend had been involved in a divorce.

Margaret became engaged to Lord Snowdon—then Anthony Armstrong-Jones—four years later.

Last night Lord Snowdon was flying to Australia to open an exhibition of his own photographs.

RODDY LLEWELLYN
Island companion

Daily Record

SCOTLAND'S BIGGEST DAILY SALE

6p   Saturday, June 5, 1976   ★★   No. 25,121

The party's over for the high life boss who ended up selling knickers

Cochrane and his beauty queen wife in prosperous days.

Times have changed and so has Cochrane

JOKER JAILED

THE jokes and the high life were over last night for former Rotary Tools boss **Maurice James Cochrane**.

He once lashed out thousands on parties. He was the most bizarre businessman Glasgow had seen.

But now he is starting a 12-month jail sentence for bribing officials with sex and gifts.

Cochrane, 51, was stunned as he left the dock at Glasgow Sheriff Court.

He could only mutter: "I've no money to pay these fines.

He had not grasped that the total of £800 in fines would not have to be paid—because the main jail sentence, of 12 months, cancelled them out.

He had been given several jail terms, to run concurrently, with the alternative of fines.

His parting words put his downfall in a nutshell.

Before the trial began almost five weeks ago, he was reduced to selling knickers and nighties at an open-air market.

The jury of nine men and six women took almost six hours to find Cochrane guilty of eight charges.

He was cleared on eight other charges.

His co-accused and former sales director at Rotary, James Drysdale, 38, was found not guilty on all charges.

On three of the charges Cochrane was convicted on the jury added riders that he had paid out money to officials under conditions and threats.

Contract

Two of these referred to payments to Walter Renfrew, of Scott's Shipyard at Greenock.

The jury found that Renfrew had made it clear that Rotary would have to give him monthly payments before the firm was allowed to tender at Scott's.

And they said Cochrane made several payments amounting to £400 to Robert McKay, the chief buyer of Chrysler at Linwood, after he threatened to terminate Rotary's contract.

Cochrane was also found guilty of providing the services of blonde model Anna Grunt to NCB production manager John Sim as an inducement or reward for showing favour to Rotary.

Sheriff Stewart Bell told him: "This is not a court of morals.

"I must try to assess sentence in the light of all the circumstances

TURN TO PAGE 2

THE ROTARY TOOLS AFFAIR

MAGIC...
That was my life wit
Cochrane

The truth about Ellie
CAROLYN last night took her place on one of Cochrane's jokes—Ellie the elephant. This was the toy on which job applicants sat—being told it was a lie detector.
" Jimmy loved it," said Carolyn.
Picture: BERT PATERSON

THE beautiful young wife of 51-year-old Maurice James Cochrane spoke yesterday of her five amazing years with former boss of Rotary Tools.

Secretary Carolyn Schulz, 27, a former public schoolgirl and beauty queen, said: " I know it's easy for people to look at the two of us now and wonder why I married him.

" But you should have seen him in those days. He was a flamboyant, forceful character.

" I know he attracted girls, and I know he was involved with some.

" But I wouldn't have married him if he was an angel. He is my sort of man.

" I must admit, it took me a few weeks to get used to him telling me to ' F . . . off ' and ' F . . . come here,' etc.

ROUGH

" But to him it meant nothing at all.

" In dictating memos, Jimmy said exactly what he thought. Sometimes they were pretty rough and hurtful.

" He would say to me: ' Send a stinking memo to so-and-so about such-and-such a thing.'

" I would therefore write a stinking memo and often Jimmy wouldn't even see it before it went out. That's how much he trusted me.

" He was always open to suggestions and also to criticisms, although sometimes he might just tell you to ' p . . . off.' "

He became easily bored with the more " sooky " members of the staff, said Carolyn, adding: " In fact, he was far too soft with many of his employees.

" My working conditions couldn't have been bettered anywhere. He gave me my own office with a communicating cloakroom.

" It was carpeted, curtained and decorated—in baby pink ! "

Carolyn found Cochrane was a complete hypochondriac. If he had the slightest sore throat or even an ache in his finger he would call a doctor.

Carolyn said: " He insisted on antibiotic injections for almost anything.

" Even when we went 20 miles by car, Jimmy insisted on taking with him a bag full of every item sold by Boots, together with a portable oxygen cylinder."

She went on: " When his health got pretty low a few years back he asked me to go and stay with him and his wife Audrey, from whom he is now divorced.

" I was not his mistress at that time. He wanted to continue his business from his bedside.

" All night long he would be awake, moaning and groaning, convinced he would die."

WORRIES

Cochrane started taking notes of all his body functions.

Carolyn said: " Every time he went to the toilet he would record what had happened, the colour of his urine and how much, the exact time, and so on.

" I was convinced he needed a psychiatrist, but he didn't take at all kindly to this idea.

" Sometimes he would call me in the small hours of the morning to discuss all his worries.

" We would talk away for hours and I would often fall asleep on the floor beside his bed.

" Eventually he left his wife and we started to live together."

Carolyn herself was mentioned in court, in one of the charges.

It was alleged Cochrane rigged the beauty contest for Miss

Airpower (GB) 19 which she won, but jury was directed return a not gu verdict.

The couple married Glasgow last summe

" Some people kept saying to me that should wait until end of the cas Carolyn said.

" But I wanted to sh him that I loved and was going to sta by him.

" I know people h suggested that he as me to marry him so t I couldn't be forced give evidence for Crown against him. that's a load of rubbi

" I think the court c happened because was just flamboy Jimmy Cochrane.

CRAZY

" If he had been businessman in p stripes living a nor dull life, he wo never have come to attention of the polic

" Jimmy just was like that. Life with was a crazy, cra existence, full of f full of tremende laughs.

" I don't like to t about sex, but rea our love wasn't that s of thing.

" Anyway, Jimmy years was so filled with tranquillisers a other sorts of pills t sex was far from thoughts."

Carolyn al spoke of the tr abroad, or in t U K, that we constantly delaye cancelled, re-arrange then cancelled again.

She said: " Once got on a plane Jim would become alm hysterical as couldn't bring hims to use the lavatory the aircraft—and needed to go at certa times, according to ' schedule.'

" Even when we we abroad, Jimmy turn down invitations to anywhere, and refused to leave bedroom and priva bathroom."

But that life is over.

HOW CAROLYN SAW THE PARTY GIRLS

CAROLYN SCHULZ saw dolly birds come and go in the crazy world of Rotary Tools.

What did she really think of them, the girls who hit the headlines, as their stories unfolded during the trial?

Carolyn liked Maretta Barnsley. " She behaved well at the several parties she attended.

" She always stayed later than the regulation hours set down by the Cosmopolitan Agency but received an extra fiver or sometimes more for this.

" Miss Barnsley was used as an escort on the night of Jimmy's birthday party, the same night when three men from Inverness were flown down for it.

" Afterwards she told us she had slept with one of the men and that she had enjoyed a lovely evening."

Of Anna Grunt, she said: " After the incident with John Sim of the Coal Board—that was the first time a girl was paid to sleep with a customer —she came into the office to pester Jimmy for more work and to be paid.

" I thought she was a ghastly type of female. She said she would do any type of work for Rotary as she needed the money to maintain her expensive life-style."

Drunk

Jennifer McGregor, she claimed, got drunk at one of Rotary's small parties and tried to get Cochrane for herself.

" She got hold of me in the office kitchen and poured hot coffee all down my new trouser suit," said Carolyn.

AND MADNESS

AMES COCHRANE set out on the road that led to his downfall long before he me to trial.

But when the fall came it was spectacular.

FROM managing director of Rotary Tools with the eet life of booze, parties, dolly birds and tinental trips.

TO a barrow boy in the open air market at gliston, near Edinburgh.

Bonkers

" Knickers ! " he boomed. " Knickers. That's what in now. Ladies' briefs and gent's Y-fronts.

" It's my kind of life."

Cochrane admitted that in business he was ruth-s, but only because he ught that was the way usiness man should

e said: " I was mad, of urse. Stark raving akers. But it was the essure of business ich made me like t.

I was a bastard, of urse I was, but it was t a big act like a farce stage.

I had a special voice shouting at salesmen o weren't doing their s properly and ther one, a softer, re encouraging one, praising them.

I was a born sales-n with plenty of drive erhaps I should have yed a salesman.

But I went to the top I played the game. n't think there was no h thing as corruption til the big bad Jimmy hrane came on the siness scene.

Theft

Bunging is a way of in business, perhaps cceptable but never-less there.

I had 1500 to 2000 tomers at Rotary and e or ten of them were ting regular cash ts.

We didn't readily e them but if certain portant customers anded it, we had to.

And they did, they d to get as much out Rotary as they could.

If word had got und that we never e hand-outs then ary could have been ned.

Cockney, Cochrane t school at the age of and ran away to join Army.

ut when they dis-ered he wasn't old ugh to shave, he was fed out.

wice more he joined but had to leave ecause of my nerves."

ver the next 30 years hrane was an actor rep, a fairground rker, a deep sea herman, a cinema nager, a dance hall endant and a sales-n.

e has also been in jail ce before.

e said: "At Glasgow riff Court in 1958 I four months for ling a van contain-

That was the way I did business

ing £100 worth of carpets.

"And at Watford in 1959, I got four years for housebreaking, office breaking, and a string of thefts.

" I'm not proud to admit it."

It was in 1965 that Cochrane started up Rotary Tools with another man in a £6-a-week office.

It went from strength to strength, and was taken over by Thistle Industrial Holdings Ltd, of Edinburgh, in 1971.

Cochrane's office was designed in the style of a Zulu kraal, the walls with spears on the furry wallpaper, his desk encased in bamboo.

Parties

In the corner was a cycling machine. He would often hold con-ferences, pedalling away on it—sometimes with little or no clothes on.

There was " Bungo-Ho," a tall polystyrene statute before which salesmen had to kneel and pray for orders.

And Ellie, the toy elephant. A girl applying for a clerkess job was asked to sit astride it by Cochrane, who told her it was a lie detector.

And then there were the lavish parties.

The big one was attended by 4000 people. Jazzman Dizzy Gillespie, hostesses, belly dancers and strippers.

It cost more than £20,000—just to cele-brate the opening of a small extension.

But now the party's over—and Cochrane is in jail.

THE OFFICE *Fur and spears on the walls, bamboo on the desk . . . this was Cochrane's Zulu den at Rotary Tools.*

THE STALL *Cochrane—without his hairpiece—takes a back seat for once as his wife Carolyn sorts through the knickers.*

Record dossier by ARNOT McWHINNIE, GORDON AIRS, TERRY HOUSTON and CHARLES BEATON

SUNDAY mail

9p   July 4, 1976   No. 3529

3 am NEWS

Troops rescue plane hostages

ISRAELI commandoes late last night rescued hostages held by pro-Palestinian terrorists at Uganda's Entebbe airport.

In a daring lightning raid, the troops poured out of three transport aircraft straight into the terminal where the hostages were being held.

Within minutes, it was all over.

But it was not until 2 a.m. that Tel Aviv announced the rescue.

A spokesman said: "Tonight IDF (Israeli Defence Forces) extricated and freed the hostages, including the Air France crew, from the airport at Entebbe."

It gave no further details.

Secret

However, the aircraft stopped briefly at Nairobi while a number of injured people were given emergency treatment on the runway.

And one of the Israelis is reported to have said:

THREAT TO OLYMPICS

THE MONTREAL Olympics came a step nearer to collapse last night—with only 13 days to go.

For the Games could now founder over politics, with the USA threatening to pull out if the Games are declared unofficial.

And the International Amateur Athletic Federation and the International Judo Federation called for the Olympics to be cancelled.

The rumpus broke when Canada refused to allow Taiwan athletes to compete as representatives of China, because Canada recognises the Communist regime.

ISRAELIS STAGE SHOCK RAID

"The operation is over. The guerrillas have been eliminated."

Meanwhile, another Air France jet, standing by in Nairobi for a possible flight to take the hostages out of Uganda after negotiations with the hijackers, was being prepared for take-off.

But there were no plans for the plane to go to Entebbe until more information was received.

The hijackers had threatened to kill all their hostages at Noon today unless their demand for the release of 53 prisoners in five countries was met.

The Airbus has been at Entebbe Airport, near Kampala, since Monday

HAPPY BIRTHDAY AMERICA
200 YEARS YOUNG TODAY

OK son, NOW you can go out to play.

| See Bing Crosby FREE! —PAGE 3 | The truth about Carter —PAGE 13 | Scotland's little America —CENTRE PAGES |

SUNDAY mail

9p   July 25, 1976   3532

1 a.m. OLYMPIC SPECIAL

GOLDEN BOY WILKIE

YOU'RE ON A WINNER WITH THE MAIL!

TODAY the Sunday Mail would like to say thanks to the thousands of new readers who have joined us in the past year.

Our sales figures for January to June show an increase of

7694

copies each week on the same period last year, bringing our circulation to

760,031

And that increase makes the Sunday Mail unique.

Every other national Sunday paper whose figures were published in the magazine Newsagent and Bookshop reported a decrease in sales.

We're delighted to have won all these new friends. We'd also like to thank the readers who have stayed with us—and our friends the newsagents who helped to make it all possible.

All in all, it's been a good week for the Sunday Mail.

● Our horse, **PUB SPY**, won his first race last week, as we report on Page 29.

● Our famous columnist **THE JUDGE** continues on his winning way; getting £200 back for a honeymoon couple; finding a family's lost furniture; keeping an innocent woman out of the hands of a debt collector. Read it all on Page 15.

It just goes to show: You're on a winner with the Sunday Mail.

Keep backing us . . . and we'll keep backing you!

FOR Scot David Wilkie, the moment has come . . . the moment he has dreamed about for years.

He has won an Olympic gold.

Victory came at Montreal last night in the 200 metres breast stroke when he shattered the world record by more than three seconds.

FUTURE

But Wilkie's race of a lifetime will also be his last. He is quitting big-time swimming. And just as soon as the Games are finished he will be flying to see mum and dad in Scotland.

He will then return to America to finish his studies before coming home for good.

THE QUEEN WORRIES AS ANNE TAKES A TUMBLE

FOR the Queen a moment of anxiety.

It came after Princess Anne took a bad tumble from her horse in Olympic cross-country trials.

For more than two minutes she lay dazed in the mud . . . then she remounted.

Last night a Royal doctor said the Princess was not badly hurt.

The full Montreal report begins on Back Page

Daily Record

SCOTLAND'S BIGGEST DAILY SALE

6p   Wednesday, December 1, 1976   No. 25,273

MAD AXEMEN KILL THREE

Mone . . . Siege in a school

McCulloch . . . He attacked a chef

Picture by **DOUGLAS SALTERI**

A NIGHT of horror is over . . . a night of horror in which three people were axed to death and two others were seriously injured.

Now the last tokens of tragedy lie beside a quiet country road . . . two battered police hats, a warder's, and a blood-stained knife.

Last night two mental patients were recaptured after four hours of violence.

Four horrifying hours in which patient Ian Simpson—a double murderer—and recreation officer Neil McLellan died inside the State mental hospital at Carstairs, Lanarkshire.

The third victim was village policeman George Taylor. He and a mate were attacked in the village near the hospital.

Last night the Scottish Office named the two escapees as Robert Francis Mone, 28, and Thomas Neil McCulloch, 26.

Stabbed

Eight years ago Mone, a private in the Gordon Highlanders, held 11 schoolgirls at gunpoint in Dundee and shot dead a woman teacher.

Thomas McCulloch was sent to Carstairs in 1973 for an attack on a chef at the Erskine Bridge Hotel.

Both were later found to be insane.

As the massive search got underway, police tried to piece together what happened after the escape.

It is thought that after the attack inside the hospital, a man donned a warder's uniform and led another man out of the hospital.

Then, in Carnwath, a few miles away, PC Taylor and PC John Gillies were approached in their Panda car.

Continued on Back Page

TWO DAYS OF HORROR—Pages 2 and 3

SCOTLAND'S ASSEMBLY

Full details of the Devolution Bill—Turn to Pages 14 and 15

SPORTS mail

It's cheers all the way for Aintree's record-breaker

TREBLE RUM!

THIS is Red Rum, the wonder horse who has made National Hunt history.

He did it by winning the Grand National for the third time at Aintree yesterday.

After taking the lead at Becher's second time round, Red Rum—9-1 joint second favourite—never looked in danger and came home alone, 25 lengths

CHARLOTTE ALMOST MADE IT

CHARLOTTE BREW, the first woman to take part in the race, faced disappointment when she had to withdraw four fences from home.

The 21-year-old, who got a tremendous reception from race fans, had kept Barony Fort clear of trouble in a great attempt to complete the course.

But her mount refused four times at that fence, leaving her well behind, and she reluctantly called it a day.

Mrs Judith Brew said of her daughter: "Charlotte was so determined to complete the course."

Wonder horse makes history

Picture: ANDREW ALLAN

clear of Churchtown Boy, last year's third Eyecatcher and The Pilgarlic.

It was the easiest win for 20 years, to a tumultuous reception, the Liverpool legend galloped the rest into the ground, as he had done when winning in 1973 and '74.

His three National victories took him to overall winnings total of £114,000—a National Hunt record.

Immediately after the

> "Since Billy Ellison left Red Rum may have been a little stale—but he's coming back to top form and there's no reason why he can't win the Grand National again if the going suits him."

race, winning trainer Ginger McCain, said: "I think he will be back again next year."

And McCain's words should be noted. For he tipped Red Rum for yesterday's race in last week's Sunday Mail.

With two seconds in the last two years, Red Rum has the remarkable record of never being out of the first two in five attempts.

As usual, Aintree's giant

● Here's what Red Rum's trainer, Ginger McCain, said in last week's Sunday Mail.

fences took their toll.

Andy Pandy, 15-2 favourite, fell when in a clear lead at Becher's on the second circuit.

Pengrail got only as far as the first fence, which also claimed Duffle Coat, Spittin' Image, Willy What and War Bonnet.

Refused

Cheltenham Gold hero Davy Lad managed only two fences more and with the fate of Inycarra, Royal Thrust and Burrator at the same third obstacle the field was quickly reduced to 33.

The front runners seemed ill-fated all through. Sebastian V fell at Bechers' first time round when in a clear lead, Boom Docker refused on the second circuit when about 15 lengths clear and

Andy Pandy also came down when way out in front.

But once Red Rum had gone clear, there was no doubt about the historic result.

Winning jockey Tommy Stack, who was in tears, said: "I was always confident I would win. The ground came just right for Red Rum and he was always going nicely."

Amateur jockey John Cardon (40), was taken to Walton General Hospital after falling with his own horse Huperade at the first fence.

Only 11 of the 42 starters completed the course

Two horses had to be destroyed. Winter Rain, which fell and broke its neck at Becher's on the first circuit, and Zeta's Son, which broke a leg in a fall at Valentine's

SCOTLAND'S bookies took a hammering with Red Rum's runaway win.

One of the worst hit was the Joe Coral chain, which featured an advert in yesterday's morning papers with the heading: "They say Red Rum will walk it in the Grand National."

And thousands of punters seemed to read no further . . . and backed the winner at a money-spinning 9-1.

BACKFIRED

If they had read the Coral ad fully, they would have also seen the words: "We think he'll be pushing his luck. And you?"

A Coral spokesman said later: "It looks as if this advert backfired on us.

"Bets of £100 or more on the horse to win were commonplace at our offices in Scotland.

"A fantastic number of small punters and housewives also had a

ONLY THE BOOKIES ARE SAD

flutter on the winner."

A spokesman for William Hill said: "We won't know how much we've lost until Monday—but it will run into thousands."

And a spokesman for William Harrower, one of the East Coast's biggest bookies said: "It's been a disaster day for us. Red Rum was a good winner, but not for the bookies— we've been taken to the cleaners."

HOW YOUR HORSE FINISHED—PAGE 39

Edited, printed and published by Scottish Daily Record and Sunday Mail Limited, Anderston Quay, Glasgow G3 8DA (041-248 7000). Registered at the Post Office as a newspaper.   ©️ Scottish Daily Record and Sunday Mail Limited 1977. A Mirror Group newspaper.

WEDNESDAY August 17 1977

Daily Record

7p   SCOTLAND'S BIGGEST DAILY SALE   No. 25,491

ELVIS DEAD

Vain battle to save dying rock king

From ANTHONY DELANO in New York

ELVIS PRESLEY, the legendary king of rock and roll, died last night in Memphis, Tennessee.

The 42-year-old singer was found unconscious in his mansion house home by his road manager Joe Esposito.

Esposito vainly tried to revive him with the kiss of life.

Presley was then rushed to the emergency unit in the nearby Baptist Hospital.

He died shortly afterwards—unable to draw breath.

Mourning

Shortly before Elvis's death, friends said he had been grieving deeply over the anniversary of the death of his mother, two days previously.

Ironically, Mrs Presley was 42—the same age as Elvis—when she died in August 1958.

In Britain, pop fans went into immediate mourning. And the Record news desk was swamped with calls—many from sobbing girls—about Elvis.

Pop radio stations across the country started playing only Elvis songs as a mark of respect.

Todd Slaughter, secretary of 12,000-strong Elvis Fan Club in Britain, said: "I am heartbroken. He was part of our lives.

"The roots of pop music have been taken

TURN TO BACK PAGE

Elvis Presley . . . recently received treatment for heroin addiction.

FAREWELL TO THE KING—Centre Pages

THURSDAY August 18 1977

Daily Record

7p   SCOTLAND'S BIGGEST DAILY SALE   No. 25,492

THE FANS WAIT AND WEEP

Thousands queue in rain to say goodbye

The king is dead . . . and one Presley fan can't hold back the tears.

THE PRIVATE HELL OF PRESLEY'S PALACE
—Pages 8 and 9

Fans jam the gates waiting to see their hero as he lies in state

GRIEF-STRICKEN fans of Elvis Presley last night fought outside his mansion in Memphis, Tennessee.

As their hero lay in state, scuffles broke out when the gates were opened so they could pay their final respects.

Heavily outnumbered, the police tried to regulate the flow of mourners, letting in groups of 50 or 60 at a time, then closing the gates on the faces of angry, frustrated fans.

Guitars

Since the news of the singer's death on Tuesday, the fans have gathered in their thousands round the 18-bedroom home at 3764 Elvis Presley Boulevard.

Last night as the heavens

From JILL EVANS in Memphis

opened up drenching them in rain hundreds broke down and wept.

Others flatly refused to believe the king was dead.

"Please tell me it isn't true," moaned one woman as she clung to the latticed gate decorated with musical notes and guitars.

Someone had pinned a white cross with pink roses to the wall. Other heart-shaped wreaths were dotted around.

Before the fans were allowed in, every now and again the gates of the mansion were opened for family members and friends.

"That's Priscilla," murmured the crowd as Presley's divorced wife went in.

The resources of Memphis have been stretched to the limit since Presley's death.

Extra telephone operators

have had to be taken on to cope with the calls from fans from all corners of the earth.

Every hotel was booked out and police and ambulancemen were worked off their feet.

Meanwhile as the fans maintained their sorrowful and sometimes violent vigil last night President Jimmy Carter joined in the flood of tributes.

"Elvis Presley's death deprives our country of part of itself," he said. "He was unique and irreplaceable."

Private

The real headache in crowd control will come at 8.15 tonight when Presley's body is laid in a family crypt at Forest Hill cemetery.

It will be a private ceremony.

The singer's mother rests in a nearby grave.

● Dr Jerry Francisco, the Memphis medical examiner, said the preliminary findings of a post mortem did not suggest Presley was a heavy drug user.

Who are Primary Five?

ANOTHER COLOUR EXCLUSIVE CENTRE PAGES

Daily Record

7p   SCOTLAND'S BIGGEST DAILY SALE   No. 25,542

BING IS DEAD

Heart attack after playing golf

Killer girl fled to have a baby

CHILD killer Mary Bell escaped from jail because she wanted to have a BABY.

She had never slept with a man—and wanted to know what it was like, it was claimed yesterday.

And she believed that if she became a mother, public sympathy would increase her chance of being released.

Mary Bell, now 21, was jailed indefinitely in Newcastle when she was only 11 years old, for strangling two boys aged four and three.

The amazing motive for her escape from an open prison last month was revealed when two men appeared in court in Derby yesterday, accused of harbouring her.

Chance

One of them was Clive Shirtcliffe. He was the first man she met in the outside world—and by sheer chance he had a fixation about her.

The court was told Shirtcliffe knew all about her from his former girlfriend, Sue Moore, who spent 10 months in jail with her.

During Bell's 50 hours of freedom, they spent two nights together, and she baby sat for two children of a family.

Shirtcliffe, 29, and Keith Hibbert, 32, both of Derby, admitted harbouring Bell. They were given six-month suspended sentences and fined £100 each.

Bing Crosby with his wife Kathryn at the London Palladium last month.

Crosby the golfer

BING CROSBY, one of the greatest showbusiness personalities of all time, died yesterday playing golf.

He collapsed with a heart attack while walking from the 18th hole of a course near Madrid. The 76-year-old singer was rushed to hospital, but it was too late.

Bing, whose "White Christmas" recording was the biggest seller ever, was in Britain just three weeks ago.

He opened a British tour before an audience of 2100 packed into the Guildhall at Preston, Lancs.

Then there was a season at the London Palladium, which ended last Saturday.

Yet the Old Groaner, as he was nicknamed, had never really recovered from an injury last March when he fell 25 feet from a stage in California. He ruptured a disc in his back.

Last night Bing's 42-year-old widow, Kathryn Grant, who flew back to the USA on Wednesday, was told of his death as she was making a TV recording in San Francisco.

She said later: "He died as he would have wished—playing a good game of golf with good friends."

The couple would

RECORD REPORTER

have been married 20 years this week.

Meanwhile, tributes were pouring in.

Frank Sinatra said: "It's more than I can take. He was the father of my career."

Bob Hope said: "I can't believe it. I'm absolutely numb."

In Britain, Prime Minister James Callaghan said: "I'm very sad. Bing Crosby's many works of charity in Britain put us deeply in his debt."

Theatre

One of those charities was the Ochtertyre Theatre in Crieff, Perthshire.

Bing became a patron in 1975.

His most famous films were the "Road" series, also starring Bob Hope and Dorothy Lamour.

The three of them had planned to do another "Road" film next Spring.

The title: "Road To The Fountain Of Youth."

YOU'LL BE THERE!

AND YOU CAN GET A SUPER FLOWER OF SCOTLAND TEE-SHIRT

TV

WEEKEND GUIDE TO THE BEST ON THE BOX

THE KING WHO MADE IT LOOK SO EASY —Page 9

Centre Pages   Starts on Page 14

SUNDAY mail

12p   January 8, 1978   3605

GROSVENOR IS GUTTED

> **'It's likely that regular firemen would have had the blaze under control long before now'**
>
> —A POLICE SPOKESMAN LAST NIGHT

THE night sky of Glasgow's West End is lit up as flames destroy a four-star hotel.

This was the scene last night at the height of the most spectacular blaze since the start of the firemen's strike.

Every available military firefighter in the city was called in as flames spread throughout the four floors of the 100-bedroomed Reo Stakis hotel in Great Western Road.

Within 30 minutes of the start of the outbreak—in the kitchen of the grill room—smoke and flames had spread throughout the length of the building.

A senior Naval officer said: "It's ablaze from end to end. The building looks a total loss."

And a police spokesman said three hours after fire fighters had arrived at the blazing hotel: "It's still spreading and there are still no signs of it being contained.

"It's likely that regular firemen would have had it under control long before now."

As flames shot more than 30ft. into the air, residents in luxury apartments adjoining the building were evacuated.

Many packed suitcases with over-night clothes. One elderly couple were seen loading a car with their collection of valuable oil paintings.

Earlier a honeymoon couple were among 15 guests who managed to escape safely from the burning hotel.

One of the hotel porters who helped alert the guests was himself trapped on a balcony. He was

Continued on Page Five

TV mail
A GREAT NEW PULL-OUT SECTION
Page 19

WHY TOWNSEND DIDN'T TELL ALL
Pages 14 and 15

£1000 AND A CORTINA MUST BE WON
Page 35

MONDAY June 5 1978

Daily Record

8p   SCOTLAND'S BIGGEST DAILY SALE   NO. 25,739

New shock for our World Cup squad

SCOTS STAR IN DRUG STORM

And here's Ally's answer to that Peru shambles

DON'T BLAME ME!

A worried and thoughtful Ally MacLeod last night
Picture: ERIC CRAIG

Willie Johnston . . . now he faces ban

ALLY MacLEOD'S position as Scotland team boss was under serious threat last night.

Football officials and fans hit out after the shame of going down 3-1 to Peru in the World Cup.

But MacLeod was defiant. He said bluntly: " Don't blame me. I did all I could in the match preparations.

" But the team were toothless tigers. How the hell it happened I do not know. We were a shambles.

GLORY

"I cannot understand it. In the opening 15 minutes I was sure we were on the way to World Cup glory."

MacLeod spoke as millions of fans at home—and the hundreds in Argentina—were giving voice to their anger after the humiliation of Saturday night's defeat.

Ally's Army feels it is the laughing stock of the world.

And there's no doubt where most of them put the blame—on the team manager.

Many fans are already planning to leave Argentina without waiting for the next two games.

Those who are staying were telling reporters: "If you see Ally MacLeod ask him one question—when is Jock Stein taking over Scotland?"

Officials, too, are deeply concerned. Chief of selectors, Tom Lauchlan, hit out: "We want to know what the blazes went wrong.

BLASTED

"We have had an informal meeting and we want answers, not excuses. We are perturbed and angry—for ourselves and the people back home."

Tommy Younger, former Scotland goalkeeper and now vice-president of the SFA, was furious. He said:

"We should have blasted them off the park in the first 20 minutes, but we collapsed.

"Yes, there will be an investigation at the top, but we must get these next two games won."

There is anger in the Scotland camp and bitterness that "Muhammad Ally," man of many words, seems to be shrugging off any criticism of himself and laying everything at the players' feet.

One official said: "I am convinced that we did not do our homework against Peru. We were left looking like babes in the wood."

It now seems certain that Ally MacLeod, without a contract, will not be in the job if Scotland have to pack their bags for home at the end of this week.

WORLD Cup star Willie Johnston plunged Scotland into a drugs scare last night.

A test made on him immediately after the defeat by Peru proved positive.

Now the winger faces expulsion from the tournament and a ban of up to a year from all international football.

The tests were made on Johnston and Kenny Dalglish—both picked at random by FIFA officials—and two Peruvians.

Banned

They should also have been informed about sleepings pills, anti-flu pills or anything of that sort.

The fact that the Scots

By KEN GALLACHER

Only Johnston proved positive.

The West Brom player takes an anti-histamine drug for hay fever. This would also show up on the computer used in the tests.

But either Johnston or the Scots team doctors were obliged to tell the FIFA officials of any such treatment at the time the tests were made.

stayed silent may weigh heavily against them.

A statement from FIFA said last night that the drug discovered in Johnston's urine was Fencamfamin.

It is on the banned list and is described as a "psycho-motor stimulant."

Mr Jim Bannerman, of the British Pharmaceutical Society, said last night: " This drug is normally used for fatigue and depression after illness.

" It has no relationship whatsoever to hay fever."

Johnston will now have another test today. An SFA spokesman refused to comment last night.

ALLY'S ANGRY ARMY

Turn to the Back Page

Daily Record

8p   SCOTLAND'S BIGGEST DAILY SALE   No. 25,792

£5000 BAIL FOR FOUR ON CONSPIRACY CHARGE

THORPE ACCUSED OF DEATH PLOT

Jeremy Thorpe . . . he smiled and chatted in the courtroom.

By SIDNEY YOUNG

JEREMY THORPE, the former leader of the Liberal Party, was accused yesterday of plotting the murder of ex male model Norman Scott.

He appeared along with three other men at a 21 minute hearing in Minehead Magistrates Court in Somerset. The others were:

DAVID HOLMES, 47, a former treasurer of the Liberal Party and best man at Thorpe's first marriage.

JOHN LE MESURIER, 44, a businessman, from St. Bride Major, Bridgend, Wales.

GEORGE DEAKIN, 35, a club boss and gaming machine company executive from Port Talbot, Wales.

The charge read "That between October 1, 1968 and November 1, 1977, in the county of Devon and elsewhere, they conspired together and with others to murder Norman Scott."

The maximum penalty for this offence is life imprisonment.

Smile

All four men were remanded on £5000 bail until September 12 and ordered to surrender, with certain conditions, their passports.

There was strict police security at the red brick courthouse on the edge of Exmoor when the defendants arrived separately in cars with their lawyers.

They were driven straight

Continued on Page Four

The decision facing Thorpe →
—See Pages 4 and 5

DAVID HOLMES

GEORGE DEAKIN

JOHN LE MESURIER

YOUR BIG WEEKEND TV GUIDE   STARTS ON PAGE 12

SATURDAY March 3 1979

Daily Record

8p   SCOTLAND'S BIGGEST DAILY SALE   No. 25,955

SCOTLAND'S VITAL VERDICTS

	YES	NO
WESTERN ISLES	6218 28%	4933 22%
ORKNEY	2104 15%	5439 39%
SHETLAND	2020 14%	5466 37%

YES: 33% NO: 31%

A NATION DIVIDED

	YES	NO
HIGHLAND	44,973 33%	43,274 32%
GRAMPIAN	94,944 28%	101,485 30%
TAYSIDE	91,482 31%	93,325 32%
FIFE	86,252 35%	74,436 31%
LOTHIAN	187,221 33%	186,421 33%
BORDERS	20,746 27%	30,780 40%

1,230,937
voted for an
Assembly

1,153,502
voted against

THE YES
MAJORITY WAS...
77,435

36% DIDN'T VOTE

	YES	NO
CENTRAL	71,296 36%	59,105 30%
STRATHCLYDE	596,519 34%	508,599 29%
DUMFRIES and GALLOWAY	27,162 26%	40,239 39%

FULL STORY AND ANALYSIS—Pages 2 and 3

SATURDAY March 15 1980

Daily Record

10p   SCOTLAND'S BIGGEST DAILY SALE   No. 26,274

JIM with manager Terry Lawless, right, and his trophy.   Picture: ERIC CRAIG

BIG FIGHT SPECIAL

BANG BANG BANG

JIM . . . a long left and Irishman Charlie Nash really feels it.

JIM FINISHES IN FOUR TO KEEP HIS CROWN

■ Jim Watt was still on top of the world last night. Scotland's pride and joy retained his world lightweight championship in around 10 minutes of whizzbang action against Ulsterman Charlie Nash. The fight was stopped in the fourth round.

■ In a 60-second shock at the Kelvin Hall Jim hit the canvas. But the champion banged his way back to cut Nash's eye and put him down three times before the referee brought the fight to a dramatic finish.

THE LOVELIEST NIGHT OF THE YEAR—BACK PAGE

YOUR WEEKEND GUIDE

TV

8 PAGES OF NEWS, VIEWS AND INTERVIEWS
START ON PAGE 17

TUESDAY   May 6   1980

Daily Record

10p   SCOTLAND'S BIGGEST DAILY SALE   No. 26,317

SIEGE BUSTERS

Hostage Sim Harris climbs over a balcony and escapes from the blazing embassy.

S.A.S. storm in—and it's all over

THE crack Special Air Service troops stormed the Iranian Embassy in London last night as the six-day siege came to a bloody end.

They were ordered into action after the embassy gunmen shot and killed two Iranian hostages.

Three gunmen died in the battle that followed and two were captured.

But there were no more casualties among the hostages, and 19, including the three Britons, were rescued unhurt.

BBC technician Sim Harris climbed through a window on the first floor of the embassy and crossed over a balcony to the building next door.

And when the SAS men stormed into the embassy, hostage PC Trevor Lock grappled with one of the Arab gunmen, who was desperately trying to hurl a grenade at the troops.

After a quick medical check, he was taken to Scotland Yard for a de-briefing and to be congratulated.

Embassy clerk Ron Morris also came through the battle unscathed.

Body

The dramatic operation to crack the siege was set in motion after gunfire erupted at the embassy.

Two bodies were brought out and the gunmen threatened to kill a hostage every half hour unless their demands for the release of prisoners in Iran were met.

After the first body was carried to an ambulance, Scotland Yard chief Peter Neivens held a street Press conference.

His voice charged with emotion, he said:

" We have tried exceedingly hard to

By RONALD RICKETTS and ROGER BEAM.

avoid just this situation developing into the tragic turn of events they have taken now.

"All we can hope is that we can try to plead with them to be sensible, to be humane, and to free those hostages that are in there."

But it was not to be. And as the SAS stormed in, a huge explosion rocked the area, shots were fired and another huge explosion followed.

The blasts were caused by SAS thunderflash grenades designed to simultaneously blind and deafen the gunmen.

At the same time the highly-trained troops slithered down ropes which had been fixed to points on the embassy roof from the start of the siege.

The troops kicked in front and rear windows and, once inside, they

TURN TO BACK PAGE

FLASHPOINT   *Hooded SAS men armed with guns and thunderflash grenades prepare to storm the building.*

HEROES . . ALL HEROES—Pages 2 and 3   **WOMEN WHO WAIT—Page 11**

Daily Record

10p   SCOTLAND'S BIGGEST DAILY SALE   No. 26,476

TOUCH AND GOLD!

Super Wells wins glory for every Scot

Scots reject music peace plan

By FRANK SULLIVAN

THE BBC are to drop their controversial plan to scrap the Scottish Symphony Orchestra . . .

But only if striking musicians agree to the axing of the Scottish Radio Orchestra.

Last night an angry and emotional meeting in Glasgow of more than 70 musicians from the two orchestras threw out the peace plan.

Rodney Mount, a member of the strike committee, said the Scots might well reject the result of the forthcoming ballot and continue strike action.

He said: "There is a distinct bias against Scotland, not only from the BBC but also from the Musicians' Union, which is London-based.

"In England there is more work for freelance players so it is much easier for players there to make up their earnings."

Action

"Our colleagues in England regard it as a reasonable offer, but there is no way BBC musicians in Scotland can make up their earnings."

Mr Mount said they would not give up until both Scottish orchestras had been saved. The strike committee will meet today to discuss further action.

Under the deal, the SSO, the Northern Ireland Orchestra and the London Studio Players would be saved.

The SRO, the Midland Radio Orchestra and the Northern Radio Orchestra would be scrapped in March, but the members would be given a pay-off and then guaranteed 66 per cent. of their earnings by working for the BBC on a freelance basis for five years.

THIS is the moment that at one time looked like never happening—Scotland's Allan Wells proudly wearing the coveted 100 metres Olympic Gold Medal.

The medal he won by a hairsbreath from Cuban Silvio Leonard, left, with Petar Petrov of Bulgaria trailing third.

But Allan's golden glory came only after an agony of waiting . . .

TEN nerve-wracking

From ALEX CAMERON in the Lenin Stadium

minutes before the judges decided he had taken first place with a nod and a push of the chest to cross the line just ahead of Leonard.

A **HOLD-UP** of two and a quarter hours before the Edinburgh sprinter was able to pass the drugs test.

Then the tension ended and 28-year-old Allan climbed the podium in the Moscow stadium to receive the Gold.

The race produced one of the most dramatic finishes of the Games.

Not even the sophisticated

electronic timing equipment could split the Scot and the Cuban—each had a time of 10.25 seconds.

When Allan saw the action replay on the stadium's huge TV screens, he was certain he had won, throwing his arms in the air and doing a lap of honour.

But for millions watching TV—and Allan's wife Margot —there were nagging doubts.

As the two sprinters crossed the line, 27-year-old Margot cupped her head in her hands, crying: "He's lost. He's lost."

Tears were streaming down her cheeks, and when the final

TURN TO PAGE TWO

OUR MESSAGE TO ALLAN LAST NIGHT

TO ALLAN WELLS

OLYMPIC VILLAGE, MOSCOW

CONGRATULATIONS FROM

EVERYONE IN SCOTLAND.

YOU'VE DONE US PROUD.

MAKE IT A DOUBLE ON MONDAY.

DAILY RECORD, GLASGOW.

WEDNESDAY December 10 1980

Daily Record

12p   SCOTLAND'S BIGGEST DAILY SALE   No. 26,589

FAREWELL TO JOHN LENNON

THE KISS

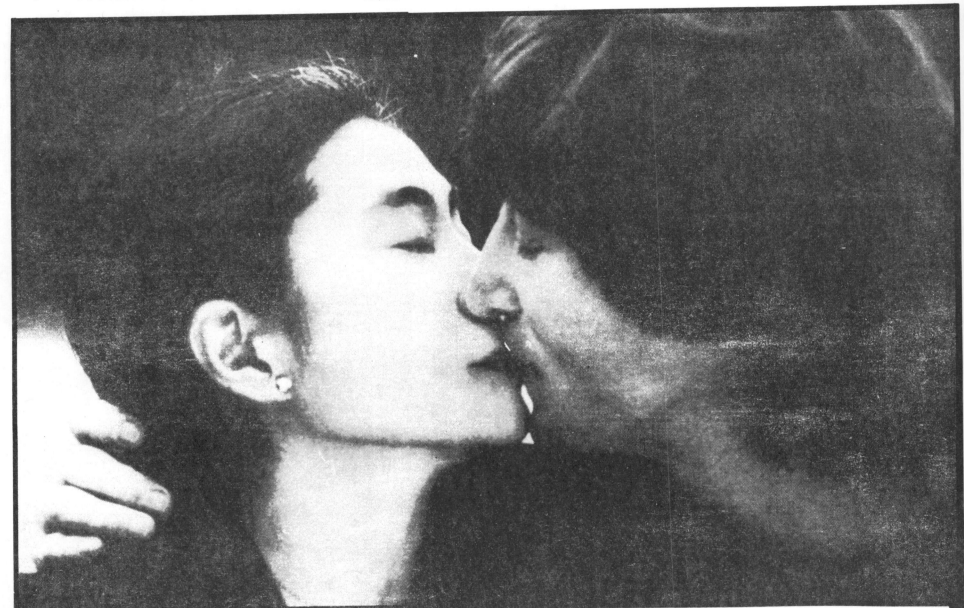

AND THE KILLER

THE GUNMAN ...
Mark Chapman

THIS picture, of John Lennon kissing his wife Yoko Ono, is how he will be remembered ... how he would want to be remembered.

For it sums up his tenderness, his love, his inner peace—his real nature hidden beneath the outward cynicism of his rebel image.

John liked the picture so much that he chose it for the cover of his latest record.

Tragically, it was partly because of that record that he died—gunned down at the age of 40 by a religious maniac who had earlier bought the album and got him to autograph it.

I'VE JUST SHOT JOHN LENNON

PAGES 2 AND 3

THURSDAY January 29 1981

Daily Record

12p. SCOTLAND'S BIGGEST DAILY SALE No. 26,628

FALL OF THE HOUSE OF FRASER

Tiny Rowland and Sir Hugh after losing the boardroom battle . . . but determined to win back power.
Picture by RICHARD PARKER

By HARRY CONROY

THE shopping empire of the Fraser family finally crumbled yesterday . . .

As chairman Sir Hugh Fraser was ousted by his fellow directors in London.

Minutes later in a dramatic move Sir Hugh's former arch-enemy, Lonrho boss Tiny Rowland announced a £155 million takeover bid for the stores chain.

And he promised: "If we win—and we will—Sir Hugh will be

THE BIG LOSER
Centre Pages

executive chairman of the House of Fraser."

But whatever the outcome, the ultimate control has passed from the hands of the Fraser family.

The group employs more than 28,000 people in stores from Arnotts in Aberdeen to Binns in Dumfries and includes Harrods in London as well as stores on the continent.

Sir Hugh's defeat at the meeting

in the House of Fraser offices in Kensington was overwhelming. Only Mr Rowland and fellow Lonrho director Paul Spicer voted for him.

Twelve Fraser directors voted against.

Bitter

The 44-year-old tycoon is replaced as boss by deputy chairman, Professor Roland Smith, who joined the Board only

last year at a salary of £50,000.

But after the meeting, the takeover bid was announced.

For the forthcoming power struggle Lonrho, which already owns 29.9 per cent of House of Fraser, can rely on Sir Hugh's own holding of 3½ per cent. Also, the Fraser family hold 6½ per cent in various trusts.

Lining up against them will be 30 per cent in the hands of various institutions—insurance companies, pension funds and so on.

So the balance of power rests with small investors who each own a few shares. Lonrho are offering 150p a share to secure a successful takeover.

At a hastily-called press conference, Mr Rowland, with Sir Hugh Fraser beside him, said: "Sir Hugh is one of the best retailers in the world."

Of the new chairman Professor Smith, a part-

Continued on Back Page

- He's OUT say the directors
- He's IN says big Tiny
- Now for the power struggle

FOOT'S FURY Page Two   BABY'S ORDEAL Page Five

Daily Record

12p SCOTLAND'S BIGGEST DAILY SALE No. 26,693

The zany life of funny girl Pamela

In Colour Centre Pages

The magic of Sir Stan Page 11

WIN A super luxury trip on Concorde Turn to Page 17

Nine seconds late Columbia touches down

JUST BEAUTIFUL!

The "all-right machine."

A triumphant wave from Robert Crippen as he is reunited with his wife Virginia after the successful landing

THEY'RE back! And everything is beautiful in the world's new space age.

That was the verdict of American astronauts Robert Crippen and John Young after their historic space shuttle flight.

As they emerged from the Columbia, 43-year-old Crippen waved to the cheering crowds and said: "It was one fantastic mission."

And Young said of the revolutionary re-usable spacecraft: "This is an all-right flying machine. Really super."

It was Young, the 50-year-old veteran of

From RONALD BEDFORD at Cape Canaveral.

five space flights, who earlier steered the Columbia safely to earth.

As it rolled to a halt on a dry lake bed in the Mojave Desert—only nine seconds late—Crippen said: "What a way to come to California."

Welcome

And mission control told them: "Welcome home Columbia. Beautiful. Beautiful."

Crippen joked: "Do I have to take it in the hangar?"

"We'll have to dust it off first," he was told.

The successful flight of the Columbia—despite the scare over its missing heat shield tiles—opened a new era in man's attempt to conquer space by proving that re-usable craft are feasible.

Millions throughout the world watched on television as the shuttle came in to land after its 54 hours in orbit.

With Young piloting the 75-ton Columbia manually like a giant glider, the shuttle coasted to a perfect landing at the desert air base.

Then, after an on-board medical check, the astronauts walked briskly down the steps and on to a plane bound for mission control in Houston.

JOHN YOUNG

ROYAL mail

A perfect match in denim

DI's in denim and Charles has a shirt to match in this new portrait of the Royal couple taken by Lord Snowdon.

Despite his divorce from Princess Margaret, Lord Snowdon is still the darling of the Royals when it comes to photography.

Even so, he and his new wife, the former Mrs Lucy Lindsay-Hogg, won't be at the wedding breakfast.

While Lord Snowdon's son, Viscount Linley, and his daughter Lady Sarah Armstrong-Jones, will be in the Royal procession, dad and step-mum will be going by car.

And they'll have a seat "somewhere" in the Cathedral.

A Buckingham Palace spokesman said: " There should be no parking problem as there is plenty of parking space beside St. Paul's."

The spokesman added: " The wedding breakfast for approximately 120 is reserved for close members of both families."

IN YOUR ROYAL MAIL . . .

● The great souvenir spree

● TV guide . . . minute-by-minute

● Scots who share the wedding fever

● How the Queen picks her outfit

● Win champagne and cake!

WEDNESDAY July 29 1981

Daily Record

14p   SCOTLAND'S BIGGEST DAILY SALE   No. 26,783

CHEERS!

Your super telly guide to the Big Day starts on Page 18

AND TOMORROW
■
ONLY IN THE RECORD
■
THE WEDDING IN COLOUR

The toast of Scotland . . . Claire McPherson and Graeme Miller drink to the Royal couple.

HAVE A NICE DAY

THURSDAY July 30 1981

Daily Record

14p   SCOTLAND'S BIGGEST DAILY SALE   No. 26,784

The Prince and Princess
Sealed with a kiss

YOUR SUPER COLOUR WEDDING SOUVENIR

MY PERFECT PRINCESS

AND NOW FOR THE HONEYMOON

The Royal couple leave St. Paul's after the magnificent wedding . . . and happiness is mirrored in their faces for all the world to see.

WEDNESDAY June 2 1982

Daily Record

15p   SCOTLAND'S BIGGEST DAILY SALE   No. 29,040

MILES OF SMILES!

—and sunshine at every step

■ IT WAS Scotland's hottest day of the year — and for 270,000 Catholics, the most joyous day ever.

Laughing, singing, waving, they greeted the Pope as he toured Bellahouston Park, Glasgow, yesterday.

For all its religious dignity, it was a day of carnival—one which the Pope enjoyed as much as his people.

GOD BLESS THEM ALL
—PAGES 8 AND 9

PILGRIM'S PROGRESS
—PAGE 17

WELCOME TO THE CARNIVAL
—CENTRE PAGES

UNITED IN JOY —BACK PAGE

Daily Record

The man of love .. and how they all loved him
UNITED IN JOY

Ecstasy for the hundreds of thousands at Bellahouston Park yesterday as they give a rapturous welcome to Pope John Paul II.

EDITED, PRINTED AND PUBLISHED IN SCOTLAND

Edited, printed and published by Scottish Daily Record and Sunday Mail Ltd., Anderston Quay, Glasgow G3 8DA (041-248 7000). Registered at the Post Office as a newspaper. © Scottish Daily Record and Sunday Mail Ltd., 1982. A Mirror Group newspaper.

TUESDAY June 15 1982

Daily Record

15p   SCOTLAND'S BIGGEST DAILY SALE   No. 29,051

THE MIDNIGHT DRAMA

' Argentine soldiers threw down their weapons. They are flying white flags. '

PREMIER MARGARET THATCHER SPEAKING IN THE COMMONS LAST NIGHT

VICTORY!

THE VICTOR
General Moore, land forces commander

SURRENDER AS ARGIE CHIEF SAYS WE'RE READY TO TALK

THE VANQUISHED
General Menendez, invasion commander

■ THE guns are silent on the Falklands. Last night a dramatic ceasefire was called after British land forces commander General Jeremy Moore made approaches to the beaten Argentine general Mario Menendez to avoid further bloodshed. Early today, terms for the surrender were being discussed in the same barracks from where the Royal Marines were driven out two months ago.

■ JUBILANT Premier Margaret Thatcher broke the news of the victory to a packed Commons. Flushed and happy she told cheering MPs: "As our forces reached the outskirts of Port Stanley the Argentine soldiers threw down their weapons. They are flying white flags over Port Stanley." When the Premier sat down she was congratulated by Michael Foot, David Steel and Dr David Owen.

■ But amid the rejoicing it must not be forgotten the high price paid for victory. The war has brought a heavy toll of men and money. Last night the Ministry of Defence, revealed another grim figure of 20 servicemen killed at the weekend in the fierce fighting around Port Stanley. This brings the total number killed or missing to more than 220. Most of them were killed by Argentine air attacks on the fleet.

THE SILENT GUNS ■ THE FINAL VICTIMS ■ THE WEEKS OF WAR

PAGES 2 and 3   PAGE 5   CENTRE PAGES

SATURDAY October 9 1982

Daily Record

16p   SCOTLAND'S BIGGEST DAILY SALE   No. 29,150

H. . . cut down in a hail of bullets leading a charge.

INSIDE THE PAPER THAT'S TOPS FOR SHOWBIZ

NYREE

MY FAVOURITE ROLE
—PAGE SEVEN

OLIVIA

LIVE FROM AMERICA
—CENTRE PAGES

TELLY'S FAMOUS FARM
—PAGE NINE

YOUR BIG TV GUIDE BEGINS PAGE 15

TWO VCs FOR THE PARAS' DEAD HEROES

FOR VALOUR

Britain honours Falklands brave

■ TWO Paratroop heroes of the Falklands conflict are to get Britain's highest gallantry award, the Victoria Cross. But, sadly, both of them are dead . . . killed in their moments of triumph as they stormed Argentine strongholds.

■ THE awards go to H . . . Lt. Col. H. Jones, 42, cut down leading a charge at Goose Green, and Sgt. Ian McKay, 29, killed at Mount Longdon as he single-handedly took a bunker. Their widows will collect the bronze cross inscribed simply "For Valour."

ROLL OF HONOUR
PAGES 2 AND 3

AWARDS FOR SCOTS

McKAY . . . killed in moment of victory.

Your chance to win

£2000

—If you're an expert on Coronation Street

IF you're one of the millions who tune in to Britain's longest-running and best-loved TV serial each week, here's your chance to put your knowledge of *Coronation Street* to the test.

Get all the answers right, and you could be the talk of your own street by winning our cash bonanza of £2000—PLUS an album selection of photographs of *Coronation Street* stars.

We've prepared 12 questions on the world-famous Granada TV programme. The first six appear today, and six more will be published tomorrow.

Just fill in the answers on the coupon provided each day and tomorrow we'll give the address where they should be sent.

The contest is FUN to solve, EASY to enter... and, as all Record contests are, entry is FREE!

The first correct entry drawn from the assembled mail after the closing date wins the super £2000 prize and album.

* * *

1. Which family lives at No. 13 Coronation Street — the Faircloughs, Ogdens or Barlows?

2. What was Emily Bishop's name before she married?

3. Actress Doris Speed plays an important role in the serial—who?

4. Which "Street" character married Steve Tanner and Alan Howard?

5. Coronation Street has been running for 16, 22 or 26 years. How many?

6. With the death of actor Graham Haberfield, Len Fairclough lost his faithful employee. Name the part Graham played.

Coronation Street contest

1..........
2..........
3..........
4..........
5..........
6..........

There will be more questions — and a name and address coupon—tomorrow.

Editor's decision is final.

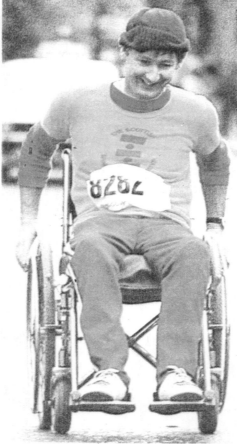

All courage . . . and none more so than chairbound competitors like Paisley's Derek Williams.

POW TO T PEOP

'They laughed and they cried or stood there, numbed by their achi

By DAVID WASTELL

THE look on his face said it all. As he neared the finishing line every nerve-pounding step of the 26 hard miles behind him was etched in the downward turn of his mouth.

Then, suddenly, it was just 100 yards to go — and in an instant the aching muscles, the sweat, the exhaustion were forgotten.

TOUGH

He knew he had done it. The crowds whistled and cheered — and he broke into a broad grin, his thumbs up triumphantly in the air.

Alan Watters, 21-year-old electrician from Motherwell, was just one runner who had completed his first-ever marathon his time was 3 hours 16 minutes.

He tottered forward to be wrapped like an oven-ready chicken in a huge tinfoil blanket to pick up his finisher's medal and to hang it proudly around his neck.

As his legs finally turned to jelly beneath him, he enjoyed the sensation shared yesterday by the thousands who finished the first Scottish People's Marathon.

They laughed and they cried, or they just stood there, numbed by their achievement.

"It's a fantastic feeling to know I can sit here and not have to move another foot as long as I want," Alan said.

Yesterday was the people's day in Glasgow, in every sense. More than 100,000 of them turned out to cheer on the 7000 runners from 15 different countries in a long figure of eight round the city.

When the field artillery gun signalled the start at 9.30 a.m., a great roar went up from the thousands gathered at the city's Saltmarket.

Runners discarded pullovers, shirts, and plastic bin-liners as they surged forward, a great mass of humanity from every layer of the social spectrum.

ENERGY

There were policemen, shipyard workers, solicitors, soldiers, engineers, housewives, top athletes and pensioners.

People hung out of their tenements to cheer them.

The runners wore T-shirts proclaiming every slogan imaginable. One had Union Jack shorts. Another completed the whole course dressed as Superman.

They were almost all sponsored for charity and are expected to raise more than £1 million.

When they finished they were

exhausted — not surpr Running a marathon takes energy as swimming eight playing three football gan row.

And a few didn't make — beaten by fatigue, cold muscles and blistered feet.

There were some pa triumphs. John Farrell, of bank, Glasgow, was the runner to take part.

Though he had to be wheelchair as soon as pleted the course, he ha that at 73 he could still

The indefatigable Sharples, Maryhill-born retr servant, was another. Ma the oldest woman runner, in 6 hours 35 minutes.

For the top athletes, the over by lunchtime.

First home, in 2 hours 17 17 seconds, was Eng Stephen Forster of Sun

First woman home was old Priscilla Welch — also — who lives in Shetland.

Leslie Watson for Scotla in a minute late under 2 hours 48

As the afterno on and the gre finally gave way they were still ce past the People' on Glasgow Gr runners, walke crawlers, bedraggled but phant.

For, in the winners wer portant.

This was eve day, everybod finished truly a — the race wh also-rans were who mattered.

All shapes . . . and two of the female contestants just can't help preening themselves and posing for the photographers as they pound along University Avenue.

Pictures by:

R E E

just
ment'

W . . . a lone piper

urs . . . and a Sikh
s it out in style.

They're all there . . . and the 7000 set out along Glasgow's High Street to test their stamina over 26 miles, 385 yards. Astonishingly, only 300 failed to complete the course.

RAIG and CHARLES DONNELLY

FRIDAY May 13 1983

Daily Record

16p   SCOTLAND'S BIGGEST DAILY SALE   No. 29,333

SONG OF SUCCESS

CITY'S TRIBUTE TO THE DONS

THREE heroes take the salute of a singing, chanting, ecstatic crowd—Dons' goalscorers Eric Black, left, John Hewitt and their manager Alex Ferguson. They brought the European Cup Winners' Cup home to a city that gave them a welcome unknown in its history. More than 100,000 people turned a victory parade into a singalong party celebrating Aberdeen's success.

COLOUR SOUVENIR CENTRE PAGES AND BACK PAGE

Daily Record

THE HAPPY HEROES
CENTRE PAGES

FERGIE STAYS PUT
Page 46

RECORD VIEW
Page 2

THE CITY STOPPERS

Record Picture Team
ERIC CRAIG
IAN TORRANCE
WILLIAM THORNTON
PETER TURNER

THE city of Aberdeen ground to a halt yesterday as the European Cup Winners' Cup was paraded through the streets, held aloft by manager Alex Ferguson.

At least 100,000 people lined the streets as the triumphant Dons took an open-top bus from the airport to Pittodrie, where 24,000 fans waited to greet their heroes.

There were cheers, songs and dances of delight as the team made their way through the city.

Virtually all of Grampian Police Force were out lining the route but with such a good-natured crowd they didn't have any problems.

One old supporter said: "Aberdeen has never seen anything like this. Not even the Coronation had scenes like these."

There were massive crowds all along Union Street and in the office windows — some people even perched on building tops.

At the Town House, Lord Provost Alex Collie was on the balcony, sporting his rosette and a dazzling red and white "bunnet."

It took the bus two hours to drive the eight miles from the airport.

And at Pittodrie, the crowd screamed their approval as skipper Willie Miller carried the cup on to the park.

EDITED, PRINTED AND PUBLISHED IN SCOTLAND

Edited, printed and published by Scottish Daily Record and Sunday Mail Ltd., Anderston Quay, Glasgow G3 8DA (041-248 7000). Registered at the Post Office as a newspaper. © Scottish Daily Record and Sunday Mail Ltd., 1983. A Mirror Group newspaper.

Rod lets it rip ... and from his smile appears to be enjoying himself as much as his thousands of fans.

Pictures: HENRY McINNES and RICHARD PARKER

DYN

IF you can't remember the time Kenny Dalglish walked Ibrox and nobody noticed, makes two of us.

But when he sat down in front of last night, that made just two of sitting down.

The other 28,598 were standing, wa tartan scarves, clapping on everyt except the beat, and generally worshippin the shrine of Rod Stew

The only time I have a reception like it was the Pope walked Murrayfield.

O-ROD!

Rod ends his show in Highland dress

Crowds of fans pack Ibrox Park as Rod takes the stage . . . in front of a huge pink lady.

By COLIN BELL

ask me to explain Rod Stewart is y well placed to preme power.

CSTATIC

Stewart Empire was no risks that anyone several miles of would miss the g of the Superstar's Scream. I have no but to concede: the guy commands total adoration.

The fans who were happy to pay £9 for a ticket, turn up at half-past four, and not get their first glimpse of Dynorod until 21 minutes past eight, were ecstatic about their idol's performance.

Across the width of the pitch and into the bowels of a stage cunningly disguised as a pin-up's navel—it was hard to recognise it really was Rod Stewart.

With my eyesight, it could have been Rod Hull, if too loudly dressed for Emu.

But 20,000 bouncing birds can't be wrong, and the distinction they drew between a distant Gary Glitter and a distant Rod Stewart was totally convincing.

One, they tolerated—the other, they lusted after, at full soprano pitch.

Somewhere in that huge box of a stadium there was Rod Stewart in the mildly jaded flesh, and somewhere, in a sound system which Hitler could have used at Nuremburg, there was Rod Stewart's voice battling against the electric elements.

There aren't words for the atmosphere which aren't already hackneyed. There are words for the security, but we don't care to use them in a family newspaper.

If you wanted to get that teeny bit closer to your hero — like out of the stand and on to the pitch, handily covered in tarpaulins — it was a mistake.

Distant as the blond mop and the blue bootees might be, this was an audience which felt it had brushed against the sleeve of Merlin.

As a matter of fact, in the Govan Stand, most of us heard more of our own singing than we heard of Rod.

For the fans, wrapped in Lions Rampant, screaming at a steady eight to the bar, it was magic.

Pop concert become World Cup Final, rock transcended into God.

There are almost certainly several people who can sing better than Stewart

But those who can sing, gyrate, and command total adoration can be counted on very limited fingers.

He isn't a singer, he's an experience.

TUESDAY September 27 1983

Daily Record

17p   SCOTLAND'S BIGGEST DAILY SALE   No. 29,450

Pat and boyfriend Tony Booth yesterday.

ELSIE QUITS THE STREET

Another shocker for TV fans .. 29 days after Len's sacking!

ELSIE TANNER is quitting TV's most famous street.

After 22 years in Coronation Street, actress Pat Phoenix has had enough.

She dropped her bombshell just 29 days after Street veteran Len Fairclough — played by Peter Adamson—was sacked from the show.

Pat's decision came as a surprise to the cast and is a body blow to Granada TV bosses. For she was always regarded as a lynchpin and corner stone of the soap opera.

Now she wants to take her chance in live theatre — for the last 10 weeks she has been playing alongside live-in lover Tony Booth in theatre in Bournemouth.

A close friend added last night: "She was upset by the sacking of Peter Adamson."

Spinster

In earlier years of the Street the two had been romantically linked.

But her resignation, delivered in a one-page letter to executive producer Bill Podmore, is far deeper than that.

For the 59-year-old star has been telling friends she is unhappy about the scripts.

Once she was the Street's sex queen. Lately she has been cast as the lonely, aged spinster.

Pat, herself, would not go into reasons for quitting last night.

"I have resigned," she confirmed. "That is definite. Beyond that I can't say anything until after my present contract expires."

Pat, who earns around £700 a week from the Street, is signed up until November. She was offered another 12-month deal, along with other members of the cast, but turned it down.

Her departure leaves the script-writers with a problem. Scripts till the end of November have already been written.

It has already been decided to "kill off" Len Fairclough. And Eddie Yeats and girlfriend Marion Wills are also to be written out.

It may be that Pat will be persuaded to stay on a few more weeks in order to dream up a suitable end for her.

Her friend added: "She also wants to do more writing as well as acting. But I think she's crazy.

"In the Street she may be a glamour girl. But life does not begin at 60 and Pat should take a long hard look in the mirror."

THE RISE OF THE PHOENIX   CENTRE PAGES

FURY OVER MAZE ESCAPE

PAGES 4 AND 5

AUSSIES' TRIUMPH

BACK PAGE

Daily Record

17p — SCOTLAND'S BIGGEST DAILY SALE — No. 29,562

Bruce boldly goes where no man has gone before

STAR TREK

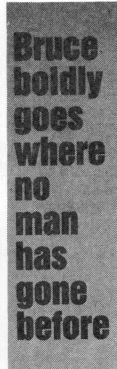

■ **FOR** the first time in history, man floats untethered in the dark void of space. It has all the elements and excitement of science fiction. But yesterday, for American astronaut Bruce McCandless and the world, it became reality.

■ **THE** 46-year-old astronaut strapped on a rocket pack and left the space shuttle Challenger. He manoeuvred around the craft, shouting with excitement when he saw the Earth below him and especially Florida, where the great adventure began.

■ **IT** was another great step for mankind. The history-making trip means that self-propelled flights can become a regular feature of shuttle missions and take life towards new horizons ... The final frontier.

THE FIRST FIRST LADY
IN COLOUR   CENTRE PAGES

JIM HITS THE BULL
PAGE 9

THE REAL IAN DURY
PAGE 10

BINGO
PAGE 21

ONE HECK OF A LEAP
FULL STORY PAGE 11

SPORTS mail CHEERS!

JUST GRAND ... the jubilant Scots celebrate in style with Edinburgh's Lord Provost Tom Morgan.

Pictures: ANDREW ALLAN and HENRY McINNES

FIFTEEN brave and bruised Scots battled their way to a place in history yesterday.

For the first time in 59 years Scotland clinched rugby's Grand Slam.

In the end the 21-12 victory over the French was emphatic. But the Scots had to fight their way back from the brink of despair.

And on a day of heroic performances at Murrayfield Peter Dods had a particularly memorable match as the Scots stormed back from 3–9 down to win in the closing minutes.

Inspiring

The Gala full-back had his right eye closed by a blow midway though the first half, but battled on to set up a new Scottish record.

His 17 points from five penalty goals and a conversion gave him a magnificent total of 50 for the season — 15 more than Andy Irvine's old record.

Skipper Jim Aitken had already established himself as Scotland's most successful postwar captain.

Dead-eye Dods day

By PETER DONALD

Coming out of retirement this year, he has now gone six games without defeat in inspiring his men to the Triple Crown and the Championship.

He said: "I wasn't happy at half-time. But it began to look good when we levelled the scores at nine-all. Then things began to click."

Ian MacGregor, in his last year as chairman of selectors, said: "No team could have done more than Scotland did today. All I can say is 'merci beaucoup' (many thanks) to the French."

French coach Jacques Fouroux said: "Scotland deserved to win. We had our chances."

Scrum-half Jerome Gallion, stretchered off in the second half, was taken to hospital for a check-up, then given the all-clear.

That was the only good news for France, who left the field to discover that the showers in their dressing-room were not working. It wasn't their day.

MAGNIFIQUE—Page 42

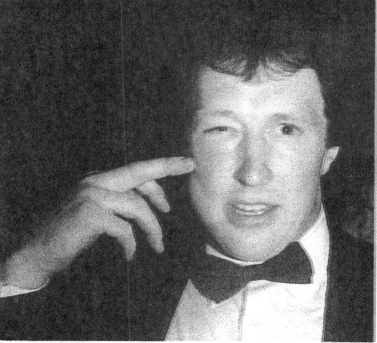

EYE-CATCHER...17 points and a souvenir for Peter Dods.

Edited, printed and published by Scottish Daily Record and Sunday Mail Limited, Anderston Quay, Glasgow G3 8DA (041-248 7000). Registered at the Post Office as a newspaper.

© Scottish Daily Record and Sunday Mail Limited 1984. A Mirror Group newspaper.

Daily Record

17p   SCOTLAND'S BIGGEST DAILY SALE   No. 29,662

They came to mourn for Eric ...

Beeb calls it a day on TV party

THE BBC has axed its controversial Saturday night rave-ups with the stars.

Saturday Night Affairs, billed as a series of informal parties, was condemned by the public and the critics.

The first programme, a fortnight ago, kicked off with Vidal Sassoon as a host. It was a disaster.

The stars were picked up by coach in London and given large amounts of drink on the journey to Pebble Mill studios in Birmingham.

In the studio, they got expensive food and more drink and were expected to entertain the viewers.

The first guests who included Bruce Forsyth, Anita Harris and Larry Grayson failed.

Uproar

The uproar from viewers was unanimous — how could the BBC spend so much public money on a load of unfunny stars when they were asking the Government to increase their licence fees.

Last Saturday, DJ Dave Lee Travis was the host, but he didn't do very much better.

Last night senior management at the Birmingham BBC studios pulled the plug on the programme, saying:

'After two programmes were transmitted and watching the material recorded so far for the remainder of the run, we were convinced that this series was not going to live up to the original expectation."

On Saturday, the late-night film will be earlier than advertised and starts in the *Saturday Night Affairs* slot.

A SORROW shared between the two people who will miss Eric Morecambe most—his widow Joan and his partner Ernie Wise.

But for the mourners at the comedian's memorial service yesterday, the tears did not last long. For Eric had the last laugh.

Only a few months before his death, he had written to his friend Dickie Henderson asking him to speak at his funeral.

And Dickie showed Eric's letter which said: "I know what a great tribute you gave to Arthur Askey. I would like you to do the same for mine to remind everyone what a great comic I was. P.S. I'll pay you when I see you ... down there."

The tears vanished and the smiles broke out. In death—as in life—Eric kept them laughing.

... but love and laughter drove away the tears

GOODBYE SUNSHINE – CENTRE PAGES

SATURDAY October 13 1984

Daily Record

18p   FORWARD WITH SCOTLAND   No. 29,774

ONLY HOURS AFTER THEY TRIED TO MURDER THE PRIME MINISTER, A CHILLING MESSAGE FROM THE IRA...

'TODAY WE WERE UNLUCKY.. BUT WE HAVE ONLY TO BE LUCKY ONCE. YOU WILL HAVE TO BE LUCKY ALWAYS'

TARGET OF HATE ... the once proud Grand Hotel, now a black monument to terror.

Christmas Record

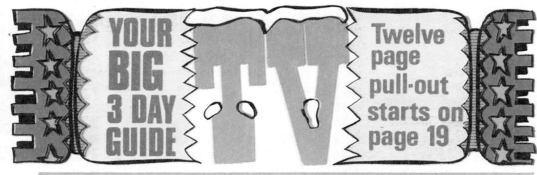

YOUR BIG 3 DAY GUIDE

Twelve page pull-out starts on page 19

IT'S A CRACKER!

18p   FORWARD WITH SCOTLAND   No. 29,835

THANK YOU!

.. to all our wonderful readers and the great guys from Band Aid

All together now. And everyone who was anyone in the pop world sang the Christmas song which touched the hearts of millions . . . and could save a million lives.

BAND WHO BRING HOPE

■ It's the miracle of Christmas ... the miracle that has linked readers of this newspaper and young folk the world over with Africa's greatest tragedy ... that has raised more than £4,250,000 so far for starving Ethiopia.

■ It's the miracle of Band Aid's chartbuster "Do They Know It's Christmas?" the biggest-selling pop record of all time. More than £2,500,000 is flowing from record shops to help the hungry millions.

■ It's the miracle of the extraordinary generosity of ordinary people. For readers of the Daily Record and the Daily Mirror have given an amazing £1,750,000 for famine relief over the last few weeks.

■ It's the miracle which must not end. For even on Christmas morning they will still be burying the dead in Ethiopia. Enjoy yourselves. And thank you for remembering those who will not. See you on Thursday.

SUNDAY mail

FORWARD WITH SCOTLAND

26p   May 12, 1985   No. 3710   TV Page 27

DISASTER

40 DIE IN FIREBALL

■ This was the horrific scene at Bradford City's soccer ground yesterday. Terror stricken fans flee for safety as fire rips through the grandstand.

■ Forty people were killed in the disaster and hundreds of others were injured as they leapt, with clothes and hair alight, from the blazing stand.

HORROR IN THE GRANDSTAND—Pages 2 and 3

Daily Record

20p   FORWARD WITH SCOTLAND   No. 30,005

THE GREATEST **ROCK** SHOW ON EARTH

MAGIC!

■ Paul McCartney's triumphant clenched fist as he finished his set said it all. It was the Greatest Rock Show on Earth, with the Greatest Rock Stars on Earth. It had the Greatest Audience on Earth. And it could be the Greatest Fund-raiser ever. For Saturday's Live Aid spectacular beamed from Wembley and Philadelphia around the world had last night raised a staggering £50 million for starving Ethiopia ... at least.

■ For 10 hours at Wembley and 11 hours in Philadelphia, more than 160,000 swaying, stamping, clapping, cheering pop fans watched the stars perform to make the charity dream of Bob Geldof come true. Billions more watched on an amazing 95 per cent of the world's TV sets. And next year's spectacular — yes, next year's — could be bigger and better. For the stars are convinced: This show MUST run and run.

SOUVENIR SPECIAL Pages 3, 15 and Centre Pages

Daily Record

20p FORWARD WITH SCOTLAND
No. 30,011

Sandy finally does it . .

MINE AT LAST

Scot's trophy triumph

A dream comes true as Sandy kisses the Open Trophy.

My dad's a champ . . son Stuart holds Sandy's trophy as Christine looks on.

A dream comes true

IN COLOUR CENTRE PAGES

IT'S the kiss that says: "It's mine . . ." The smile that says: "I've done it."

For last night Sandy Lyle became the first Scot to win the Open for 54 years.

It was a lifetime's dream come true for 27-year-old Sandy, who started playing golf as a three-year-old.

Honour

And the husky, broad-shouldered golfing great was in tears as he savoured the ultimate triumph in his career.

As his wife Christine, herself a top golfer, cuddled their toddler son,

By ALISTER NICOL

Stuart at chilly Royal St. George's club in Sandwich, Kent, he wiped his eyes as he received the trophy.

He told the delighted crowds: "It's a great honour. I'd like to thank the greenkeeper for putting the pins in their right position.

"And I'll be back next year to defend my title at Turnberry — one of my favourite courses."

Sandy, who first qualified for the Open as a 15-year-old, won the title which makes him a millionaire virtually overnight with a battling par round under the most severe pressure.

For his historic victory — the first Scot to win since naturalised American Tommy Armour in 1931 — he won £65,000, the Open Trophy, and a replica of the original Open Championship belt from the first tournament at Prestwick in 1860.

There to see him win

TURN TO BACK PAGE

TINA'S ON THE WARPATH

Colour Special Page 8

PLUS

BINGO

ANOTHER SUPER CHANCE TO WIN

Daily Record

20p FORWARD WITH SCOTLAND No. 30,058

The Lisbon Lions join football's greats to mourn Jock Stein

THE PRIDE AND THE GRIEF ... Lisbon greats Tommy Gemmell, Jim Craig and Billy McNeill join other mourning stars.

TEARS FOR THE BIG MAN

Denis Law bites back the tears.

■ Football mourned a legend yesterday ... Jock Stein, The Big Man. There were stars of the past, like Celtic's immortal Lisbon Lions, and the present, like Scotland's World Cup squad. Stars of showbiz, like Rod Stewart, and stars of TV sport, like Lawrie McMenemy, Denis Law and Pat Crerand.

■ The unknown stars were there, too ... the fans who cheer Scotland from the terracing. In their thousands they turned out to line the funeral route. It was a day for unashamed grief. And hundreds, like Denis Law, simply could not contain their tears.

HE WAS JUST MAGIC ...
Pages 8 and 9.

As the nation mourns one of football's legends,

SEE JOCK . . . HE

Rod Stewart follows Graeme Souness into the service.

LAST RESPECTS ... Lawrie McMenemy chats to Sir Matt Busby and Pat Crerand.

THEY said goodbye to Big Jock yesterday ... the rich and the famous, the poor and the unknown.

They crowded into a little chapel of rest to bid the Big Man of Scottish football farewell.

They silently stood three-deep at the pavements as the funeral cortege passed by.

And they wept. From superstar Rod Stewart to an unknown punk teenager. They wept for Jock Stein, the man who was Scotland's soccer king.

FINAL

Big Jock died on Tuesday, just after the team he loved fought a draw with Wales in a vital World Cup clash in Cardiff.

And yesterday his body made the final journey of a few miles from his home in Glasgow to the city's Linn Crematorium.

More than 10,000 fans, unashamed of their tears, paid their last respects on the funeral route. And 500 of soccer's top names, past and present, gathered inside in a football Who's Who—names like Busby, Law and Crerand, Jock's famous Lisbon Lions, and the stars who grab the headlines today.

But it was not just a day for the world of football. It was a day of deep personal sorrow for Jock's family, his wife Jean, daughter Rae and son George.

GENIUS

They huddled together with a few close friends and wept quietly as they heard the Rev. James Martin talk of "the two men" they were mourning...

"Jock, football genius without peer. And John, husband, father, grandfather ... warm-hearted and generous, loving and beloved. He will be sadly missed."

Another soccer legend, Denis

Farewell to the Big Man

By JAMES McBETH and MIKE RITCHIE

Law, tears streaming down his face, summed up the feelings of thousands.

"When death hits a family, that family feels it. When a man like Jock dies, it affects a whole nation."

The words were echoed in the mountain of tributes that flowed into the chapel of rest ... from the famous, like Rod Stewart's blue and white saltire of blooms, and from the teams, like Celtic, and the present World Cup squad.

At the end, the big names filed slowly out into the blustery afternoon — McNeill, Auld, Lennox and Jinky from the Lisbon Lions, Jock Wallace, Willie Waddell, Willie Henderson, John Greig and Bobby Shearer from Rangers.

SPECIAL

International managers mourned — Bobby Robson of England, and Mike England of Wales. Scotland's football bosses — Alex Ferguson, Davie Hay, John Blackley rubbed shoulders with English team bosses Lawrie McMenemy and Donald Mackay.

Said Bobby Robson: "Jock was an ordinary man — and a very special man. He will be missed terribly."

But it was left to a Glasgow fan, Alex McGregor, 54, of Castlemilk, to sum it up:

"SEE THAT BIG MAN. HE WAS MAGIC..."

one fan's words sum it all up..

WAS MAGIC

As he stands with Willie Henderson, Denis Law can't hold back the tears.

From the Lisbon greats to today's young lions . .

LAST RESPECTS...from left, Celtic's Murdo McLeod, chief scout John Kelman, Bobby Lennox, Mo Johnston, Davie Provan, Tommy Burns and physio Brian Scott.

PICTURES BY ERIC CRAIG, JAMES ROBERTSON AND ROBERT HOTCHKISS

THURSDAY July 24 1986

Daily Record

20p   FORWARD WITH SCOTLAND   No: 30,299

COLOUR SOUVENIR

That's for you, Duchess!

It's a smacker for a smasher as Andy shows off his bride

■ It was what the crowds had waited for. And the Grand Young Duke of York obliged. On the balcony at Buckingham Palace, he delivered a smacking kiss to his beautiful Duchess as thousands cheered below. It had been a day of pomp and pageantry. And their kiss made it a day of simple love.

SEALED WITH A KISS

INSIDE TODAY:

All the super pictures and stories

Daily Record

SCOTLAND THE PROUD ... and the boys who carry a nation's hopes acknowledge the friendly waves from the crowd at Meadowbank.

FRIENDS ACROSS THE GLOBE

THE Scots boys looked braw in their kilts. And the Sheilas from Down Under looked equally stunning in their blazers.

The Friendly Games certainly lived up to their reputation — Old Friends made sure of that!

GREAT TO BE HERE ... the bonny lassies from the Australian team enjoy their welcome.

EDITED, PRINTED AND PUBLISHED IN SCOTLAND

Published by Scottish Daily Record and Sunday Mail (1986) Ltd. (041-248 7000) and printed by British Newspaper Printing Corporation (Scotland) Ltd., Anderston Quay, Glasgow G3 8DA. Registered at the Post Office as a newspaper. © Scottish Daily Record and Sunday Mail Ltd. 1986. A Mirror Group newspaper.

Daily Record

20p   FORWARD WITH SCOTLAND   No. 30,455

JENNY ... a long affair with the tycoon.

Randy Ralph's other love..

A SECOND secret love of millionaire Burton's boss Sir Ralph Halpern was named last night ... glamorous estate agent Jenny Singleton, a former model.

Randy Ralph, 48, who hit the headlines at the weekend over his sexy high jinks with 19-year-old nude model Fiona Wright, began his romance with Jenny when she was 17.

Now aged 23, red-haired Jenny lived in her married lover's luxury Hampstead flat until last year.

They split up after heartbroken Jenny, a stunning six-footer, found out he was seeing another woman.

SIR RALPH

TAILOR-MADE FOR DISASTER
Pages 6 and 7

New fear for Waite in arrest mystery

ENVOY TERRY IS HELD

RECORD REPORTER

FEARS were growing last night that peace envoy Terry Waite had been seized in Lebanon.

Reports reaching London said the Archbishop of Canterbury's special envoy was "under house arrest".

Frantic efforts were being made by the Archbishop's staff to find out exactly what has happened to him.

According to the Kuwaiti sources Mr Waite was taken prisoner by Shi'ite Moslem gunmen he was negotiating with for the release of two American hostages.

His attempt at a deal fell through and they seized him.

None of the many warring militias in the Lebanese capital, Beirut, could confirm the report.

But they did say that the Druze Progressive Socialist Party Militia, which escorted Mr Waite to his meeting with the kidnappers, was now increasingly worried about his whereabouts.

A spokesman for the Archbishop, Dr Robert Runcie, said: "We are aware of the report that Terry Waite has been detained and we are seeking clarification as a matter of urgency.'

Mr Waite dropped out of sight seven days ago, believing it was the best way to fulfil his latest Beirut mission to free Western hostages.

But the Archbishop's staff repeatedly insisted he was in good hands.

Two unidentified Westerners were kidnapped yesterday, bringing the total seized in the last two weeks to 12.

Daily Record

20p   FORWARD WITH SCOTLAND   No. 30,540

FINAL AGONY OF SIR HUGH

SIR HUGH...wealth and power but luck was against him.

TRAGIC TYCOON IS KILLED BY LUNG CANCER

■ **MILLIONAIRE** tycoon Sir Hugh Fraser died yesterday at 50 — just five days after he'd been told he was suffering from lung cancer and had only a few weeks left to live.

■ **CHAINSMOKING** Sir Hugh — he got through 80 to 100 cigarettes a day — inherited a glittering £100 million empire which included the world-famous Harrods and other stores at 30.

■ **BUT** luck was never on his side. The next twenty years included two broken marriages, a string of failed love affairs and at least £1.5 million lost at the gaming tables.

THE STORY IN FULL *PAGES 2, 3, 9 AND CENTRE PAGES*

UNITED'S EUROPE CHALLENGE

COLOUR SOUVENIR SPECIAL

PAGE 34 AND BACK PAGE

WEDNESDAY August 19 1987

Daily Record

22p   FORWARD WITH SCOTLAND   No. 30,630

It's the same the world over..

The wife is left to amuse the kids .. and husband is off with the lads

Minder Mum . . . as Harry plays.

PRINCE OF DRAMS!

- **ACTION**-man Prince Charles had a day out with the lads yesterday ...and a couple of large drams to boot!

- **AND** after a spot of daredevil tightrope walking, his new mountain rescue mates presented him with a Glencoe ice axe.

- **BUT** while dad was off having fun, Diana, like mums the whole world over was left to amuse the kids — having a ball at Balmoral.

Walking the tightrope ... Pages 6 and 7

GIRLS .. WIN A FABULOUS WEDDING DRESS   /   *A SUPER CONTEST —CENTRE PAGES*